SMITH'S REVIEW SERIES

Torts
FOURTH EDITION

MYRON G. HILL, JR.
Adjunct Professor of Law,
Antioch School of Law
Member of District of Columbia,
Ohio and U.S. Supreme Court
Bars

HOWARD M.
ROSSEN
Director, Ohio Bar Review and
Writing Seminar
Member of Ohio,
District of Columbia,
Florida, Pennsylvania and
U.S. Supreme Court Bars

WILTON S. SOGG
Adjunct Professor of Law,
Cleveland-Marshall
College of Law,
Cleveland State University
Lecturer on Law,
Harvard Law School
Member of Ohio,
District of Columbia,
Florida, U.S. Tax Court and
U.S. Supreme Court Bars

SMITH'S REVIEW SERIES

Torts
Fourth Edition

Keyed to Leading Casebooks
for Law School, Bar and College
Examinations

Keyed to Multistate Bar
Examination Test Specifications

WEST PUBLISHING COMPANY
St. Paul, Minnesota © 1983

Library of Congress Cataloging in Publication Data

Smith, Chester Howard, 1893–1964.
    Smith's review of torts.

    (Smith's review series)
    Rev. ed. of:Torts, for law school and bar examina-
tion/Myron G. Hill, 3rd ed. 1975.
    Includes index.
    1. Torts—United States—Examinations, questions,
etc. I. Hill, Myron G., 1936–   . II. Rossen,
Howard M., 1936–   . III. Sogg, Wilton S., 1935–
IV. Hill, Myron G., 1936–   . Torts, for law school
and bar examinations. V. Title. VI. Series.
KF1250.Z9S56 1983   346.7303'076   83–6847
                          347.3063076

ISBN 0–314–71911–3

To Our Parents

PREFACE

The Smith Review Series was initiated by Professor Chester H. Smith in 1958. Since his death these Reviews have been revised regularly in an effort to bring to the student the best study guide available.

Since the last edition of this Review was published, the law of torts has undergone many significant changes and important developments. Further, the advent of the Multistate Bar Examination, made up completely of multiple-choice questions and adopted in most states, has created a new emphasis in preparation for examinations in torts. In this Fourth Edition the authors have endeavored to reflect these changes and developments in subject matter and new emphasis in bar examinations.

To this end, all of the text has been completely updated. All material covered on the Official Outline for the Multistate Bar Examination in torts has been covered fully.

In order to enable the student to prepare for the Multistate Bar Examination itself, or any multiple-choice style examination in the field of torts, the authors have included the Test Specifications for Torts and selected actual questions from the Multistate Bar Examination. These, together with the official answers and the authors' explanation of those answers, appear in the Appendix at the end of this volume.

This Review contains a Study Outline of Torts. The authors have attempted to provide a structural outline of the subject together with a word-phrase presentation of the elements of the key concepts and principles of law in each of the basic subject areas.

The principles of each topic within a chapter are numbered. If the principle is brief, clear and easily understood, it is left simply in the form of a statement. If the principle is a bit complex or may not be easily understood, it is illustrated by an example immediately following. If the principle is very important or difficult to understand, it is illustrated by a Case which follows the topic. The Case is also intended to present an effective method of constructing an opinion in the solution of a legal problem. CAVEAT and NOTE have been used throughout this Review to alert the student to important areas of difficulty, change and development.

It is hoped that this method of presentation, (a) will give the student an over-all, bird's-eye view of the most important principles in this particular subject, (b) will enable him to see and understand more clearly those basic principles, and (c) will enhance his capacity in choosing the appropriate principles, in applying those principles to the facts, and in constructing effective opinions, in the solution of legal problems.

The authors have combined their teaching experience and practical knowledge to make this Review the clearest, most complete and accurate study guide available to students of Torts. Suggestions for further improvement of future editions may be directed to the authors in care of West Publishing Company.

Apart from the cases cited, the citations in this Review are as follows:

"Cary" refers to William L. Cary, Cases and Materials on Corporations, Fourth Edition–Unabridged, 1969, by The Foundation Press, Inc.; "Dobbs" refers to Dan B. Dobbs, Handbook on the Law of Remedies, 1973, by West Publishing Co.; "Franklin" refers to Marc A. Franklin, Cases and Materials on Tort Law and Alternatives, 1979, by The Foundation Press; "Green" refers to Leon Green, et al., Torts, Cases and Materials, 1977, by West Publishing Co.; "Gregory" refers to Charles O. Gregory, Harry Kalven, Jr., and Richard A. Epstein, Cases and Materials on Torts, Third Edition, 1977, by Little, Brown and Company; "Henn" refers to Harry G. Henn, Handbook of the Law of Corporations and Other Business Enterprises, Third Edition, 1983, by West Publishing Co.; "Keeton" refers to Page Keeton and Robert E. Keeton, Cases and Materials on the Law of Torts, Second Edition, 1977, by West Publishing Co.; "Morris" refers to Morris on Torts, Second Edition, 1980, by The Foundation Press; "P & W" refers to William L. Prosser, John W. Wade, and Victor E. Schwartz, Torts, Cases and Materials, Seventh Edition, 1982, by The Foundation Press; "Perkins" refers to Rollin H. Perkins, Criminal Law, Second Edition, 1969, by The Foundation Press, Inc.; "Prosser" refers to William L. Prosser, Law of Torts, Fourth Edition, 1972, by West Publishing Co.;

"Shulman" refers to Harry Shulman, et al., Torts, Cases and Materials, 1976, The Foundation Press, Inc.; "Shapo" refers to Marshall S. Shapo, Tort and Compensation Law, 1976, West Publishing Co.

This volume would not be complete without thanks to Stephen J. Werber, Professor of Law at Cleveland-Marshall College of Law, Cleveland State University, for his assistance in the preparation of the chapter on Products Liability.

MYRON G. HILL, JR.
HOWARD M. ROSSEN
WILTON S. SOGG

Washington, D.C.
Cleveland, Ohio
April, 1983

SUMMARY
OF CONTENTS

TABLE OF CONTENTS

OUTLINE OF TORTS

I. INTRODUCTION—OVERVIEW

A. Basis of liability
1. intentional aggression
2. negligence
3. liability without fault
B. Analysis of problems
1. establish liability
2. consider other issues, including:
a. required state of mind
b. legal causation
c. damages
d. defenses
e. immunities
3. procedural issues
a. burden of proof
b. joinder of parties
c. evidence

II. INTENTIONAL TORTS

A. Assault
1. elements by defendant
a. force set in motion toward P
b. which is wrongful
c. and with the intent to injure
2. elements by plaintiff
a. P did not consent
b. there is apparent present ability, and
c. P reasonably apprehends immediate injury
B. Battery
1. elements
a. intentional start of force toward P
b. which is wrongful
c. against P's will
d. causing physical contact
2. apprehension *not* necessary
3. touching sanctioned by social custom is *not* a battery

4. transferred intent doctrine—D's intent to hit X is transferred to Y where Y is hit instead
5. technical battery—doctor exceeds patient's consent; battery unless an emergency

C. Intentionally causing emotional distress
  1. intentional tort of words or act
    a. done to cause fright or anxiety
    b. which causes such mental disturbance
  2. contrast to assault—can occur without threat of physical contact
  3. contrast to battery—can occur without actual contact
NOTE—Emotional distress may also result from another tort, in which case damages for emotional distress are included in the compensatory damages awarded for that tort

D. False imprisonment and false arrest
  1. false imprisonment—elements
    a. unjustified, substantially total confinement
    b. intent to confine
    c. against will of P, and
    d. P was conscious of the confinement
  2. false arrest—arrest without legal authority
    a. constitutes sufficient restraint for false imprisonment
    b. storekeepers and shoplifters
      i. common law—detaining innocent customer was false imprisonment
      ii. modern view—frequently by statute—with probable cause customer may be detained a reasonable time to investigate

E. Trespass to land
  1. protects interest in exclusive possession of land
  2. a trespass action *can* be brought by
    a. a person in wrongful possession
    b. the owner, if in possession
  3. a trespass action *cannot* be brought by
    a. a licensee or holder of an easement
    b. a tenant at will
    c. an owner not in possession
  4. liability for trespass if
    a. wrongful entry onto land
    b. remaining on land after right to do so expires
    c. failing to perform duty to remove something from land
  5. actual injury to land not necessary—used to test title
  6. intention to trespass not necessary
  7. rights of possessor to sue for trespass
    a. surface—if any part entered
    b. earth below—if area which can be used is penetrated
    c. air above—if interference with surface use
      i. zone theory
      ii. unused airspace theory
      iii. privilege
      iv. nuisance

F. Trespass to chattels
  1. interest in possession and physical condition protected by
    a. trespass—minor interference
    b. conversion—substantial interference
  2. remedies
    a. trespass—nominal or compensatory damages
    b. conversion—value of goods at the time of conversion

G. Defenses to intentional torts
   1. privilege
      a. prevents existence of tort
      b. based on consent or law
   2. mistake and unavoidable accident
      a. reasonable mistake is no defense
      b. unavoidable accident excuses D's act
   3. consent
      a. can be express or implied
      b. usually a valid defense but statute sets age of consent for some torts
   4. self defense—requirements
      a. reasonable belief of danger
      b. reasonable force used
   5. defense of others—elements
      a. immediate necessity
      b. reasonable force used
   NOTE—Honest, reasonable mistake still permits defense of self defense, but many courts make D liable if defending others
   6. defense of property
      a. can use reasonable force to defend real or personal property
      b. cannot set trap for trespasser
      c. cannot use force to evict wrongful occupant of land— must use civil remedy
      d. defense of habitation—may take life if:
         i. attack against inhabitants, and
         ii. to commit a felony
      e. duty to retreat
         i. if outside house, must retreat before taking life, but,
         ii. not so inside house
   7. recapture of chattels
      a. permitted if
         i. wrongfully taken
         ii. prompt recapture
      b. UCC rule—may recapture only if no breach of peace occurs
      c. Due Process Clause of Constitution—permits recapture after default if
         i. supervised by judge, and
         ii. bond posted, and
         iii. prompt judicial hearing guaranteed
   8. necessity—act to prevent injury from cause not connected with P, *e.g.* a storm or other act of nature
      a. public necessity avoid public disaster—no liability on D
      b. private necessity—protect person or property of D or another—liability for harm caused to P
   9. legal process and arrest
      a. acting under court order is complete defense
      b. arrest without warrant by officer—allowed at common law for
         i. felony
            (a) if person committed felony or
            (b) probable cause to believe person committed felony

        ii.   misdemeanor—only if
            (a)   breach of peace and
            (b)   committed in officer's presence
NOTE—Modern statutes expand authority of officer to arrest and generally allow private parties to arrest for any offense committed in their presence

10. discipline
    a.   parent or teacher may use reasonable force to discipline
    b.   courts divided on whether to allow suit for "discipline" of one spouse by the other

III. NEGLIGENCE—CONDUCT WHICH INVOLVES AN UNREASONABLY GREAT RISK OF CAUSING DAMAGE

A. Elements of a cause of action in negligence
   1. D owed P a duty of due care
   2. D breached that duty
   3. P was injured
   4. D's negligence was the proximate cause of P's injury

B. Standard of care
   1. *objective test*—reasonable, prudent person
   2. must consider all surrounding circumstances
   3. balance these factors
      a.   probability harm will be done
      b.   seriousness of resulting injury
      c.   burden of adequate precautions
   4. infants
      a.   *subjective test*—age and experience considered part of surrounding circumstances
      b.   if engaged in adult activities, treated as an adult

C. Duty of care
   1. misfeasance—affirmative act violating duty of care
   2. nonfeasance—failure to act when duty to do so
   3. if no duty to assist is owed
      a.   no liability for failure to act
      b.   voluntarily assisting creates duty to do so carefully
      c.   liable for injury caused for negligence while assisting
   4. rescue doctrine—if rescuer injured he may recover from tortfeasor who could have foreseen as "danger invites rescue"
   5. good samaritan statutes—alters standard of care to encourage assistance in emergency

D. Violation of statute
   1. standard of care set by statute
   2. to maintain action under statute
      a.   P must be in protected class
      b.   P was injured in way statute designed to prevent
      c.   injury would not have occurred if statute not violated
   3. violation excused if reasonable diligence used, unless absolute duty imposed
   4. licensing statutes—do not create liability

E. Extent of liability—interests secured
   1. interests in tangible property protected
   2. interests in physical person protected
   3. mental disturbance sometimes protected:
      a.   physical impact + physical injury = protection
      b.   physical impact + no physical injury = no protection

      c.   no physical impact + physical disorders = protection under majority rule

      d.   no physical impact + no physical disorders = no protection

NOTE—If mental disturbance results from willful, wanton or a vindictive wrong recovery may be permitted

F.   Duty to unborn children—prenatal injuries

   1.   injuries

      a.   unborn viable child—separate entity—may recover

      b.   fetus not viable—split of authority—many courts permit recovery

   2.   wrongful death

      a.   if viable—recovery

      b.   if nonviable—recovery in only a few courts

G.   Proximate cause and liability

   1.   "causation in fact"—series of events which combine to produce a result

   2.   proximate cause—events which produce a result and impose legal liability for it

      a.   negligence must cause injury

      b.   mere possibility not enough

   3.   two negligent persons act to cause one inseparable injury—each liable for entire damage

   4.   two persons act to cause injury but only one is negligent—negligent person liable for entire damage

   5.   two negligent persons act to cause different injuries—each liable only for own damage

   6.   test for proximate cause—does negligent act result in foreseeable danger?

NOTE—Negligence is not based on failure to anticipate extraordinary events

H.   Vicarious liability

   1.   imputed negligence—A's negligence imputed to B who is then liable

   2.   arises because of special relationship

      a.   master servant (employer-employee)

         i.   respondeat superior—master responds for servant's acts within scope of employment

        ii.   includes intentional and negligent torts

      b.   family automobile doctrine

         i.   makes owner of car responsible for tort of user

        ii.   requirements for liability

            (a)   A owns a car

            (b)   A lets members of family use it

            (c)   A gives permission to X to use

            (d)   X is a member of A's family

      c.   joint enterprise

         i.   usually a business venture

        ii.   partners considered to be agents of each other

        iii.   partner can be held for torts of another in scope of venture

I.   Proof of negligence

   1.   P has burden of proving negligence by preponderance of evidence

   2.   D has burden of proving contributory negligence

   3.   the court

      a.   directs a verdict for P or D if reasonable persons could not differ

      b.   jury decides where reasonable persons could differ

J. Res Ipsa Loquitur—the thing speaks for itself
1. elements
a. circumstances of P's injury indicate someone negligent
b. D had exclusive control of instrumentality
c. injury not due to voluntary act by P
2. procedural effect of doctrine
a. creates *inference* of negligence—not a presumption
b. jury may accept or disregard
c. D can rebut
d. minority of courts hold a *presumption* of negligence is created
i. rebuttable presumption—continues until D overcomes it
ii. conclusive presumption—only one conclusion is permitted

IV. DEFENSES TO NEGLIGENCE

A. Contributory negligence—complete defense where P is negligent
NOTE—P may use last clear chance to avoid defense of contributory negligence where:
1. D was aware of P
2. D was aware of P's peril
3. D could have acted to avoid injury
B. Comparative negligence—damages apportioned according to relative fault of parties
C. Assumption of risk—P encounters a known risk voluntarily
D. Imputed negligence—negligence of one person charged to another and this imputed contributory negligence may prevent recovery
E. Intervening cause—requirements for defense
1. D's negligence and a second cause produce injury
2. the second cause was not reasonably foreseeable
3. the intervening cause came after D's negligence and contributed to P's injury
F. Liability insurance—"no-fault"
1. uninsured motorist coverage
2. medical expenses paid
3. Keeton-O'Connell Plan

V. OWNERS AND OCCUPIERS OF LAND

A. Categories of persons
1. trespasser—comes without permission
2. licensee—comes with permission for own purpose
3. invitee—comes with permission for owner's benefit
B. Duty to trespasser
1. trespasser assumes risks
2. cannot set traps for trespasser
3. cannot injure by active negligent conduct
C. Duty to licensee
1. warn of known concealed dangers
2. cannot injure by active negligent conduct
D. Duty to invitee
1. make premises safe

      2. liable for
        a. visible dangers
        b. known concealed dangers
        c. unknown concealed dangers discoverable with due care
        d. active negligent conduct
  E. Modern concept of duty
      1. eliminate trespasser, licensee and invitee classifications
      2. base duty on
        a. foreseeable risk
        b. inconvenience to avoid
        c. what reasonable person would do under circumstances which includes how entry was made and "moral blame" attached to D's conduct
  F. Duty to children trespassers—attractive nuisance
      1. requirements
        a. trespass by children foreseen
        b. condition on premises is artificial (not natural)
        c. child would not recognize danger
        d. usefulness to occupier slight compared to danger involved
      2. when child older, defenses of contributory negligence and assumption of risk available

VI. LIABILITY WITHOUT FAULT

  A. Owners of animals—common law
      1. naturally harmless animals—no liability
      2. domesticated animals
        a. trespassing—strict liability unless
          i. dog or cat
          ii. cattle driven along highway
        b. not trespassing—no liability unless
          i. knowledge of vicious propensities (scienter)
      3. wild animals—strict liability
      NOTE—Statutes often change common law rules and impose strict liability except for those naturally harmless, *e.g.* a canary
  B. Abnormal (ultrahazardous) activities
      1. liability without fault imposed if occupier of land
        a. maintains dangerous condition on land, or
        b. engages in dangerous activity on land, and
        c. either a or b was the proximate cause of injury
      2. use of land must be unnatural or extraordinary
      3. condition or activity must threaten injury because
        a. it is inherently dangerous, and
        b. located where it threatens others
      4. condition or activity must cause damage
  C. Defenses
      1. Act of God
      2. act of third person
      3. assumption of risk—usually a defense
      4. contributory negligence—never a defense

VII. PRODUCTS LIABILITY

  A. Liability of manufacturer and suppliers may be based on
      1. negligence
      2. breach of express or implied warranty

3. strict liability
4. violation of statute
5. tortious misrepresentation
6. res ipsa loquitur

B. Negligence
  1. privity of contract not required—duty owed to all foreseeable users
  2. must make goods safe for foreseeable use
  3. must warn of dangerous design even if product not manufactured negligently
  4. must test and inspect adequately
  5. crashworthiness doctrine allows recovery for enhanced injuries even if defect not cause of initial injury

C. Recovery for breach of warranty
  1. implied warranty
    a. merchantability
    b. fitness for a particular purpose
  2. express warranty
    a. promise by seller
    b. any description of goods
    c. any sample or model
  3. privity of contract not necessary to recover from manufacturer

D. Strict liability
  1. privity not necessary
  2. negligence not necessary
  3. liability imposed for sale of *any* defective product if
    a. seller in business of selling such products
    b. reaches user without substantial change
  4. also applies to bailors and lessors
  5. does not apply to services
  6. design, rather than manufacturing, defect
    a. most courts require that product be "unreasonably dangerous" to user for strict liability to apply
    b. other courts require defectiveness of product to be evaluated by its "reasonably foreseeable use"
    c. defense—risk benefit standard—do benefits of design outweigh risk inherent in design

E. Product misrepresentation
  1. emerging theory of liability
  2. liability for innocent, negligent, or intentional misrepresentations
  3. intentional or reckless misrepresentation may also be fraud

F. Defenses
  1. P must have proven
    a. P was injured by the product
    b. P was injured because product was defective
    c. product defective when it left D's possession
  2. contributory negligence
  3. assumption of risk
  4. intervening cause
  5. disclaimers, exclusions and limitations by manufacturer under UCC

G. Consumer Product Safety Act
  1. Federal statute to protect consumers from unreasonable risks from products

  2. administered by government agency which can
   a. set safety standards for products
   b. ban hazardous products
   c. direct manufacturer to
    i. recall or repair defective product
    ii. replace with non-defective product
    iii. refund purchase price
  3. civil penalties for violation of standard
  4. criminal penalties for willful violation
  5. private suits permitted if no government action

VIII. MISREPRESENTATION

 A. Includes:
  1. fraud and
  2. deceit
 B. Elements
  1. statement of a material fact
  2. statement is false
  3. defendant knows it is false
  4. defendant intends to deceive
 C. P must
  1. reasonably rely on statement
  2. be injured thereby
 D. Action *not* supported by:
  1. prediction of future event
  2. promise to do something in future
  3. statement of opinion
 E. Silence may be misrepresentation if:
  1. latent defective condition
  2. only part of truth told
  3. fiduciary relationship, trade custom, or other circumstances may require disclosure of fact
  4. subsequently acquired information making earlier statement false
 F. If there is no intent to deceive recovery is possible on theory of
  1. negligence—liability for negligently made statements
  2. warranty—the statement constitutes a warranty of condition
 G. Remedies
  1. damages for tort of deceit
  2. damages for making negligent statement
  3. contract damages for breach of warranty
  4. rescission and restitution
 H. Misrepresentation may also be used as a defense
 I. Damages for tort of deceit are either:
  1. loss of bargain, or
  2. out of pocket

IX. UNJUSTIFIABLE LITIGATION

 A. Suits based on legal action taken in bad faith
  1. malicious criminal prosecution
  2. malicious civil proceedings, whether judicial or administrative, such as
   a. involuntary bankruptcy

        b. liquidation proceedings
        c. arrest
        d. execution against property
     3. abuse of process
  B. Interests protected by these torts
     1. physical integrity and freedom from restraint
     2. reputation as an asset
     3. personal dignity and honor
     4. financial integrity
  C. Elements of malicious prosecution
     1. commencement of legal proceedings
     2. proceedings terminate in favor of defendant
     3. proceedings brought without probable cause
     4. malice on part of person bringing proceedings
  D. Abuse of process—using civil or criminal process for a purpose not intended
  E. Elements of abuse of process
     1. intentional, wrongful use of legal process
     2. for an improper purpose
     NOTE—Lack of probable cause and termination of proceedings in defendant's favor NOT required as in malicious prosecution action

X. DEFAMATION

  A. Tort protects right to acquire and maintain good reputation
  B. Tort includes
     1. libel, which is written and seen
     2. slander, which is spoken and heard
  C. Elements of defamation
     1. false and defamatory language
     2. words published to third person
     3. language "of or concerning" plaintiff (P)
        a. P named or identified to a reasonable person
        b. P is part of small group named
     4. reputation injured
  D. Strict liability after publication of matter defamatory per se
     1. crimes
     2. loathsome disease
     3. words affecting business
       e.g. X lawyer is a "shyster"
     4. unchastity to a woman—courts divided
  E. If language not defamatory on its face P must prove
     1. innuendo making statement defamatory
     2. damages sustained
  F. Defenses
     1. truth—an absolute defense
     2. publication by accident without negligence
     3. common law privileges
        a. absolute privilege in
           i. judicial proceedings
           ii. legislative proceedings
           iii. government officers when administering laws
        b. qualified privilege—no specific test—considerations
           i. reasonable publication for proper purpose
           ii. important private interest to protect or public interest in publication

NOTE—Malice cuts off qualified privilege, but not absolute privilege
   4. constitutional privileges (CHART IV)
      a. official conduct of public officials—P must show "actual malice" to recover (N.Y. Times v. Sullivan)
      b. public affairs of public figures—P must show intentional falsehood or reckless disregard for the truth to recover (Curtis Publishing v. Butts)
      c. private individual involved in event of public interest—P may recover compensatory but not punitive damages (Gertz v. Welch)
      d. when right of privacy is balanced against freedom of the press, freedom of the press prevails in absence of showing of "reckless disregard of the truth" (Time v. Hill)
   5. consent by person defamed
   6. partial defenses—damages mitigated by
      a. good faith
      b. P's reputation was already bad
      c. publication of retraction

XI. RIGHT OF PRIVACY

   A. Tort of invasion of privacy protects right of a person to maintain privacy and live an individual life free from unreasonable prying or publicity
   B. Tort protects against
      1. unreasonable intrusion
      2. unreasonable disclosure of another's private life
      3. placing another in a false light
      4. appropriation of another's name or likeness
      NOTE—In contrast to defamation, the fact that disclosure is truthful is no defense to the tort of invasion of privacy
   C. Right of privacy cannot be sustained
      1. by a "public figure"
      2. privilege of publication
      3. consent to publicity
      4. if published to only a few people
      5. child too young to appreciate privacy
      6. a partnership or corporation
   D. Damages for this tort include
      1. harm to interest in privacy
      2. mental distress and personal humiliation
      3. special damages
      4. punitive damages may be limited by Gertz v. Welch decision

XII. INTERFERENCE WITH ADVANTAGEOUS RELATIONS

   A. Law recognizes right to
      1. make contracts, and
      2. engage in a business
   B. Intentional interference with those rights is a tort
      1. inducing someone to break a contract
      2. business competition violating generally accepted business ethics

C. Main defense is privilege
    1. D was furthering a valid interest by lawful means
    2. competition
D. Domestic relationships also protected
    1. interference with marriage or parent-child relation is actionable
    2. good faith advice not actionable

XIII. NUISANCE

A. Describes a field of tort liability
B. Types
    1. public—unreasonable interference with right common to all members of the public
    2. private—substantial and unreasonable interference with use and enjoyment of land by person in possession
C. Pivotal element—reasonableness of D's conduct on the average person, determined by
    1. extent of harm
    2. character of harm
    3. social value of conduct
    4. suitability of conduct to character of locality
    5. ease of preventing harm to burden of avoiding it
D. Remedies
    1. damages
    2. injunction if damages inadequate and continuing acts
    3. abatement by self-help

XIV. IMMUNITY

A. Defense to a tort based on public policy
B. Contrast to privilege
    1. *privilege* eliminates existence of tort
    2. *immunity* avoids liability for the tort without denying the existence of a tort
C. Intra-family
    1. common law—no action between husband and wife or child and parents for personal torts
    2. trend of recent decisions—suits for all personal torts permitted
D. Charitable immunity
    1. traditionally—charities immune
    2. present decisions—"rapid overthrow" of charitable immunity
E. Governmental immunity
    1. common law—full immunity—"the king can do no wrong"
    2. common law applied to Federal and state governments—must give consent to suit
        a. Federal government consents in Federal Tort Claims Act except for
            i. intentional torts
            ii. discretionary functions
        b. state and local governments—trend to limit or abolish immunity by
            i. statute, or
            ii. court decision

3. Eleventh Amendment grants states immunity from private suits
4. exception—when state denies Constitutional rights

XV. DAMAGES

A. Damages—money given for an injury
　1. nominal—small sum of money for a wrong which does no real injury
　2. compensatory—money for actual loss suffered and nothing more
　　a. general damages—flow from wrong complained of
　　b. special damages—not proximate consequence of wrong; must be specifically pleaded
　3. punitive—money in excess of compensatory damages to punish a willful or wanton act
　　a. malice required
　　b. discretionary with jury
B. Contribution—right of one of several joint defendants who has discharged a liability common to all to recover proportionate share from others
C. Indemnity—shifts entire loss from defendant tortfeasor to another—damages not apportioned
D. Damages—wrongful death
　1. basis for recovery—pecuniary loss to survivors and not total amount of decedent's future earnings
　2. mental suffering of survivors not considered
　3. unborn child—split of authority on recovery
　4. distinguish from survival statutes which:
　　a. permit recovery for conscious pain and suffering of decedent, property damage and hospital bills prior to death
　　b. are independent of wrongful death statutes
E. Loss of consortium—services and conjugal affection of spouse
　1. common law—granted only to men
　2. today—remedy available to women because of Equal Protection Clause
F. Remittitur and Additur—remedies for "grossly excessive" or "grossly inadequate" jury verdicts
　1. remittitur—order P to release D from part of damages awarded by jury or submit to a new trial
　　a. recognized at common law
　　b. utilized when appropriate
　2. additur—order D to pay more than jury award or submit to a new trial
　　a. constitutional problem
　　　i. not recognized at common law
　　　ii. denies P right to jury trial of Seventh Amendment. P has no choice
　　　iii. rarely used in Federal courts
　　　iv. state courts divided on constitutional issue

TEXT CORRELATION CHART

Smith's Review Torts	Franklin	Green	Gregory	Keeton	Prosser and Wade	Shapo	Shulman
Chapter II							
Assault	605–611	5–26	907–913	8–10, 24–26	34–36	58–63	1010–1018
Battery	605–611	6, 17–20, 75–79	903–907	5–8, 26–40	30–33	64–74, 90–93	1010–1018
Battery—Special Rules	607–611	55, 162	6–14	52–54	28–29	181–191	1022–1027
Emotional Distress	233–238, 651–659	20–27	933–952	113–123	50–70	94–105	
False Imprisonment & False Arrest	634–642	37–48	920–933	41–43	37–49, 125–127	113–115, 145–156	1039–1048
Trespass to Land			915–919	136–138, 161	70–81	941	
Trespass to Chattels			86–88	141–143	81–96	117	
Defenses—Privilege							
Mistake and Unavoidable Accident						461	
Defenses—Consent	607–611, 620–622	17	14–17	45–51	97–111	180	1022–1023
Defense of Self and Others	611–613, 622–624	27–33	18–23	63–67, 104–105	113–116	119–131	
Defense of Property	613–615		22–23	73–90	116–124		
Defenses—Necessity	615–629	424–426	33–42	150–160	129–136	459–472	45–50
Legal Process and Arrest				90–103	137–138	153–162	
Defenses—Discipline				104–113	138–140		
Chapter III							
Historical Development		552–554	60–74	161–165	6–12, 143–144	215–217, 752–754	
Reasonable Person Concept	36–66, 109	160–162, 562–567	109–110, 130–155, 208–211	207–229, 249–252	144–216	251–270, 314–317	171–212
Standard for Children	54–57	79, 668–669	136–148	234–238	177–184	398–403	156
Misfeasance and Nonfeasance	167–191	89–95, 135, 182	338–360	252–266, 401–405	434–458	708	308
Violation of Statute	569–573	667	183–202	278–280, 331–332	220–246	265–277	210–216, 334–338
Mental Distress	246–253	114–126	952–975	367–383	417–434	629–631	504–518
Duty to Unborn Children		1072–1076		197–202	258–268		553
Proximate Cause	131–162	562–597	247–312	313–347	284–334	734–776	339–373
Master—Servant	366–378		701–709	293–303	688–692	383–389	103–112
Family Automobile Doctrine	382–385	699–701		307–309	697		
Res Ipsa Loquitur	71, 85–93	166–174, 708–709	222–246	266–278	251–280	546–554	249–284
Chapter IV							
Contributory Negligence	291–306	556–557	381–404	166, 495–502	591–603	358–403	374–402
Assumption of the Risk	308–324		406–416	517–537	617–636		

Smith's Review Torts	Franklin	Green	Gregory	Keeton	Prosser and Wade	Shapo	Shulman
Imputed Negligence	300–301	699	716–734	305–306, 502–514	693–704		
Last Clear Chance	295–299	719–722	400–408	166–168, 495–502	599–603	409–413	403, 405
Comparative Negligence	324–341	711–723	426–440	537–551	603–617	413–421	428–440
No Fault Insurance	793–839	739–755	833–888	775–834	1300–1324	797–859	666–670
Chapter V General Duty			447–449	406–408	481–486	241–244	
Analysis of Duty	191–194	501–539	449–459		487–504	240–244	619–644
Attractive Nuisance	204–206	468–494	459–468	418–423	510–515	389–398	591–596
Modern Concept of Duty	194–211	508–509	474–485	408–417	517–522	244–245	
Chapter VI Injury from Animals		326–329	488–495	573–578	705–709		97–99
Abnormal Activities	392–419	365–378	495–514	579–595	709–726	421–428	53–67
Defenses	419	401–402	514–517		729–736		
Chapter VII Negligence and Privity	211–217, 487–488	254–261	360–372, 549–573	631–640, 661–666	738–744	203–209, 943–944	671–680, 702, 731
Warranty Theory	440–441, 545–568	266–280	561, 566–573, 580–589	640–660	749–755	776–786	701–721
Strict Liability	473–528	299–306	573–598, 609–631	429–448, 668–730, 747–758	756–794	429–448	438–442, 722–740
Product Misrepresentation	444	280–291	554–566	667–668	744–748, 840–841, 962–963		680–682
Defenses	528–545, 563–568		571–573, 620–622	730–746	785–786	453–459, 943–944	701–702, 725–726
Chapter VIII Actionable Misrepresentation	1019–1068	777–786, 797–798, 914–926		835–933	911–913, 936–942		747–839
Chapter IX Malicious Prosecution	634–650	1339–1348		1104–1130	1119–1143	646	1049–1060
Abuse of Process	650–651	1339–1342		1130–1133	1144–1148	632–638, 646	1049–1060
Chapter X Common Law Defamation (Libel and Slander)	884–902	1206–1236	977–1039	934–981	977–1022	61–64, 981, 1003–1004	840–865
Common Law Defenses	934–936	1236–1244	1039–1040	1080–1103	990, 1079–1081		866–872
Privileges	936–956	1258–1305	1040–1081	1042–1080	1058–1078	1013–1025	872–879
Constitutional Privileges	902–934	1166–1199	1081–1129	981–1041	1023–1057	980–1013	880–948
Defenses— Procedural Aspects	956–959	1186–1188, 1261–1262	983, 1039–1040	970–975	1019–1020		844–845
Chapter XI Privacy Interests Protected	965–1018	25–27, 1000–1026, 1194–1206	1131–1190	1135–1170	1083–1118	1–12, 954–958, 1026–1044	953–989

Smith's Review Torts	Franklin	Green	Gregory	Keeton	Prosser and Wade	Shapo	Shulman
Chapter XII							
Interference with Advantageous Relations Interests Protected	1086–1150	818–824, 868–876, 932–937		1175–1176	1149–1210	954–978	
Chapter XIII							
Public and Private Nuisances	420–424	408–410	521–524	621–626	846–855	933–953	86–94
Actionable Conduct	420–424		517–532		861–872		
Defenses					895–898		71–78
Remedies	424–436	402–406	536–546	603–621	882–894	926–932	78–86
Chapter XIV							
Intra-family Immunities	346–355	1088–1099	735–747	477–486	643–653		455–459
Charitable Immunity	341–345	186–192	747–750	490–495	653–657	1044–1056	137–138
Governmental Immunity	355–364	214–239	750–761	455–470	657–677	1056–1080	120–137
Chapter XV							
Compensatory Damages	710–721	583	677–689	180–189	537–560	850–856	477–480
Joint Tortfeasors		724–739	441–445	323–324	406–410	647–652	301–306
Contribution	330–335, 755–759	724–737		552–555	392–396	653–667	
Indemnity	330–331, 386–391, 755–759	737–739		555–559	399–403	653–669	
Wrongful Death	268–282	1042–1068	690–700		570–590	473–512	
Loss of Consortium	259–266	1099–1110		1182–1190	1208		546–557
Remittur and Additur					546–547		

I INTRODUCTION

Summary Outline

A. Basic Concepts

B. Basis of Liability

C. Analysis of Torts Problems

BASIC CONCEPTS

1. A tort is a breach of a noncontractual legal duty. It is a private or civil (as opposed to criminal or public) wrong for which the law provides a remedy.

   (a) It may be intentional aggression against another person such as assault or battery.

   (b) It may be the invasion of an owner's interest in the exclusive possession of land, as by a trespass.

   (c) It may be the wrongful interference with intangible interests, such as libel or slander which injures the good reputation of another.

2. The source of the duty which is breached in a tort may be a court decision or a statute.

   e.g. Courts impose the duty on all persons to refrain from creating an unreasonable risk of harm to others by their conduct. Statutes require persons to obey traffic regulations.

3. The same act may be both a tort and a crime. A tort is a private injury redressed by suit of the injured party, and a crime is an offense against the public which is prosecuted by state or federal authorities.

   e.g. The unjustified hitting of another person is a battery. It is both a tort and a crime.

4. The person who has been injured may bring a civil action for money damages or some other remedy. The person filing suit is called the plaintiff.

5. The person who is sued is called the defendant.

6. When the plaintiff files suit he alleges the facts on which he relies in a document called a complaint.

7. The defendant files an answer to the complaint in which the facts alleged are admitted or denied. The defendant may also move to dismiss the complaint on the ground that even if the facts as stated by the plaintiff are true there is no legal basis upon which the plaintiff may recover.

8. The plaintiff's action is generally tried before a judge and jury.

   (a) The judge rules on matters of law.

   (b) The jury resolves any factual disputes between the plaintiff and the defendant.

9. At trial the plaintiff must establish a "prima facie case." The usual usage of that term is that the plaintiff must produce evidence sufficient to render reasonable a conclusion in favor of the allegation contained in the complaint, such as the commission of a tort by the defendant which was the proximate cause of an injury to the plaintiff. In other words "prima facie case" means that the evidence is sufficient to establish the plaintiff's

case if all other evidence is disregarded. See Husbands v. Pennsylvania, 395 F.Supp. 1107, 1139 (D.C.Pa.1975).

10. When the plaintiff has established a prima facie case the defendant is subject to liability. However, that does not mean that the defendant is in fact liable to the plaintiff. The defendant may escape liability by presenting a valid defense.

11. After the trial court enters judgment for one of the parties, the other party may appeal to an appellate court.

    (a) The party who takes the appeal to set aside the judgment is called the appellant.

    (b) The party who is appealed is called the appellee.

    NOTE—The student will encounter many unfamiliar terms during this course. For an explanation of those terms the student should consult the Index under the heading "Definitions" or under the particular word for a reference to the page where the term is explained.

1. The elements for a tort action are:

    BASIS OF LIABILITY

    (a) a legal duty,

    (b) a breach of that duty, and

    (c) an injury to such person which is the proximate result of the breach of the duty.

2. All tort liability is based on one of three grounds:

    (a) intentional aggression,

    (b) negligence, or

    (c) "liability without fault", when there is neither intentional aggression, nor negligence.

3. Intentional aggression may be toward:

    (a) property, personal or real, or

    (b) the person, physical or mental.

    See Chapter II, Intentional Torts, below.

4. Negligence may result from doing an affirmative act without using due care, or in negligently failing to do an act which is required by law to be done. See Chapter III, Negligence, below.

5. If an actor has been negligent, there are various defenses which may be applicable to negate all or part of the liability. See Chapter IV, Defenses to Negligence, below.

6. There are special duties imposed on owners and occupiers of land. These duties traditionally depend on the status of the

person who comes onto the land. See Chapter V, Owners and Occupiers of Land, below.

7. Liability without fault, also called strict liability or absolute liability, is liability imposed on one engaged in an activity peculiarly dangerous to others. Liability is imposed even though the activity was conducted carefully and no harm was intended to others. This is based on public policy for the protection of the general welfare. See Chapter VI, Liability Without Fault, below.

8. The liability of the manufacturer or supplier of a product which causes personal injury to the user may be based on:

    (a) negligence,

    (b) strict liability,

    (c) warranty of the product, or

    (d) one of several emerging theories.

    See Chapter VII, Products Liability, below.

9. The law imposes liability for other acts or conduct in certain situations. These include the torts of:

    (a) fraud and misrepresentation, see Chapter VIII, Misrepresentation, below,

    (b) malicious prosecution and abuse of process, see Chapter IX, Unjustifiable Litigation, below,

    (c) libel and slander, see Chapter X, Defamation, below,

    (d) invasion of privacy, see Chapter XI, Right of Privacy, below,

    (e) wrongful interference with the business or contractual relations of another, see Chapter XII, Interference with Advantageous Relations, below, and

    (f) unreasonable interference with another's use and enjoyment of land, see Chapter XIII, Nuisance, below.

10. Even though the elements of a tort are present and there is no defense available, there may be no civil liability because of:

    (a) the relation of the parties, or

    (b) the status of the actor.

    See Chapter XIV, Immunity, below.

11. After liability has been established, the damages which may be recovered must be determined. See Chapter XV, Damages, below.

1. In analyzing any torts question, the student must go beyond a mere "pigeonholing" of the basic area of tort liability in question. Once the facts have been analyzed to determine the tort or torts which may be the basis of liability, there remain issues of:

   (a) defenses,

   (b) immunities,

   (c) requisite intention or state of mind,

   > *e.g.* The tort of malicious prosecution requires a showing of malice. The tort of false imprisonment does not require malice, but if malice is shown, punitive damages may be awarded to punish the willful or wanton wrongful act.

   (d) legal causation, and

   (e) damages.

2. In addition to these substantive issues, the problem may contain procedural issues, such as burden of proof or joinder.

3. The student should be continually aware that as to any given set of facts there may be more than one applicable theory of liability, and thus all possible alternative or overlapping theories, and their related defenses, and measures of damages, should be considered.

   > *e.g.* In a products liability problem, there may be liability based on negligence, breach of warranty, strict liability, or some other theory. The remedy may be different depending on the theory urged by the plaintiff. Further, the defenses available to the defendant may also be different depending on the theory of recovery urged.

4. The three bases of liability described above (see Basis of Liability, number 2) all refer to kinds of *conduct* on the part of the defendant. The student must also be aware of the *interest* of the plaintiff which has been invaded by the conduct in question. Different interests are protected by different torts.

   > *e.g.* The interest in one's personal reputation is protected by the tort of defamation, and the interest in freedom from unwarranted publicity is protected by an action for invasion of privacy. Therefore, in each fact situation the student must look for all interests of the plaintiff which may have been invaded by the defendant's conduct to determine the torts which may have been committed.

5. The nature of the defendant's conduct is always important. This may determine whether or not liability will be imposed, and if liability is imposed the extent of liability.

e.g. If D's negligence causes an injury to P, D may have the defense of contributory negligence available which will prevent P from recovering because P was also negligent. By contrast, if D committed an intentional tort thereby injuring P, the contributory negligence of P would not be a defense.

II INTENTIONAL TORTS

Summary Outline

INTRODUCTION **1.** Intentional torts constitute the first of the three basic categories of torts. These categories include:

    (a) intentional torts,

    (b) negligence, and

    (c) liability without fault.

2. The intentional tort may be directed towards:

    (a) property, personal or real, or

    (b) the person, physical or mental.

3. An element, common to all of the intentional torts, is the requisite frame of mind of the defendant. The defendant must intend to commit the tort.

4. Intentional torts against the person include:

    (a) Assault,

    (b) Battery,

    (c) Intentionally causing emotional distress,

    (d) False imprisonment and false arrest.

5. Intentional torts to property include:

    (a) Trespass to land, and

    (b) Trespass to chattels.

6. In addition to the defenses which are traditionally analyzed with respect to specific individual intentional torts, there are a number of defenses which are generally available to all intentional torts.

These include:

    (a) Privilege,

    (b) Consent,

    (c) Self-defense,

    (d) Defense of others,

    (e) Mistake,

    (f) Unavoidable accident,

    (g) Defense of property,

    (h) Recapture of chattels,

    (i) Necessity,

    (j) Legal process and arrest, and

    (k) Discipline.

7. The intentional torts and defenses thereto outlined above are the traditional intentional torts, all of which are discussed in this Chapter. In addition thereto, the following intentional torts are discussed elsewhere in this Review:

   (a) Invasion of privacy,

   (b) Interference with advantageous relationships,

   (c) Defamation,

   (d) Misrepresentation,

   (e) Malicious prosecution, and

   (f) Abuse of process.

1. The essential elements of an assault at common law are these: **ASSAULT**

   (a) On the part of the defendant—

      (1) The defendant must *intentionally set in motion a force towards* the *plaintiff.*

      (2) Such force must be *wrongfully set in motion* by the defendant.

      (3) The defendant's intention must be that of causing a harmful or offensive contact with a person of the plaintiff, or a third person, or an imminent apprehension of such a contact.

   (b) On the part of the plaintiff—

      (4) The force set in motion towards the plaintiff must be *without* the plaintiff's *consent* and *against his will.*

      (5) To the plaintiff as a reasonable person there must be *apparent present ability* on the part of the defendant to inflict immediate bodily injury on him.

      (6) The plaintiff must *reasonably* be apprehensive of *immediate bodily injury.*

2. The gist of the injury in assault is the apprehension in the mind of the plaintiff caused by the threat of the defendant's act.

   e.g. D went to a tavern to buy a bottle of wine. He found the tavern closed and struck the door with his hatchet. P leaned out of the window and told D to stop. D struck at P with his hatchet, but missed her. P sued for damages for assault. May P recover even though D did not hit her?

   Answer. Yes. An assault may be committed even though no bodily harm resulted. The fact that D missed P when he swung at her is not a defense. P recovered damages. See I. de

S. and Wife v. W. de S., Liber Assisarum, folio 99, placitum 60 (1348 or 1349).

3. The force must be such as would put a reasonable person in fear, not merely one who is super-sensitive or "scared of his own shadow". Note, however, that if the defendant's conduct is intended to create the required apprehension in the plaintiff, and it achieves that result, then there is liability for an assault, even though a person of ordinary courage would not have had such apprehension. See Restatement, Second, Torts § 27.

4. "Apprehension" does not mean "fear"; it is awareness of the defendant's conduct. See Prosser, pp. 38–40.

5. Mere words, looks or gestures, without more, however violent or insulting, cannot constitute an assault under the general rule. The defendant must be able to carry out his threat immediately and there must be some affirmative act to do so. See Western Union Telegraph Co. v. Hill, 25 Ala.App. 540, 150 So. 709 (1933); Prince v. Ridge, 32 Misc. 666, 66 N.Y.S. 454 (1900).

> *e.g.* P filed suit alleging that D displayed a blackjack and stated that he would beat P unless P left the premises. The court dismissed the suit because words alone, no matter how threatening do not constitute an assault. The mere possession of blackjacks by D and others with him did not convert the unactionable words into a cause of action. To convert a threat into an assault there must be some act to show that a battery will follow immediately. The complaint did not allege that the blackjacks were shown to P in a manner that would amount to an offer to commit a battery. Therefore, P's complaint was dismissed. See Cucinotti v. Ortmann, 399 Pa. 26, 159 A.2d 216 (1960). See also Read v. Coker, 13 C.B. 850, 138 Eng.Rep. 1437 (1853).

NOTE—Although insulting or abusive language, which is not accompanied by some act or slight body movement and threat of immediate battery, does not constitute an assault under the general rule, words alone may be sufficient to impose liability for some other tort, such as intentionally causing emotional distress. See Emotional Distress, below.

6. The defendant need not actually intend to harm the plaintiff. It is the apparent intention to act, the *apparent meaning* of the words and act to a reasonable person under the circumstances, which determine whether fear was reasonably created in the plaintiff.

CAVEAT—The *civil* action in tort for assault must be distinguished from the *crime* of assault. The tort of assault requires that there be *apparent* present ability to assault, but the crime of assault requires present *actual* ability.

e.g.   P rented an apartment from D, but was behind in rent payments.   While P was having her furniture moved out of the apartment, D pointed a pistol at P and threatened to shoot her in order to prevent P from moving her furniture.   P sued D for assault, and D contended no assault could be committed because of the lack of evidence that the pistol was loaded.   The court found D guilty of assault.   Even if there were no actual present ability to shoot P, the apparent present ability is just as effective in causing fright as though the gun were loaded.   Actual ability is not necessary.   Therefore, D committed the tort of assault.   See Allen v. Hannaford, 138 Wash. 423, 244 P. 700 (1926).

NOTE—By contrast, however, apparent present ability is not sufficient to constitute the common law crime of assault.   There must be actual present ability.   See Restatement, Second, Torts § 22, comment b.   See also Restatement, Second, Torts §§ 21–34.   Today, many courts apply the tort test to criminal assault.

See generally, Gregory, pp. 907–913; Keeton, pp. 8–10, 24–26; P & W, pp. 34–36; Prosser, pp. 37–41.

Conditional threat is not an assault   Case 1

P sued D for assault.   D contended that the assault was justified because P put his hand on his sword and said, "If it were not assize time, I would not take such language from you."   Were P's words an assault justifying D's subsequent assault?

   Answer. *No.   P's words did not constitute an assault at common law because they did not show a present intention to do anything.   If the words used by D are taken at their face value, there is no present threat of immediate bodily injury to P because it was, in fact, assize time.   There was no present threat.   No assault can be based on a threat of future injury.   Without both apparent present ability, and reasonable apprehension of immediate bodily contact, there can be no assault.   Thus, D's defense that P assaulted him is not valid.*

   See Tuberville v. Savage, 1 Mod. 3, 86 Eng.Rep. 684 (King's Bench 1669).

Assault—required elements   Case 2

P was in a hotel dining room.   D walked up to P carrying a stick and threatened to "whip hell out of" P unless P signed "an apology and retraction" which D had prepared.   P signed and later sued for assault.   May P recover?

Answer. Yes. All the elements of an assault are present. (1) D directed a force towards P intentionally. (2) The force was wrongful. (3) Such force was without P's consent and against her will. (4) There was apparent present ability by D, to any reasonable person in P's position and condition to (5) inflict immediate bodily injury on P if P violated the condition which D had no right to impose. If one can escape threatened and immediate bodily injury only by leaving a place where he has a right to be, or to do an act which he otherwise would not have done, there is an assault.

See Trogden v. Terry, 172 N.C. 510, 90 S.E. 583 (1916).

Case 3   *Assault—plaintiff unaware*

D pointed a loaded rifle at P intending to kill P. Before D pulled the trigger a friend of P stuck a revolver in D's ribs and said, "Put that gun down or you will get it too." Thereupon, D put his gun down. P did not see what happened and was not aware of the threat until he was told about it later. P sues D for damages for assault. The court directed a verdict for D. Was the court correct?

Answer. Yes. The fact that D was a "bad egg" does not make him liable for assault if the essential elements of the tort are not present. In this case D intentionally directed a hostile force towards P. There was not only apparent present ability, there was actual present ability as is required generally in criminal assault. Any reasonable person in P's position would have been put in fear of immediate bodily injury had he seen what D did. But that is the element of the tort which is absent. There can be no assault without the plaintiff's being conscious of the threat to his physical integrity. Without P's being aware of the threat from D, he could not be and was not put in fear of immediate bodily injury. Hence, this element being absent, the court was correct in directing a verdict for the defendant.

See State v. Barry, 45 Mont. 598, 124 P. 775 (1912).

BATTERY 1.   The essential elements of a battery at common law include:

(a) The defendant must *intentionally* by an act set in motion a force towards the plaintiff, or a third person.

(b) The force must be *wrongful,* not justified by the usages of men.

(c) The force directed towards the plaintiff must be *without his consent* and *against his will.*

(d) The force must cause *physical contact* with the person of the plaintiff.

2. The gist of the offense in battery is the unpermissible touching of the person of the plaintiff without his consent.

    NOTE 1—The intent to harm is not necessary to establish a battery, but rather the intent to bring about some offensive bodily contact. See Baldinger v. Banks, 26 Misc.2d 1086, 201 N.Y.S.2d 629 (1960), where a six year old was held liable. See also Restatement of Torts, § 13, Comment e.

    NOTE 2—An insane person is held liable for his torts. Usually this is based on public policy. In McGuire v. Almy, 297 Mass. 323, 8 N.E.2d 760 (1937), the court held an insane person liable for assault and battery. The court stated that the decision would encourage custodians and those interested in the estate of the insane person to keep him under control.

3. A touching of the person which is sanctioned by the usages of society is not a battery.

    e.g. D taps P on the shoulder merely to get his attention to point out to him a comet in the sky. P is jostled in a crowd leaving a football game and D just happens to be a person whose body brushes against P. These may be offensive to P but they are not batteries.

4. It is not essential that the plaintiff be aware of the battery when it is inflicted on his person.

    e.g. D sneaks up behind P and hits him on the head with a club causing P's immediate unconsciousness. P neither sees nor hears D, but there is a battery.

5. There must be some volitional act by the defendant for a battery. Mere passivity cannot constitute a battery.

    e.g. P attempted to enter the dining room of a hotel, but was prevented from entering by a policeman stationed at the door. P sued for assault. The court held that if the policeman was passive, and merely stood in the doorway blocking the entrance, there was no assault. However, if the policeman pushed P back when P attempted to enter the room, there would be an assault and battery. See Innes v. Wylie, 1 C & K 257, 174 Eng.Rep. 800 (1844).

6. The contact need not be with the physical person directly; it is enough if the contact is with a thing which is so connected with the person as to be identified with it such as one's clothing, jewelry, or a book in one's hand.

    e.g. P attended a buffet style luncheon with others. P was standing in line waiting to be served when D snatched the plate from P's hand and shouted that P, a Negro, could not be served. Although P was not actually touched, the unpermitted and intentional taking of the plate constituted a battery. P was permitted to recover for actual damages which included mental suffering and exemplary damages for D's malicious conduct. See Fisher v. Carrousel Motor Hotel, Inc., 424 S.W.2d 627 (Tex. 1967). See also Alcorn v. Mitchell, 63 Ill. 553 (1872) where punitive damages were awarded for maliciously spitting in a person's face, and Chapter XV, Damages, below.

7. The least possible unpermissible touching, even though no actual injury results, is a battery; such touching is damage as a matter of law. See Cole v. Turner, 6 Modern Rep. 149, 90 Eng.Rep. 958 (Nisi Prius, 1704), Restatement, Second, Torts §§ 13–20.

See generally, Keeton, pp. 5–8, 26–40; Gregory, pp. 903–907; P & W, pp. 30–33; Prosser, pp. 34–37.

Case 4 *Battery—indirect causation of harm*

P, an arthritic woman, was about to sit down in a chair when D, aged five years, nine months, suddenly and without warning, pulled the chair from under her. P fell to the ground and was injured. P sued D for damages in battery. May she recover?

Answer. Yes. Even a joke may result in a battery if the essential elements are present. If the pulling of the chair from under P by D was intentional and done with substantial certainty that P would attempt to sit where the chair had been, there is a battery. It was none the less so because it was intended as a joke. Such force exercised by D towards P was without P's consent and against her will. The removal of the chair caused the physical contact between P's body and the ground. These facts constitute a battery for which P may recover in tort. The types of situation in which a battery may exist are almost as varied as the activities of men. D's yelling at the horse on which P is riding, causing the horse to rear and throw P to the ground; D's spitting in P's face; D's knocking a paper rudely from P's hand; D's turning the sun's rays, by a mirror, against the helpless body of P and burning it; D's putting poison in candy in New York and sending it to P in San Diego, which is eaten by P causing illness; all these are illustrative of facts which constitute batteries.

See Garratt v. Dailey, 46 Wash.2d 197, 279 P.2d 1091 (1955). See also Clark v. Downing, 55 Vt. 259 (1882).

BATTERY—SPECIAL RULES

1. In determining the existence of the requisite elements of the tort of battery a number of special rules or so-called "doctrines" have developed. These are:

   (a) The *doctrine of transferred intent*—which supplies an otherwise missing element of intent.

(b) the *technical battery,* which negatives the defense of consent, and

(c) the *emergency doctrine,* which supplies the otherwise missing consent as the defense.

2. Under the doctrine of transferred intent, if D intentionally directs some force against X but instead hits Y, D's intent is said to be "transferred" from X to Y.

3. The doctrine of transferred intent was adopted to supply the requisite intent for the tort of battery which would otherwise be missing. By virtue of this doctrine the actor is said to be responsible for the natural consequences of his act. See CASE 5, below.

    CAVEAT—The doctrine of transferred intent is also applicable to other intentional torts and in criminal law fact situations as well.

4. A technical battery occurs when a physician or dentist, in the course of treatment, exceeds the consent given by a patient. Although no wrongful intent is present, and in fact there may be a sincere purpose to aid the patient, recovery is permitted unless there is an emergency. However, if the patient benefits from the battery only nominal damages may be recovered. See CASE 6, below.

5. The doctrine of technical battery serves to negative the "consent" of the patient, which would otherwise be a defense to the tort.

6. In an emergency situation when medical service is required for an adult who by virtue of his physical condition is incapable of giving consent, or with respect to a child, whose parent or other guardian is absent, and thus incapable of giving consent, the law implies the consent required to administer emergency medical services. See Prosser, p. 104.

    e.g. P, an adult, is injured in a traffic accident, and is rendered unconscious. D, a doctor, determines that immediate surgery is required to stop internal bleeding. P, by reason of his unconsciousness, is incapable of consenting to the surgery. After the surgery, P recovers, and brings an action against D for the surgery as being unrequested and unconsented to. D defends on the basis of the emergency doctrine, contending that circumstances were such that a reasonable man in P's position would have consented to the surgery at that time. Can P recover?

    Answer. No. This fact pattern is exactly that which is contemplated by the emergency doctrine. To hold otherwise would put D, the defendant doctor, at his peril in rendering medical services which were reasonably required, and would put people in the position of plaintiff, generally, in danger of not receiving required medical services.

See generally, Gregory, pp. 6–14; Keeton, pp. 52–54; P & W, pp. 28–29, 100–105.

Case 5 *Battery—transferred intent doctrine*

D saw two boys on the roof of one of his sheds. D ordered the boys to get down and they began to do so. Before they were down D took a stick and threw it in the direction of the boys. The stick did not hit them, but it hit another boy, P, in the eye causing the boy to lose the sight of the eye. P sued for damages. D did not intend to hit P. The jury was instructed that if they concluded that D threw the stick intending to hit one of the boys on the shed, and that was an unreasonable force under all the circumstances, then D would be liable. The jury found for P. Was the instruction a correct statement of the law?

Answer. Yes. D is liable to P for battery and for all the damages which are the natural and proximate result of D's act. When one intends to commit a battery on one person, but misses the one intended and hits another, it is a case of what is called, "transferred" intent. It is none the less a battery on the person who is hit, and the actor is liable for the tort so committed, and for all the damages which flow therefrom. The right of P to recover was properly made to depend on D's intent to hit someone and to inflict an unwarranted injury upon someone. The judgment in P's favor was affirmed.

See Talmage v. Smith, 101 Mich. 370, 59 N.W. 656 (1894).

Case 6 *Technical battery—exceeding consent*

D, an ear specialist, advised P to have an operation on her right ear and she consented. While P was under an anaesthetic in the operating room D examined her and concluded that the condition of P's right ear was not so serious as to require an operation, but that P's left ear should be operated upon. D told these facts to P's family physician, who was present in the operating room at P's request to "calm her fears" of the operation. D suggested the operation on P's left ear and P's family physician made no objection. D performed the operation which was successful and P benefited therefrom. P sued for assault and battery. May P recover damages?

Answer. Yes. P did not consent to the operation on her left ear and her physician did not have authority to consent. D's act went beyond P's consent to an operation on her right ear and, therefore, D's act was tortious. D committed what is known as a "technical battery" and P may recover. A patient's consent is necessary for an operation except when: (1) the injured person is unconscious or unable to consent and prompt medical attention is necessary, or

(2) during the operation consented to conditions are discovered which require that the operation be extended. In the present case the condition was discovered before the operation began, and it could have been postponed to obtain P's consent. Thus P is entitled to damages.

 See Mohr v. Williams, 95 Minn. 261, 104 N.W. 12 (1905).

 NOTE—The *Mohr* decision is followed in most jurisdictions today. However, some courts have taken the position that a patient's consent to an operation, in the absence of evidence to the contrary, will be construed as general in nature rather than being limited to a specific operation. Under that construction the surgeon may extend the operation to remedy any abnormal or diseased condition in the area of the original incision when the surgeon, in the exercise of sound professional judgment, determines that the operation originally contemplated should be extended.

 e.g. P consented to an appendectomy. During the operation the surgeon discovered cysts on P's ovaries and punctured them in accordance with usual medical procedures. P sued for battery because her consent to the operation was exceeded. There was no allegation that P's surgeon exercised bad judgment or that the extended operation was not dictated by sound surgical procedure. Recovery was denied because the court concluded that P's consent should be construed to authorize an extension of the intended operation where sound medical judgment indicated that should be done. See Kennedy v. Parrott, 243 N.C. 355, 90 S.E.2d 754 (1956).

EMOTIONAL DISTRESS

1. The intentional causing of emotional distress or mental disturbance is recognized as a tort separate and apart from assault and battery in most jurisdictions.

2. This tort recognizes a right to recover for a severe disturbance of mental or emotional tranquility resulting from an unprivileged act committed intentionally or recklessly, even though there is no physical injury or independent tort committed. See cases collected at 64 A.L.R.2d 100, 119.

3. "One who by extreme and outrageous conduct intentionally or recklessly causes severe emotional distress to another is subject to liability for such emotional distress and for bodily harm resulting from it." Restatement, Second, Torts, § 46(1).

 NOTE—The Restatement further states: "Liability has been found only where the conduct has been so outrageous in character, and so extreme in degree, as to go beyond all possible bounds of decency, and to be regarded as attrocious, and utterly intolerable in a civilized community." Restatement, Second, Torts § 46, comment g.

4.   This tort may exist without either the threat of physical contact involved in assault, or the actual contact involved in battery. This is a developing area of the law and the limits of this tort have not yet been defined.

5.   The tort may be committed by intentionally using words or doing an act with the purpose in mind of causing to another, fright, terror, anxiety or distress of mind and which actually causes such mental disturbance. See CASE 7, below.

    (a)   The landlord, D, locked P out of her apartment although she had paid her rent. When she went to D to complain and seek assistance, D refused to allow P to enter her apartment, and said that P could not have the apartment any more. D also yelled at P, saying that he would not rent to P any more. D's conduct caused P to become frightened, and suffer an upset to her glandular system. It resulted in nervousness, headaches, loss of sleep and inability to carry on her normal activities. P recovered damages for intentionally causing emotional distress, and D appealed. The court rejected D's contention that there could be no cause of action for personal injuries arising from fright caused by spoken words, and affirmed the judgment for P. See Emden v. Vitz, 88 Cal.App.2d 313, 198 P.2d 696 (1948).

    (b)   D decided to commit suicide in P's kitchen by cutting his throat. When P discovered "the gory and gastly sight" of the corpse and blood all over her kitchen she was shocked, became nervous, and had difficulty sleeping thereafter. P sued D's estate. May she recover?

        Answer. Yes. The appellate court reversed a directed verdict for D's estate and held that recovery should be permitted if the jury found that D's suicide was willful even though P's injury was caused by fright. See Blakeley v. Shortal's Estate, 236 Iowa 787, 20 N.W.2d 28 (1945).

    (c)   An association of rubbish collectors threatened to beat P and burn his truck unless he paid money that he collected in a territory assigned to someone else. P became ill from fright, and he was permitted to recover damages and cancel notes given in payment of the unlawful demand. See State Rubbish Collectors Association v. Siliznoff, 38 Cal.2d 330, 240 P.2d 282 (1952).

6.   There can be no recovery for mental disturbance alone, unless the circumstances are aggravated and the injury real and substantial; mere annoyance, hurt feelings or exaggerated mental injury will not support the action. See Wallace v. Shoreham Hotel Corp., 49 A.2d 81 (D.C.Mun.App., 1946); Restatement, Second, Torts § 46, comment d.

    CAVEAT—In the analysis of any case involving emotional distress, or mental disturbance, the student must look for the

CAUSE of that mental disturbance, and determine if it is negligent or intentional. The student must also look to see if the mental disturbance was accompanied by, or was followed by, physical injury.

   (a) In an ordinary negligence action there is no recovery for mental disturbance, unless accompanied by contemporaneous physical injury. See Prosser, pp. 328–333. Historically, the fear of vexatious suits and fictitious claims led to this result. See discussion under Negligence, below.

   (b) Where there is intentional or reckless causing of mental or emotional distress, no physical injury or independent tort is required for recovery under modern authorities.

   (c) Mental disturbance may also result from other torts, such as Defamation and Invasion of Privacy, which are discussed below. Analysis of any fact situation involving mental disturbance, or emotional distress, must also include consideration of such alternative theories of liability. For example, where there is no "publication" to complete the tort of defamation, there may be the intentional causing of emotional distress. The interests protected by these torts are similar, and care must be taken to distinguish between them.

See generally, Gregory, pp. 933–952; Keeton, pp. 113–123; P & W, pp. 50–70; and Prosser, pp. 49–62.

Intentional infliction of mental distress   Case 7

D, as a practical joke, told P that her husband had been seriously injured in an accident and she must go at once to bring him home. There was no truth to the statement and D knew it was untrue. The statement caused P such worry and anxiety that she herself was made violently ill and suffered permanent physical harm. P sues D for damages for her injury. May she recover?

Answer. *Yes. D played a heartless and cruel joke on P, intending that it should have the effect of upsetting her peace of mind and causing her worry and anxiety. This was not only the foreseeable and proximate result of his words, but it was the very effect he had in mind subjectively when he used those words. D has no interest which the law should protect. D should be subjected to liability for his words and acts as a tort, wholly apart from any threat of physical contact. This is the modern view.*

   See Wilkinson v. Downton, 2 Q.B. 57 (1897). Recovery was also permitted in Barnett v. Collection Service Co., 214 Iowa 1303, 242 N.W. 25 (1932) which involved extreme collection letters and in

Jeppsen v. Jensen, 47 Utah 536, 155 P. 429 (1916) where D pointed a pistol at P's husband, swore at him and threatened to kill him.

NOTE—The purpose of the early law in recognizing assault as a tort was not to protect the individual against mental disturbance or to insure his peace of mind. It was to prevent a breach of the peace, because threats of physical contact often result in fights. However, it was natural that some of the earlier cases of mental disturbance should be pinned to the action for assault, or to the breach of an implied contract. Giving damages for insulting language and mental abuse which was intended to cause mental suffering, first appeared in the public utility cases on the theory that the utility violated its implied contract to treat the public with decency and respect. See Knoxville Traction Co. v. Lane, 103 Tenn. 376, 53 S.W. 557 (1899); and Lipman v. Atlantic Coast Line Railroad Co., 108 S.C. 151, 93 S.E. 714 (1917). Such liability was gradually extended. Today when mental suffering is intentionally inflicted under circumstances of aggravation, recovery is permitted regardless of physical contact.

FALSE IMPRISONMENT AND FALSE ARREST

1. False imprisonment is the confining of one person by another person within bounds, so as to deprive him of his liberty of motion and locomotion. Some cases still analogize the required restraint to the original cases where the defendant locked the plaintiff in a castle dungeon because the restraint must be substantially total as distinguished from an obstruction to go in a particular direction. See CASES 8 and 9, below.

   NOTE—An arrest without proper legal authority is a false arrest and because an arrest restrains the liberty of a person it is also false imprisonment. See number 7 below and CASE 11. See also, Legal Process and Arrest, below.

2. The gist of the tort is protection of the personal interest in freedom from restraint of movement.

   NOTE—Neither ill will nor malice are elements of the tort, but if these elements are shown, *punitive damages* may be awarded in addition to compensatory or nominal damages. See Chapter XV, Damages, below.

3. The following elements must be present for false imprisonment:

   (a) The plaintiff's *restraint* must be *substantially total*. The restraint necessary for the tort may be apprehension of force reasonably implied from the circumstances, even though no force is used or expressly threatened. See Stevens v. O'Neill, 51 App.Div. 364, 64 N.Y.S. 663 (1900), affirmed 169 N.Y. 375, 62 N.E. 424 (1900).

   (b) The restraint must be *against* the *plaintiff's will*.

(c) The plaintiff must be *conscious* of the restraint when it occurs or the plaintiff must be harmed by the confinement. See Restatement, Second, Torts § 42 and Herring v. Boyle, 1 Cromp. M & R 377, 149 Eng.Rep. 1126 (1834).

(d) The *defendant must impose the restraint* on the plaintiff.

(e) The defendant must *intend* to impose the restraint.

(f) The *restraint* must be legally *unjustifiable.*

4. Typical cases where false imprisonment would be found today include:

   (a) A storekeeper detains a customer-plaintiff an unreasonable time or in an unreasonable way, to investigate whether the plaintiff paid for his purchases. See Montgomery Ward & Co. v. Freeman, 199 F.2d 720 (4th Cir. 1952). See also CASE 10, below.

   (b) A storekeeper retains the purse of one of its customers to search it, even if the customer is free to leave. See Ashland Dry Goods Co. v. Wages, 302 Ky. 577, 195 S.W.2d 312 (1946).

     NOTE—The common law rule made a storekeeper liable for false imprisonment if he detained a customer to investigate suspected shoplifting and the customer was blameless. Today many states have statutes which permit a storekeeper to detain a customer a reasonable time if the storekeeper has probable cause to believe that the customer has taken something even if, in fact, he has not. Thus, probable cause is made a defense by statute.

   (c) An employer detains an employee-plaintiff an unreasonable time or in an unreasonable way, to investigate whether the plaintiff has stolen or misappropriated some of the employer's property. But if the employer calls the employee into the office to question regarding a theft, and the employee asks permission to leave to which the supervisor answers that he wants the employee to stay, there is no false imprisonment. The interview was lawful and no force was used to detain the employee. See Weiler v. Harzfeld-Phillipson Co., 189 Wis. 554, 208 N.W. 599 (1926).

   (d) D wrongfully repossessed a car sold to P under a conditional sales contract and towed it away with P still inside it. See National Bond & Investment Co. v. Whithorn, 276 Ky. 204, 123 S.W.2d 263 (1938).

   (e) The defendant refuses to stop a speeding automobile so that the plaintiff who is riding inside can leave.

5. There is no false imprisonment if there is a means of escape which is reasonably safe and reasonably apparent to the plaintiff.

6. Merely obstructing one's way is not a false imprisonment.

    e.g. D fenced off a public footpath going over a bridge without authority to do so. P tried to climb the fence but was prevented by D's agents. P left using the road that was still open. Was this false imprisonment?

    Answer. No. There must be confinement within some boundary for false imprisonment. Although D wrongfully blocked the road, P could leave the way he came so there was no imprisonment. See Bird v. Jones, 7 Q.B. 742, 115 Eng.Rep. 668 (1845).

7. The restraint required for false imprisonment may be imposed upon the plaintiff under an asserted legal authority. If the plaintiff submits to that authority, it is an "arrest"; and if there is no proper legal authority for the arrest it is a "false arrest". This constitutes false imprisonment because of the unlawful restraint imposed. See CASE 11, below. See also, Restatement, Second, Torts §§ 35–45A.

    See generally, Gregory, pp. 920–933; Keeton, pp. 41–43; P & W, pp. 37–49, 125–127; Prosser, pp. 42–49.

Case 8 *False imprisonment—elements of cause of action*

D and his girl friend, P, were taking a ride in D's automobile. D made improper advances toward P which made her angry. She demanded that he stop the automobile and permit her to depart therefrom. They were riding in a park of a city. There were many people in the vicinity and means of transportation to P's home was readily available by bus. Furthermore, P had "mad money" in her purse with which to pay her transportation home on a bus. D speeded up the car to prevent P's exit therefrom, and refused to permit P to leave his automobile unless she were to run the risk of serious injury by getting out when the car was moving rapidly. P sues D for damages for false imprisonment. May P recover?

Answer. Yes. The elements of the tort are present: (1) P was substantially and totally deprived of her liberty for she could not get out of D's car without taking an unreasonable risk of serious injury. (2) P's restraint was against her will. (3) She was quite conscious of the restraint. (4) D imposed the restraint on P. (5) D's imposition of the restraint was intentional for the facts state that he speeded up the car to prevent P's escape. (6) There was no legal justification for the restraint. This would be true even though D thought it was for P's own good or welfare, that he keep P in the car. All the elements of false imprisonment being present, P may recover damages from the defendant.

See Cieplinski v. Severn, 269 Mass. 261, 168 N.E. 722 (1929).

False imprisonment—elements of cause of action   **Case 9**

P and her husband were members of a religious sect which had colonies in the state of Maine and in Jaffa, Syria. A yacht owned by the sect transported members between those places. P was in Syria and desired to return to America. However, P did not want to return on the yacht for fear that she would not be permitted to leave until she had been "won to the movement" again. D assured P that she would not be detained on the ship after it arrived at port. The ship arrived May 8, 1910 and P was not permitted to leave until June 6, 1910 when a writ of habeas corpus was issued. No physical force or threats were used to keep P aboard the ship; P was just refused a rowboat to take her to shore. P sued for damages for false imprisonment. Did D's actions constitute false imprisonment?

Answer. Yes. *All of the elements of the tort of false imprisonment were present. The restraint was physical and not merely a moral influence. There was actual physical restraint because it was impossible for P to leave the ship; actual force was not necessary. D intended to, and did impose the restraint on P against her will. The facts are analogous to a person who falsely imprisons another by locking him in a room and refusing to give him the key. In the present case D kept P on the ship and refused to permit her to use a rowboat to get ashore. This constitutes the tort of false imprisonment.*

See Whittacker v. Sandford, 110 Me. 77, 85 A. 399 (1912).

False imprisonment—shopkeeper's privilege to detain   **Case 10**

A private policeman employed by D's store stopped P after she left the store and said that someone in the store had told him that P had put some jewelry into her purse without paying for it. P denied that she had taken anything, but complied with the request to empty her purse and produce sales slips for items purchased. P was then permitted to leave. P sued for false arrest. What standard is used to judge D's conduct?

Answer. The court adopted the view of the Restatement, Second, Torts, § 120A, which recognized the privilege of a merchant to detain for reasonable investigation a person whom he reasonably believes has unlawfully taken some property. This privilege is necessary to protect a shopkeeper from the increasing problem of shoplifting. He may reasonably detain a suspect without arresting him and being liable for damages. This privilege applies whether the suspect is in the store or is in the immediate vicinity of the store, such as a parking lot. In the present case the jury must first determine whether D reasonably believed that P had taken anything. If the jury concludes that D's belief was reasonable, it secondly must determine whether the detention was reasonable under all the cir-

cumstances. The case was remanded because of error in the instructions to the jury.

See *Bonkowski v. Arlan's Department Store, 12 Mich.App. 88, 162 N.W.2d 347 (1968), affirmed 383 Mich. 90, 174 N.W.2d 765 (1970).*

Case 11 *Unprivileged arrest—police officer liable*

D, a police officer, suspected P of stealing a pair of shoes from a store while it was on fire. D went with two deputies at night to P's home and said, "Consider yourself under arrest. You must go back to Granite Falls with us." P asked to see D's warrant. D refused because he did not have a warrant to arrest P. Finally P said, "I will go with you." D told P that he did not have to return with them if P would promise to go to town the next day. P promised and went into town the next day, but he was never indicted. P sued D for false arrest. May he recover?

Answer. Yes. Two questions arise on this set of facts: (1) Was there an arrest of P? (2) If there was an arrest, was it justified? (1) An arrest by an officer does not require physical force to deprive one of his liberty. If the victim submits to restraint of his liberty simply because he does not wish to resist the apparent authority of law, and not because he consents thereto, he is arrested. In this case P did not give up his liberty voluntarily. He went into town only because he did not want to be guilty of resisting D's apparent authority. Therefore, when P acted, he did not do so voluntarily. The law does not require the victim to resist and thereby compel the officer to use physical force before he has a cause of action for wrongful arrest. Had P run away from D when D told him he was under arrest, there would have been no arrest. Of course, had D put his hands on P and physically detained him, there would have been an arrest. This case is between these two, and constituted an arrest of P. (2) A peace officer may, without being liable for false imprisonment, arrest in three cases involving felonies: (a) He may arrest a felon, that is, one who has actually committed a felony. (b) If a felony has been in fact committed and there is reasonable grounds for believing this person committed it, the officer may arrest. (c) If there has been no felony committed but there is reasonable ground for believing one has been committed, then the officer may arrest. These are privileges which the law grants to its peace officers. But when the officer arrests a person without the benefit of the privilege, that is, beyond the authority accorded him, then he acts at his peril in taking away one's liberty, even if he makes an honest mistake in doing so. In this CASE the facts disclose that there had been no felony committed and that there was no reasonable grounds for believing P had committed a felony. Nevertheless, D arrested P. Having taken away P's liberty without privilege or justification, D must pay damages for the false arrest of P.

See Martin v. Houck, 141 N.C. 317, 54 S.E. 291 (1906). See also Restatement, Second, Torts § 121.

1. The gist of the tort of trespass to real property is protection of the interest in exclusive possession of the land, with the physical condition thereof remaining intact: **TRESPASS TO LAND**

   (a) *Neither* a *licensee* nor the *holder of* an *ordinary easement* in land, *can maintain* an action in *trespass* because neither is possessed.

   (b) By the better rule a *tenant at will cannot maintain trespass* because his possessory interest is too ephemeral.

   (c) However, *one* who is *wrongfully possessed may maintain an action in trespass.*

   e.g. O is the owner of Blackacre. P wrongfully evicts O from the land and takes possession thereof. D then enters the domain occupied by P, without P's permission. P may maintain trespass against D.

2. One who is not in possession of land cannot maintain an action for trespass on the land.

   e.g. L, owner of Blackacre, leases it to T for 5 years. While T is in possession, B, without permission, comes onto the land wrongfully. L, out of possession, cannot sue B for the trespass, because such action is to protect the exclusive possession of the possessor. T, the tenant, can maintain the action of trespass against B, because T has the right of exclusive possession.

3. Liability for the tort of trespass to land arises when the defendant:

   (a) enters land in the possession of the plaintiff, or causes a thing, or a third person to do so, see Dougherty v. Stepp, 18 N.C. 371 (1835),

   (b) remains on the land, or

   (c) fails to remove something from the land which he is under a duty to remove.

4. There is liability for a trespass in these situations, even if the conduct causes no harm to the plaintiff. See Restatement, Second, Torts § 158.

5. Fright and mental anguish are elements of damage if they arise out of a trespass which causes physical injury.

   e.g. D's agent attempted to enter P's apartment to read the gas meter instead of entering the basement through a side door. P's nurse opened the door but refused to let D's agent enter. D's agent would not permit the nurse to close the door. The argument with P's nurse at the door frightened P and caused P to have a miscarriage the following day. The actions of D's agent constituted a trespass. P was permitted to recover for her fright and mental anguish as well as for physical injuries from the miscarriage because this was caused by the trespass.

See Bouillon v. Laclede Gaslight Co., 148 Mo.App. 462, 129 S.W. 401 (1910).

6. A trespass to land may take place under certain circumstances when the defendant has originally entered the land without committing any wrong. This is called a "trespass ab initio," and occurs when the defendant has entered the plaintiff's land under a privilege or a license, and then by misconduct abuses or exceeds such right. This misconduct, which must amount to a trespass, is treated as to relating back to the beginning ("ab initio"), to the original entry onto the land thus making it tortious.

e.g. The failure to pay for drinks after lawfully entering an inn is not sufficient for "trespass ab initio" because the omission is not a trespass. See Six Carpenters Case, 8 Co.Rep. 146a, 77 Eng.Rep. 695 (1610). See also Keeton, pp. 137–138, Prosser, pp. 129–131.

NOTE—Prosser states that "the entire doctrine is on its way to oblivion" as an increasing majority of courts reject the doctrine of trespass ab initio. See Prosser, pp. 130–131. The Restatement has also rejected the doctrine. See Restatement, Second, Torts §§ 214(2), 136, 278.

7. The rights of the possessor of land include:

   (a) the soil on the surface of the land,

   (b) the earth below the surface to the extent that it can be effectively used presently or in the future, and

   (c) the air space above the surface.

8. The following conclusions are sound common law doctrine:

   (a) On the surface, anyone who, without permission, penetrates the imaginary domain of the possessor of land, which is sometimes referred to as "breaking the close", and thereby interferes with his exclusive possession, is liable for trespass. See CASE 12 and Chapter XIII, Nuisance, below.

   (b) In the area below the land surface, anyone who, without permission, penetrates the imaginary domain of the possessor of the land at a depth above which the possessor can presently or in the future put such soil or area to use, is liable for trespass.

   (c) In the space above the land surface, anyone who, without permission, penetrates the imaginary domain of the possessor of the land at a height below that which is essential to the surface use by the possessor and materially interferes with that surface use, is liable for trespass.

e.g. A hunter who fired his shotgun over P's land was held liable for trespass even though the hunter was not on P's land and the bullets did not fall on P's land. The court found that the shots were a danger to P's cattle and interfered with his enjoyment of the land. Therefore, there was a trespass. See Herrin v. Sutherland, 74 Mont. 587, 241 P. 328 (1925).

NOTE—From the above three propositions it necessarily follows that one who penetrates the space above the land, at a height which does not interfere with the surface use, or does an act beneath the surface at such a depth that it cannot interfere with any use of such space or soil by the surface possessor, either presently or prospectively, is not liable for trespass.

9. Four theories have been applied in balancing the interests of the possessor of land against the interests of flight above his land.

   (a) The "zone" theory divides airspace into two zones, based on the outer limit of the owner's "effective possession", and limits the owner's rights to the lower zone so established. See Smith v. New England Aircraft Co., 270 Mass. 511, 170 N.E. 385 (1930).

   (b) The "actual use" or "unused airspace" theory holds that there is no ownership of airspace which the owner is not putting to present use. One court held that there would be no trespass from flights within five feet of the surface of unoccupied waste land unless there was interference with the present enjoyment or possession of such land. See Hinman v. Pacific Air Transport, 84 F.2d 755 (9th Cir. 1936), certiorari denied 300 U.S. 654, 57 S.Ct. 431, 81 L.Ed. 865 (1937).

   (c) The "privilege" theory holds that the owner of land has unlimited ownership of the space upward, above his land, subject to the privilege of reasonable flight by others. See Strother v. Pacific Gas & Electric Co., 94 Cal.App.2d 525, 211 P.2d 624 (1949).

   (d) The "nuisance" theory provides a remedy based on nuisance or negligence for actual interference with the use of the land, and does not concern itself with the extent of ownership above the surface. It considers whether the flight seriously interferes with the use and enjoyment of the land by a reasonable person. This is a factual question which must be determined by the circumstances in each case. See Atkinson v. Bernard, Inc., 223 Or. 624, 355 P.2d 229 (1960).

NOTE—None of the above theories can be said to represent the current prevailing view of a majority of courts. Prosser states that the "nuisance" theory appears to be the trend of the courts. See Prosser, p. 72.

10. For one to be liable in trespass to land there must be an act, but an intention to trespass is not required.

(a) D had a hedge of thorns on his property along the boundary with P's land. D cut the thorns and they fell on P's land. D picked them up as soon as he could. P sued for trespass. Did D commit a trespass?

Answer. Yes. D intentionally entered upon P's land and he thereby committed a trespass. It does not matter that D's act was otherwise lawful. See The Case of the Thorns, Y.B. 6 Ed. 4, 7a, pl. 18 (1466).

(b) D was physically carried onto P's land by other persons and P sued D for trespass. Did D commit a trespass?

Answer. No. D did not intentionally enter upon P's land so he is not guilty of trespass. However, those who put D on P's land, even if they did not actually step on the land themselves, committed a trespass. See Smith v. Stone, Style 65, 82 Eng.Rep. 533 (1647).

(c) Twelve armed men threatened to kill D unless he stole a gelding from P. D stole the gelding and P sued for trespass. Did P commit a trespass?

Answer. Yes. D performed the act intentionally and, therefore, he was a trespasser. If the threats of another were a defense, then P could not obtain satisfaction for the wrong done to him. See Gilbert v. Stone, Style 72 (Eng.Rep. 1648).

(d) P and her husband gave D permission to place a snow fence on their property and D agreed to remove it at the end of winter. In removing the fence D failed to remove one post. P's husband hit it while on a mowing machine and he was thrown to the ground and died. Was there a trespass?

Answer. Yes. The failure to remove something placed on the land of another when it is time to do so results in a continuing trespass for which D is liable. See Rogers v. Board of Road Commissioners for Kent County, 319 Mich. 661, 30 N.W.2d 358 (1948).

See generally, Gregory, pp. 915–919; Keeton, pp. 136–138, 161; P & W, pp. 70–81; Prosser, pp. 63–75.

Trespass—right of flight and "taking" of property   **Case 12**

P, a farmer, owned a five acre tract on which he operated a small dairy and chicken farm. Airplanes belonging to the United States flew over P's land when taking off and landing. The planes flew 67 feet above P's house, 63 feet above his barn and 8 feet above his highest tree. As a result of these flights his chickens failed to lay eggs and his cows failed to give milk in quantities as they did before these flights began. The chickens flew against the fences and walls and killed themselves. P and his family were frightened, made nervous and their sleep was disturbed by the vibrations, noise and bright lights of landing planes. P sued the United States claiming that his property had been taken and that under the Fifth Amendment of the Constitution he was entitled to just compensation. Is he correct?

Answer. Yes. Every land owner has a right to protection in the enjoyment of his land either: (1) on the theory that he owns the space above his surface to the sky, which is the ad coelum doctrine, subject to the right of flight, or (2) on the theory that he owns the air space above his land to such height as he can effectively possess. Under either theory he has a right not to have the enjoyment of his land materially interfered with by air traffic. This means that planes in flight must remain at such a height as not to interfere substantially with the surface use and enjoyment of land over which they fly. In this case the United States has not touched the ground with its planes, but it has committed a trespass and rendered P's land uninhabitable for dwelling purposes. Of course, it might still be used for raising grain provided the flights were not so low and so frequent as to render any use practically impossible. But the present use for raising chickens and producing milk has been eliminated by the government's use of the air space. This constitutes a diminution of the value of P's property and is a taking of property within the Fifth Amendment. Here there was direct and immediate interference with P's enjoyment of his land. Hence, P is entitled to "just compensation" for the "taking" of property.

See United States v. Causby, 328 U.S. 256, 66 S.Ct. 1062, 90 L.Ed. 1206 (1946).

NOTE—The Causby case is an example of inverse condemnation. That occurs when governmental activity interferes with the use of property prior to the start of any condemnation proceedings. It constitutes a "taking" for which compensation must be paid under the Fifth Amendment.

TRESPASS TO CHATTELS AND CONVERSION

1. The interest in the exclusive possession and physical condition of personal property is protected by two related tort actions:

    (a) trespass to chattels, and

    (b) conversion.

2. The purpose of the tort of trespass to chattels is to remedy minor interferences to chattels which are not sufficiently serious, or sufficiently important to be a conversion. See Prosser, p. 76. Compare Restatement, Second, Torts § 217 (trespass to chattels) with § 223 (ways of committing conversion).

    e.g. P left his horse with D to be fed. While it was in D's possession D took a brief ride on the horse for pleasure. D's actions were not sufficiently serious to constitute a conversion of the horse, but they were a trespass. See Johnson v. Weedman, 5 Ill. 495 (1843).

3. Conversion results from a major interference with a chattel, or with the plaintiff's rights in it, which are so serious, and so important, as to justify the forced judicial sale of it to the defendant. This is the distinguishing feature of the action for conversion.

    e.g. A cotenant took possession of the house owned in common with P and put P's furniture in storage. P's goods were not used or damaged. P sued for conversion and was awarded the full monetary value of the goods. Was the verdict correct?

    Answer. No. There was no substantial interference which would constitute conversion. P has a cause of action for trespass, and he may recover for the actual damages he suffered due to the impairment of his property and loss of its use. However, P may not recover the full value of his property because there was no conversion. P's property is in storage for him. See Zaslow v. Kroenert, 29 Cal.2d 541, 176 P.2d 1 (1946).

4. Today when one, without justification or excuse, *intentionally interferes with the possession, dominion, or condition of a chattel in the possession of another*, it *is* a *conversion*. The *remedy* is an action for damages, which is the value of the goods at the time of the conversion.

    (a) X steals wheat from P and sells it to D, a bona fide purchaser. Over a year later P learns of this transaction and demands the return of the wheat or its value. The wheat had risen in value from 30 cents a bushel to $1.03 a bushel when the demand was made. What, if anything, may P recover?

    Answer. X stole the wheat so he cannot pass title to it to D. When D bought the wheat he exercised dominion and control over it. The conversion took place at that time, and D's good faith is not a defense. The damages are the value at the time of the conversion. By the better rule, an action for conversion may be maintained without a demand, so the value of the wheat at the time of the demand is not used to determine damages. See Hovland v. Farmers Union Elevator Co., 67 N.D. 71, 269 N.W. 842 (1936).

(b) P employed D as a salesman on commission and shipped him goods to be sold. P later requested the return of the goods. To comply with this request D called X Express Co. An impostor representing himself to be employed by X called for the goods and D gave them to him. In this way the goods were stolen and P sues D for their value. May P recover?

> *Answer.* Yes. The absence of bad faith or of gross negligence by D is no defense. P had title to the goods and had the right to have them returned upon demand. Since D did not return the goods he is liable for the conversion which occurred when he gave them to the impostor. See Baer v. Slater, 261 Mass. 153, 158 N.E. 328 (1927).

(c) P loaned his horse to D for the purpose of going to point X, and told D not to use the horse to go further to point Y. D rode the horse to X and then on towards Y. When half way to Y, the horse dropped dead due to the altitude and hard climbing. Here *misuse of the horse,* exceeding the permission given by P, which caused its death, *constituted* a conversion by D, for which D is liable to P. See Restatement, Second, Torts §§ 216–222 (trespass to chattels) and §§ 222A–244 (conversion).

(d) D was using ordinary care in managing his horses, but they became frightened and ran against a lamp post on P's land thereby breaking it. P sued D. The court held that mere ownership of the horses did not render D liable. D was not liable because: (1) he did not intend the injury, and (2) he was not negligent or at fault for the actions of his horse. See Brown v. Collins, 53 N.H. 442, 16 Am.R. 372 (1873).

5. The following remedies are available to the owner of chattels:

(a) for trespass, only nominal damages or compensatory damages,

(b) for conversion, damages are normally the value of the goods at the time and place of conversion. See Chapter XV, Damages, below.

See generally, Gregory, pp. 86–88; Keeton, pp. 141–143; P & W, pp. 81–96.

1. In the analysis of any tort problem, after exploration of the basic issues of liability the student must consider all possible de-

DEFENSES— INTRODUCTION

fenses to each cause of action. See Chapter I, Analysis of Tort Problems, above.

    (a) Specific defenses may be available as to specific torts.

       e.g. Truth, as a defense to an action for defamation.

    (b) Certain defenses may be applicable to all or most tort claims.

       e.g. Consent.

2. The following defenses to intentional torts against persons or property are considered:

    (a) privilege,

    (b) mistake and unavoidable accident,

    (c) consent,

    (d) self-defense and defense of others,

    (e) defense of property and recapture of chattels,

    (f) necessity,

    (g) legal process and arrest without a warrant, and

    (h) discipline.

NOTE—In addition to substantive defenses, such as those outlined in number 2, the analysis of any fact situation should also include a review of other defenses of general applicability. These include the statute of limitations, improper joinder, or the presence of a release or covenant not to sue. "Immunity" may also serve as a defense to a tort action. See Chapter XIV, Immunity, below. See also Restatement, Second, Torts §§ 895A–895G. The Restatement, in addition to its discussion of defenses as related to specific torts, discusses defenses of justification and excuse which are applicable to all tort claims. See Restatement, Second, Torts §§ 888–895.

DEFENSES— PRIVILEGE

1. A privilege is any immunity which prevents the existence of a tort.

2. "Privilege" denotes the fact that conduct which, under ordinary circumstances, would subject the defendant to liability, under particular circumstances does not do so. See Restatement, Second, Torts § 10.

3. The defense of privilege may be asserted by a defendant whose action has such social importance that it is entitled to protection even though the plaintiff has suffered some injury. See Prosser, p. 98.

4. A privilege may be based upon the consent of the injured party, or may be created by law, irrespective of the injured party's consent. Privileges created by law are divided into "absolute" and "conditional" privileges.

  (a) A privilege created by law may be based upon the value attached to the interest protected by its exercise. In such a case, the privilege protects the defendant only if his conduct in question is done for the purpose of protecting the interest in question. This is a "conditional" privilege.

  (b) A privilege created by law may be given to persons who perform certain public functions, so that nothing that they do in carrying out these functions will subject them to liability, or to the annoyance, or expense incident to even unsuccessful litigation. In such a case, neither an improper motive, nor an improper purpose can destroy the privilege. This is an "absolute" privilege. See Restatement, Second, Torts § 10, Comment d. See also Restatement, Second, Torts § 890.

  See generally, Prosser, pp. 98–99.

1. If an act is done under a mistake of fact it is usually no defense to an intentional tort even if the act was reasonable.

MISTAKE AND UNAVOIDABLE ACCIDENT

  (a) B steals X's book and sells it to C, a bona fide purchaser, who has no knowledge of the theft. C sells the book to Y. X sues Y for converting the book. It is no defense that Y honestly but mistakenly believed that he was the owner of the book. A thief cannot pass good title.

  (b) D mistakes P for X and commits a battery on X. P may recover for D's battery even though the battery would have been privileged if P had been X.

CAVEAT—Mistake may make the defense of privilege available.

  e.g. D reasonably believes that P is attacking him. Although D is mistaken, D is privileged to defend himself. See Courvoisier v. Raymond, 23 Colo. 113, 47 P. 284 (1896), and Privilege, above.

2. An unavoidable accident excuses the defendant's act. See CASE 16, below. See also Prosser, pp. 99, 140.

3. Mistake must be distinguished from an unavoidable accident.

  (a) An unavoidable accident is an event which was not intended and which could not have been foreseen by a reasonable, prudent person in the defendant's position.

e.g. D's horse became frightened through no fault of D and ran onto P's land. This is a trespass, but D may defend a suit by P for damages by showing that it was an unavoidable accident.

(b) In a mistake, the defendant intended the result. However, he acted under a reasonable but erroneous belief, which if correct would justify the act. This is usually not a valid defense.

e.g. D intentionally rides his horse onto P's land at night thinking that it is D's own land. D is liable for trespass even though the act was done because of a mistake.

See generally, Prosser, pp. 99–101.

DEFENSES— CONSENT

1. "Consent" denotes willingness, in fact, on the part of the plaintiff, that an act, or an invasion of an interest, shall take place. See Restatement, Second, Torts § 10A.

2. Consent is usually a valid defense. Consent may be:

   (a) expressed by words, or

   (b) implied from action, inaction, or silence.

   NOTE—The test as to implied consent is whether a reasonable person in the position of the plaintiff would act or speak under the circumstances if the person were not willing to permit the conduct to occur. Words, conduct or inaction which are reasonably understood to be consent may be treated as consent in fact even where the plaintiff subjectively does not intend to consent. Custom and usage may also confer consent. See Restatement, Second, Torts § 892.

3. If a person with capacity to consent manifests assent to the conduct of another, in the absence of duress, fraud or substantial mistake as to the risk involved, such person may not maintain an action for harm resulting from such conduct.

   (a) D offered a free vaccination to immigrants on its ship so they could lawfully enter the U.S. P waited in line, but told D's doctor that she had been vaccinated before. The doctor said that it left no mark and it should be repeated. P held out her arm and was vaccinated. P entered the U.S. and sued for assault. The court held that P's actions in holding out her arm constituted consent to the vaccination. Words are not necessary for consent and P's secret feelings do not overcome the apparent consent demonstrated by her outward actions. See O'Brien v. Cunard Steamship Co., 154 Mass. 272, 28 N.E. 266 (1891).

(b) If consent is given because of fraud or deceit, it will not prevent a plaintiff from recovering damages. See De May v. Roberts, 46 Mich. 160, 9 N.W. 146 (1881).

(c) If consent is given to do one act and then it is exceeded, the defense may not be available.

> *e.g.* P gave D permission to put stones on his vacant lot, but D covered it with boulders. D exceeded the consent given and is liable. See Wheelock v. Noonan, 108 N.Y. 179, 15 N.E. 67 (1888).

4. Statutes may fix the age of consent for certain acts, such as sexual intercourse, in order to protect a certain class of persons. In such a case an underage female is not legally capable of consent and she may maintain a civil action for damages. In such a case the defendant may *not* use consent as a defense. See Bishop v. Liston, 112 Neb. 559, 199 N.W. 825 (1924).

NOTE—The rule in number 4 above which negatives consent as a defense in certain circumstances, applies both to civil cases, *e.g.* the age at which a binding contract may be signed, and to criminal cases, *e.g.* statutory rape.

5. On the civil, as *distinguished* from the criminal, side of the law, *consent* by the plaintiff *is a defense* to the defendant in an action for damages for *intentional interference with person or property*.

(a) Where a state statute made prize fighting illegal, a minority of courts have held that the fighter who lost may not hold the other liable for injuries because both consented to the fight. This rule is based on the maxim *volenti non fit injuria* (the volunteer suffers no wrong). That rule has been adopted in the Restatement, Second, Torts § 60. See Hart v. Geysel, 159 Wash. 632, 294 P. 570 (1930).

(b) In another case, where the fight was conducted without a license in violation of a law providing criminal penalties, the promoter was held liable for injuries suffered in the bout, regardless of the rights between the contestants. This result comes from the public policy expressed in the law requiring the license and overrides the fact that the injured party consented to the match. See Hudson v. Craft, 33 Cal.2d 654, 204 P.2d 1 (1949).

See generally, Gregory, pp. 14–17; Keeton, pp. 45–51; P & W, pp. 97–111; Prosser, pp. 101–108.

1. The privilege of self-defense is based on the necessity of permitting a man who is attacked to take reasonable steps to prevent harm to himself where there is no time to resort to the law.

DEFENSE OF SELF AND OTHERS

2. Self-defense is available as a defense if the following conditions coexist:

    (a) The defendant has a reasonable belief that he is in real danger. A reasonable, but mistaken, belief that a man advancing toward defendant was about to attack him would justify an act of self-defense. See Courvoisier v. Raymond, 23 Colo. 113, 47 P. 284 (1896).

    (b) The force used is reasonably necessary, or appears so, to protect against the threatened injury. Great bodily injury need not be threatened to justify an ordinary battery. See Boston v. Muncy, 204 Okl. 603, 233 P.2d 300 (1951).

3. The privilege to defend other persons is recognized if:

    (a) the necessity for defense is immediate, and

    (b) the defendant uses only reasonable force to defend another just as if he himself were attacked.

4. An honest mistake as to the need for defense of others will subject the person defending another to liability in most jurisdictions. This rule is criticized by Prosser for the reason that a person should be given the same right to defend others as he has to defend himself. See Prosser, p. 113.

    See generally, Gregory, pp. 18–23; Keeton, pp. 63–67, 104–105; P & W, pp. 113–116; Prosser, pp. 108–113.

DEFENSE OF PROPERTY

1. One may use reasonable force when apparently necessary *to defend* his *possession of personal or real property*. The issue of the reasonableness of the force is a fact question for the jury. See CASE 14, below.

2. The owner or occupier of land must ordinarily ask a trespasser to leave the property before using any force. If the trespasser refuses to leave, physical force may be used. Setting a trap, such as a spring gun, for a trespasser renders the owner liable for injuries caused by the trap because there is no request to leave.

3. If a person is wrongfully occupying land, most states do not permit the use of force to evict the occupant. See Newton v. Harland, 1 Man. & G. 644, 133 Eng.Rep. 490 (1840). However, most states provide for a prompt civil remedy by statute to evict the occupier.

4. One's habitation is his castle, the place or house in which he lives. The common law rule that one must retreat until his back is to the wall before he takes life in defense, does not apply to one's habitation. This is the sole distinction between habitation and other property. Within his habitation one may

stand his ground and take life if necessary in protecting himself and his family therein from death or serious bodily injury.

5. Life may be taken, if necessary, to protect one's habitation against attack, in two instances only:

   (a) when the attack is not against the property as property, but against the inmates of the habitation; then the rules of self defense apply; and

   (b) when the attack is to commit a felony within the habitation.

6. If one has committed larceny, a felony, and is retreating with the stolen goods, his life may be taken to prevent his escape on the ground that he is a felon.

7. *Forcible recapture* of a chattel can be *justified* only *when* it has been *taken* from the recapturer *wrongfully* and the *recapture* is made promptly. Only reasonable force may be used and the burden of proof is on the recapturer to show that he is entitled to the chattel. The recapturer is liable for damages if he makes a mistake.

   (a) P made false representations to D in order to buy a stove from him. P gave a promissory note to D and left with the stove. D soon discovered the fraud and overtook P. D retook the stove by force. P sued D for trespass and assault and battery. Is P entitled to damages?

   Answer. No. Self help may be used to recapture a chattel if it was wrongfully taken and the recapture is immediate. A wrongful taking includes acquiring goods by fraud. In such a case the owner may rescind his consent. Although the recapture was not immediate in this case, there was no undue lapse of time between the sale and the recapture so the judgment for P was reversed. See Hodgeden v. Hubbard, 18 Vt. 504 (1846).

   (b) If goods are sold under a conditional sales contract, the seller may not use violence to repossess the goods after a default. He may retake possession only if he can do so peaceably. See Lamb v. Woodry, 154 Or. 30, 58 P.2d 1257 (1936). See Restatement, Second, Torts §§ 100–111.

NOTE 1—After the sale of a chattel under a conditional sales contract, under the UCC, a secured party has the right after default to take possession of the property unless there is an agreement to the contrary.

   (a) In taking possession, the secured party may proceed without judicial process, so long as no breach of the peace occurs.

   (b) If a breach of the peace does occur, the mortgagee is deemed to be converting the mortgagor's equity in the chattel.

(c) A clause in a chattel mortgage, giving the mortgagee the right on default to break into any premises where the chattel may be found, is against public policy and, therefore, void.

NOTE 2—Rights afforded under the Due Process Clauses of the Fifth and Fourteenth Amendments must be considered in any situation where goods are repossessed.

> *e.g.* Household goods were purchased under an installment sales contract. The seller retained a vendor's lien to secure the unpaid balance of the purchase price. After a default by the buyer, the seller obtained a writ of sequestration for repossession of the goods under state law by: (a) filing an affidavit with the court; (b) posting a bond; and (c) obtaining an order from a judge authorizing the repossession. Under the applicable state law the debtor had a right to a prompt hearing *after* the goods were repossessed and, unless the seller proved valid grounds for repossession, which is the existence of the debt, the lien and the delinquency, the debtor was entitled to damages and attorney's fees in addition to the return of his property. The debtor claimed that his constitutional rights were violated by the repossession of the goods without a prior hearing. Does this procedure of repossessing chattels prior to a judicial hearing violate the Due Process Clause of the Fourteenth Amendment?

> ***Answer.*** No. The law balances the rights of the buyer and seller. There is judicial control of the repossession and the risk of wrongful repossession by a seller is kept to a minimum. The seller has a substantial interest in the property because of the lien and should be protected from waste or destruction of the merchandise. See Mitchell v. W. T. Grant Co., 416 U.S. 600, 94 S.Ct. 1895, 40 L.Ed.2d 406 (1974).

NOTE 3—The Court in the Mitchell case distinguished Fuentes v. Shevin, 407 U.S. 67, 92 S.Ct. 1983, 32 L.Ed.2d 556 (1972) which found a state statute providing for repossession unconstitutional for lack of due process. In the Fuentes case the repossession of the merchandise was without judicial order, approval or participation. The writ of replevin was issued by the court clerk on the bare assertion that the party seeking the writ was entitled to it. In Mitchell, the nature of the claim, the amount due and the grounds relied on for issuance of the writ had to be clearly set forth. This was determined by a judge rather than "court functionaries." Furthermore, the *guarantee* of a *prompt* hearing for the debtor and damages for wrongful use of the writ offered more protection in the Mitchell case. In Fuentes the law only provided for an "eventual" hearing and damages were only awarded if the property was "wrongfully detained" which is a broader standard than in Mitchell. Therefore, the state law considered in the Fuentes case was declared unconstitutional because it violated the Due Process Clause of the Fourteenth Amendment.

(c) D employed P as a bookkeeper. D discovered that some money belonging to his company was missing and held P responsible. D deducted the money from P's pay. Some time later D gave P some money to pay the employees. P accepted the money, took what was due him, and handed the rest back to D saying that he was going to leave. D grabbed P to take back the money and they fought. P was injured in the fight and sued for damages. Was D justified in using force to retake the money from P?

> *Answer.* No. D voluntarily gave the money to P. P came into possession lawfully in the usual course of business, without trick or fraud. Therefore, D may not use force to retake the money, but D must look to his legal remedy for satisfaction. See Kirby v. Foster, 17 R.I. 437, 22 A. 1111 (1891).

> See generally, Gregory, pp. 23–33; Keeton, pp. 73–90; P & W, pp. 116–124; Prosser, pp. 113–124.

1. One who acts "to prevent a threatened injury from some force of nature, or some other independent cause not connected with the plaintiff, is said to be acting under necessity." Prosser, p. 124.

DEFENSES— NECESSITY

(a) D kills P's dog which had come on his property to protect his hens from the danger of being killed by the dog. D is not liable to P for the killing of the dog. D's privilege of intentionally killing the dog is a necessity to protect his own hens, and is a good defense to an action by P against D. See Ex Parte Minor, 203 Ala. 481, 83 So. 475 (1919).

(b) An entry upon the land of another to save goods which are in jeopardy of being lost or destroyed is not a trespass. See Proctor v. Adams, 113 Mass. 376 (1873). Similarly, one may enter upon the land of another if it is necessary to save property.

> *e.g.* A storm arose while P and his family were sailing. In order to save his ship and the lives of his family P moored his ship to D's private dock. D unmoored the ship and set it adrift in the storm. As a result the ship was driven upon the shore and destroyed. P and his family were injured. P sued D for damages. The court permitted P to recover because P was privileged to moor his ship at D's dock out of necessity. Thus, because of P's privilege to protect his

property D was not permitted to unmoor P's ship even though the dock belonged to D and he did not give P permission to use it. As is shown in the example under (c) below, if the dock had been damaged during the storm, D would have been afforded compensation. See Ploof v. Putnam, 81 Vt. 471, 71 A. 188 (1908).

(c) A violent storm came up while D's boat was moored to P's dock. The wind buffetted the boat back and forth against the dock. The boat was saved undamaged, but the dock was severely damaged by the beating from the boat in the wind. P sued D for injury to the dock. D's defense was that it was necessary to hitch his boat to the dock to save it. Does the defense of necessity prevent P from recovering?

> *Answer.* No. Here two private interests are involved. D has acted so as to save his own property at the expense of another's property. This private necessity negatives the existence of the tort of trespass, but does not eliminate liability for harm actually done to P's property. The privilege created by the necessity is thus a "partial" or "incomplete" one. Hence, D must pay for injury to P's dock. The recovery is not based on a tort, but it is because of D's unjust enrichment. See Vincent v. Lake Erie Transportation Co., 109 Minn. 456, 124 N.W. 221 (1910).

2. The law distinguishes between "public" and "private" necessity.

(a) The distinction turns upon the interest which the defendant seeks to protect. If he seeks to avoid a *public* disaster, this is a "public necessity", and if he is protecting the person, or property of himself, or a third person, this is a "personal necessity."

e.g. In the course of fighting a fire, D, a city official blew up P's house in order to prevent the spread of the fire. D is not liable for the damage to P's house because D was acting to avoid a public disaster, and thus was acting within a privilege created by public necessity. See Surocco v. Geary, 3 Cal. 69 (1853).

(b) The significance of the difference between public and private necessity lies in the existence or absence of liability for any harm caused by the exercise of the privilege created by the necessity.

(i) When the defendant's conduct is to protect the person, or property of himself, or another (private necessity) he is liable for any harm caused thereby.

(ii) By contrast, there is no liability imposed on the defendant for any harm caused in avoiding a public disaster (public necessity).

(c) Because of the liability for any harm caused in pursuit of a private necessity, the privilege created by such necessity is said to be an "incomplete" privilege. Recovery is awarded to the plaintiff on a theory of unjust enrichment, not on a tort theory. See Restatement, Second, Torts §§ 196, 197, 262, and 263.

See generally, Gregory, pp. 33–42; Keeton, pp. 150–160; P & W, pp. 129–136; Prosser, pp. 124–127.

LEGAL PROCESS AND ARREST

1. A court may authorize the interference with the rights of a person by seizure of his property, arrest, or some other restraint imposed by a public official. This is a privilege granted by legal process and constitutes a complete defense to a suit against the public officer for performing the authorized act.

2. An arrest is the taking of a person into custody under circumstances and in a manner authorized by law.

3. An arrest may be made either:

   (a) with a warrant, or

   (b) without a warrant.

4. A warrant of arrest is a written order from a court directed to a peace officer, or to some other person specifically named, commanding him to arrest a person.

5. At common law an *officer* could make an arrest:

   (a) with *a warrant,* of any person described in the warrant, whether for a felony or misdemeanor,

   (b) *without a warrant for a felony if:*

      (i) the person arrested has committed a felony,

      (ii) there has been in fact a felony committed and there is probable cause to believe the person arrested committed it, or

      (iii) there is probable cause to believe the person arrested committed a felony, even if no felony has been committed,

   (c) *without a warrant for a misdemeanor* only when it amounts to a breach of the peace and is committed in the officer's presence.

6. The common law authority to arrest has been changed by statute in most states, and the extent of an officer's authority to

arrest has been increased. The principal change from the common law permits officers to arrest without a warrant for certain designated misdemeanors which are not committed in the officer's presence where there is probable cause.

e.g. Such arrests are generally permitted under shoplifting statutes.

7. Modern statutes generally permit private persons to arrest for any offense committed in their presence.

8. Legal authority is a defense to a civil action based on the intentional arrest of a person, or seizure of property.

   (a) A court with jurisdiction issued a warrant for the arrest of X and a writ of execution for the seizure of X's automobile. The warrant and writ were placed in the hands of Sheriff D. The Sheriff proceeded to locate X and his car. However, he made a mistake and arrested P and seized P's automobile, thinking P was X. P sues Sheriff D for false arrest of P's person and for D's conversion of P's car. May he recover on either count?

   Answer. Yes, P may recover on both counts. The warrant described X as the person to be arrested. It would have protected the Sheriff from liability had he arrested X. The writ described X's automobile as the property to be seized. Had the Sheriff seized X's car, the writ would have afforded him a complete defense. But these papers give Sheriff D no protection or immunity from liability for arresting the wrong person, or from seizing the wrong property. Therefore, Sheriff D is liable for his intentional interference with P's liberty and for seizing P's car. See Hays v. Creary, 60 Tex. 445 (1883); Johnson v. Weiner, 155 Fla. 169, 19 So.2d 699 (1944); Symonds v. Hull, 37 Me. 354 (1853); Buck v. Colbath, 70 U.S. (3 Wall.) 334, 18 L.Ed. 257 (1865).

   (b) H spat in P's face, which constituted a misdemeanor. On the following day, P told Policeman D about the battery. D inquired of others and learned that there was no doubt about the fact. Without procuring a warrant, D arrested H for the alleged offense. H sues D for false arrest. May he recover?

   Answer. Yes. The common law rule is that neither an officer, nor a private person, has a right without a warrant to arrest for a misdemeanor which does not constitute a breach of the peace. Nothing appears in this case to show that H's spitting constituted a breach of the peace. Therefore, D's arrest of H without a warrant was without lawful authority and subjects D to liability for his intentional interference with H's liberty. See Restatement, Second, Torts §§ 112–136. See also State v. Mobley, 240 N.C. 476, 83 S.E.2d 100 (1954).

NOTE—An arrest without proper legal authority is a false arrest, and because an arrest restrains the liberty of a person it is also the tort of false imprisonment. See False Imprisonment and False Arrest, above.

9. Although an officer or a private person may have authority to make an arrest, the authority to use force in accomplishing the arrest is circumscribed by the law.

   (a) Whether the arresting party is an officer or a private person, the general rule is that the arrester is privileged to use reasonable force in making the arrest.

   (b) At common law the use of deadly force was never permitted to stop one who was fleeing from arrest for a misdemeanor.

   (c) At common law one was privileged to kill a fleeing felon. This was so because all felonies were punishable by death.

   NOTE—Because most felonies no longer carry the death penalty, the traditional rule permitting the use of deadly force to stop a fleeing felon is undergoing change. The Model Penal Code, § 3.07(2), would restrict the use of deadly force to an authorized peace officer or one assisting a person he believes to be an authorized police officer. The use of such force would be further limited to those situations in which the force used creates no substantial risk of injury to innocent persons. The person using such force must believe either that the crime for which the arrest is made involved conduct including the use or threatened use of deadly force, or, that there is a substantial risk that the person to be arrested will cause death or serious bodily harm if his arrest is delayed.

10. Under the common law a person was permitted to use reasonable force, which would ordinarily be non-deadly, to resist an unlawful arrest by a police officer. Today many courts hold that force may not be used to resist an unlawful arrest.

   See generally, Keeton, pp. 90–103; P & W, pp. 137–138; Prosser, pp. 127–136; Smith's Review, Criminal Procedure, Chapter II, Arrest, pp. 27–30.

DEFENSES— DISCIPLINE

1. The necessity of maintaining order by one in charge of others confers a privilege on the person in charge to use reasonable force.

2. A person who has authority over a child, such as a parent or teacher, may use reasonable force to discipline the child. See Steber v. Norris, 188 Wis. 366, 206 N.W. 173 (1925).

   e.g. P, an eighth grade student, put on the gloves of another student at the start of class. The teacher, D, told P to take them off. When this was not done promptly D hit P several times on the head rupturing P's eardrum. The lower court directed a verdict for D and P appealed. Was the evidence sufficient to go to the jury?

Answer. Yes. Whether discipline is reasonable depends on: (a) the form of the punishment and the resulting injury to the pupil, (b) the pupil's conduct which gave rise to the punishment, (c) the teacher's motive in administering the discipline, and (d) whether the teacher was angry at the time because a punishment administered in anger is more likely to be intemperate. Using these criteria a jury could have found for P so the case should have gone to the jury for decision. The case was remanded for a new trial. See Tinkham v. Kole, 252 Iowa 1303, 110 N.W.2d 258 (1961).

3. The common law recognized the husband as head of the household and permitted him to discipline his wife.

4. There is a split of authority today on whether a wife is permitted to recover from her husband for torts. See Chapter XIV, Intra-family Immunities, below.

NOTE—In addition to substantive defenses, such as those outlined in this chapter, the analysis of any fact situation should also include a review of other defenses of general applicability such as the statute of limitations, improper joinder, or the presence of a release or covenant not to sue. "Immunity" may also serve as a defense to a tort action. See Chapter XIV, Immunity, below. See Prosser, pp. 859–864.

See generally, Keeton, pp. 104–113; P & W, pp. 138–140; Prosser, pp. 136–138.

Case 13 *Defense of self and others—examples of reasonable and excessive force*

P, age ten, and three playmates were throwing snowballs at passing cars. A snowball hit D's car and he stopped. D chased the boys and caught P. D took P by the arm to his car and drove P into the village where he held P by the arm until he could turn him over to a police officer. P sued D for false imprisonment and assault and battery. D explained that he was trying to protect motorists from the dangerous actions of the boys. The jury found for D and P appealed. Is D liable to P for any of his actions?

Answer. *Yes. D's restraint of P constituted false imprisonment and holding P's arm was a battery unless D was legally justified in taking reasonable steps to prevent further dangerous activities. The court concluded that D used reasonable force in bringing P to his car and admonishing him. However, the court ruled as a matter of law that D could not take P into custody and drive him into town. P's parents lived across the street and he could have taken him there. The jury's verdict, in effect, found D's conduct reasonable and this will stand up to the point D drove P into the village. The ride in the car was false imprisonment and holding P by the arm after they arrived in the village until they found a police officer was a battery, though nominal. The case was remanded for a determination of compensatory damages due P. The court noted that there was no malice by D so no punitive damages were allowed. Furthermore, the record would* not *support substantial compensatory damages.*

See Drabek v. Sabley, 31 Wis.2d 184, 142 N.W.2d 798 (1966).

Excessive force not permitted in defense of real or personal property   Case 14

P went onto D's property and began to tear down D's fence. D protected his property by using his hands, feet and sticks to hit P, thereby wounding him. P sued for damages. D contended that his actions were justified because he was protecting his property. There was a verdict for P and D appealed. Was D justified in wounding P to protect his property?

Answer. *No. An assault and battery may be justified to protect real or personal property, but here D used excessive force and wounded P. P contended that D should have pleaded* moliter manus imposuit, *which literally means he gently laid hands upon. That plea would have required D to have requested P to depart before he used force. The court said that where a plaintiff in possession of property was attacked by actual force no such request to desist was necessary. Where possession is invaded by* implied force *only, injuries in the defense of the possession ought to be justified by way of moliter manus.* Actual force *is breaking open a gate or door, or trespassing with force and arms. In that event the owner may lay hands on the intruder immediately. Where possession is invaded without using actual force, the law will imply a force, but there must be a request to depart before the possessor can lay hands on the trespasser and throw him out. In the present case P's entry by tearing down a fence was* actual force *and justified an assault and battery. However, P did not commit an assault on the person of D which would justify the use of additional force by D. Thus D was not justified in wounding P, even though D had a valid defense to the assault and battery charged. The verdict for P was affirmed.*

See McIlvoy v. Cockran, 9 Ky. (2 A. K. Marsh.) 271 (1820).

NOTE—Whether the force used to protect property is reasonable is usually a factual question for the jury to determine. However, it is established that force which can cause death or serious injury may not be used to protect property other than one's dwelling and in cases involving arson, burglary and robbery. This is because the value of human life outweighs property interests. For this reason setting a trap with a spring gun to shoot a trespasser is not justifiable. The owner may not do indirectly with a trap that which he could not do directly if he were present. See Bird v. Holbrook 4 Bing. 628, 130 Eng.Rep. 911 (1828); Katko v. Briney, 183 N.W.2d 657 (Iowa 1971).

III | NEGLIGENCE

Summary Outline

INTRODUCTION

1. Negligence is the second of the three basic forms of tort liability.

2. Negligence may result from:

   (a) *doing* an affirmative act without using due care, or

   (b) negligently *failing to do* an act which is required by law to be done.

3. A careful distinction should be made between:

   (a) negligence, as a form of conduct, and

   (b) a cause of action based upon negligence.

   CAVEAT—All too frequently in analyzing fact patterns and answering examination questions students merely make reference to the conduct in question as "negligence" or "negligent". They do not analyze the rest of the fact pattern to determine whether all of the elements of a *cause of action* in negligence are present. It is not sufficient to impose liability on the defendant merely because he acted negligently. The balance of the elements of the cause of action must be established, and there must be no defense available to the defendant.

4. The analysis of a negligence problem includes consideration of:

   (a) the basis for liability,

   (b) the interest of the plaintiff which is protected,

   (c) the standard of care required of the defendant,

   (d) problems of proof of negligence,

   (e) duty of care, including misfeasance and nonfeasance,

   (f) proximate causation, and

   (g) extent of liability.

5. Having determined that a cause of action exists in favor of the plaintiff, analysis of the fact pattern must then be made to determine if a defense is available to the defendant. See Chapter IV, Defenses to Negligence.

PREREQUISITES OF NEGLIGENCE

1. Negligence is an *unintentional* tort. It is conduct "which falls below the standard established by law for the protection of others against unreasonably great risk of harm." Restatement, Second, Torts § 282. See also, Prosser, p. 145.

2. There is a cause of action based on negligence if the plaintiff can show that the following elements exist:

(a) that the defendant owed the plaintiff a duty to use due care,

(b) that the defendant breached that duty by being negligent,

(c) that the plaintiff was injured, and

(d) that the defendant's negligence proximately caused the plaintiff's injury.

3. The question of law for the court is: whether the relationship between the parties is such that there is a duty of due care owed by the defendant.

4. The questions of fact for jury are:

(a) whether the defendant was negligent,

(b) whether the plaintiff was injured and, if so, the extent thereof, and

(c) whether the negligence of the defendant caused the plaintiff's injury.

NOTE—If the answers to the factual questions above are so clear that reasonable men could not differ thereon, they are questions of law for the court.

5. In a negligence case, the fact that the defendant did not intend to injure the plaintiff is immaterial. State of mind is not important, but only the conduct of defendant.

6. The analysis of a negligence problem includes consideration of:

(a) the basis for liability,

(b) the interest of plaintiff protected,

(c) the standard of care required of the defendant,

(d) proof of negligence,

  e.g. res ipsa loquitur,

(e) duty of care including misfeasance and nonfeasance,

(f) causation,

(g) extent of liability, and

(h) defenses.

See generally, P & W, p. 144.

Negligence—elements of cause of action **Case 15**

A statute provided that one should not drive an automobile faster than 15 miles per hour in a business district. D drove his automo-

bile at a speed of 25 miles per hour and otherwise negligently in a business district which negligence and excess speed caused injury to P. P sues D. May he recover?

Answer. Yes. This is a typical case of actionable negligence. Every element of a cause of action is present: (a) When one undertakes an affirmative course of conduct, he creates a risk of injury to others. He owes to all who may be injured by his affirmative acts a duty to use due care in the performance of such acts. Therefore, D owed to P a duty to use due care in the operation of his automobile. (b) There are two reasons for saying D breached his duty to use due care: (1) the facts say D drove his car at a speed of 25 miles per hour in a 15 mile zone. This statute limiting speed was enacted for the safety of the public. When a statute is placed on the books for the purpose of protecting the public, a violation of that statute is negligence per se. (2) The facts say that D was otherwise driving negligently. Therefore, on both grounds, D was breaching his duty of due care by being negligent. (c) The facts state that P was injured. (d) The facts also state that the excessive speed and negligence caused P's injury. Hence, there are present in this case all the elements required for a cause of action based on negligence. Therefore, P may recover from D.

See Restatement, Second, Torts §§ 281, 282.

HISTORICAL DEVELOPMENT

1. Negligence, as a distinct and specific basis for tort liability, is a newcomer in the common law. It has been so recognized for little more than a century.

2. Prior to the emergence of negligence, tort liability as we know it today, was usually founded on:

    (a) intentional aggression, or

    (b) the doctrine of liability without fault.

    > *e.g.* P and D went into the forest to cut trees. D swung his ax in cutting down a tree. By pure accident the head of D's ax flew off the handle and injured P. In the early law D was liable to P irrespective of fault. It was a theory of act-injury-liability. The loss fell on the actor simply because he was the actor.

3. The basis for liability in the field of negligence is fault. The doctrine of "no liability without fault" began to emerge in the early part of the 19th century, and today is the basis for much litigation in the field of torts.

4. The theory underlying our tort law is this: *let the loss lie where it falls, unless there is reason for shifting it.*

5. The law does recognize three reasons for shifting the loss:

    (a) intentional wrongdoing,

    (b) negligence, and

    (c) situations justifying the imposition of absolute liability or liability without fault, also called strict or absolute liability.

6. These concepts rule out any liability for pure accident.

    (a) P and D were walking their dogs when the dogs began to fight. D tried to separate the dogs by hitting them with a stick. When D raised the stick it hit P in the eye. P sued D for damages. D was not held liable because he was doing a lawful act with due care. D's hitting P was accidental so D is not liable. See Brown v. Kendall, 60 Mass. (6 Cush.) 292 (1850).

    (b) P alleged that D shot him and thereby injured him. P did not allege that D acted negligently or that he shot P intentionally. The court dismissed the suit because the mere fact that P was injured by D's act, without more, does not establish liability. See Fowler v. Lanning, 1 All E.R. 290 (Q.B.D.1959). See generally, Keeton, pp. 162–165; P & W, pp. 6–12, 143–144.

Unavoidable accident—no liability without fault   **Case 16**

D was driving his automobile along the street at a speed of 5 miles per hour when P, a child of 5 years of age following a ball, ran directly in front of the car and was injured. D was wholly without fault because no amount of effort or care could have avoided the result. P sues D. May he recover?

Answer. *No.* An accident is an event which cannot be avoided by the exercise of due care. *In this case there is such an event. P, a child of 5 years, cannot be negligent as a matter of law. D was wholly free from fault. He was not negligent. He was exercising due care. He did not run into P intentionally. And finally, this is not a situation recognized by the law where liability should be imposed without fault. Hence, this is an accident for which no one is liable. Therefore, the loss must lie where it falls, that is, on the child P. D is not liable and P cannot recover from him.*

See *Uncapher v. Baltimore & Ohio Railroad Co.,* 127 Ohio St. 351, 188 N.E. 553 (1933).

NOTE—In a similar case, D was driving his car at a reasonable rate of speed when he suddenly became ill and fainted. The car went off the road and crashed, injuring two passengers, P and Q, who sued D for damages based on his negligence in losing control of the car. D had never fainted before and was in good health. Is D liable to P and Q?

Answer. No. Here is an accident which neither foresight nor the exercise of due care could have avoided. It is an event over which D had no control and which rendered him incapable of doing any act. The things which happened after D became unconscious are merely events in the external world for which no one incurs any liability in tort or otherwise. It is an accident for which no one is liable. Therefore, the loss must lie where it falls—on P and Q. Both D, and Q are innocent persons and there exists no reason for shifting the loss from where it fell. Hence, P and Q cannot recover. See Cohen v. Petty, 62 App.D.C. 187, 65 F.2d 820 (1933).

REASONABLE PERSON CONCEPT

1. The standard of conduct required of the actor in the field of negligence is that care and caution which:

   (a) a reasonable, prudent person would exercise

   (b) under the circumstances.

   CAVEAT—The applicable standard may be stated either as that of a reasonable, prudent person, or that of a reasonable and prudent person. However, it is not correct gramatically to state the standard as that of a reasonably prudent person.

2. This so-called reasonable, prudent person is a non-existent, hypothetical imaginary person who is established as a standard. His or her conduct would represent the conduct of the average person in the community, acting under the circumstances which surrounded the defendant at the time of his alleged negligence.

3. The reason for requiring every adult to conform to the standard pattern of conduct is this: When an adult moves among other persons in the external world there is danger to the general welfare. Therefore, the law places a duty on the adult person to compel him or her to conform to the minimum standard of conduct for the purpose of protecting the general security of others.

4. The standard of care required in any given situation depends on a balancing of three factors:

   (a) the probability that some damage will be done,

   (b) the seriousness of the resulting injury, and

   (c) the burden of adequate precautions.

   See United States v. Carroll Towing Co., 159 F.2d 169 (2d Cir. 1947), rehearing denied 160 F.2d 482 (1947).

5. It is impossible to define "negligence" in the abstract. It can exist only in a setting, and therefore a jury must consider all the circumstances surrounding the negligent act. For this reason it is reversible error for the court, when instructing the jury on the defendant's being required to act as a reasonable, prudent person, to omit the words, "under the circumstances". Defendant

must act as a "reasonable, prudent person under the circumstances". Louisville & Nashville Railroad Co. v. Gower, 85 Tenn. 465, 3 S.W. 824 (1887).

6. In general, the standard to which all adults must conform is objective. It is whether the defendant acted as a "reasonable person of ordinary prudence" in the circumstances and not whether the defendant himself acted honestly and bona fide to the best of his judgment. See Vaughn v. Menlove, 3 Bing.N.C. 468, 132 Eng.Rep. 490 (1837). This is the first case in which this standard is mentioned.

    (a) In applying the standard many of the individual idiosyncracies of the actor are eliminated and he is compelled at his peril, to conduct himself in conformity with the minimum standard required of the reasonable, prudent person.

        e.g. If the actor is sluggish, hotheaded, thoughtless, excitable, inefficient, or has poor judgment—all of these personal characteristics are eliminated from consideration and the actor is compelled to act as though he were not sluggish, not hotheaded, not thoughtless, not excitable, not inefficient, not possessed of poor judgment. He is held to account for his acts and the consequences thereof as though he were acting as the reasonable, prudent person. If the actor's conduct does not meet that standard and causes injury, there is liability.

    (b) However, the standard applied is "not necessarily a supercautious individual devoid of human frailties and constantly preoccupied with the idea that danger may be lurking in every direction about him at any time." Whitman v. W. T. Grant Co., 16 Utah 2d 81, 395 P.2d 918, 920 (1964); Public Service Co. of New Hampshire v. Elliott, 123 F.2d 2 (1st Cir. 1941).

    (c) There are certain objective attributes of the actor which are taken into consideration when the test is applied.

        e.g. The actor's sex and age, his physical condition, whether he is blind, deaf, lame, has only one arm or leg, his knowledge and mental capacity, together with his education and training, are all items included within the phrase, "under the circumstances".

CAVEAT—A person with a physical handicap is not required to meet a standard of conduct which is physically impossible. However, such a person must act in a reasonable and prudent manner taking the physical handicap into consideration.

    e.g. A blind person may be negligent in taking a risk which is unreasonable because of that handicap. Blindness is one of the factors a jury must consider in determining whether a person acted as a reasonable, prudent person. See Hill v. City of Glenwood, 124 Iowa 479, 100 N.W. 522 (1904).

(d) By the expression, *under the circumstances,* the jury may consider a multitude of other items apart from the condition of the actor's body and mind, such as instinctive action in an emergency situation where there was no time to reflect on the best course of action. See Whicher v. Phinney, 124 F.2d 929 (1st Cir. 1942). See also Cordas v. Peerless Transportation Co., 27 N.Y.S.2d 198 (1941).

(e) A person is not required to guard against extremely improbable events, but only against those events which are reasonably foreseeable.

(i) D installed water mains and fire hydrants in a city. The hydrant opposite P's house was constructed with due care and D provided against normal frost damage. However, in an unprecedented frost the mechanism of the hydrant was upset, and water leaked through the ground and damaged P's house. The court held that P could not recover because D was not negligent. D was not required to provide against the unprecedented frost because that was not a contingency against which a reasonable person would provide under the circumstances. See Blyth v. Birmingham Waterworks Co., 11 Exch. 781, 156 Eng.Rep. 1047 (1856). See also CASE 59, below.

(ii) D, a father, left his golf club on the ground in his back yard. D's child found the club, and negligently hit P while playing with it. P may not recover from D, the father, because there was little possibility that D's conduct would result in injury to another. In other words, a reasonable, prudent person could not foresee the harm which resulted from D's child's conduct. See Lubitz v. Wells, 19 Conn.Sup. 322, 113 A.2d 147 (1955).

(iii) D left a loaded gun by his fence. A boy passing by picked it up, and thinking that it was not loaded, shot it and injured P. D was held liable for the injury to P. This is so because the event to be guarded against could have been reasonably foreseen. See Sullivan v. Creed, 2 Ir.R 317 (K.B.1904).

7. The fact that defendant acted just as others would have acted under the circumstances does not necessarily mean that the act was not negligent. However, a jury may consider the customary way of conducting a business and this will ordinarily negate any inference of negligence, unless the custom would be recognized by all prudent persons to be dangerous. See Bandekow v. Chicago, Burlington & Quincy Railroad Co., 136 Wis. 341, 117 N.W. 812 (1908).

8. Meeting the custom of care in an industry is not conclusive evidence that due care was used in a negligence action.

(a) P brought a malpractice action against her ophthalmologists for failure to test for and determine that she had glaucoma after numerous complaints and examinations. As a result, P suffered permanent damage to her vision. The evidence showed that standards for the profession did not require tests for glaucoma for patients under forty because the disease rarely occurred in that age group. P was 32. However, such tests should be given if symptoms reveal that glaucoma should be suspected. The court noted that following the standard in the community does not prevent a finding of negligence. The test for glaucoma is relatively simple, and persons under forty are entitled to protection from disease. Therefore, the standard that should have been followed was to test P for glaucoma, and failure to do so was negligence by the doctors which proximately resulted in P's injury. P may recover. See Helling v. Carey, 84 Wn.2d 514, 519 P.2d 981 (1974).

(b) The owner of a tug, which was lost in a storm with two barges, was liable for the loss of the cargo because the tug was not equipped with a radio which would have warned of the storm and prevented any loss. This was so even though it was not the usual practice to have such radios on ocean tugs. See The T. J. Hooper, 60 F.2d 737 (2d Cir. 1932), certiorari denied 287 U.S. 662, 53 S.Ct. 220, 77 L.Ed. 571 (1932). In accord, see Mayhew v. Sullivan Mining Co., 76 Me. 100 (1884).

NOTE—It is for the jury to determine whether a plaintiff exercised the care required. If the defense of contributory negligence is raised, the jury also decides that factual issue. The jury determines these issues based on all the circumstances. See Pokora v. Wabash Railway Co., 292 U.S. 98, 54 S.Ct. 580, 78 L.Ed. 1149 (1934).

See generally, Gregory, pp. 101–133, 154–183, 208–211; Keeton, pp. 12–14, 208–230, 249–252; P & W, pp. 144–216.

Duty of care—no liability for unavoidable accident　　　　　Case 17

A box was given to D in New York for shipment to California. It was put on a steamship and shipped. The box was leaking an unknown substance when it arrived, and it was taken to D's office for examination. No one knew that the box contained nitro-glycerine. While the box was being opened it exploded killing the bystanders and damaging the building. The owner of the building sued D for damages to his building based upon D's negligence. Is D liable for damages to the building?

Answer. No. *The mere fact that an injury has been caused is not sufficient, by itself, to establish liability. No one is responsible for injuries resulting from an unavoidable accident while engaged in a lawful business. D accepted the box in the usual course of business and there was no duty to inquire as to its contents. There was nothing to indicate its contents were dangerous. When it was discovered that the box was leaking, it was taken to D's office for inspection according to its customary practice. Nitro-glycerine had been discovered only a few years before, and its use for blasting was just being explored. D used ordinary care and that is all that was required. The consequences of the accident must be borne by the sufferer of the misfortune. Thus D was not liable for the damage to the building because reasonable care was exercised.*

See The Nitro-Glycerine Case, 82 U.S. (15 Wall.) 524, 21 L.Ed. 206 (1872).

Case 18   *Failure to maintain the standard of care*

P purchased a drum of gasoline for use on his farm. When P attempted to remove the bunghole cap from the drum a spark was produced because of the condition of unrepair in the threads of the bung cap. This caused a sudden outburst of fire which severely burned P. The drum had been in use for nine years and D knew that the threads on the bung cap were broken from repeated hammering on the bung cap during the course of its use. P sued D manufacturer and others for his injuries. D contended that there should be no liability because the occurrence was so unusual and improbable that it could not be foreseen. Is D liable for the injuries to P?

Answer. Yes. *A person must guard against the reasonably foreseeable consequences of his act, but it is not necessary to guard against extremely improbable occurrences. "The test as respects foreseeability is not the balance of probabilities, but the existence, in the situation in hand, of some real likelihood of some damage, and the likelihood is of such appreciable weight and moment as to induce, or which reasonably should induce, action to avoid it on the part of a person of a reasonably prudent mind." In the present case the standard of care required of D is that of a person of ordinary prudence and D should reasonably have anticipated that a sudden fire or explosion could be caused by the disrepair of the cap. The fact that the occurrence of injury was remote does not absolve D from liability because P need not show that his injury was likely to occur. P established that the injury should have been foreseen by D in these circumstances and, therefore, P may recover.*

See Gulf Refining Co. v. Williams, 183 Miss. 723, 185 So. 234 (1938). See also Heaven v. Pender, 11 Q.B.D. 503 (1883); Marsh Wood Products Co. v. Babcock & Wilcox Co., 207 Wis. 209, 240 N.W. 392 (1932).

1. The standard of conduct of a reasonable, prudent person is flexible. Its application to certain classes of persons requires knowledge of special rules.

   (a) Infants are held to the reasonable, prudent person standard with age, intelligence and experience considered as part of the circumstances in determining whether the child was negligent.

   (b) Insane, mentally subnormal, and voluntarily intoxicated persons are held to the same reasonable, prudent person standard as adults.

   (c) Persons whose mental faculties have been impaired by age have that fact considered as part of the surrounding circumstances in determining whether they were negligent.

2. *The test for children is primarily subjective, dealing with the capacity of a particular child to recognize and avoid risk and harm, taking into consideration this child's age, his intelligence and his experience.* This test recognizes that children develop at different rates even in the same age group, and acquire capacity individually, and not in conformity to any presupposed pattern. See Kuhns v. Brugger, 390 Pa. 331, 135 A.2d 395 (1957); Restatement, Second, Torts §§ 283A, 464; CASE 19, below.

3. When children engage in activities normally pursued only by adults, such as driving a car or flying an airplane, they are held to the same standard as an adult. Courts reason that if children engage in such an activity which could be dangerous to the minor and other persons, the minor should be held to the adult standard of care. See CAVEAT after CASE 19, below.

4. With respect to mentally subnormal persons, a jury is permitted to consider mental condition in determining whether the person was contributorily negligent. See Lynch v. Rosenthal, 396 S.W.2d 272 (Mo.App.1965).

5. In only one case, according to Prosser, was a mentally subnormal, although not insane, person held to the same standard of conduct as a normal adult person in determining whether there was contributory negligence. P's decedent was found to have been contributorily negligent by accepting an automobile ride with an intoxicated person, and thus P could not recover. See Wright v. Tate, 208 Va. 291, 156 S.E.2d 562 (1967); Prosser, p. 153; and Restatement, Second, Torts, § 464(g).

6. The general rule with respect to insane persons is that the reasonable, prudent person test is applied, and there is liability if that standard is not met. The rule which holds an insane person to the same standard as a normal person is based on public policy:

   (a) to allocate loss on the person who occasioned it where one of two innocent persons must suffer,

STANDARD FOR CHILDREN AND OTHERS

(b) to induce those interested in the estate of the insane person to restrain and control the person, and

(c) to prevent false claims of insanity in order to avoid liability.

7. Some courts have recognized an exception to the general rule that insane persons are responsible for their own torts. Where there was no forewarning of the mental disorder the person is treated the same as one who suffers a heart attack or some other sudden illness without sufficient warning. Where such illness could not reasonably have been foreseen, there is no liability.

e.g. While D was driving her automobile she had the mental delusion that God was operating her car. D saw a truck approaching and stepped on the gas to become airborne. However, there was a collision with P who brought suit for damages. D contended that there was no negligence because D could not have reasonably forseen that she would have a mental delusion. P contended that insanity is no defense, and in any event there was forewarning because P had visions of God prior to the accident. D appealed a jury verdict for P. The court held that "where the driver is suddenly overcome without forewarning by a mental disability or disorder which incapacitates him from conforming his conduct to the standards of a reasonable man under like circumstances" the general rule that insanity is no defense does not apply. However, in the present case the prior visions of P were sufficient for a jury to conclude that P had warning or knowledge that she might have a mental delusion while driving. Since P had some reason to believe that her condition might endanger others, the jury verdict for P should not be overturned on that ground. See Breunig v. American Family Insurance Co., 45 Wis.2d 536, 173 N.W.2d 619 (1970).

8. Persons whose mental faculties have been lessened by age are treated as children. That is, they are held to a standard of conduct with due consideration given to their age and mental capacity.

See generally, Gregory, pp. 136–148; Keeton, pp. 234–238; P & W, pp. 177–184; Prosser, pp. 152–157.

Case 19 *Standard of care—children*

D, age 17, while driving an automobile struck and killed P's three year old son. P sued D for damages for negligence. The court instructed the jury that if they found that the defendant, D, exercised the care and caution of a reasonable, prudent person, taking into consideration the defendant's age, intelligence and experience, under the circumstances then surrounding the defendant, then they should find for the defendant. The jury found for the defendant. The plaintiff appealed contending that the court should have treated any youth who is permitted by law to drive an automobile exactly the same as an adult. Was there error?

Answer. *No. The instruction given is a proper statement of the law. The test for determining the proper conduct of an adult in the field of negligence is objective. It is that of the reasonable, prudent person under the circumstances. The age factor is ignored and all adults must meet the standard or be liable for falling short of it. However, it would be highly prejudicial to children if their conduct were judged by the same standard which is applied to a mature person. In some jurisdictions children who have attained the age of 14 or over are treated as adults. In other states every child is required to act according to the standard conduct of a child of his own age. In still others the courts arbitrarily hold a child of 17, 18, 19 or 20, to the same standard of conduct as an adult. Each of these tests is arbitrary, inflexible and objective. The fundamental fault is that any such test presupposes that children develop uniformly in point of age or time which simply is not true. The test applied to children should be uniform and primarily subjective. It should allow for varying degrees of development of children of different ages and also for those of the same age. The instruction given by the court in this case permitted the jury to consider not only the care and caution of a "reasonable, prudent* person," *but also the "defendant's age, intelligence and experience", under the circumstances. To the extent that the infant is treated as a "reasonable, prudent person" the test may be said to be objective. To the extent that the particular child's age, intelligence and experience, may be taken into consideration, the test is subjective. The instruction to the jury in this case, was fair to the infant and a proper protection for society. Judgment for D was affirmed.*

See Charbonneau v. MacRury, 84 N.H. 501, 153 A. 457 (1931).

CAVEAT—The rule in the Charbonneau case is no longer applied to minors when they engage in adult activity. The case illustrates the rule and judicial reasoning applicable to minors when they are NOT engaging in adult activity. The New Hampshire court subsequently changed the rule in the Charbonneau case and held that where minors engage in adult activities, such as operating an automobile or motorcycle, they should be treated as adults. The court reasoned that it would be unfair to the public to permit a minor to operate a vehicle and not require the same standard of care expected of others. Further, traffic laws apply to "any person," which indicates a legislative intent to have all drivers exercise a single standard regardless of age and experience. Therefore, a more lenient standard for minors in the operation of a motor vehicle is unrealistic and contrary to public safety and legislative policy. See Daniels v. Evans, 107 N.H. 407, 224 A.2d 63 (1966).

MISFEASANCE AND NONFEASANCE

1. In the field of negligence a legal duty is the obligation of one person to use due care not to injure another.

2. A defendant cannot be liable in negligence to a plaintiff to whom no duty is owed, either individually or as a member of a class.

3. Liability for negligence may be founded on either misfeasance or nonfeasance.

   (a) Misfeasance is affirmative action which violates the duty to act with due care.

   e.g. D moved some casks of brandy without consideration for P and negligently damaged them. P may recover for D's breach of his duty to act with due care. See Coggs v. Bernard, 2 Ld.Raym. 909 (K.B. 1703).

   (b) Nonfeasance is the negligent failure to act when there is a legal duty to act. Liability for nonfeasance must be based either on a specific relationship, or on statute. See CASE 20, below.

   e.g. D's minor son often assaulted and mistreated smaller children. D knew this, but he did not try to prevent this misconduct and he permitted his son to play with other children. D's son assaulted and injured P who sued D for damages. May P recover?

   Answer. Yes. A parent who knows of the dangerous propensities of his child must take reasonable care to control the child. D's failure to take reasonable measures to prevent the occurrence of a *definite* type of misconduct known to D is negligence, and P may recover. See Linder v. Bidner, 50 Misc.2d 320, 270 N.Y.S.2d 427 (1966).

   NOTE—Contrary to the popular belief among laymen, parents are not liable for the torts of their children in the absence of special circumstances such as those in the example above, or as a result of a special statute.

4. Nonfeasance is the failure to act. It cannot be the foundation of liability if there is no legal duty owed the person in a perilous position.

   (a) P and D were business partners and they discussed insurance for a ship they owned. D said that he would obtain insurance, but he did not do it. The ship sank and was a total loss. The court held that D was not liable for P's loss because D never attempted to obtain insurance, and his failure to perform the promise, which was made without consideration, was not actionable. By contrast, D would be liable for misfeasance, such as securing insurance on the wrong boat or in an inadequate amount, but not for nonfeasance. See Thorne v. Deas, 4 Johns 84 (1809).

NOTE 1—Although the decision in Thorne v. Deas has been criticized, the distinction between misfeasance and nonfeasance continues to the present time in tort law. The tort aspect of the decision is still good law. See P & W, pp. 437–438; Restatement, Second, Torts § 323.

NOTE 2—When Thorne v. Deas was decided the contract doctrine of promissory estoppel, which is a substitute for consideration, had not been developed. Today that doctrine might be applicable and change the result. See Restatement, Second, Contracts § 90.

(b) D saw X drowning after X's canoe overturned. D was an expert swimmer, and had a boat and rope with which he could rescue X. However, D sat on shore and watched X drown. The law does not recognize D's moral obligation to rescue X. D had no legal duty to act and, therefore, D is not liable. See Osterlind v. Hill, 263 Mass. 73, 160 N.E. 301 (1928). See also Handiboe v. McCarthy, 114 Ga.App. 541, 151 S.E.2d 905 (1966).

(c) Plaintiff's husband drowned as a result of being taunted by defendant to jump into a water filled basin on defendant's property. In denying recovery the court found that decedent had voluntarily placed himself in danger and was owed no duty of rescue by defendant. See Yania v. Bigan, 397 Pa. 316, 155 A.2d 343 (1959). See also, Buch v. Amory Manufacturing Co., 69 N.H. 257, 44 A. 809 (1898).

5. It is said that "danger invites rescue." Therefore, it is foreseeable that someone will attempt to rescue a person in danger. This is known as the rescue doctrine, and under it a rescuer who is injured during a reasonable attempt to assist the person endangered by the wrongdoer may recover.

(a) P and his cousin, H, boarded a commuter train and were standing just inside the door. The train started, but the door was not closed. There was a sudden lurch and H was thrown out of the car. The train was stopped and P walked back along the tracks to look for H. It was dark, and P missed his footing and fell. P brought suit against the railroad for his injuries. The railroad contended that P was contributorily negligent, and therefore, should not recover. The court noted: "Danger invites rescue." The risk of rescue must be placed on the wrongdoer unless the rescue attempt is foolhardy. In this case the questions of whether H's fall was due to the railroad's negligence, and whether P's rescue attempt was reasonable considering the emergency confronting him, were for the jury to determine. See Wagner v. International Railway, 232 N.Y. 176, 133 N.E. 437 (1921).

(b) D negligently caused her automobile to overturn. P, seeing D's situation, attempted to assist D and injured his back while rescuing D. P was permitted to recover against D for his injuries even though the person in peril was D herself. See Britt v. Mangum, 261 N.C. 250, 134 S.E.2d 235 (1964).

(c) P intervened to rescue his wife from D's assault, and P was hit and injured by D. P recovered damages as D's defense of assumption of the risk was rejected. See Farber v. Bryce, 40 Misc.2d 899, 244 N.Y.S.2d 212 (1963).

NOTE—Rescuers of rescuers are also covered by the rule.

6. If one owes no legal duty to another, but undertakes affirmatively to assist such other, and in such voluntary assistance acts negligently causing injury, then there is liability.

(a) P, age 6, who was accompanied by his mother, fell and got his finger caught in the escalator in D's store. D was not liable for the initial injury because there was no negligence in maintaining the escalator. However, D was held liable for the aggravation of the initial injury caused by unreasonable delay in stopping the escalator. See L. S. Ayres & Co. v. Hicks, 220 Ind. 86, 41 N.E.2d 195 (1942).

(b) D undertook to render medical aid to P although he was under no duty to do so. However, D kept P in an infirmary for six hours without any medical care. Because of this D is actionably negligent. If D had done nothing initially perhaps some passerby would have called an ambulance for P. See Zelenko v. Gimbel Brothers, 158 Misc. 904, 287 N.Y.S. 134 (1935).

(c) D's Siamese cat bit or scratched P. Prior to that time the cat had never exhibited any vicious traits. It had always been gentle, and there was no negligence by D in allowing the cat to run freely. Both P and D were aware of the dangers if the cat had rabies. D said that she would keep the cat under observation for fourteen days until it could be determined whether the cat was rabid. However, no special precautions were taken and a few days later the cat escaped. When it returned a month later it was healthy. However, the escape of the cat necessitated P having the Pasteur treatment, which was very painful. P sued for damages. The court noted that D was not liable for the initial bite or scratch of the cat because there was no negligence or reason to believe that the cat was dangerous. When D volunteered to restrain the cat, but failed to use ordinary care to prevent the cat's escape, D was liable to P for damages sustained for failure to use ordinary care. D could have had public authorities restrain the cat, but relied on P's statements. When the cat escaped P was forced to undergo painful medical treatment which would otherwise have been unnecessary. Therefore, although P was not liable for the initial scratch, P was liable for damages caused by the failure to perform her promise to restrain the cat for observation, upon which D relied. See Marsalis v. La Salle, 94 So.2d 120 (La.App.1957); Lacey v. United States, 98 F.Supp. 219 (D.C.Mass.1951).

7. In order to avoid imposing liability on the good samaritan who causes injury during his assistance, some jurisdictions have enacted statutory protection. This alters the standard of care required in such circumstances to encourage assistance in an emergency by those who might otherwise be afraid to risk liability.

e.g. Ohio Revised Code § 2305.23 provides that "No person shall be liable in civil damages for administering emergency care or treatment at the scene of an emergency outside of a hospital, doctor's office, or other place having proper medical equipment for acts performed at the scene of such emergency, unless such acts constitute willful or wanton misconduct". The statute applies both to laymen and to those with medical training who fall under its protection. The exculpatory provisions in this statute do not apply, however, where care or treatment is rendered for payment.

See generally, Gregory, pp. 325–360; Keeton, pp. 252–266, 384–404; P & W, pp. 434–458; Prosser, pp. 338–350.

Doctor has duty to warn of danger posed by patient   Case 20

X was an out-patient at D hospital and receiving treatment from a psychologist. During the treatment X told the psychologist that X intended to kill T because she had spurned X's romantic advances. The psychologist notified campus police who detained X. A panel of D's doctors reviewed the matter and concluded that it was not necessary to confine X. X discontinued his psychotherapy treatments at that time, and two months later X killed T. T's parents brought suit against D hospital and its doctors for failure to confine X and failure to warn T of X's threat. The defendants moved to dismiss on the ground that there was no duty to warn third persons. Should the motion be granted?

Answer. No. In an analogous situation it has been held that a doctor who negligently fails to diagnose a contagious disease is liable to persons infected by the patient. Similarly, if a doctor diagnoses the illness but fails to warn members of the patient's family he is also liable. In the present case X was a patient with a mental illness and potentially dangerous proclivities. A doctor or psychotherapist treating such a patient with mental illness, just as a doctor treating a physical illness, has a duty to give threatened persons such warnings as are necessary to avert foreseeable danger arising from the patient's condition or treatment. Once a person has undertaken to render a service he must exercise reasonable care. If that care requires the giving of warnings the person must do so. Therefore, the Ds' motion to dismiss was denied. T's parents may recover if the defendants negligently failed to give a warning.

See Tarasoff v. Regents of University of California, 13 Cal.3d 177, 118 Cal.Rptr. 129, 529 P.2d 553 (1974), vacated 17 Cal.3d 425, 131 Cal.Rptr. 14, 551 P.2d 334 (1976).

NOTE—The defendants contended that unless information revealed by a patient was covered by a physician-patient privilege, the patient will not make the full disclosure necessary for proper diagnosis and treatment. The court said that the importance of such a privilege must be weighed against the public interest in safety. Here the public interest prevails. There can be no patient-psychotherapist privilege where there is reasonable cause to believe that the patient may be dangerous to himself or others and disclosure of the communication is necessary to prevent the threatened danger.

Case 21   *Misfeasance distinguished from nonfeasance*

D is the engineer on a locomotive which is being taken to a roundhouse for repairs. P is a brakeman who is standing in front of the engine signaling to D when to put on the brakes and stop the engine. When P gives D the signal to stop the engine, D negligently fails to stop the locomotive which runs against P and injures him. (a) Is the negligence of D "misfeasance" or "nonfeasance"? (b) May P recover from D?

Answer. *(a) D's negligence is "misfeasance". (b) P may recover from D. (a) There was a duty owed to P by D to stop the engine. This he negligently failed to do. Considering only the failure to perform that duty, there would appear to be "nonfeasance". But in this case failure to stop the engine was only a part of the entire conduct on the part of D in his operation of the locomotive. He had undertaken an affirmative course of conduct which included starting, running, slowing and stopping the engine. When any one of these was done negligently, it was operating the engine negligently. Therefore, D's negligent act in failing to stop the engine, was negligent operating of the locomotive and constituted "misfeasance". (b) When one undertakes an affirmative course of conduct, as D did in this case, he owes a duty of reasonable care to all those who may be anticipated to be injured if he acts negligently. Within the scope of such duty of D in this case is P who is D's brakeman, whose injury must be anticipated and foreseen by D if he were to be negligent in operating the locomotive. Therefore, the very anticipated injury having happened, P may recover from D for "misfeasance". When "nonfeasance" is involved the duty to act must be* *based on a specific relationship between the injured person and the defendant who negligently fails to act. Even if we should call D's failure to stop the engine nonfeasance, D would be liable to P because of the relationship which existed between them requiring D to stop the engine and not run it against P.*

See Dahlstrom v. Shrum, 368 Pa. 423, 84 A.2d 289 (1951); West v. Cruz, 75 Ariz. 13, 251 P.2d 311 (1952). See also Restatement, Second, Torts § 281, comment c.

Misfeasance—undertaking an affirmative duty   Case 22

D railroad had employed a watchman at a heavily traveled crossing for a number of years. P was a passenger in a truck, the driver of which was aware of D's practice. When the truck with P approached the crossing the watchman gave no signal and the truck proceeded onto the tracks and there was a collision. P sued for damages. D defended by showing that there was no law requiring it to employ a watchman at the crossing. D contended that its failure to perform a voluntary act should not make it liable. May P recover?

Answer. *Yes.* The court reasoned "where there is no duty prescribed by statute or ordinance, it is usually a question for the jury whether the circumstances made the employment of a watchman necessary in the exercise of due care. . . . Where the voluntary employment of a watchman was unknown to the traveler upon the highway, the mere absence of such watchman could probably not be considered as negligence toward him as a matter of law, for in such there is neither an established duty positively owing to such traveler as a member of the general public, nor had he been led into reliance upon the custom. The question would remain simply whether the circumstances demanded such employment. But where the practice is known to the traveler upon the highway, and such traveler had been educated into reliance upon it, some positive duty must rest upon the railway with reference thereto." *The court held that D could not discontinue its practice without giving reasonable warning to travelers of such discontinuance. By acting it had created a duty for itself. Since that duty had not been met, P may recover.*

See Erie Railroad Co. v. Stewart, 40 F.2d 855 (6th Cir. 1930).

1.   The standard of care defines the "duties" of the defendant to the plaintiff. The standard may come from a variety of sources, including: **VIOLATION OF STATUTE**

    (a)   the relationship between the parties,

    (b)   a rule of law determined by the courts,

    (c) the requisite standard in a given situation, as found by the jury on all the facts,

    (d) a standard of conduct as established by statute.

2.   The standard of care required in any given situation is not always a question of fact for the jury to determine. Sometimes the required conduct is prescribed by either a civil or criminal statute.

3.   A violation of the standard of care, whatever its source, constitutes negligence. Thus, violation of a statute may be "negligence".

4.   A violation of a statute is said to be "negligence per se". This does *not* mean that a complete cause of action has been proven. Rather it means that a legal duty and its breach have been established. The remaining elements of the cause of action still must be proven.

5.   To base a negligence action on a violation of a statute the plaintiff:

    (a) must be within the class of persons which the statute was designed to protect, see Erickson v. Kongsli, 40 Wn.2d 79, 240 P.2d 1209 (1952), and

    (b) must have been injured in a way that the statute was designed to prevent, see Reque v. Milwaukee & Suburban Transport Corp., 7 Wis.2d 111, 97 N.W.2d 182 (1959), and Ross v. Hartman, 78 U.S.App.D.C. 217, 139 F.2d 14 (1943), and

    (c) must show that the injury would not have occurred if the statute had not been violated. In other words, the violation of the statute was the proximate cause of the injury.

6.   The following examples illustrate the application of the elements in number 5:

    (a) A clerk in D's store sold poison without labeling it "Poison" as required by statute. The purchaser, unaware that it was poisonous, partook of it and died. P, the purchaser's administrator, sued for damages based on the violation of the statute. Can P recover?

        Answer. Yes. The purpose of the statute is to protect the public against the dangerous qualities of poison. D's clerk neglected to perform the duty imposed by statute, and that neglect was the proximate cause of the death of a person whom the statute was meant to protect. In those circumstances the failure to comply with the standard set by statute was conclusive evidence of negligence. P may recover. See Osborne v. McMasters, 40 Minn. 103, 41 N.W. 543 (1889).

(b) P was riding in a buggy which was driven by her late husband. It was dark and the buggy had no lights, which violated a criminal statute. The buggy was struck by D's auto at a curve in the road. D was coming in the opposite direction and was left of the center line when he hit the buggy. Is P entitled to damages?

> ***Answer.*** No. The unexcused omission of the lights required by statute was negligence in itself. Lights are intended for the guidance and protection of other travelers on the highway. If the absence of lights on the buggy is a contributing cause of the collision, P may not recover. Here the absence of lights in violation of the statute is negligence which contributed to the accident. This contributory negligence bars recovery by P. A verdict was directed in D's favor. See Martin v. Herzog, 228 N.Y. 164, 126 N.E. 814 (1920).

(c) D, a shipowner, agreed to transport P's sheep. D did not keep the sheep in special pens as was required by a statute. During the voyage a number of sheep were washed overboard and lost. P sued D for the loss, contending that D's violation of the statute was negligence per se. D contended that the purpose of the statute was to prevent the animals from communicating any infectious disease to other animals. D reasoned that since the purpose of the statute was not to prevent the harm which occurred, its violation did not impose liability. The court denied recovery. The purpose of the statute was not to prevent the harm which occurred. Therefore, its violation was not negligence per se. If the sheep had died from a contagious disease then P could recover based on the statute. However, since the purpose of the statute was unrelated to the harm which occurred, P may not recover merely because D violated the statute. See Gorris v. Scott, L.R. 9 Exch. 125 (1874).

7. Most courts hold that the unexcused violation of a statute which causes the injury complained of is negligence "per se," as contrasted to mere evidence of negligence. See Martin v. Herzog, number 6(b), above; Hardaway, Auto Owners Insurance Co. v. Consolidated Paper Co., 366 Mich. 190, 114 N.W.2d 236 (1962); Restatement, Second, Torts § 288B.

(a) If the defendant's conduct is negligence per se (majority view) there is no factual question for the jury to decide. The judge will conclude that the defendant was negligent as a matter of law.

(b) If the defendant's violation of the statute is only evidence of negligence (minority view) the jury decides the ultimate question of whether the defendant was negligent based on all the circumstances.

8.   The violation of a statute which is due to circumstances beyond the control of the defendant, who exercised reasonable diligence to obey the statute, is excused unless the statute imposes an absolute duty.

(a)   A state statute required that all brakes on automobiles be maintained in good order and capable of stopping within certain distances and at certain speeds. D's brakes did not comply with that standard and D's car collided with another vehicle because it would not stop. The brakes worked properly prior to the accident. Periodic lubrication and servicing did not reveal the defect in the brakes which caused the malfunction. Is D liable?

Answer. No. The court held that the violation of the statute was excusable if the defect could not have been discovered by the exercise of the highest degree of care. D exercised the highest degree of care and did not discover the defect and, therefore, he is not liable. See Ainsworth v. Deutschman, 251 Or. 596, 446 P.2d 187 (1968), and Pozsgai v. Porter, 249 Or. 84, 435 P.2d 818 (1967).

(b)   These cases explain and expand the rule in McConnell v. Herron, 240 Or. 486, 402 P.2d 726 (1965), in which the court stated that a violation could be excused if it was impossible to comply with the statute by the exercise of the highest degree of care.

9.   Statutes which require a license, such as to practice medicine or drive a car, are usually held by courts to create no liability where the actor is competent but unlicensed. This is because the failure to procure a license is not the proximate cause of the injury. Rather, a negligent act which must be shown.

e.g. D did not have a license to practice medicine, but he gave P chiropractic treatments which caused her to become paralyzed. P sued for damages and the jury was instructed that noncompliance with the statute might be considered "some evidence" of negligence. Was the instruction correct?

Answer. No. "The purpose of the statute is to protect the public against unfounded assumption of skill by one who undertakes to prescribe or treat for disease. In order to show that the plaintiff has been injured by defendant's breach of the statutory duty, proof must be given that defendant in such treatment did not exercise the care and skill which would have been exercised by qualified practitioners within the state, and that lack of skill and care caused the injury. Failure to obtain a license as required by law gives rise to no remedy if it has caused no injury." Thus P must prove that the treatment was improper to recover. The mere violation of the licensing statute did not warrant the legal conclusion that D's treatment of P was negligent. See Brown v. Shyne, 242 N.Y. 176, 151 N.E. 197 (1926).

See generally, Gregory, pp. 183–202; Keeton, pp. 278–280, 331–332; P & W, pp. 220–246; Prosser, pp. 190–204.

1. The issues of standard of care and duty of care go to the basic question of whether there is any liability whatsoever for negligence.   **EXTENT OF LIABILITY**

2. An entirely separate question is that of the *extent* of liability, once liability for negligence has, in fact, been established by failure to meet the standard of care.

3. The question of the extent of liability for negligence is analyzed in a variety of ways and under a variety of "rules" or doctrines. In essence, each of them is approaching the question of the extent of liability in a different manner. These include:

(a) the question of mental injury,

(b) the question of duty to the unforeseen plaintiff,

(c) the question of prenatal injuries and/or duty to the unforeseen (because unborn) plaintiff,

(d) the question of causation,

(e) the question of vicarious liability, which is the question as to who, beyond the actual actor, should be liable, and

(f) damages.

1. *All interests* which one may have *in physical tangible property* are *protected* by law *against* injury by *negligent conduct*.   **MENTAL DISTRESS**

2. *All interests* which one has *in* his *physical person* are *protected* by law *against* injury by *negligent conduct*.

3. The protection afforded freedom from mental or emotional distress by the law of negligence is illustrated in the following cases, which assume a negligent act on the part of the defendant and causation.

(a) If there is *injury to the physical person,* then *damages for mental suffering* are *permitted* as an inseparable part of the physical injury.

e.g. D negligently runs his automobile into and over P, causing cuts, bruises and a broken leg. P may recover both for the physical cuts, bruises, broken leg, and for the pain and mental suffering which accompany such physical injuries.

(b) Under the traditional rule, damages were permitted for mental distress only if there were some physical impact, even if the impact itself caused no actual injury.

e.g. D negligently drives his automobile against P and knocks him down. The impact and the fall cause no actual physical injury, but P's fright and nervous shock are substantial. P may recover from D damages for the mental suffering. That is known as the "impact" rule. The purpose of the impact requirement is to give some protection against fabricated claims.

NOTE—The "impact rule" is being repudiated by an increasing majority of courts due to advances in medical science that have made it possible to trace a resulting physical injury back to show causation. This decreases the possibility of fraudulent claims and justifies the modern view. See Hughes v. Moore, 214 Va. 27, 197 S.E.2d 214 (1973).

(c) Under the modern rule if there is *no physical impact but* the negligent act is accompanied or followed by *physical disorders* such as a miscarriage, then *damages* are *permitted* for the *mental suffering.*

e.g. D negligently drove his carriage into a public house. P was working behind the bar at that time and the shock and fright from the collision caused P to become ill and give premature birth to a child. P may recover damages for her injuries because they are directly attributable to D's negligent act. The fact that D's carriage did not hit P did not prevent recovery. See Dulieu v. White & Sons, 2 K.B. 669 (1901).

(d) If there is *no physical impact* and the negligent act is *not accompanied* or followed *by* any *physical disorder,* but does cause mental disturbance, generally there is *no recovery permitted.*

e.g. P was in a horse drawn buggy driven by her husband. D's agent raised a gate for them to cross railroad tracks. As they started across a train appeared and almost ran them down. The buggy was not hit, but P sustained severe nervous shock and became ill. May P recover damages?

Answer. No, under the common law where this case arose. Since there was no physical impact there could be no recovery. Negligently causing mental shock was not actionable, even though it resulted in physical illness under the common law. See Victorian Railways Commissioners v. Coultas, 13 App.Cas. 222 (P.C.1888).

NOTE 1—If the Coultas case had been decided under modern law P could recover because she suffered physical illness from D's negligence. However, if P only suffered fright from the apprehension of a collision she could not recover in most jurisdictions today because there was no physical injury from D's negligence.

NOTE 2—There are two special cases where recovery is permitted in some jurisdictions for mental suffering alone, even though there is no "impact": (a) the negligent transmission of a message which would obviously cause mental suffering if incorrect, such as a telegram announcing death. See Western Union Telegraph Co. v. Redding, 100 Fla. 495, 129 So. 743 (1930); (b) negligent or unauthorized handling of corpses. See CASE 25, below.

4. If the mental disturbance to the plaintiff results from impending harm to another person, ordinarily recovery is denied on the grounds that the defendant could not reasonably foresee such an injury and, therefore, no duty of care is owed to the plaintiff. See King v. Phillips, 1 Q.B. 429 (1953).

(a) If P is in danger of being injured by a vehicle out of control, but P is not hit and suffers physical harm from the apprehension of danger to her child being hit by that vehicle, it has been held that she may recover. See Hambrook v. Stokes Brothers, 1 K.B. 141 (1925).

(b) A few courts in the United States have permitted recovery for mental distress by a person not in danger from the impending harm. In those jurisdictions courts consider the following factors as bearing on the degree of foreseeability.

(i) whether the plaintiff was near the scene of the accident,

(ii) whether the plaintiff observed the accident and there was a direct emotional impact, and

(iii) whether the plaintiff and the victim were closely related.

e.g. While driving his automobile negligently, D struck and killed P's daughter. P was near the accident and saw it, but was never in any danger of being struck by D's car. In a suit for wrongful death of the child P sought damages for fright and mental distress. The court held that the harm to P was reasonably foreseeable, and therefore, D owed a duty to P. P may recover for nervous shock together with mental and physical pain resulting from D's negligence. See Dillon v. Legg, 68 Cal.2d 728, 69 Cal.Rptr. 72, 441 P.2d 912 (1968); contra Whetham v. Bismarck Hospital, 197 N.W. 2d 678 (N.D.1972).

CAVEAT—By contrast to the rule in negligence, if the mental suffering results from a willful, wanton or vindictive wrong directed to one person, then recovery for mental suffering is permitted if it results to another person. See Halio v. Lurie, 15 A.D.2d 62, 222 N.Y.S.2d 759 (1961) and Chapter II, Emotional Distress, above.

See generally, Gregory, pp. 952–975; Keeton, 367–383; P & W, pp. 417–434.

Case 23 *Mental distress—physical impact doctrine*

P was driving his automobile along a three lane paved highway and in the right lane thereof. A large passenger bus driven by D moving in the same direction as P's car, undertook to pass P's car by running in the center lane. Before the bus had entirely passed P's car the driver negligently turned the bus into the right lane so sharply that it forced P's car off the road but there was no impact of the bus against P's car. But the bus did, while negligently turning in front of P's car and into the right lane of the highway, cause dust from the highway to blow into P's eyes. P stopped his car in the shallow ditch beside the highway. He wiped the dust out of his eyes with his handkerchief. From the fright and shock caused by D's negligent driving of the bus, P suffered a nervous collapse which caused his hospitalization. There was no injury to P's eyes from the dust and there was no injury to P's car. (a) May P recover from D? (b) If P may recover, for what items of damage may he recover?

Answer. (a) P may recover. (b) P may recover both for his nervous collapse necessitating hospitalization and for his mental suffering. Here there was no impact with P's car. But the slightest physical impact with the person *has been considered sufficient voucher for the genuineness of the plaintiff's injuries, physical and mental. This is true even though the impact itself has caused no damage or injury. In this case the negligence of D in forcing P off the road caused dust from the highway to enter P's eyes. It actually caused no injury to P's eyes. But such trivial impact is laid hold of by the courts to support the action for negligence which causes mental suffering. In this case then, there being a harmless physical impact caused by the negligent act of the defendant, the plaintiff can recover for the damages caused by the nervous shock and fright, including his nervous collapse and the mental suffering which accompanied such, as the result of the defendant's negligent driving of the bus.*

NOTE—The requirement of this totally immaterial "impact" is an anachronism which should be eliminated from the legal consciousness for it serves no useful purpose. If the defendant's negligence causes mental distress through fright or shock, which in turn, causes physical injury, there should be recovery with or without physical contact or impact in the first instance. In these cases there is real danger of feigned and fictitious injury. But protection against such should be found not in requiring "impact" but in requiring more substantial and objective evidence of the injury, beyond the self-interest, subjective evidence by the plaintiff as to his mental suffering, shock and fright.

See Porter v. Delaware, Lackawanna & Western Railroad Co., 73 N.J.L. 405, 63 A. 860 (1906); Prosser, pp. 330–333.

Physical injury resulting from mental distress   Case 24

M operated a small dairy from which he supplied a few close neighbors with milk. M bought his cow feed from D. Through the negligence of D there was sold to M a quantity of poisoned feed which had been prepared for the eradication of rodents. M's cows became sick and died from the poison. M had delivered to his customers milk from the cows while they were poisoned. M became so worried for fear he had poisoned his customers with the milk that he suffered severe nervous shock which caused heart failure and M's death. M's executor, P, sues D for the wrongful death based on D's negligence. May he recover?

Answer. Yes. This is a case in which there was no impact whatsoever with the decedent, but the defendant's negligence brought about nervous disorders which resulted in physical injury and death. The better considered cases permit recovery of damages for negligence which causes mental suffering which in turn results in physical injury. In such cases there is less opportunity for feigning injury because the actual physical illness or injury provides reasonable voucher for the genuineness of the mental suffering than in the cases where there is mental disturbance or suffering only. The only real question then is the question of whether or not the negligence actually caused the mental suffering which brings on the physical illness. It is quite natural for one to worry about his own safety, or the safety of the members of his immediate family, but how far from such persons may a plaintiff claim that the defendant's negligent act causes such worry that the defendant should be held liable for the plaintiff's injury from such mental disturbance? In this case the worry was for the safety, not of himself or his family, but for those with whom he occupied a relationship of supplier and customers of food. This would seem to be near the borderline of the extent to which the cases have yet gone. However, in this case there was the additional important fact that the decedent had done an affirmative act of supplying milk to his customers for whose safety he was worrying. Thus D's negligence resulted in M's death and recovery is permitted.

See Rasmussen v. Benson, 135 Neb. 232, 280 N.W. 890 (1937).

Case 25   *Recovery for mental suffering alone—autopsy of corpse*

P's husband died and D, a surgeon, performed an autopsy on the body without P's permission. P claimed that D's acts mutilated the corpse and interfered with her exclusive right of sepulchre. P sued D for mental pain and suffering. D demurred (moved to dismiss) because P did not suffer any physical injury. The trial court granted D's motion and P appealed. May P recover for her mental suffering?

Answer. Yes. *This case is an exception to the general rule which denies recovery for mental suffering where there is no physical injury or physical consequences. P had the right to the body of her husband in its condition at the time of death so P could provide for burial. Only P could authorize an autopsy on the body, unless the death occurred under circumstances where an autopsy was required by statute. In the present case D had no authority to perform the autopsy, and his unauthorized act was an invasion of a right of P. Therefore, P may recover for the mental suffering endured as a consequence of D's invasion of that right. The decision of the lower court was reversed and the case was remanded for trial.*

See Alderman v. Ford, 146 Kan. 698, 72 P.2d 981 (1937).

Case 26   *Recovery for emotional harm permitted*

P's mother was a patient in D hospital. There was another patient in D hospital who had the same name as P's mother, and who died. D negligently informed P that it was her mother who died. In fact, P's mother was alive and well. When P viewed the deceased at a funeral parlor P realized that the deceased was not her mother. P became hysterical. P was unable to work for eleven days and had nightmares. P brought suit for funeral expenses and emotional harm. May P recover?

Answer. Yes. *P may recover for emotional harm sustained by her as a result of the negligent misinformation transmitted by D that P's mother had died. This is based on D's duty to inform the proper next of kin of the death of a patient. The funeral expenses and serious psychological impact on P were foreseeable upon breach of that duty. Although courts have been reluctant to permit recovery for negligently caused psychological trauma (injury) in the absence of physical injury, two exceptions have been recognized at least in some jurisdictions. Recovery has been permitted for: (a) emotional harm resulting from negligent transmission by a telegraph company of a message announcing death, and (b) emotional harm to a close relative resulting from the negligent mishandling of a corpse. The facts of the present case come within those exceptions so P may recover damages for all harm suffered.*

See *Johnson v. State*, 37 N.Y.2d 378, 372 N.Y.S.2d 638, 334 N.E.2d 590 (1975).

DUTY TO UNBORN CHILDREN

1. Prior to 1946, courts denied recovery to a child or its estate for prenatal injuries. That result was reached on these grounds:

   (a) the difficulty in determining the existence of a causal relationship between the prenatal injury and the resulting death or damage,

   (b) a fear of false or fraudulent claims, and

   (c) no duty owed to one not in existence at time of defendant's action.

2. Today nearly all jurisdictions grant recovery for prenatal injuries because the reasons stated in number 1, above are no longer considered valid. See CASE 27, below.

3. An unborn viable child is capable of independent physical existence and is regarded as a separate entity apart from its mother. Thus an action for wrongful death of a viable unborn child can be instituted by the child's estate in many jurisdictions. See Leal v. C. C. Pitts Sand & Gravel, Inc., 419 S.W.2d 820 (Tex. 1967); Poliquin v. MacDonald, 101 N.H. 104, 135 A.2d 249 (1957); Libbee v. Permanente Clinic, 518 P.2d 636 (Or.1974), rehearing denied 520 P.2d 361 (1974).

   (a) A stillborn viable child was held to be a person within the meaning of "person" in the Ohio Constitution which gives every injured person a legal remedy. See Stidam v. Ashmore, 109 Ohio App. 431, 167 N.E.2d 106 (1959).

   (b) Other jurisdictions have held that a wrongful death action may not be maintained for the death of a viable, unborn child since the damages which are recoverable by the parents in their own right redress the wrong done. See Endresz v. Friedberg, 24 N.Y.2d 478, 301 N.Y.S.2d 65, 248 N.E.2d 901 (1969). See also State ex rel. Hardin v. Sanders, 538 S.W.2d 336 (Mo.1976).

4. Recovery for wrongful death of a nonviable stillborn child has been granted in only a few jurisdictions. See Prosser, p. 338 and CASE 27, below.

   See generally, Green, pp. 1072–1076; Keeton, pp. 197–202; P & W, pp. 258–268; Prosser, pp. 335–338.

Prenatal injuries—recovery by mother permitted   **Case 27**

P, who was one month pregnant, was driving her automobile when it was hit in the rear by D. P alleged that as the result of pre-birth injuries the child was born Mongoloid. P, suing on behalf of the child, alleges that D caused the accident by his negligence. D demurred (moved to dismiss) to the complaint on the ground that it failed to state a cause of action. D contended that no legal duty was owed to an unborn child to use due care toward it, and that it was not a "person" entitled to relief from negligence because it was still a part of P, the mother. D also contended that the cause of action, if any, belonged only to the mother. The trial court sustained the demurrer and dismissed the suit. Was the court correct?

Answer. No. The court erred. The complaint stated a cause of action and the demurrer should have been overruled. Prior to the year 1946 the courts rather uniformly held as the trial court held in this case and placed their decisions mainly on three bases: authority and stare decisis, fear of imposition because of unfounded suits and that such suits would clog the courts, and the child is part of the mother till born and the remedy, if any, belongs only to the mother. None of these is a valid or substantial reason for denying an unborn viable child a remedy for his injuries if they were in fact caused by the negligence of the defendant. (1) It has been demonstrated that a child prematurely born may be viable, that is, have developed sufficiently so that it can exist independently of the mother. If a viable child is born alive and crippled because of the negligence of the defendant, it should have a remedy. Otherwise, the common law fails to keep abreast of changing conditions and progress. (2) The argument that such suits if allowed will clog the courts is wholly without justifiable foundation for two reasons: (a) it is not true, and (b) even if it were true, it involves no greater difficulty in determining causation than in many other difficult cases with which the courts and juries have to deal in their daily routine. (3) When medical science has shown that the viable child can live separate and apart from the mother, it is entitled to be considered as a "person" to whom a duty of due care is owed by those who do affirmative acts and can anticipate that injury to the mother will also injure her unborn child. This is true in the field of torts whether the child is alive and suing for his injuries or is the subject of litigation for wrongful death. Otherwise, the plaintiff goes through life with negligently caused injuries and having no remedy against the wrongdoer who caused those injuries. These are the views of recent cases. Therefore, the court concluded that D owed a duty to the unborn infant. In the present case P's child was not viable at the time of the accident. That does not affect the basic right to recover because the fetus is regarded as having existence as a separate creature from the moment of conception. The case was remanded for trial. P may recover if she can show that D's negligence caused injury to the fetus even though it was not viable at the time of the accident.

See Williams v. Marion Rapid Transit, Inc., 152 Ohio St. 114, 87 N.E.2d 334 (1949).

1. The law of negligence distinguishes between:

    (a) causation *in fact,* and

    (b) legal cause or proximate cause.

2. "Causation in fact" refers to a series of events or set of circumstances such that one may be traced to another, then to another, and so on through the entire sequence of events leading from the first, to the last.

    e.g. D's friend, X, calls D and invites him to his home for a visit. On the way, D, driving negligently, injures P. It may be said that X, the friend's phone call was a cause *in fact* of P's injury, because "had it not been for" the phone call and the invitation, D would not have been driving at all, let alone negligently. However, no liability is imposed upon X, the friend, on these facts, even though there is "causation in fact".

3. Proximate causation or legal causation means a sequence of events so connected that the law imposes liability upon the defendant for the sequence of events arising out of or following from his negligence.

    e.g. The defendant, while negligently driving, injures the plaintiff. The plaintiff, while riding in an ambulance to the hospital is injured, once again, when the ambulance driver negligently drives the ambulance. The plaintiff in turn is injured further through the negligence of the doctor after he reaches the hospital. During the period of recuperation from the injury inflicted by the negligent doctor the hospital is struck by an earthquake and the plaintiff is further injured by falling plaster from the roof of his hospital room. The injury from the falling plaster may be said to have been caused "in fact" by the original defendant's negligence in driving. However, the law imposes a limit and at some point in the chain of factual causation says that liability ceases. This is because the injury to the plaintiff has not been "proximately" or "legally" caused by the conduct of the defendant.

4. There is no liability for a negligent act if the negligence does not cause injury. This is called the "but for" rule.

    (a) If the injury would not have occurred *but for* the negligent act, there is liability because the negligence is a cause in fact of the injury.

    (b) If the injury would have occurred regardless of the negligent act, there is no liability because the negligence was not a cause in fact of the injury.

    e.g. P made a left hand turn as D was approaching from the opposite direction about 150 to 200 feet away. P thought D was parked and did not look at D after he began the turn. D collided with P who sued for damages. D

sine qua non
or
"but for" rule

claimed that P was contributorily negligent because he did not signal before making the turn. The evidence showed that even if P had signaled D would not have seen it. Here P was negligent but this did not contribute to the accident. Therefore, D does not have a valid defense. This is called the *sine qua non* or *but for* rule. It means that a person's negligent conduct is not the cause in fact of the accident if the accident would have occurred without such negligence. See Rouleau v. Blotner, 84 N.H. 539, 152 A. 916 (1931). See also, Cole v. Shell Petroleum Corp., 149 Kan. 25, 86 P.2d 740 (1939), and Prosser, pp. 238–239.

misfeasance = doing something negligently

nonfeasance = failure to do something that results in an injury, or failure to take necessary precaution to prevent an event from happening.

5. There is *liability* for negligence *when the negligence causes injury,* whether the negligence be active misfeasance or passive nonfeasance.

(a) P was a passenger on D's horse car. D negligently started to drive the car across railroad tracks as a train approached. The railroad gateman negligently lowered the gate preventing D's car from getting across the tracks. P was injured as the other passengers rushed to get off the car. The gate was raised in time for D's car to get across without a collision. D is liable to P for its negligence which resulted in an injury to P even though the negligence of someone else contributed to the injury. See Washington & Georgetown Railroad Co. v. Hickey, 166 U.S. 521, 17 S.Ct. 661, 41 L.Ed. 1101 (1897).

(b) A spark from D's locomotive started a fire which combined with a fire of unknown origin to destroy some property owned by P. D is liable because D negligently started a fire which was a material factor in destroying P's property. The fact that the other fire would have destroyed P's property regardless of D's negligence is no defense because D's negligently caused fire was a material factor in the destruction of P's property. See Anderson v. Minneapolis, St. Paul & Sault St. Marie Railway Co., 146 Minn. 430, 179 N.W. 45 (1920); Kingston v. Chicago & Northwestern Railway Co., 191 Wis. 610, 211 N.W. 913 (1927).

6. Causation is essential to liability for negligence, but the fact that a negligent act causes injury does not necessarily make the actor liable. The negligent act must be the proximate cause of the injury: the injury must be foreseeable. See CASES 28 and 29, below, illustrating the existence of causation, but not imposing liability for lack of duty owed to the plaintiff for lack of foreseeability.

(a) As P was leaving a hotel room a piece of glass fell from the transom above the door and cut his forehead. Some time later skin cancer developed at the point where P had been cut. P sued for damages. There was medical testimony at trial that there was a possibility that skin cancer could have been caused by P's injury, but there was no such probability. A verdict for P was appealed. The court held that the mere possibility that an injury was caused by some past event was not sufficient evidence for a jury to base its verdict. P must show that his injury was caused by the defendant's negligence. There was insufficient proof of causation of the cancer. P may recover for the cut on his forehead, but not for the skin cancer. See Kramer Service, Inc. v. Wilkins, 184 Miss. 483, 186 So. 625 (1939).

(b) The mere possibility that the injury would have occurred without the defendant's negligence is not sufficient to relieve the defendant of liability. See Reynolds v. Texas & Pacific Railroad Co., 37 La.Ann. 694 (1885).

7. The decision as to how far in time and space a negligent actor should be held liable for the consequences of his negligence is a matter of social policy. The modern cases tend to determine liability on the concept of "duty" rather than on "causation." The law creates a zone of demarcation, *within* which there is, and *outside* of which there is not, legal responsibility for negligent conduct. This zone is created by holding:

(a) that negligence is determined by the test of foreseeability,

(b) that a legal duty is owed only to one who is within the field of foreseeable danger, and

(c) that there is no liability without both:

(i) the existence of foreseeability, and

(ii) causation in fact.

e.g. A woodshed belonging to D railroad caught on fire due to sparks from one of its locomotives. P's house was located 130 feet from the shed, and it was soon set on fire due to heat and sparks from the woodshed. The fire then spread to several other houses. P brought suit for the value of his house which was destroyed by the fire. The court stated the general principle that a person is liable for the proximate results of his own acts, but not for remote damages. The first building destroyed by the sparks which were thrown from the engine was D's own woodshed. That was the foreseeable result of the negligence. That the fire would spread to other buildings was not a necessary result of the first fire. Whether the fire spreads depends on the wind, degree of heat and materials used to construct the other buildings. The negligent party has no control over those circumstances and is not responsible for their effects. P may not recover because the fire that destroyed his house was not the result of the negligence of D's employees. The result of their negligence was the destruction of D's shed. Further damages are too remote to allow recovery. See Ryan v. New York Central Railroad Co., 35 N.Y. 210, 91 Am.Dec. 49 (1866).

NOTE—The reason the New York court limited liability to the first building burned was public policy. Liability for fire damage could extend indefinitely unless there was some cut-off point for liability. Other jurisdictions have rejected the New York rule. See Prosser, pp. 252–253.

8. If two or more persons act negligently, in concert or separately, and their combined negligence causes a single injury, each may be liable for the entire damage.

e.g. X and Y were hunting quail. Both negligently fired at the same time and one shot hit P in the eye. P sued X and Y for his injury, but P could not establish who fired the shot which hit him. P may recover from both X and Y because they acted together. To hold otherwise would exonerate both from liability, although both were negligent, and deny redress to the injured person. See Summers v. Tice, 33 Cal.2d 80, 199 P.2d 1 (1948).

9. If two or more persons act, and only one of them is negligent, and the force of their combined acts causes injury, the negligent actor may be liable for the entire damage.

e.g. Through the negligent act of D in driving his automobile, his car collides with the car of X which hits Y's car and injury therefrom results to P, who was only hit by Y's car. D is liable to P for the entire damage caused to P, since D was the only negligent actor.

10. If two or more persons act negligently but separately, and the negligence of each takes effect separately, causing separate injuries, then each is liable only severally for the injury he has caused if the damages can be separated.

(a) P was injured in an automobile accident through D's negligence and sued D for damages. By the time the case came to trial P had been injured in three other accidents, all involving the same area of P's body. The jury must apportion damages as well as possible among the various accidents. If a rough apportionment is not possible the damages must be divided equally. This is true even if P cannot recover for the other accidents because of contributory negligence or the statute of limitations. See Loui v. Oakley, 50 Hawaii 260, 438 P.2d 393 (1968). See also, McAllister v. Pennsylvania Railroad Co., 324 Pa. 65, 187 A. 415 (1936); Johnson v. City of Fairmont, 188 Minn. 451, 247 N.W. 572 (1933).

(b) Of course, if X and Y are both negligent in performing a duty, such as maintaining a party wall, both are liable for injury to P caused by the wall falling. This is so because P would not have been injured unless both X and Y were negligent. See Johnson v. Chapman, 43 W.Va. 639, 28 S.E. 744 (1897).

CAVEAT—Where there have been two negligent acts which combined to cause damage, the passage of time between the two negligent acts may render the first act of negligence a remote cause, as contrasted with proximate cause, and thus no liability will attach to the first act.

e.g. X negligently installed electric wires and Y city negligently failed to inspect and maintain them. As a result P's house was damaged 18 months after installation of the wires. The court held Y city liable to P for Y's failure to inspect and maintain the wires as Y agreed to do in its contract with X. However, X was not liable because of the passage of time. See Goar v. Village of Stephen, 157 Minn. 228, 196 N.W. 171 (1923). See also, Stultz v. Benson Lumber Co., 6 Cal.2d 688, 59 P.2d 100 (1936).

11. If D creates a dangerous condition by a negligent act which foreseeably could cause injury, D is liable for such injury even though it was brought about in an unforeseeable way.

   (a) A railroad tank car derailed through the negligence of D railroad. Gasoline from the tank car ran into the street and X ignited it with a match which injured P, who was a bystander. The evidence was in conflict as to whether X's act was intentional or inadvert. P sued D railroad and a verdict was directed for D. Was the ruling correct?

   Answer. No. If X's act was inadvertent or negligent P may recover because D's negligence was one cause of P's injuries. If X's act was done maliciously, then D is not liable because it could not be anticipated. This is a factual question for the jury to determine. The case was remanded for a new trial. See Watson v. Kentucky & Indiana Bridge & Railroad Co., 137 Ky. 619, 126 S.W. 146 (1910), *modified* 137 Ky. 619, 129 S.W. 341.

   (b) A car derailed through the negligence of D railroad and ran across the street, over two curbstones and into the front of a house. P was on the sidewalk near the house and saw the car coming at full speed. P ran away from the car, but fell and injured herself. May P recover?

   Answer. Yes. D put P in danger through its negligence. P sustained her injury in a reasonable attempt to escape. Thus P is entitled to damages for her injuries even though they happened in an unexpected way. See Tuttle v. Atlantic City Railroad Co., 66 N.J.L. 327, 49 A. 450 (1901).

   (c) A motorist negligently hit a wooden pole maintained by D as part of its street railway system. The pole fell and injured P. P filed suit against D, alleging that the pole was rotten and ready to fall, that D knew or should have known of its condition, and that D failed to take reasonable precautions. D moved to dismiss on the ground that there was no liability because it was not foreseeable that a motorist would hit the pole and cause it to fall on P. The court stated the rule to be that if D's conduct was a substantial factor in bringing harm to P, the fact that D could not have foreseen the extent of the harm or the manner in which it occurred did not absolve D of liability. If the facts are as alleged by P, and a properly maintained pole would not have broken, P may recover. On the other hand, if a sound pole would have broken under the impact of the collision, then D would not be liable. Those are questions for the trier of fact to resolve. The motion should be denied. See Gibson v. Garcia, 96 Cal.App.2d 681, 216 P.2d 119 (1950).

NOTE—If an act does not result in a foreseeable danger, either directly or from an intervening cause, then there is no liability. Negligence is not based on the failure to anticipate extraordinary events.

e.g. The roof of D's premises fell on and killed X during a storm. If such storms were usual in the area, D is liable for failure to maintain the roof to withstand reasonably foreseeable weather conditions. If the storm was extraordinary, then D did not have a duty to anticipate it and there is no liability. See Kimble v. MacKintosh Hemphill Co., 359 Pa. 461, 59 A.2d 68 (1948).

12. If X places a person in danger by his negligence, X is liable for injuries sustained by a rescuer of the person placed in danger. This is true regardless of whether the rescue attempt was foreseeable as "the risk of rescue, if only it be not wanton, is born of the occasion." Wagner v. International Railway Co., 232 N.Y. 176, 133 N.E. 437 (1921). This rule also protects the rescuer of one who attempts to commit suicide. See Talbert v. Talbert, 22 Misc.2d 782, 199 N.Y.S.2d 212 (1960). See also Misfeasance and Nonfeasance, number 5, above.

See generally, Gregory, pp. 247–312; Keeton, pp. 313–347; P & W, pp. 284–334.

Case 28   *No liability to unforeseeable plaintiff*

P was standing on a platform of D railroad after buying a ticket. While P was waiting for her train, X ran to catch another train as it was pulling away. As X climbed aboard the train, he was assisted by a guard who reached forward to pull X inside, A, another guard on the platform, pushed X from behind to help him board. While this was happening X dropped a package which contained fireworks. The fireworks exploded when they fell. The shock from the explosion caused some scales at the other end of the platform to fall and injure P, who sued for damages. May P recover?

Answer. *No, according to the four judges who wrote the majority opinion. They held that "foreseeability" is the test and determines the extent of one's legal duty in a negligence case; the three dissenting judges answered the question in the affirmative, thus saying that the negligent actor is liable for all injuries naturally and proximately caused by his negligent act, whether or not such plaintiff or his injury is foreseeable. The argument in favor of the majority opinion is this: (a) the scope of liability for a negligent act is limited to the area of apparent danger, (b) a duty is not owed to P, who is outside the area of apparent danger, (c) as to P who is outside the area of apparent danger, any injury should be treated as though it were an unavoidable accident, i.e., there was no negligence as to P, (d) as a matter of policy and administration, the liability for a negligent act should be restricted within reasonable bounds, and (e) to permit duty of due care and liability for its breach, to extend indefinitely to all persons who are actually injured, may impose liability out of all proportion to the seriousness of the original negligent act. Section 281, comment c, of the Restatement, Second, Torts has adopted this view.*

The argument against this view and in favor of the dissenting judges, that the duty to use due care extends not only to those whose injury can be foreseen, but to all those who are actually harmed by the negligent act, is this: (a) every person owes a duty to use due care to protect society generally, (b) such duty is not limited to those whose injury can be foreseen because they are within the apparent danger zone, (c) every person who is actually injured by the negligent conduct of the actor has a right to be compensated when in fact his injury has been caused by the negligent act, and (d) no theory of duty should prevent his recovery. Between the injured person and the negligent actor, the innocent person who is injured is in a more favorable position than the negligent actor and should be permitted to recover. P was not permitted to recover under the majority opinion because P was not foreseeable.

See Palsgraf v. Long Island Railroad Co., 248 N.Y. 339, 162 N.E. 99 (1928). In accord see Mauney v. Gulf Refining Co., 193 Miss. 421, 8 So.2d 249 (1942), Petition of Kinsman Transit Co. ("Kinsman No. 1"), 338 F.2d 708 (2nd Cir. 1964); and Petition of Kinsman Transit Co. ("Kinsman No. 2"), 388 F.2d 821 (2d Cir. 1968).

NOTE—The cases since the *Palsgraf* case are about evenly divided on the question. Prosser states that there is a trend in favor of the rule and probably a small majority of jurisdictions have adopted the rule. See extended discussion, Prosser, p. 254 et seq., including citations of the cases on both sides of the question.

Injury must be foreseeable   Case 29

A freighter owned by D negligently discharged oil into the bay where it was moored. The oil did minor damage to the slipways of

P's wharf, but P did not attempt to obtain damages from D. Some time later P's workmen dropped molten metal into the bay which ignited cotton waste floating on the surface and that in turn ignited the oil. The resulting fire damaged P's wharf and two ships owned by others. The trial court found that D did not know and could not reasonably have known that there was a danger of the oil being set on fire because of its high flash point. May P recover for damages suffered as a result of the fire?

Answer. *No. An act of negligence which results in trivial foreseeable damage will not make the actor liable for all consequences of the negligent act however unforeseeable even though they are "direct". A man is responsible only for the probable consequences of his act and to make him responsible for more would be too harsh a rule. Since the damage by fire was not a foreseeable consequence of the negligent act, D is not liable.*

See Overseas Tankship (U.K.) Limited v. Morts Dock & Engineering Co., Limited ("Wagon Mound No. 1") Privy Council, 1961, A.C. 388.

NOTE 1—The effect of CASE 29, above was to overrule what had been the leading case in the area, In re Arbitration between Polemis and Furness, Withy & Co., Limited, 3 K.B. 560 (1921). In that case P charted a ship to D to carry cargo. As the cargo was being unloaded a plank was negligently permitted to fall into the hold where petrol was stowed. This caused a spark which ignited petrol vapor. There was an explosion and fire which completely destroyed the ship. P sued D for the value of the ship and the court held D liable for the damage because it resulted from his negligence. Although the causing of the spark from the falling board could not have been reasonably foreseen as a consequence, some damage to the ship might have been anticipated. D was negligent and the fact that it resulted in the loss of P's ship in an unexpected way does not relieve him of liability.

NOTE 2—The owners of the two damaged ships in CASE 29, above sued D in a separate action alleging that D created a nuisance by his negligence and should be liable for the damages caused by such nuisance. The court found that D's chief engineer should have realized that it was possible for the oil to ignite, although it was not likely. D's engineer could easily have prevented the nuisance by not discharging the oil. A reasonable person would not have discharged the oil because of the possibility of fire. Since a reasonable person would have foreseen the risk and could easily have prevented it, D is liable for damages to the ships because he created the nuisance which caused the damage. See Overseas Tankship (U.K.) Ltd. v. Miller Steamship Co. ("Wagon Mound No. 2") Privy Council, 1966, 1 A.C. 617. See also Chapter XIII, Nuisance below.

Liability imposed for foreseeable negligence of third party   **Case 30**

D radio station sponsored a promotion whereby motorists were to locate a special red car. Messages from the car broadcast its location, which changed from moment to moment. The first person to approach the car at each location was given the opportunity to win a cash prize by answering a question. One motorist who heard the broadcast sped along a freeway at eighty miles per hour in order to reach D's car first. That negligent or reckless driving forced P's car off the road and P was killed. Suit was brought for damages against the motorist and D. May D radio station be held responsible for the negligent acts of a motorist responding to its promotion?

Answer. Yes. All persons must use ordinary care to prevent others from being injured as a result of their conduct. Foreseeability of risk is a primary consideration in establishing the element of duty. In the facts of the present case it was foreseeable that D's listeners would race to the announced site to win a prize, and in their haste disregard the demands of highway safety. It is no defense that P's death was caused by others acting negligently. The intervening negligent act by the motorist was foreseeable. The reckless driving was stimulated by D's affirmative act, promoting the contest, and that exposed P to an unreasonable risk. Therefore, D radio station is liable for P's death.

See Weirum v. RKO General, Inc., 15 Cal.3d 40, 123 Cal.Rptr. 468, 539 P.2d 36 (1975).

1. Vicarious liability is liability imposed upon a person, who is otherwise free of fault, holding him responsible for the tortious conduct of another.   **VICARIOUS LIABILITY**

2. Vicarious liability for the negligent conduct of another is called *imputed negligence.*

   CAVEAT—Imputed negligence as a basis of liability applies to a defendant. This should be distinguished from imputed contributory negligence which is a defense and applies to the plaintiff. See Chapter IV, Imputed Negligence, below.

3. Vicarious liability arises because of some special relationship between the negligent actor and the person held vicariously liable.

   This often occurs in the following cases:

   (a) master-servant (employer-employee) relationship,

   (b) family automobile doctrine, or

   (c) joint enterprise.

   See CASES 39 and 40, below.

See Chapter IV, Imputed Negligence and Contributory Negligence, below.

MASTER–SERVANT

1. In many situations a master is liable to third persons for the torts committed by his servants. Modern terminology would be employer-employee rather than master-servant.

2. This rule is sometimes referred to as the doctrine of Respondeat Superior which means "let the master respond".

3. The gist of the theory of vicarious liability in the relationship of master-servant is that the master has the right to control the details of the servant's performance and he is in a better financial position to respond to the third party for the torts committed by its servants.

4. Under the doctrine of Respondeat Superior the master is liable for the negligent torts committed by its servant which occur within the scope of the employment and in furtherance of the master's business. Both elements are necessary factors in determining liability.

5. In addition to negligent torts, the master may also be liable for the intentional torts committed by his servant, provided that the servant was acting within the scope of the employment and the servant's intentional act was related to carrying forth the master's business.

6. There are two key factors to be considered in imposing liability of the master for intentional torts of his servant:

   (a) Was the servant acting within the scope of his employment? If the servant was motivated by purely personal reasons the master is generally not liable. See Restatement, Second, Agency §§ 234 and 236.

   e.g. Plaintiff purchased a train ticket and took his baggage to the check room. There an argument arose between the plaintiff and the baggage master. The baggage master struck the plaintiff with a hatchet which was in no way related to his employment. The court held that there was no liability imposed on the railroad for its servant's intentional tort of assault and battery since the servant was motivated by purely personal reasons and thus was considered to be on a frolic of his own. The servant, however, would be personally liable for the assault and battery committed.

   (b) Was the servant acting to further the business interests of the employer? If so, the master is generally liable.

   e.g. S is employed as a bouncer in M's tavern. Plaintiff is seriously injured by S who forcibly ejects P from M's tavern. The use of excessive force by S imposes liability on M since the servant's act is directly related to carrying forth the master's business and is not motivated by purely personal reasons. Thus the master will be liable for the intentional torts of assault and battery of the bouncer and the plaintiff may recover directly from M.

7. The master may be insulated from liability for the acts of his servant where, in fact, the servant has gone on "a frolic of his own" and thus has been held to have abandoned the course of conduct on behalf of the master. Courts very often look to the purpose of the mission and the distance traveled in determining whether the servant has abandoned the course of employment or has merely deviated from the master's employment. Where there is a "mere deviation" the courts tend to fasten liability on the master, whereas in the case of an abandonment the courts generally absolve the master from liability for the torts committed by the servant.

8. Procedurally both the master and the servant may be joined in a single tort action, and a judgment may be taken against one or both, but only one full satisfaction is permitted by the plaintiff.

NOTE—If the master is not liable under the doctrine of Respondeat Superior it is still possible for the master to be liable in negligence for the negligent hiring and/or retention of his servant, rather than for the negligent act of the servant itself.

See generally, Gregory, pp. 701–709; Keeton, pp. 293–303; P & W, pp. 688–692; Smith's Review, Agency, Chapter VIII, Relation Between Principal and Third Person in Tort; Restatement, Second, Agency §§ 219–236.

Vicarious liability—master's right over against servant   Case 31

M was riding in the rear seat of his automobile which was being driven by his chauffeur, D. Through the negligent driving by D the automobile was driven against and over P. P sues both D and M as defendants for his injuries. M enters a cross-complaint against D, seeking judgment for such amount as P recovers against M. (a) May P recover from D and M? (b) May M recover on his cross-complaint against D?

Answer. *(a) Yes. (b) Yes. (a) There is a master-servant relation between M and D. The master is liable for the negligent acts of the servant which are performed within the scope of his employment. Since D drove the car negligently within the scope of his employment, and caused injury to P, both D and his master, M, are liable to P for D's negligence. However, it should be noted that only D is negligent in fact. Liability is imposed on the master vicariously as a matter of policy through the doctrine of respondeat superior. Therefore, P may recover from both D and M. Having* *judgment against both, P may collect from either or both to the extent of a full recovery. (b) As between the master and servant, the master has a right of recovery over against his negligent servant who, through negligence, caused liability to be imposed on M as a matter of law. Therefore, M has a right to be made whole or indemnified for any loss which has been imposed upon him because of D's negligence. This cross-complaint is for indemnity, not for contribution. Hence, M may recover against his servant, D, on the cross-complaint.*

NOTE 1—See Royal Indemnity Co. v. Becker, 122 Ohio St. 582, 173 N.E. 194 (1930); Restatement, Restitution, § 96. This case should be distinguished from the case of joint tortfeasors. M is not a joint tort-feasor with his servant, D. M is liable only because he occupied the legal position of master. There was no negligence in fact on the part of the master, M. In the case of joint tortfeasors, all are wrongdoers, and therefore, courts refuse to entertain a suit for contribution among them.

NOTE 2—It is equally true that a servant who negligently drives his master's car and causes injury to the master is liable to the master for such. For example, M hires S as a chauffeur. S drives M's car negligently while M is riding in the rear seat. M is injured and the car is damaged due to S's negligence. M may sue and recover damages from his servant, S, for injury to himself and to his car. See Darman v. Zilch, 56 R.I. 413, 186 A. 21 (1936).

FAMILY AUTOMOBILE DOCTRINE

INTRODUCTORY NOTE—Not infrequently, automobile accidents caused by minors take place when they are driving their parents' cars. Since the child seldom has the financial ability to satisfy a judgment taken against him, resourceful counsel for plaintiff have pursued a variety of theories upon which to impose liability on the parents. The Family Automobile Doctrine (or family purpose doctrine) is one of these. Counsel have often alleged facts tending to show that the child was the servant of his parent. Basically, when the driver is "judgment proof," the attempt is to impose liability on the owner on a respondeat superior theory.

1. The Family Automobile Doctrine (or Family Purpose Doctrine) holds the owner of an automobile which was purchased and maintained for the pleasure of his or her family liable for injuries inflicted by the vehicle while it was being used by members of his family for their own pleasure.

   e.g. D, owner of a car and head of a family, keeps his car for family as distinguished from business purposes. He permits his son, X, to use the car for the purpose of taking his girl friend to a dance. X drives the car negligently and injures P who sues D. Under this doctrine, even though X was on a "frolic of his own", D is liable to P because: (a) D was owner of the car, (b) he kept it for family purposes, (c) he gave X permission to use the car, and (d) X was a member of D's immediate family. About half the states follow the doctrine, see *e.g.* King v. Smythe, 140 Tenn. 217, 204 S.W. 296 (1918). For states repudiating the doctrine see *e.g.* Klein v. Klein, 311 Pa. 217, 166 A. 790 (1933); McMartin v. Saemisch, 254 Iowa 45, 116 N.W.2d 491 (1962).

2. Liability is imposed on the head of the household on the basis of the dangerous character of the vehicle.

3. In some states liability is imposed by statute on the bailor of the auto because the bailor permits use of the vehicle by the bailee. There is no master-servant relationship, but rather liability is imposed by a so called "permissive use statute."

4. In those states which do not impose liability either under the general rule or by statute, the head of the household is generally liable only if the driver is in fact acting as his servant.

See generally, Keeton, pp. 307–309, 515–517; P & W, p. 697; Prosser, pp. 483–487.

1. The burden of proving negligence by a preponderance of the evidence is on the plaintiff.   **PROOF OF NEGLIGENCE**

   (a) P slipped on a banana peel in D's railroad station and sued for damages. P offered no evidence as to how the banana peel got there or how long it had been there. May P recover?

   Answer. No. Since P offered no evidence to show that the railroad was negligent in some way, P may not recover and it was proper for the court to direct a verdict for D. See Goddard v. Boston & Maine Railroad Co., 179 Mass. 52, 60 N.E. 486 (1901).

   (b) If P had been able to show that the banana peel was dry, gritty, black in color and stuck to the floor, P would have presented sufficient facts for a jury to conclude that the banana peel had been there for some time. If that were true, a jury could find the railroad negligent in not removing the banana peel. See Anjou v. Boston Elevated Railway Co., 208 Mass. 273, 94 N.E. 386 (1911).

2. By contrast the burden of proving *contributory negligence* by a preponderance of the evidence is on the defendant since contributory negligence is an affirmative defense. See Chapter IV, Contributory Negligence, below.

3. These two propositions which place the burden on the plaintiff to prove negligence and the burden on the defendant to prove contributory negligence, spring from the presumption that all

persons act carefully in the absence of a showing to the contrary.

4. In a negligence case it is the function of the court:

   (a) to direct a verdict for the defendant if the evidence of negligence is so slight that reasonable persons could only reach the conclusion that there was no negligence,

   (b) to direct a verdict for the plaintiff if the evidence of negligence is so clear that reasonable persons could only reach the conclusion that there was negligence, and

   (c) to submit to the jury the question of negligence or no negligence if the evidence of negligence is such that reasonable persons could differ as to whether the evidence does or does not show negligence.

   See generally, Gregory, pp. 218–222; Keeton, pp. 206–207; P & W, pp. 247–250; Prosser, pp. 205–211.

RES IPSA LOQUITUR

1. *Res Ipsa Loquitur* literally means "the thing itself speaks" or "the thing speaks for itself." This so-called "doctrine" is available only to the plaintiff in a negligence case and, if applicable, has two legal effects:

   (a) it will prevent a directed verdict in favor of the defendant, and

   (b) it permits the jury to consider the question of whether or not the defendant was negligent in causing some event which injured the plaintiff. But the jury is at liberty either to find the defendant negligent or not negligent.

2. The court is justified in submitting the question of negligence to the jury under *res ipsa loquitur* if:

   (a) the plaintiff's injury was caused under circumstances which in the experience of mankind does not occur unless there has been negligence by some one, and

   (b) such injury is caused by an agency or instrumentality within the exclusive control of the defendant, and

   (c) such injury was not due to any voluntary act or contribution on the part of the plaintiff.

3. Recent cases have taken the view that commercial air travel has become so safe that planes engaged in regularly scheduled commercial flights do not crash unless someone has been negligent; that such planes in flight are within the exclusive control of the defendant; and that no voluntary act of the plaintiff as a passenger could contribute to the accident. Hence the doctrine of res ipsa loquitur applies to such cases. See Cox v. North-

west Airlines, Inc., 379 F.2d 893 (7th Cir. 1967), certiorari denied 389 U.S. 1044, 88 S.Ct. 788, 19 L.Ed.2d 836.

4. The "exclusive control" requirement has been eased by the courts in certain cases. Some courts eliminate this element entirely in cases involving the explosion or breaking of bottles containing liquids. Other courts which still cling to this element permit recovery for an explosion if plaintiff proves careful handling after the product has left defendant's possession. See Bornstein v. Metropolitan Bottling Co., 26 N.J. 263, 139 A.2d 404 (1958). See also CASE 34, below.

5. There is an increasing tendency to include automobile accidents caused by a sudden unexplained loss of control within the doctrine of res ipsa loquitur. For example:

   (a) an auto suddenly swerving off good hard-surfaced road injuring passenger. See Johnson v. Foster, 202 So.2d 520 (Miss.1967); Bullington v. Farmer's Tractor & Implement Co., 230 Ark. 783, 324 S.W.2d 517 (1959) and,

   (b) a truck skidding on slippery surface and crossing into wrong lane and striking plaintiff-passenger. See Pfaffenbach v. White Plains Express Corp., 17 N.Y.2d 132, 269 N.Y.S.2d 115, 216 N.E.2d 324 (1966). This case discredited the earlier case of Galbraith v. Busch, 267 N.Y. 230, 196 N.E. 36 (1935), which refused to apply the doctrine to a car which suddenly went out of control, reasoning that the accident may have been caused by an unknown mechanical defect as well as by the negligence of the driver.

6. The further application of res ipsa loquitur is illustrated by the following situations:

   (a) In a collision between a street car and another vehicle, a passenger on the street car may use the doctrine against the street car company, but not against the other vehicle involved in the collision. This is because the operator of the street car owed its passengers a high degree of care and had control of the vehicle. Passengers are not expected to watch out for accidents or collisions with other vehicles. Thus, when a collision occurred, that circumstance alone was sufficient to permit a jury to infer that the carrier was negligent. See Capital Transit Co. v. Jackson, 80 U.S.App. D.C. 162, 149 F.2d 839 (1945).

   (b) D who was operating a bingo game gave a chair to P so she could play after P paid a fee. After a while the chair collapsed because some screws were missing and P was injured. A jury may apply res ipsa loquitur and find for P even though the chair was not in D's exclusive possession. See Benedict v. Eppley Hotel Co., 159 Neb. 23, 65 N.W.2d 224 (1954).

(c) A piece of a chandelier broke and fell on a theatre patron causing injury. The court held that merely showing that the chandelier had been inspected every week for years without discovering any defect did not overcome the inference of negligence as a matter of law and the case was properly sent to the jury. See Goldstein v. Levy, 74 Misc. 463, 132 N.Y.S. 373 (1911).

7. Res ipsa loquitur has been applied in medical malpractice cases to prove negligence in the absence of expert medical testimony.

   (a) The doctrine was held applicable against doctors and hospital employees where plaintiff was unconscious at time of injury. See CASE 35, below.

   (b) Some courts refuse to apply this doctrine to medical malpractice cases. See Ayers v. Parry, 192 F.2d 181 (3rd Cir. 1951).

   (c) Other courts grant recovery on theories, such as respondeat superior and ordinary negligence involving joint tortfeasors where physicians collaborate for treatment or diagnosis. See Shannon v. Jaller, 6 Ohio App.2d 206, 217 N.E.2d 234 (1966) and Sprinkle v. Lemley, 243 Or. 521, 414 P.2d 797 (1966).

   For an article discussing defenses against this doctrine in malpractice cases, see Rossen, "Defense Against Res Ipsa in Medical Malpractice", 13 Clev.-Mar.L.Rev. 128 (1964).

8. Procedurally, most courts hold that res ipsa creates only an *inference* of negligence which may be disregarded by the jury. A minority of courts consider res ipsa loquitur a rebuttable presumption.

   CAVEAT—Discussions of res ipsa loquitur sometimes confuse inferences with presumptions. It is important that the student distinguish an inference from a presumption. Whereas the trier of fact is at liberty to draw or refuse to draw an *inference* from proven facts, the trier of fact is bound to give effect to a *presumption*. The key is whether the trier of fact *may* find either way, an inference, or is *compelled* to reach a particular conclusion, a presumption. See CASE 36, and Inferences and Presumptions, below.

   See generally, Gregory, pp. 222–246; Keeton, pp. 266–278; P & W, pp. 251–280; Prosser, pp. 228–231.

Case 32 *Application of res ipsa loquitur*

P was walking by D's place of business when a barrel of flour fell out of the building on him and injured him. P sued D for damages and presented evidence that the barrel was being lowered from D's window when it fell on him. The trial court dismissed P's suit because no evidence of D's negligence was presented. Was that ruling correct?

Answer. *No. It is not necessary to prove negligence where the circumstances of the accident speak for themselves, and the accident would not have occurred unless D was negligent. This is known as the doctrine of res ipsa loquitur and it is applicable to the facts of the present case. The barrel would not have fallen unless someone was negligent. It was in D's custody. D occupied the premises and was a dealer in flour. D is responsible for the acts of his employees who had control of the barrel. The fact that it fell on P from D's building is prima facie evidence of negligence. Once these facts are established P does not have to show that the barrel could not have fallen without negligence; the burden is on D to present evidence that he was not negligent. Since D did not do this, D is liable for P's injuries.*

See Byrne v. Boadle, 2 H. & C. 72 (Exch.1863).

Res ipsa loquitur—no exclusive control   Case 33

P, while walking on the sidewalk, just stepped out from under the marquee of D hotel and was struck on the head and injured by an armchair which fell on her. P sued D hotel for damages. May P recover?

Answer. *No. To recover under the doctrine of res ipsa loquitur P must prove: (1) that there was an injury, (2) that the thing or instrumentality which caused the injury was at the time and prior thereto under the exclusive control and management of the defendant, and (3) that the injury was such that in the ordinary course of events, the defendant using ordinary care, the injury would not have happened. Applying that rule to the present case the elements of exclusive control and ordinary care are absent. A hotel does not have exclusive control of its furniture. Guests have control of furniture in their rooms and a hotel using ordinary care cannot prevent guests from throwing furniture out of windows—unless they put bars on windows or stationed a guard in each room, which is not required. Thus the accident could occur despite ordinary care by D. Since P could not establish the required elements for res ipsa loquitur, P may not recover.*

See Larson v. St. Francis Hotel, 83 Cal.App.2d 210, 188 P.2d 513 (1948).

Res ipsa loquitur—application to exploding bottle cases   Case 34

P purchased a bottle of Coca-Cola at D's grocery store. While he was leaving the store with the bottle in his hand, it exploded caus-

ing substantial damage to his hand by the flying glass from the bottle. P sues D for negligence. D offers no evidence. P insists that he has a right to a directed verdict because the doctrine of res ipsa loquitur applies and that such doctrine gives him the benefit of a presumption *of negligence on the part of the defendant. The court submitted the question of the defendant's negligence to the jury. The jury found for the defendant. Was the court correct?*

Answer. Yes. This is a typical case for the application of the doctrine of res ipsa loquitur. (a) Bottles containing beverages for human consumption do not, in the experience of mankind, usually explode unless some one has been negligent. (b) The fact that the bottle happened to be in the hand of the plaintiff when it exploded, does not mean that it was within the "control" of the plaintiff. Control in this instance means that the method of preparing the beverage for bottling and the method used in sealing the beverage in the bottle, were wholly and exclusively within the control of the defendant in the bottling process. Therefore, the instrumentality causing the accident was within the exclusive control of the defendant. (c) There was no voluntary act on the part of the plaintiff which contributed to the accident, so long as he was merely carrying it in his hand which was exactly what the defendant presupposed, foresaw and hoped would happen in the market places. Hence, this is a proper case for applying the res ipsa loquitur doctrine. But, assuming that to be true, what is the effect of applying such doctrine? While some courts do hold that it amounts to a presumption *of negligence on the part of the defendant and entitles the plaintiff to a directed verdict in the absence of contrary evidence on the part of the defendant, that is not the majority rule. Properly analyzed, the doctrine is a phase of circumstantial evidence. It is applied as a matter of common sense when there is no direct evidence concerning the issue of negligence of the defendant. It is applied only when the accident is of such a type that the experience of mankind is relatively clear that this kind of accident just does not happen unless there was negligence. Even with such possibility or even probability that there was negligence on the part of the defendant, still the mere fact of the accident is not conclusive that the defendant was negligent. It is merely a sufficient base from which an inference* may be drawn. The *effect of res ipsa loquitur is merely to let the issue of negligence be submitted to the jury, from which evidence of the accident itself, the jury may, but need not, draw the inference that there was negligence in fact* on the part of the defendant. *Therefore, the court was quite right in submitting the question to the jury, and it was quite within the province of the jury to do as it did in this case, find or infer that the defendant was not negligent.*

See Zentz v. Coca Cola Bottling Co., 39 Cal.2d 436, 247 P.2d 344 (1952); Honea v. Coca Cola Bottling Co., 143 Tex. 272, 183 S.W.2d 968 (1944).

Res ipsa loquitur applied to medical procedure

An appendectomy was performed on P with his consent. Immediately upon recovering from the anesthetic P noticed a pain in his right shoulder. The pain became worse despite treatment, and P developed paralysis and atrophy (wasting away) of the muscles around his shoulder. P brought suit against all medical personnel involved in the operation. There was medical evidence that P's condition was due to trauma (injury from extrinsic agent), but P relied on res ipsa loquitur to place liability on defendants. Defendants moved to dismiss on the ground that there was no showing that any particular defendant caused P's injuries, and holding all defendants liable would make some defendants liable for acts for which they were not responsible. Should P's action be dismissed?

Answer. No. The purpose of res ipsa loquitur is to place the duty of producing evidence on the party charged because such evidence is inaccessible to the injured person. The present case comes within the reason and spirit of the doctrine. P's injury was not due to his own conduct, and the evidence showed that P's injury was not the type which would occur without someone's negligence. This is so because P's shoulder was normal before the operation and the operation did not involve his shoulder. The number of defendants and their relationship to each other, such as employees or independent contractors, does not determine whether the doctrine of res ipsa loquitur is applicable. Each defendant was bound to exercise ordinary care to see that no unnecessary harm came to P. Each defendant would be liable for breach of that duty. Furthermore, each defendant had control of an instrumentality which, at one time or another, could have caused P's injury. Since P was unconscious he could not explain how he was injured. P may rely on the doctrine of res ipsa loquitur to place the burden on the defendants to explain what occurred. Thus, where a patient receives unusual injuries while unconscious and in the course of medical treatment, all persons who had control over the patient's body or instrumentalities which might have caused the injuries, may be required to meet the inference of negligence by explaining their conduct. The motion of defendants was denied.

See Ybarra v. Spangard, 25 Cal.2d 486, 154 P.2d 687 (1944).

Jury decides weight accorded inference of negligence

P sued D city for damages to his property caused by a split in a water main which D laid nine years before. P did not introduce any other evidence. D showed that the pipe was new when laid, that it had been tested by its field inspectors before being laid, and that it was installed at the approved depth. The evidence also established that such pipe will last for decades unless affected by chemicals in the ground or in the water. The trial judge granted P's motion for a directed verdict. He reasoned that D's evidence did not rebut the inference of negligence because if the pipe was not defective when laid, it would not break in nine years unless it were improperly laid or it were subjected to some exceptional force, which was not shown. Was that ruling correct?

*   **Answer.** *No. Res ipsa loquitur means that an inference of negligence may be drawn from the facts, not that they compel a presumption of negligence. An inference which is "compelled" is, in fact, a presumption. The inference of negligence may be rejected by the jury just as other circumstantial evidence may be rejected. In the present case D was not required to inspect the buried water mains. D did not show what caused the break, but that was not necessary. Conclusive affirmative proof by D that all reasonable care was used in the inspection and laying of the pipes would rebut the presumption in P's favor. No such proof was presented in the present case, but the evidence was sufficient to go to the jury. It was the function of the jury to weigh the inference of negligence arising from P's evidence against the care used by D, and a directed verdict in favor of P preempted the function of the jury. The case was remanded for a new trial.*

*   *See George Foltis, Inc. v. City of New York, 287 N.Y. 108, 38 N.E.2d 455 (1941).*

NOTE—If a plaintiff by pleading and proof makes out a prima facie case of res ipsa loquitur and the defendant overcomes such prima facie case by showing no negligence on his part, then res ipsa loquitur is no longer applicable. The burden of proof is always on the plaintiff. Hence, at this point the plaintiff must go forward with the evidence to establish the negligence of the defendant. This is done by presenting specific proof of negligence just as though res ipsa loquitur had played no part in the case.

INFERENCES AND PRESUMPTIONS

1. An *inference* is a process of reasoning by which a fact or proposition sought to be established *may* be deduced as a logical consequence from other facts, or state of facts, already proved or admitted.

2. When the law *requires* that an unknown fact be inferred from the existence of a known fact or group of facts, this is called a *presumption*.

3. A presumption is either:

    (a) *rebuttable*, which means that it continues until overcome by evidence to the contrary, or

    (b) *conclusive*, which means that the trier of fact is bound by only one conclusion upon which no evidence to the contrary can be presented.

    See Smith's Review, Evidence, Chapter III, Inferences and Presumptions—Civil.

IV | DEFENSES TO NEGLIGENCE

Summary Outline

INTRODUCTION　　INTRODUCTORY NOTE—Chapter III explained the elements necessary for a plaintiff to establish a cause of action based on negligence.　However, that is only part of the answer to any given factual situation.　This Chapter analyzes the various defenses which may be available to a defendant.

1.　Although a plaintiff has established a prima facie case based on the negligence of the defendant, there are certain defenses which may be available to a defendant which prevent recovery by the plaintiff.　The basic defenses to a negligence action include:

(a)　contributory negligence,

(b)　assumption of the risk,

(c)　intervening cause, and

(d)　unavoidable accident, see CASE 16 above.

2.　The defense of contributory negligence, no matter how slight, is an absolute defense to a cause of action in negligence.　Because of the harshness of this rule the doctrine of last clear chance has developed.

(a)　This doctrine negatives the defense of contributory negligence.

(b)　The doctrine has two different forms:

(i)　conscious last clear chance, and

(ii)　unconscious last clear chance.

3.　The doctrine of imputed contributory negligence may be available in master-servant and joint enterprise situations to prevent recovery.　See Imputed Negligence, below.

4.　Because of the harshness of the doctrine of contributory negligence, many states by statute or court decision, have adopted the concept of comparative negligence which allots the fault of each party.

e.g.　If the plaintiff was twenty percent at fault in causing the accident, the plaintiff may recover only eighty percent of his damages.　See Comparative Negligence, below.

5.　Because of the difficulties arising from the applicability of contributory negligence to automobile accidents, and other shortcomings in the law of negligence, there is a growing trend to enact no fault insurance laws.　See No Fault Insurance, below.

6.　An intervening cause is a new and independent event occurring after the defendant's negligence.　It acts upon the situation which the defendant created and contributes to the plaintiff's injury.　This is a valid defense only where the intervening cause could not be reasonably foreseen.

e.g. D negligently left dynamite caps where children played. X, who was ten years old, took some of the caps home. X's mother saw X playing with the caps. Although she knew that X found them somewhere, and that they were for some kind of explosives, she did nothing. X traded the caps to a friend of his, P. While P was playing with them a cap exploded, resulting in the amputation of P's hand. P sued D. The court stated the issue to be whether D's negligence in leaving the caps where children could take them was the proximate cause of P's injury. The general rule is that "if, subsequent to the original negligent act, a new cause has intervened, of itself sufficient to stand as the cause of the injury, the original negligence is too remote" for liability. Here the conduct of X's mother broke the causal connection between D's negligent act and the later negligence of X's mother. X's possession of the caps when he traded them to P was referable to the permission of X's mother and not D. Therefore, D's negligence was not the proximate cause of P's injury, and P may not recover from D. See Pittsburg Reduction Co. v. Horton, 87 Ark. 576, 113 S.W. 647 (1908). See also Chapter III, Proximate Cause and Liability, above; Prosser, pp. 270–289.

NOTE 1—Where the intervening negligent act causing injury could be foreseen, liability will be imposed on the original wrongdoer. See CASE 30, above.

NOTE 2—Where the intervening cause could not be reasonably foreseen and is a valid defense, it is sometimes called a "superseding cause". See Restatement, Second, Torts § 440.

7. Unavoidable accident, although sometimes referred to as a defense to negligence is not, strictly speaking, a defense because a defense negatives liability. An unavoidable accident which serves as a defense means that there is no liability on the part of the defendant because there was no negligent act which caused the injury and thus, there can be no liability. See CASE 16 and Chapter III, Historical Development, above.

CONTRIBUTORY NEGLIGENCE

1. Contributory negligence is the failure of a person, who is later plaintiff in a suit, to use the care of a reasonable, prudent person in the protection of himself or his property, which failure is a legally contributing cause to his damage.

2. The failure to discover or appreciate the consequences of some risk, as well as the intentional exposure to risk, may constitute contributory negligence. However, a person is not required to forgo some right, such as the reasonable use of land, merely to guard against the possible negligence of another.

e.g. P stacked 700 tons of straw on its land, seventy feet from D's railroad tracks. D's employees operated a locomotive negligently causing it to emit large quantities of sparks and live cinders. A high wind carried sparks to the straw, starting a fire which destroyed all of P's straw. P sued for damages. D contended that P was contributorily negligent in storing the straw too near the tracks. The court held that the doctrine of contributory negligence should not be applied to the present case. P had the right to make reasonable use of its property, and such use should not be limited by the possible negligence of others. D may make reasonable use of its property, even though operating a railroad may cause persons on nearby property to suffer some inconveniences. However, neighboring property owners are not expected to accept risks from D's negligent operation of its railroad. P made lawful use of its property, and the defense of contributory negligence is not available to D. See LeRoy Fibre Co. v. Chicago, Milwaukee & St. Paul Railway, 232 U.S. 340, 34 S.Ct. 415, 58 L.Ed. 631 (1914).

3. Contributory negligence is a complete defense to an action based on negligence. It is an affirmative defense and the burden of proving it rests on the defendant.

4. Contributory negligence is not a defense to an action based on willful, wanton or intentional aggression.

   e.g. P and D get into an argument. D swings at P and hits P in the nose. If P sues D for assault and battery, D may not avoid liability by claiming that P was contributorily negligent by not ducking to avoid the punch. See P & W, pp. 602–603.

   NOTE—The defense of contributory negligence should be distinguished from the defense of "avoidable consequences". Contributory negligence is negligence by the plaintiff before or concurrent with any negligent act of the defendant and fully bars recovery. The doctrine of "avoidable consequences" is applicable only after the defendant has acted negligently and the plaintiff can avoid some of the consequences of defendant's act. If plaintiff fails to act reasonably so as to avoid the consequences of defendant's act, then he may not recover for such additional injuries.

   > *e.g.* P's arm is broken by D's negligence, but P does not seek medical treatment promptly. As a result P is required to have his arm amputated. D is liable for the broken arm, but not for the amputation which P could have avoided by seeking medical treatment promptly. See Prosser, pp. 422–424.

5. If the defendant's negligence is based on the violation of a statute, the plaintiff's contributory negligence bars recovery. See Restatement, Second, Torts § 483; Prosser, p. 426 et seq.

   See generally, Gregory, pp. 381–404; Keeton, pp. 166, 495–502; P & W, pp. 591–603; Prosser, pp. 416–427.

Contributory negligence bars recovery   **Case 37**

D, in the course of making some repairs to his house, put a pole across part of the roadway. P was riding his horse "violently" down the road at dusk. P hit the pole, was thrown from his horse and injured. The evidence showed that the pole could be seen 100 yards away at the time of the accident. P sued for damages. The jury was instructed that if P, using ordinary care, could have seen and avoided the obstruction, then P was guilty of contributory negligence and could not recover. The jury found for D and P appealed. Was the instruction correct?

Answer. Yes. At common law contributory negligence of the plaintiff is a complete defense to the defendant, whether the plaintiff's contributory negligence was slight, ordinary, or gross, and whether it caused 99% or 1% of the damage. The reason is that he has contributed to his own injury. The common law did not recognize in such cases any degrees of negligence, nor the doctrine of comparative negligence. To recover P must show: (a) an obstruction in the road by the fault of D, and (b) no want of ordinary care to avoid the obstruction by P. Here (b) is not present. P contributed to the accident by his own conduct and, therefore, P may not recover. The instruction to the jury was correct.

See Butterfield v. Forrester, 11 East 60, 103 Eng.Rep. 926 (1809). See also Restatement, Second, Torts § 463.

1. The defense of assumption of the risk may arise when the plaintiff voluntarily encounters a known risk created by the defendant. It involves the following elements:

   (a) a voluntary choice to enter or remain in the area of the risk,

   (b) manifestation of consent to accept the risk, and

   (c) actual knowledge of the risk and appreciation of its danger.

2. When a plaintiff consents to assume the risk of injury from a particular hazard, it may constitute a complete defense in favor of the defendant.

3. The assumption of the risk by a plaintiff must be a voluntary choice. If the defendant wrongfully requires the plaintiff to choose between two alternatives then there can be no free choice and assumption of the risk does not apply.

   (a) P rented a house from D. There was a detached privy which P and other tenants used. P knew that the floor of the privy was not well maintained. However, P used the facilities, fell through the floor, and injured herself. P sued D for damages, and D contended that P assumed the risk by using the privy knowing of its defective condition. The court recognized that P "had no choice, when impelled by

ASSUMPTION OF THE RISK

the calls of nature, but to use the facilities placed at her disposal by the landlord, to wit, a privy with a trap door in the floor, poorly maintained. We hardly think this was the assumption of a risk; she was not required to leave the premises and go elsewhere." D had a duty to maintain the privy which P had a right to use. P was not required to give up her legal right to use the privy, and therefore, P did not assume the risk. P was not obligated to select her alternative choice, which was to leave the premises, so P may recover. See Rush v. Commercial Realty Co., 7 N.J. Misc. 337, 145 A. 476 (1929). See also CASE 54 (Marshall v. Ranne) below; Prosser, pp. 450–455.

(b) Similarly, the risk is not assumed where the plaintiff has no reasonable alternative or the plaintiff acts out of necessity to avert harm to himself or another. See Restatement, Second, Torts § 496E.

4. The consent to assume the risk:

(a) may be by express agreement.

e.g. P bank contracted with D armored car service to transport P's money. The contract limited D's liability to $30,000 per shipment. D lost a shipment of $165,450 due to its negligence and P sued D for that amount. D contends that his liability is limited by the contract. May a bailee limit his liability by contract?

Answer. Yes, when the two parties have equal bargaining power. P and D were in business and made the contract with full knowledge of the risks involved. A bailee may not limit his liability where the parties have unequal bargaining power and public policy is involved. Since those factors are not present, P's recovery is limited by his contract. P assumed the risk that the contract limit on liability would not be enough. See Jefferson County Bank of Lakewood v. Armored Motors Service, 148 Colo. 343, 366 P.2d 134 (1961).

(b) may be implied from the facts.

(i) D hotel just completed cementing a flight of stairs and covered them with loose planks. P, a guest in the hotel, saw the planks, and was aware that the stairs were dangerous. P used the stairs although there were other exits that she could have used. P fell and was injured and sued D for damages. May P recover?

Answer. No. P's use of the steps when she was fully conscious of their danger, without knowing additional facts, would not make P negligent. But, where other stairs unattended by danger were reasonably convenient, which she could have used, P may not recover because she voluntarily accepted the risk. See

Hunn v. Windsor Hotel Co., 119 W.Va. 215, 193 S.E. 57 (1937).

(ii) D employed P who assisted D in loading logs onto a truck. The logs were lifted onto the truck by a cable attached to a tractor which was being driven forward and backward according to D's signals. When the logs were loaded P was putting a chain around them when a log rolled off the truck and injured him. P sued D for damages. Did P assume the risk inherent in such work?

> ***Answer.*** No. To apply the doctrine it must be shown that P had actual or implied knowledge of the specific danger involved and an appreciation of the magnitude thereof. These elements are lacking in this case as precautions had been taken to prevent slipping and P reasonably thought he was safe when the log slipped. Thus P did not assume the risk and he may recover. See Guerrero v. Westgate Lumber Co., 164 Cal.App.2d 612, 331 P.2d 107 (1958).

(iii) It has also been held that P assumed the risk when teaching D to drive an automobile, where D lost control and injured P. See Richards v. Richards, 324 S.W.2d 400 (Ky.1959).

CAVEAT—The key element of both express and implied assumption of the risk is the plaintiff's consent. Assumption of the risk arises regardless of the due care used by the plaintiff. This should be contrasted to contributory negligence where the issue is the due care exercised by the plaintiff.

5. The plaintiff's knowledge of the danger and appreciation of its consequences are measured subjectively. Therefore, even if a reasonable person would consider an activity dangerous, a plaintiff who does not appreciate the risk because of age, inexperience or poor judgment will not be held to have assumed the risk. However, contributory negligence may be a defense if the plaintiff's conduct is unreasonable, using the reasonable, prudent person standard.

e.g. P parked his vehicle in an alley between two buildings in order to make some repairs. Although the alley was partially blocked by P's vehicle, P believed that there was enough room for other vehicles to use the alley. D attempted to drive his tractor down the alley but hit P's vehicle causing it to move forward on P, fatally injuring him. P's surviving spouse sued D. D contended that P assumed the risk of injury by blocking the alley. The court rejected D's defense because P had not assumed the risk of negligent driving by persons using the alley. "Although one may assume the risk of the negligence of another if he is fully informed of such negligence, one is not, under the doctrine of assumption of risk, bound to anticipate the negligent conduct of others. . . . The standard to be applied is a subjective one, of what the particular plaintiff in fact sees, knows, understands and appreciates." The evidence showed that several vehicles had safely driven past P. Therefore, P thought it was safe and cannot be said to have assumed the risk of D's negligence. See Hilderbrand v. Minyard, 16 Ariz.App. 583, 494 P.2d 1328 (1972).

6.   Some states have held that the risk cannot be assumed in certain situations, such as:

(a)   the violation of a safety statute, see Guerrero v. Westgate Lumber Co., 164 Cal.App.2d 612, 331 P.2d 107 (1958),

(b)   the breach of the duty of the driver of an automobile to a passenger, see McConville v. State Farm Mutual Automobile Insurance Co., 15 Wis.2d 374, 113 N.W.2d 14 (1962), and

(c)   the breach of the duty of an employer to provide a safe work place for employees.

e.g. An employee was hit by a hook on a door when it was opened. Although the employee knew of the hook, she was permitted to recover. The court said that the employer had a duty to provide a safe place to work, and the employee did not assume the risk by accepting employment. See Siragusa v. Swedish Hospital, 60 Wn.2d 310, 373 P.2d 767 (1962).

NOTE 1—Some courts have refused to recognize implied assumption of the risk. Instead, those courts base their decisions either on the defendant's duty to the plaintiff and negligence, or on contributory negligence. The factual question is presented to the jury of whether plaintiff, knowing of a danger acted as a reasonable and prudent man under the circumstances by incurring the known risk or in the manner the plaintiff proceeded in the face of that risk. If the jury determines that plaintiff acted unreasonably it will deny recovery based on contributory negligence rather than assumption of the risk in those jurisdictions. See Springrose v. Willmore, 292 Minn. 23, 192 N.W.2d 826 (1971); Meistrich v. Casino Arena Attractions, Inc., 31 N.J. 44, 155 A.2d 90 (1959); Rosas v. Buddies Food Store, 518 S.W.2d 534 (Tex. 1975).

NOTE 2—Courts which follow the above view and have abolished implied assumption of the risk as an independent defense continue to apply the traditional assumption of the risk defense where the risk has been expressly assumed and in strict liability cases.

See generally, Gregory, pp. 406–416; Keeton, pp. 517–537; P & W, pp. 617–636; and Prosser, pp. 439–457.

Attendance at baseball game—assumption of risk   **Case 38**

P was sitting in the grandstand at a baseball game and was injured when a foul ball hit him. P sued for damages contending that D was negligent in not maintaining a screen to protect patrons. D defended by showing that there was an area protected by a screen near where P sat. By voluntarily sitting in the area which was not screened P was guilty of contributory negligence and assumed the risk of the accident and injury. May P recover?

Answer. *No. Initially the court answered the question affirmatively because there was no warning given of the danger involved and there was an implied representation by D that the seat was reasonably safe. However, upon a rehearing that decision was overruled. The court reasoned that P could have sat behind the screen, but he voluntarily chose to sit somewhere else. P was familiar with baseball and knew the risk involved, and since he voluntarily chose the more dangerous seat, he may not recover.*

See Kavafian v. Seattle Baseball Club Association, 105 Wash. 215, 177 P. 776, reversed 105 Wash. 215, 181 P. 679 (1919).

NOTE 1—Compare Lee v. National League Baseball Club of Milwaukee, 4 Wis.2d 168, 89 N.W.2d 811 (1958) where P was injured at a baseball game by other spectators who were trying to get a foul ball. The court held that P did not assume the risk of being injured by other spectators and permitted recovery of damages. See Gregory, pp. 409–410.

NOTE 2—P was hit by a puck at a hockey game, while sitting in unscreened stands. The court permitted P to recover because the puck does not ordinarily leave the playing area and, therefore, this was not a risk assumed by a spectator. See Morris v. Cleveland Hockey Club, Inc., 157 Ohio St. 225, 105 N.E.2d 419 (1952).

NOTE 3—D produced a fireworks display under a license granted by the city. Although an area was roped off for the protection of spectators, several persons standing behind the ropes were injured by the explosion of a bomb or shell. The injured persons brought suit against D. At trial D showed that in firing the bomb he exercised reasonable care, and it was a common type of fireworks long in use. The plaintiffs contended that a city ordinance prohibited issuance of a license to use the bomb which injured them. The court rejected that argument. It was held that "a voluntary spectator, who is present merely for the purpose of witnessing the display, must be held to consent to it, and he suffers no legal wrong if accidently injured without negligence on the part of any one, although the show was unauthorized. He takes the risk." Therefore, the spectators assumed the risk that they might be injured in the absence of negligence and may not recover. See Scanlon v. Wedger, 156 Mass. 462, 31 N.E. 642 (1892).

IMPUTED NEGLIGENCE

1. Imputed negligence means that the negligence of one person may be charged to some other person.

2. Imputed contributory negligence may serve as a defense by imputing negligence to the plaintiff thus making him contributorily negligent. See CASE 39, below.

3. Generally, contributory negligence is imputed to a plaintiff only to prevent recovery by the plaintiff where there is a master-servant (employer-employee) relation or a joint enterprise which involves the plaintiff and a wrongdoer.

   (a) P operated an auto rental business. P leased a car to X for a fixed sum plus a charge for mileage. During the rental period X was involved in an accident with an automobile driven by D. Both X and D were negligent. P sued D for damage to its automobile. D contended that the negligence of X, who rented the car from P, should be imputed to P and bar recovery by imputed contributory negligence. The court reasoned that since X was using the automobile for his own purpose and not for P's benefit, and because P had no control over X's activities, X's negligence could not be imputed to P to bar recovery. See Continental Auto Lease Corp. v. Campbell, 19 N.Y.2d 350, 280 N.Y.S.2d 123 227 N.E.2d 28 (1967).

   (b) P employed X to deliver supplies. During the course of X's employment X was involved in an automobile accident with D. Both X and D were negligent. P may not recover damages from D for repairs to the vehicle operated by X, because X's negligence will be imputed to P. This is so because of the employer-employee relationship and the fact that X was acting within the scope of his employment and in furtherance of P's business.

4. In a joint enterprise the negligence or contributory negligence of one is imputed to others in the enterprise preventing them from maintaining a suit because of contributory negligence.

5. Courts frequently require the following elements for a joint enterprise:

   (a) an agreement, express or implied, among the members of the group,

   (b) the group has a common purpose,

   (c) the group has a pecuniary interest in accomplishing its purpose, and

   (d) each member of the group has an equal right of control over the enterprise.

   e.g. A partnership is a joint enterprise, but usually the objective of a joint enterprise is more limited than a partnership business.

See Restatement, Second, Torts § 491, comment c.

6. Where the Family Automobile Doctrine applies (See Chapter III, Family Automobile Doctrine, above) most courts hold that contributory negligence of the driver is not imputed to the owner of the car in a suit for damage to the car.

e.g. D was driving an automobile owned by P who was a passenger. D was negligent and collided with Blank who was driving another car. P was killed in the accident, and P's estate brought suit against D and Blank. Should D's negligence be imputed to P and prevent recovery because P would then have been deemed contributorily negligent?

Answer. No. The court held that a driver's negligence will not be imputed to a passenger unless the relationship between the driver and passenger was such that the passenger would be vicariously liable as defendant for the driver's negligence. This only occurs where there is a master-servant relation or a joint enterprise. The facts of the present case do not show that relationship, so D's negligence may not be imputed to P, and P's estate may recover. See Smalich v. Westfall, 440 Pa. 409, 269 A.2d 476 (1970). See also Mills v. Gabriel, 259 App.Div. 60, 18 N.Y.S.2d 78 (2d Dept. 1940).

NOTE—The rule in the Smalich case is known as the "both-ways" test. Although the rule has been criticized, it is applied in a number of jurisdictions. Other courts refuse to impute the driver's negligence to a passenger in any situation and allow recovery. See P & W, p. 703.

See generally, Gregory, pp. 716–734; Keeton, pp. 305–306, 502–514; P & W, pp. 693–704; Prosser, pp. 475–491.

Joint tort liability for persons engaged in joint enterprise　　　**Case 39**

D and T often went on automobile journeys for pleasure. After D obtained permission to use his father's car, D and T took two women automobile riding. D and T alternated driving. While T was driving he negligently killed P's wife. May P sue D for damages for T's negligent operation of the car?

Answer. Yes. If D and T were engaged in a joint enterprise at the time of the accident and they had joint control of the automobile at that time, then D is liable for T's negligence. The court said, "An enterprise is simply a project or undertaking, and a joint enterprise is simply one participated in by associates acting together. The basis of liability of one associate in a joint enterprise for the tort of another is equal privilege to control the method and means of accomplishing the common design." The control necessary for liability is not actual steering of the wheel in this case, but the fact that D and T had equal authority to decide how to use the car. D and T both borrowed the car to take the girls riding. The girls were guests but neither D nor T was a guest of the other, or a mere passenger while the other was driving. D and T had equal authority to decide where to go, how long to stay there and who was to drive the car. Thus there was a true joint enterprise so D is liable for T's tort.

See Howard v. Zimmermann, 120 Kan. 77, 242 P. 131 (1926).

NOTE—Many courts require a business venture, in contrast to a social venture, before they will find a joint enterprise. In those jurisdictions the decision above would not be followed.

Case 40   *Employer's negligence not imputed to employees*

Plaintiffs' decedents were employed on Ship X which collided with Ship Y because of the mutual negligence of those in charge of each ship. The trial court imputed the contributory negligence of those in charge of the ship to the decedents and denied recovery. P appealed. May the negligence of those in charge of a ship be imputed to the ship's employees to deny them recovery?

Answer. No. The employees were not negligent and they had no control over the persons whose negligence caused the collision. The employees could not have prevented the collision, so there is no valid reason to deny them recovery. If D were suing for negligence there would be no need to join the plaintiffs herein although the master was held liable for the conduct of his servant, because there is no relationship between the owner and his employees that would make them vicariously liable. Therefore, in the present case the master's negligence cannot be imputed to the employees and they may recover. If the employees had been negligent instead of the master, their negligence would have been imputed to the ship-owner just as the master's negligence.

See Mills v. Armstrong (The "Bernina"), 13 App.Cas. 1 (1888). See also Weber v. Stokely-Van Camp, Inc., 274 Minn. 482, 144 N.W.2d 540 (1966).

LAST CLEAR CHANCE

1. The last clear chance doctrine came into being as an attempt to avoid the harshness of contributory negligence as a complete defense.

   CAVEAT—The Last Clear Chance Doctrine is NOT a defense to negligence. It is, rather, a theory which avoids the application of contributory negligence as a complete defense.

2. The doctrine is *in favor* of the *plaintiff only*, and only he can claim its benefit.

3. It is usually justified on the ground that the defendant's negligence is "the proximate" or "sole" cause of the plaintiff's injury, because it was later in point of time.

4. Court decisions concerning the existence of the doctrine of last clear chance and its application vary substantially from state to state. CHART I, below, summarizes the rules generally applicable, but compare exceptions and refinements to the general rules in numbers 5 through 11, below.

5. Last clear chance includes two different concepts:

   (a) conscious last clear chance,

   > *e.g.* P was driving his automobile and made a left hand turn, although D was approaching from the other direction. D saw P and could have avoided an accident by applying the brakes of his car immediately, but D did not do so. In this situation P negligently subjected himself to a risk from D's subsequent negligence, and P was unable to avoid harm by the exercise of reasonable care. D saw P and knew of P's peril, but D was negligent by failing to use reasonable care. There was an accident and P was injured. This is known as the "helpless plaintiff" situation because after P's negligence P was unable to avoid injury. P may recover. See CASE 42 below; Restatement, Second, Torts § 479(b) (i).

   (b) unconscious last clear chance,

   > *e.g.* P was negligent and unable to avoid injury by the exercise of reasonable care (helpless plaintiff situation). D had a duty to discover P's peril, but failed to use reasonable care and discover it. If D had exercised due care D would have discovered P's situation and avoided injury to P. If P is injured most states would hold D liable. See CASE 43, below; Restatement, Second, Torts § 479(b)(ii). However, there is a split of authority and many other states would not hold D liable on these facts.

6. The helpless plaintiff situation, number 5, above, should be distinguished from cases where the plaintiff is inattentive. If the plaintiff is inattentive, meaning that the plaintiff could have discovered the danger with reasonable vigilance after the initial negligent act, the plaintiff can recover only if the defendant:

   (a) had actual knowledge of the plaintiff's situation,

   (b) had reason to realize that the plaintiff would not discover her peril, and

   (c) thereafter failed to exercise reasonable care.

   See Restatement, Second, Torts § 480.

7. Last clear chance is distinguished from contributory negligence by answering three questions concerning the facts of the given case:

    (a) Who was present at the crisis of the accident?

    (b) Who was acting at the crisis of the accident?

    (c) Were the negligences of the parties simultaneous or successive?

8. If both parties were present and acting at the time of the accident, then their negligence was simultaneous, and it is a case of contributory negligence, and neither can recover.

9. If only the defendant, was present, or both parties were present but the plaintiff was unable to act, and their negligence was successive (that is the plaintiff's negligence came first, and the defendant's negligence came later), then last clear chance applies and the plaintiff can recover. See Restatement, Second, Torts § 479 and Prosser, p. 427 et seq.

e.g. P tied the forefeet of his donkey and let it graze on a public highway, which was illegal. D negligently drove his team of horses down the highway and they hit and killed P's donkey. P sued for damages. Will the fact that P put the donkey in the road prevent him from recovering?

> ***Answer.*** No. By exercising ordinary care D could have avoided hitting the donkey. D had the duty to proceed down the highway at a speed that would not cause injury to others. Even if the donkey were illegally on the road, the consequence of P's negligence in tying the donkey was avoidable. By exercising ordinary care D had a "last clear chance" to avoid the accident. Therefore, D is liable for his failure to exercise care which would have avoided the accident. See Davies v. Mann, 10 M. & W. 546, 152 Eng. Rep. 588 (1842).

10. If the defendant discovers the peril of the plaintiff, but acts in willful or wanton disregard of that peril, as distinguished from mere negligent conduct, the defendant may not use the plaintiff's contributory negligence as a defense.

e.g. D's subway train was brought to an emergency stop. The motorman knew that this could have occurred from the blowing of a valve, a passenger pulling an emergency strap, or by the operation of a tripping device under the car indicating that something had come into contact with it. The motorman reset the breaks and started the train without investigating. The car was stopped automatically again and he started it again without any investigation. After a third emergency stop the motorman investigated and found the deceased wedged under a car. A wrongful death action was initiated invoking the doctrine of last clear chance. Under this theory it was argued that the decedent could have been saved if the motorman had investigated after the first or second stop. The subway showed that decedent should not have been on the subway tracks and he was contributorily negligent. The court held that the facts should have gone to the jury on plaintiff's theory. The motorman knew that someone might be in danger, and his indifference showed willful negligence. Since there was evidence that decedent might have been saved by an investigation after the first or second stop, recovery is permitted because D had a last clear chance to avoid the death after the first stop. The defense of contributory negligence does not supersede the doctrine of last clear chance. See Kumkumian v. City of New York, 305 N.Y. 167, 111 N.E.2d 865 (1953).

NOTE—Some states which have abandoned the doctrine of last clear chance use this rule to reach the same result as if the doctrine were used. See Restatement, Second, Torts § 481.

11. Where the defendant's negligence consists in the lack of preparation for the situation which results in injury to the plaintiff, most courts hold that the plaintiff may not recover.

e.g. P drove onto railroad tracks without looking for trains. A train approaching P saw him and could have stopped if its brakes had not been defective. However, the brakes were defective and the train hit P because it could not stop in time. P's estate sued for damages for wrongful death and the railroad defended on the basis that since P was contributorily negligent in proceeding onto the tracks without looking, there could be no recovery. The court held that since the accident resulted from the railroad's negligence in not maintaining adequate brakes, and this prevented it from avoiding the results of P's negligence, the railroad was liable. Contributory negligence does not prevent recovery where the exercise of due care by defendant would have avoided the accident. See British Columbia Elec. Ry. Co. v. Loach, 1 A.C. 719 (Privy Council, 1916). This is the minority view in America. Most courts would decline to distinguish between the negligence of a defendant in maintaining good brakes and the negligence of a plaintiff which placed him in danger and thus would deny recovery to the plaintiff.

See generally, Gregory, pp. 400–408; Keeton, pp. 166–168, 495–502; P & W, pp. 599–603; Prosser, pp. 427–433.

CHART I		
LAST CLEAR CHANCE		
SUMMARY OF VARIATIONS OF DOCTRINE		

Position of Plaintiff	Position of Defendant	Majority Rule	Restatement, Second, Torts
Helpless P	D knows of peril	D liable CASE 41	§ 479
Helpless P	D inattentive	D liable[1] CASE 42	§ 479
Inattentive P	D knows of peril	D liable	§ 480
Inattentive P	D inattentive	D not liable[2]	§ 480

1. Many states would not hold D liable in this situation.

2. The Missouri humanitarian doctrine, applied in only a few states, would hold D liable at least in railroad and automobile collisions.

CAVEAT—The application of the doctrine of last clear chance varies widely from state to state, and there are exceptions to the general rules outlined above. Some states have abolished the doctrine completely.

Case 41 *Last clear chance and contributory negligence compared and contrasted*

P was standing on a railroad track watching a passing train when another train came from the opposite direction on the track where P was standing. P was not looking for this second train and it hit him. P sued for damages and D claimed that P was guilty of contributory negligence which barred recovery. P claimed that D had a last clear chance to avoid the accident and that excused his contributory negligence. There was a jury verdict for P and D appealed. Did D have the burden of proof in establishing that there was no last clear chance to avoid the accident?

Answer. *No. P was negligent in standing on railroad tracks with no heed to the danger therein. To avoid the defense of contributory negligence, the burden of proof is on P to show: (1) that the defendant is aware of the plaintiff's presence, (2) that he is also aware of the plaintiff's ignorance of his peril or of his inability to save himself, and (3) that the defendant may then in due course act to avoid injury. In the present case it was P's burden of proof to show that he was ignorant of his peril or could not meet it, and that D knew it. Since the trial court instructed the jury that the burden was on D as part of his defense of contributory negligence to show that there was no last clear chance to avoid the accident, the case was remanded for a new trial.*

See Clark v. Boston & Maine Railroad, 87 N.H. 434, 182 A. 175 (1935).

Conscious last clear chance by defendant allows recovery   Case 42

P, a minor, was riding a motor scooter toward an intersection. D was approaching the same intersection on another street in his car. When D was 75 feet from the crossing D saw P about 50 feet from it and P was looking back over his shoulder. D, who had the right of way, then looked to the right and when D looked back P was 5 or 6 feet from him still looking over his shoulder. D accelerated to avoid the collision, but P hit the rear of D's car and was injured. D, assuming that P would see him and stop, did not blow his horn or do anything else to warn P. P sued for damages based on the doctrine of last clear chance. May P recover?

Answer. Yes. The last clear chance doctrine is not limited to situations where P is physically helpless to prevent the accident. It also applies to the inattentive plaintiff. When D first saw P, P was unaware of the danger and, for that reason unable to avoid it at that time. The continuing negligence of P does not bar him from recovery if the other person nevertheless had a last clear chance to avoid the accident. The fact that D expected P to exercise due care and avoid the accident is no defense. P did not know of the impending danger when D saw him and a reasonable, prudent man in D's position would have taken steps at that time to avoid an accident rather than look the other way to see if there was any danger. Since D knew that P was unaware of the impending danger and took no steps to avoid it, D is liable for damages to P.

See Peterson v. Burkhalter, 38 Cal.2d 107, 237 P.2d 977 (1951).

Unconscious last clear chance by defendant allows recovery   Case 43

P was driving a truck and about to enter a highway. P saw D's truck approaching, but P thought he could "make it" and pulled onto the highway. As P reached the center of the highway and before P could turn, D's truck hit him. D could have avoided the accident if he had started to slow down when P started onto the highway, but D was negligent in not keeping a lookout so he did not see P when P started out. May P recover?

Answer. Yes. If D had been keeping a lookout while driving, D would have seen the danger when P started out. D could then have slowed down and avoided the accident. Since D's negligence was later in time than P's, D could have avoided the accident by the exercise of due care. Thus D is liable for P's injuries. P's negligence in entering the highway was not contributory negligence because: (a) only the defendant was present, (b) only the defendant was acting, and (c) the negligent acts of the plaintiff and defendant were successive, that is, the negligence of the plaintiff was prior to the negligence of the defendant. D could have prevented the accident if he had not been negligent. Thus he is said to have had an unconscious chance to avoid the accident and he is liable.

See Independent Lumber Co. v. Leatherwood, 102 Colo. 460, 79 P.2d 1052 (1938); contra, Menke v. Peterschmidt, 246 Iowa 722, 69 N.W.2d 65 (1955).

NOTE—The rule in CASE 43 above does not apply where the defendant sees the danger but makes an error in judgment in trying to avoid it.

e.g. P's intestate, a young boy was killed when hit by D's locomotive. The engineer saw the boy and shouted to him to get off the tracks, but the boy did not move. Then the engineer applied the brakes, but could not stop. P may not recover. Last clear chance does not apply because the engineer took action immediately to avoid hitting P's intestate. He made a reasonable effort to avoid the peril in that emergency situation and he was not negligent. See Woloszynowski v. New York Central Railroad Co., 254 N.Y. 206, 172 N.E. 471 (1930).

COMPARATIVE NEGLIGENCE

1. Traditionally, contributory negligence of the plaintiff, no matter how slight, has served as a *total* defense to a cause of action in negligence. Thus, regardless of the relative fault of the two parties the plaintiff bears the total loss and the defendant is free of liability for damages.

2. The injustice created by this rule has prompted *most* states to adopt a system of comparative negligence to be applied at a minimum in certain situations.

3. There are two basic types of comparative negligence systems:

(a) "Pure" comparative negligence permits a plaintiff to recover regardless of the degree of fault.

e.g. Compensatory damages due a plaintiff (P) without fault are $20,000. If P is found to be sixty percent negligent and D forty percent negligent, P may recover forty percent ($8,000) as her damages.

(b) "Partial" comparative negligence has been adopted in most states which have abolished contributory negligence. Under this system the plaintiff may only recover where she was less than fifty percent at fault. Where the plaintiff's negligence equaled or exceeded that of the defendant, the plaintiff may not recover.

(i) If P is found to be sixty percent negligent and D forty percent negligent, P may not recover.

(ii) If P is found to be fifty percent negligent and D is fifty percent negligent, P may not recover.

(iii) Some states permit P to recover where fifty percent of the fault has been apportioned to the plaintiff. In this variation of the rule stated in example (ii), above, P is entitled to her proportional recovery if her negligence was equal to or less than the defendant's negligence.

NOTE—The partial comparative negligence system appears to be a compromise which retains some aspects of contributory negligence. It is based on the view that where a plaintiff is substantially responsible for her own injury, compensation should be denied.

4. Although the ability of a jury to properly apportion fault, and with it, damages, has been called into question, supporters of comparative negligence argue that this defect is less objectionable than denying any recovery to the plaintiff.

5. An open issue under many statutes is the question of whether last clear chance applies in the presence of comparative negligence.

e.g. It may be argued that since last clear chance developed to eliminate the all or nothing effect of contributory negligence, it should have no application in comparative negligence situations. Thus some courts have held that under comparative negligence statutes damages are always apportioned, even though the defendant had a last clear chance to avoid the accident. This is considered the better rule. See Last Clear Chance, above.

6. Most courts which have considered the question of whether to adopt a comparative negligence system have held that such a decision is for the legislature and that it is not for the courts to change the contributory negligence rule. See, *e.g.*, Maki v. Frelk, 40 Ill.2d 193, 239 N.E.2d 445 (1968). A few courts have instituted a comparative negligence system without formal legislation. See CASE 44, below.

See generally, Gregory, pp. 426–440; Keeton, pp. 537–551; P & W, pp. 603–617; Prosser, pp. 433–439.

Comparative negligence rule adopted by court without legislation   Case 44

P was driving her automobile and made a left hand turn at an intersection. D, driving at an unsafe speed in the opposite direction, entered the intersection after the traffic light had turned yellow. There was a collision in which P was injured. P sued for damages based on D's negligence. The court found that D was negligent, but denied recovery because P was contributorily negligent. P appealed, contending that contributory negligence should not be a complete defense. Should the court declare the doctrine of contributory negligence no longer applicable and replace it with the doctrine of comparative negligence which assesses liability in proportion to fault?

Answer. Yes. *Contributory negligence bars all recovery when P's negligence has contributed as a legal cause in any degree to the harm suffered by her. That rule has been criticized because it fails to distribute responsibility in proportion to fault. Initially, the court concluded that state law did not prevent the court from changing the law of contributory negligence by judicial decision. The court then examined practical arguments against a comparative fault system. Where there are multiple plaintiffs or defendants it may be difficult to apportion damages. This would be especially difficult if not all persons were parties to the suit, and it could create problems of contribution and indemnity. In addition, assigning a specific percentage to the negligence of each party could be difficult for a jury. The court concluded that guidelines could be given to the jury, perhaps with special interrogatories, to help it focus on the issues. Therefore, these reasons should not prevent a court from adopting a comparative negligence system.*

The court also concluded that the doctrine of last clear chance should be abandoned since it was not needed when "pure" comparative negligence replaced contributory negligence. The court adopted a system of "pure" comparative negligence. Responsibility for damages must be assigned in proportion to the negligence of each party under this system, and P may recover that proportion of damages attributed to the negligence of D regardless of whether D's negligence was greater or less than P's negligence.

See Li v. Yellow Cab Co. of California, 13 Cal.3d 804, 119 Cal. Rptr. 858, 532 P.2d 1226 (1975).

NOTE 1—This case illustrates the trend to replace contributory negligence with a comparative negligence system. Here, the court, rather than the legislature, selected the "pure" form of comparative negligence because under the alternative system of partial comparative negligence a slight difference in proportional fault may bar recovery. Thus a plaintiff who is charged with 49 percent of the total fault may recover, but a plaintiff charged with 51 percent of the total fault is denied any recovery if the partial comparative negligence were adopted. In that example the plaintiff would recover 51 percent or 49 percent of her total damages under a "pure" comparative negligence system.

NOTE 2—The change from contributory to comparative negligence has usually been legislative, but a few courts, such as the California court in the Li case, above, have imposed it on their own initiative.

NO FAULT INSURANCE

1. Liability insurance involves a contract between the insurer, an insurance company, and the insured, a policyholder, in which the insurer agrees to indemnify the insured against specified losses to third persons. See Prosser, pp. 541–542.

2. The fault-oriented system of providing redress for personal injuries with respect to automobile accidents has been subject to increasing criticism. Statutory reform and reform of current insurance programs have been suggested.

3. The fault-oriented system has been subjected to criticism.

   (a) Even where there is insurance, currently, there is liability only where there is fault.

   (b) Even where there is insurance, and even where that insurance is required by statute, the required minimum limits, typically $10,000–$20,000, are totally inadequate.

   (c) Despite statutory requirements for insurance, under many circumstances many plaintiffs' claims go unredressed because:

      (i) an irresponsible and judgment-proof defendant carries no insurance,

      (ii) the plaintiff may not be able to prove negligence, or

      (iii) the plaintiff may be contributorily negligent or be deemed to have assumed the risk.

   (d) The fault-oriented system may produce inequitable results, especially with respect to minor claims (nuisance suits).

   (e) Our present judicial process of resolving automobile accident claims, with its protracted delays, extensive litigation, and excessive costs related to attorneys' fees and other expenses has been subject to increasing demands for reform and change.

4. One of the principal areas of reform has been the insurance coverages related to automobile accidents.

5. Although approach to reform is not infrequently referred to under the umbrella of "no fault" insurance, in fact there is a variety of plans and proposals which have been discussed and adopted. Two insurance techniques have already been rather widely accepted:

   (a) The first is the so-called "uninsured motorist coverage." The driver obtains insurance against the event that a potential defendant is himself uninsured.

   (b) The second is the "medical pay" portion of many policies. This provides for the payment of a certain stipulated amount of medical expenses for either party, regardless of fault.

6. The great majority of proposed plans for dealing with automobile accidents draw their analogies from workers compensation statutes which have the following five basic elements:

   (a) strict liability,

(b) compulsory insurance,

(c) a schedule of compensation,

(d) a commission or other administrative body rather than courts and a jury, and

(e) a limitation of attorney's fees.

See Prosser, p. 560.

7. Some states have attempted to require "compulsory insurance," but these programs have generally proven to be inadequate.

8. The most widely discussed "no fault" plan is referred to as the Keeton-O'Connell Plan, deriving its name from the co-authors of a study of the subject.

    (a) The concept of the Plan is that an individual carries his own insurance for personal injuries up to $10,000.

    (b) The insurance coverage *replaces* any traditional cause of action for damages if personal damages are less than $10,000 and damages for pain and suffering are less than $5,000.

    (c) If damages exceed these amounts the traditional negligence cause of action is retained, although recovery is reduced by these amounts.

        See O'Connell, Taming the Automobile, 1964, 58 Minn.L. Rev. 299; Keeton and O'Connell. Basic Protection—A Proposal for Improving Automobile Claims Systems, 1965, 78 Harv.L.Rev. 329; O'Connell, Basic Protection—Relief for the Ills of Automobile Insurance Cases, 1967, 27 La.L.Rev. 647.

9. The first statute adopting such reforms became law in Puerto Rico in 1968 and took effect in 1969. The Massachusetts' statute, based upon the Keeton-O'Connell Plan, was adopted in 1970 and became effective in 1971. Today, at least half of the states have enacted some form of no fault insurance. These statutes have been held constitutional.

e.g. A state no fault insurance system was challenged by an accident victim as violative of the Due Process and Equal Protection Clauses of the U.S. Constitution. State law did not allow recovery for pain and suffering if medical expenses were less than $500. Civil suits for damages, including pain and suffering, could be brought only in certain specified circumstances. Coverage under the law was compulsory for all motorists. The state claimed that the legislation had a legitimate purpose, which was to reduce court cases and provide prompt awards to injured persons, and that the no fault statute was a legitimate means to accomplish those purposes. Was the no fault legislation constitutional?

Answer. Yes. Initially, it should be recognized that no preexisting vested right was abolished since the law was not retroactive. The statute merely changed the substantive rights of recovery or limited the plaintiff's method of enforcing her rights. Although a plaintiff may not recover for pain and suffering in certain circumstances, the defendant is not liable for such damages under the no fault law. Further, motorists who were negligent could not recover for injuries under prior law. The new statute permits them to recover as if they were not negligent. Thus the new law, considered as a whole, was not one-sided or arbitrary. The no fault system bore a rational relationship to valid state objectives. It was not arbitrary or discriminatory towards a class of persons. Therefore, the law was valid. See Pinnick v. Cleary, 360 Mass. 1, 271 N.E.2d 592 (1971); Montgomery v. Daniels, 38 N.Y.2d 41, 378 N.Y.S.2d 1, 340 N.E.2d 444 (1975).

10. The new statutory plans have been subject to the following criticism by lawyers and insurance companies:

    (a) Lawyers, fearing loss of a lucrative specialty, have decried destruction of traditional causes of action and labeled such programs socialistic.

    (b) Insurance companies have been concerned over the possible increased costs of such coverage in relationship to currently existing premiums.

See generally, Gregory, pp. 833–888; Keeton, pp. 775–834; P & W, pp. 1300–1324; Prosser, pp. 541–570.

*

V | OWNERS AND OCCUPIERS OF LAND

Summary Outline

A. Introduction
B. General Duty
C. Analysis of Duty
D. Attractive Nuisance
E. Modern Concept of Duty

INTRODUCTION   1. The general principles relating to negligence and defenses to negligence (Chapters III and IV, above) have special application to owners and occupiers of land because their duty to others may be greater or lesser depending on certain circumstances.

    (a) Generally, liability of owners and occupiers of land is based on negligence. The owner is not usually an insurer of the safe conditions of the land. This principle is explained in this Chapter.

    (b) An owner may be strictly liable without fault in certain circumstances. See Chapter VI, Liability without Fault, below.

2. Where liability is based on negligence, the defendant may avail himself of normal defenses to negligence, such as contributory negligence.

3. The crucial element in the law of negligence is the duty of the defendant to the plaintiff. In the law of owners and occupiers of land the law has structured the liability of a defendant based on essentially three different degrees of duty to three different classes of plaintiffs, namely:

    (a) trespassers,

    (b) licensees, or

    (c) invitees or business invitees

4. For the purpose of tort liability a person may have one of three relationships to land. He may be:

    (a) an owner,

    (b) an occupier claiming to be an owner, such as an adverse possessor, or

    (c) a possessor claiming no right of ownership, such as a tenant. This Review treats occupiers and possessors as one and the same; this does not include a tenant at will or by sufferance.

5. An owner of land, for this purpose, is one who is a vendor or a landlord, but not one who is in possession. An owner who is in possession of the land either actually or constructively (one having title to vacant land) is an occupier.

6. An occupier is one in possession of land and who has control thereof.

    e.g. an owner, a lessee, an adverse possessor.

7. The condition of land may be either safe or dangerous. If it is safe, then neither owner nor occupier has any liability to anyone.

8. The dangerous condition of land exists in three forms:

(a) visible dangers,

(b) concealed dangers, known by the owner or occupier, or

(c) concealed dangers which are unknown but which by the exercise of due care in making an inspection would be discovered.

9. This Chapter also considers:

(a) the attractive nuisance doctrine, which examines the duty to children who are trespassers, and

(b) the modern approach to defining the duty of owners and occupiers of land.

1. By the general rule the owner of land is not liable to anyone for the dangerous condition of the land sold or leased, because the doctrine of caveat emptor, "let the buyer beware," applies both to sales and leases of land.

GENERAL DUTY

2. Courts have recognized the following exceptions whereby liability may be imposed on a vendor or lessor.

(a) A *vendor or lessor may be liable for a nuisance or dangerous condition* which he has maintained on the land, *for some time after he has sold or leased the land.*

e.g. D maintained a gutter from the roof of a building which discharged water onto a sidewalk. The water turned to ice and P fell on it thereby injuring himself. P may recover. The occupier of the land erected the gutter which caused water to flow onto the public sidewalk creating a public nuisance and causing the injury. See Tremblay v. Harmony Mills, 171 N.Y. 598, 64 N.E. 501 (1902). See also Leahan v. Cochran, 178 Mass. 566, 60 N.E. 382 (1901).

(b) A vendor or lessor has a duty to warn his vendee or lessee of a known concealed danger on the land, which a reasonable inspection of the land would not disclose to the vendee or lessee.

e.g. D leased a house, which included an outhouse, to L. The outhouse was built over an abandoned well contrary to a city ordinance. D negligently permitted the timbers supporting the floor to become rotten and did not repair them. The rotten supporting timbers were concealed from view and L could not discover their condition. P, a guest of L, was using the outhouse when the floor gave way causing injuries to P. P sued D for damages. May P recover?

Answer. Yes. "If there is a concealed danger on the premises, known to the landlord and unknown to the tenant at the time of the lease, the landlord is liable to the tenant or to his licensees, who may without negligence be injured thereby, though the landlord does not covenant to make repairs." Ames v. Brandvold, 119 Minn. 521, 138 N.W. 786 (1912).

3. Generally, an occupier of land is not liable for a dangerous natural condition on his land, such as a swamp, or for natural growth on his land, such as the branches of his trees hanging over his neighbor's land.

> *e.g.* A tree which had been dead for several years fell and injured P who was driving on a seldom used public highway. D, the owner of the land, did not know of the dead tree. The court held that D did not have the duty to inspect his property, which was forest land in a sparsely settled area. See Lemon v. Edwards, 344 S.W.2d 822 (Ky.1961).

CAVEAT—The rule in number 3, above, applies only to unaltered natural conditions. If a natural condition on land has been changed, thereby creating or increasing a risk, the owner may be held liable for the resulting harm.

4. An occupier may be liable to others off the land for maintaining either a nuisance, public or private, or a dangerous condition on the land which causes injury.

(a) D owned land on which a baseball park was located. D rented the park to baseball teams. During an average game 16 to 18 foul balls were hit out of the park onto a public street. There was a ten foot fence to protect pedestrians along part of the street, but two or three foul balls were hit over that fence during every game. P was walking along the street and was injured by a foul ball hit over that fence. The court held that P could recover from D. The public had the right to free and unmolested use of the public street. D, the abutting landowner, was not permitted to use land so as to interfere with the rights of persons lawfully using the street. Under the circumstances the precautions taken by D to protect persons using the street were insufficient. D knew or should have known that the fence was inadequate protection, so P may recover. See Salevan v. Wilmington Park, Inc., 6 Terry 290, 72 A.2d 239 (Del. Super.1950).

(b) P missed a turn while driving his car down the highway on a foggy morning and unintentionally drove onto D's property and was injured by a depressed railroad track. D was held liable for the failure to place a light or barrier at the end of street since D could have anticipated that a traveler might accidently come onto D's property and drive over the depressed track, thus injuring himself. See Louisville & Nashville Railroad Co. v. Anderson, 39 F.2d 403 (5th Cir. 1930). See also Downes v. Silva, 57 R.I. 343, 190 A. 42 (1937).

See generally, Gregory, pp. 447–449; Keeton, pp. 406–408; P & W, pp. 481–486.

1. The *liability of an occupier to persons who come onto his land,* centers around three principal classes of persons, which are defined below, and the duty to each:

ANALYSIS OF DUTY

(a) trespassers,

(b) licensees, and

(c) invitees.

   (i) A *trespasser* is one who *comes onto* the *land* of another *without right or permission.*

   (ii) A *licensee* is one who *comes onto* the *land* of another *for his own purposes,* but who comes on *with* the *occupier's consent.* The consent may be expressed or implied by conduct. It includes a *social guest,* one who steps inside a doorway to get out of the rain, one who follows a path for a shortcut, a parent in search of a child, one who comes for information or to borrow books, tools or equipment, or a customer in a store who goes to a non-selling area with the owner's permission after making his purchase to get a box. See Whelan v. Van Natta, 382 S.W.2d 205 (Ky.1964).

   (iii) An *invitee* is one who *comes onto* the *land* of an occupier *at* the *occupier's invitation* under circumstances where a representation may be implied that reasonable care has been exercised to make the premises safe. It includes:

      (1) *business guests,* such as customers of stores even though they have not made a purchase, see Campbell v. Weathers, 153 Kan. 316, 111 P.2d 72 (1941), banks, theaters, filling stations, cleaning establishments, commercial parking lots and amusement centers, cafes,

      (2) *non-business guests* who have been invited by the occupier but involving no pecuniary benefit to the occupier, such as those attending free lectures, movies, amusement centers, swimming pools, parks, libraries, golf courses, and

      (3) others such as a policeman checking a building while making his rounds (Cameron v. Abatiell, 127

Vt. 111, 241 A.2d 310 (1968)), and a guest of a tenant using a common stairway in an apartment house, see Taneian v. Meghrigian, 15 N.J. 267, 104 A.2d 689 (1954).

e.g. P went to a clinic which provided free baby care. While there P fell on some steps which the clinic had permitted persons such as P to use for a number of years. A jury could conclude from D's conduct that the stairs were for the use of P and, therefore, P was an invitee, rather than a licensee, and may recover. The court rejected the older view that D must receive some "economic benefit" for P to be an invitee. See Dowd v. Portsmouth Hospital, 105 N.H. 53, 193 A.2d 788 (1963).

See CHART II, Liability of Occupier of Premises, below.

2. An *occupier* of land *may use reasonable and necessary force to eject a trespasser* from his land; other than that *he is liable for wanton and willful injury of the trespasser,* including setting traps for him, such as spring guns or vicious dogs.

(a) The *trespasser* assumes the risk of the condition of the premises on which he trespasses, and there is no liability on the occupier to him.

(b) The *licensee* assumes the risk of the condition of the premises as to visible dangers, but the occupier owes a duty to the licensee to warn him of known hidden dangers.

(c) As to the *invitee*, the occupier assumes the risk of the condition of the premises, has a duty to use due care in making the premises safe for the invitee's reception, and is liable for his negligence as to such condition.

3. The following outline illustrates the liability of the occupier to trespassers, licensees and invitees.

(a) *liability of occupier of land to trespassers:*

(i) The occupier *owes no duty to* and *is not liable to* an *unperceived, unanticipated trespasser.* He need not look out for him and he need not keep the premises safe for him. A duty not to injure a trespasser only arises after he is discovered. See Sheehan v. St. Paul & Duluth Railway Co., 76 F. 201 (7th Cir. 1896); and CASE 45 below.

(ii) The occupier owes *no duty* of due care *to make the premises safe for* an *anticipated trespasser;* but he does owe a *duty* of due care *to discover* the *anticipated trespasser* and thereafter to treat him as a *perceived* trespasser. See Frederick v. Philadelphia Rapid Transit Co., 337 Pa. 136, 10 A.2d 576 (1940).

(iii) The occupier owes *no duty* of due care *to make the premises safe for* a *perceived trespasser;* but he does owe a *duty not to injure him by active negligent conduct.* The trespasser is not an outlaw, and being discovered, is entitled to the same protection as other persons as to active conduct. See Herrick v. Wixom, 121 Mich. 384, 80 N.W. 117 (1899),

(b) *liability of occupier of land to licensee:*

(i) The occupier is *not liable* to use due care to make the premises safe for the licensee *as to visible dangers.* As to such visible dangers the risk is assumed by the licensee.

(ii) The occupier *owes a duty* of due care *to warn* the *licensee of known concealed dangers* on the premises so that he will not be injured by such as though they were a trap. There is *no duty to make* such known *concealed dangers safe for the licensee.*

CAVEAT—The duty to warn the licensee extends only to dangerous conditions which the owner would not expect the licensee to discover. Where the danger is open and obvious some courts consider that as a factor bearing on the owner's negligence in failing to warn, and as bearing on the contributory negligence or assumption of risk by the licensee, and not as a limitation to the duty of the owner.

(iii) The occupier *owes a duty of due care not to injure the licensee by active negligent conduct.*

(c) *liability of occupier of land to invitee:*

(i) The occupier *owes a duty of due care to the invitee to make* the *premises safe as to visible and known concealed dangers.*

(ii) The occupier owes a duty of due care to the invitee to make the premises safe as to unknown concealed dangers which could be discovered by the exercise of due care.

(iii) The occupier owes a duty of due care to the invitee not to injure him by active negligent conduct.

(iv) The occupier owes a duty to invitees to warn of impending danger, such as the fact that the bank is being robbed. See Sinn v. Farmers' Deposit Savings Bank, 300 Pa. 85, 150 A. 163 (1930).

4. An invitee or a licensee may become a trespasser by going into an area where he has not been invited because he has exceeded the permission given. See CASE 47 below.

5. Where premises are leased, generally only the tenant is liable for breach of the duty of care. The landlord is not liable even

where the condition existed before the lessee took possession unless:

(a) the landlord knew or had reason to know of a concealed dangerous condition, or

(b) the dangerous condition is on part of the premises over which the landlord retained control.

> *e.g.* For common areas, such as hallways or elevators used by all tenants and their visitors, the landlord has the duty to discover and make safe any dangerous condition.

NOTE 1—Where the landlord has agreed to make repairs most courts impose tort liability for failure to repair. Further, statutes in many states also impose a duty on the landlord to repair leased premises. See CASE 48 below.

NOTE 2—The traditional concepts and classifications relating to the liability of owners and occupiers of land are illustrated in CHART II, below. The student must also consider recent court decisions relating to these concepts. See Modern Approach, below.

See generally, Gregory, pp. 449–459; P & W, pp. 487–504.

CHART II

LIABILITY OF OCCUPIER OF PREMISES *

TRESPASSERS

(1) unperceived and unanticipated	—the occupier is not liable for dangerous condition of the premises or for active negligent conduct thereon—trespasser assumes all the risk
(2) anticipated but unperceived	—the occupier is not liable for dangerous condition of the premises but owes duty to discover trespasser and after he is discovered, must treat him as perceived trespasser
(3) perceived	—the occupier is not liable for the dangerous condition of the premises but owes a duty not to injure him by active negligent conduct on the premises

LICENSEES
(Social guests—See Note 1)

(1) visible dangers	—the occupier is not liable
(2) known concealed dangers	—the occupier is not liable for such but must warn the licensee of their existence
(3) active negligent conduct	—the occupier is liable to the licensee for injury due to occupier's active negligent conduct

INVITEES

(1) visible dangers	—the occupier is liable
(2) known concealed dangers	—the occupier is liable
(3) unknown concealed dangers discoverable by use of due care	—the occupier is liable
(4) active negligent conduct	—the occupier is liable

* IN NONE OF THE CASES ABOVE IS THERE LIABILITY UNLESS THE OCCUPIER IS NEGLIGENT

NOTE 1—A social guest is considered a licensee even though the guest has been invited onto the premises. Thus there is no duty to inspect the premises or make them safe for a social guest. This classification has been criticized, but only two states, Louisiana and Michigan, have held a social guest to be an invitee.

NOTE 2—Recent decisions involving active operations conducted on property, such as operating machinery or backing up a truck, impose a duty to exercise reasonable care so as not to injure a possible trespasser, licensee or invitee.

NOTE 3—MODERN VIEW—The categories of trespasser, licensee and invitee are not considered. The duty owed is that of reasonable care depending on the surrounding circumstances, which include how the entry was made. This view has been adopted in only a few jurisdictions.

Duty owed by owner and third persons to trespassers   Case 45

A transmission line of D electric company was damaged by a flood. D made temporary repairs by running a temporary electric line across T's property with T's permission. D did the work negligently which caused a wire fence on T's property to become charged with electricity. P and a companion were hunting and trespassed on T's property. They came into contact with the fence. P was injured and his companion was electrocuted. P sued D for damages and the court directed a verdict for D reasoning that D owed no duty to a trespasser on T's land. Was the ruling correct?

Answer. *No. P was a trespasser and was not owed any duty by T, the landowner. P must accept the land in the condition he finds it, as T had no duty to keep his land safe for trespassers. However, T's defense that no duty is owed to a trespasser is not available to D, whose act of putting the temporary power line across T's property caused the fence to become electrified. Thus if P can show that D was negligent in installing the power lines and this caused the fence to become electrified, P can recover. The case was remanded for a new trial.*

See Humphrey v. Twin State Gas & Electric Co., 100 Vt. 414, 139 A. 440 (1927). See also, Ehret v. Village of Scarsdale, 269 N.Y. 198, 199 N.E. 56 (1935).

Liability of occupier to a licensee   Case 46

D invited P to her home. During the visit P went downstairs for a blanket at D's request. D knew that the steps were defective but

did not warn P of their condition. P fell while using the steps and sued D and her husband for damages. May P recover?

Answer. Yes. P, a social guest, is recognized as a licensee and does not have the rights of an invitee. A licensee comes onto the land for his own purposes and not for the purposes of the occupier of the premises. Hence, the licensee, like the trespasser, assumes the risk of the dangerous condition of the premises. Consequently, in this case had D not known about the dangerous condition of the stairs, D would not have been liable and the loss would have remained on P. However, the occupier, having consented to the licensee's coming onto the land, has a duty to warn the licensee of any concealed dangerous condition on the premises of which the occupier has knowledge. In this case D had such knowledge, and it was a breach of this duty for D to fail to warn P of the danger involved. Thus D is liable for P's injuries. D's husband, who was joined in the suit because he was co-owner, did not know of the dangerous condition of the steps, and he was held not liable.

See Laube v. Stevenson, 137 Conn. 469, 78 A.2d 693 (1951).

NOTE—As a customer of a store P was an invitee. P slipped on ice in the store's parking lot. P knew there was ice and was walking carefully, but slipped nevertheless. The trial directed a verdict for D because of contributory negligence of P in walking where it was known to be slippery. On appeal the court held that if the ice presented an unreasonably dangerous condition D could be liable even though P knew of the ice. That was a question for the jury to determine. The directed verdict for D was reversed and the case was remanded for the jury to determine the factual question presented. See Dawson v. Payless for Drugs, 248 Or. 334, 433 P.2d 1019 (1967).

Case 47 *Change in status from invitee to trespasser negates liability*

D was the owner and operator of a feed grinding plant. He was chairman of a committee of his college alumni group. He called the members of his committee consisting of P and X, and invited them to meet with him at his office in his plant for the purpose of preparing a program for the alumni group. P arrived in D's office about 15 minutes before time for the meeting. D's clerk invited P to have a chair in the office and wait for D who was "somewhere in the plant". P had never been in D's place of business before. Without anything more being said, P opened a door which lead from D's office into the main part of the plant where D's feed grinding operations were being carried on. The floor in that part of the plant consisted of loose planks laid on crossbeams below. P stepped on the edge of one of these planks. The plank turned over and P's foot became caught in a turning grain auger which was under the plank and P was injured. P sues D. May he recover?

Answer. *No. The first question to be determined is the status of P on D's premises. An invitee is one who comes onto the premises for some purpose of the occupier. But the general rule includes not only those persons from whom the occupier expects some pecuniary benefit to follow, but includes also other persons who are "invited" to the premises by the occupier but from whom no pecuniary benefit is contemplated, such as those who are invited to attend free lectures, swimming pools, parks, amusement centers or golf courses. Either the "invitation" or the "expectation of pecuniary benefit" may be considered as for the occupier's purpose, under this general rule. Following such concept in this case D's invitation to P to attend the committee meeting would make P an invitee "at his (D's) office in the plant". Consequently, had P been injured while he was in D's office, P could have claimed all the rights of an invitee. He could then have recovered had he shown that D was negligent as to either: (a) visible danger, or (b) concealed danger known to D, or (c) concealed danger unknown to D but which could have been discovered by D in the exercise of due care. Of course, P, being an adult, would be bound by any contributory negligence or, had he known about the dangerous condition, he would not be permitted to recover. But P was not injured in D's office, the part of the occupier's premises to which he was invited. He was injured in a part of the premises to which he was not invited. In the main part of D's plant where the injury occurred, P was not only not invited, he was not even encouraged to enter. The clerk had asked P to be seated in the office and to wait there for D. Hence, P could not even claim to be a licensee in that part of the plant where he was injured. The liability of the occupier of the premises is only coextensive with his invitation. Therefore, P could claim the protection due to an invitee only while he was in the office of D. As to the place in the plant where P was actually injured, P must be considered as a trespasser and as such, he assumed all the risk of the condition of the premises. The condition of the premises under the plank may be considered one of such risks. Furthermore, even if it should be considered that the moving auger under the plank were active conduct on the part of D, still P could be no more than an unanticipated, unperceived trespasser, for which active conduct, D is not liable to P. Hence, because P was not an invitee but a trespasser in the place where he was injured, and because as such trespasser, D owed no duty to P, there can be no recovery by P.*

See Guilford v. Yale University, 128 Conn. 449, 23 A.2d 917 (1942); Lerman Bros. v. Lewis, 277 Ky. 334, 126 S.W.2d 461 (1939).

Case 48   *Duty of landlord to repair*

P agreed to lease a house owned by D. At that time the back porch needed to be repaired where the top step joined the porch. D agreed to make the necessary repairs or furnish materials for P to do it when the lease was signed. P took possession and D subsequently repeated his promise, but D did nothing to keep his promise. P fell and injured herself and sued for damages. D moved to dismiss on the grounds that he did not have the duty to repair the premises. D's motion was granted and P appealed. Was the ruling on D's motion correct?

Answer. No. A lessor of land is liable for injuries to his lessee, and others on the land with the consent of the lessee, which are caused by the disrepair of the leased premises if: (a) the lessor has contracted to keep the premises in repair, (b) the disrepair creates an unreasonable risk, and (c) the lessor fails to exercise reasonable care to perform his contract. The reason for the rule is to protect tenants who are likely to be impecunious and unable to make the repairs, to recognize the special relationship between a landlord and tenant, and to require the landlord to take reasonable care of his property to keep the premises safe. The court concluded that P stated a cause of action because of his agreement with D and the case was remanded for trial. Since the court was ruling on a motion to dismiss it did not consider any possible contributory negligence by P.

See Reitmeyer v. Sprecher, 431 Pa. 284, 243 A.2d 395 (1968).

NOTE—The rule in CASE 48 above is contained in the Restatement, Second, Torts § 357. It has been adopted in a slight majority of jurisdictions and reflects the trend of decisions. See Prosser, pp. 408–412.

ATTRACTIVE NUISANCE

1. Children are treated differently from adults when they trespass onto land. They are given greater protection because:

    (a) they are immature and lacking in judgment to appreciate possible dangers, and

    (b) public policy favors the safety and welfare of children.

2. The special protection afforded children when they trespass is known as the attractive nuisance doctrine.

3. The occupier of land is liable to trespassing children under the "attractive nuisance" doctrine in most states, if four requirements are met.

    (a) A trespass by children on the premises must be reasonably foreseen by the occupier. See Goll v. Muscara, 211 Pa. Super. 93, 235 A.2d 443 (1967).

(b) The condition of the premises must be artificial, not natural, and such that the occupier would recognize as being reasonably dangerous to a child.

(c) The child would not recognize the condition as dangerous. This is a factual question for the jury. However, if a child is 14 years or older this doctrine will seldom apply.

(d) The usefulness to the occupier of maintaining the condition must be slight compared to the risk of injury to the child.

See Keffe v. Milwaukee & St. Paul Railway Co., 21 Minn. 207, 18 Am.Rep. 393 (1875); King v. Lennen, 53 Cal.2d 340, 1 Cal.Rptr. 665, 348 P.2d 98 (1959); Harrison v. City of Chicago, 308 Ill.App. 263, 31 N.E.2d 359 (1941); Restatement, Second, Torts § 339; and CASE 41, above.

4. A few jurisdictions have rejected the doctrine of attractive nuisance as based on sympathy rather than law or logic. See Bottum's Administrator v. Hawks, 84 Vt. 370, 79 A. 858 (1911).

5. When a child is old enough to comprehend the risk, the defenses of contributory negligence and assumption of the risk are available to the defendant. See Parzych v. Town of Branford, 20 Conn.Supp. 378, 136 A.2d 223 (1957)—two fifteen year old boys denied recovery from exploding gunpowder found in defendant's building.

See generally, Gregory, pp. 459–466; Keeton, pp. 418–423; P & W, pp. 510–515; Prosser, pp. 364–376.

Application of attractive nuisance doctrine   **Case 49**

P, age 7, went onto D's golf course with other boys to play. A golfer hit P with a golf ball and injured him. Children were permitted on the golf course during the winter months to play, but they were not permitted during golfing season. However, D knew that children often trespassed on the course. P sued D for damages claiming that D maintained an attractive nuisance which resulted in an injury to P. D contended that P was a trespasser and, therefore, D did not owe any duty of care to P. The jury found for P, but the judge granted D's motion for judgment notwithstanding the verdict. Was the trial court correct in granting D's motion?

Answer. No. D is liable under the attractive nuisance doctrine, which requires that four conditions be met: (a) There must be a trespass by children which was reasonably foreseen by the occupier. D knew that children played on the course by going through holes in the fence which surrounded the course, or, by climbing over the fence. (b) The dangerous condition of the premises must be artificial, as distinguished from natural, and the occupier must recognize the condition as dangerous to children. D was aware of the speed golf balls travel, the force with which they can hit someone, and the fact that a golfer might hit a ball almost anywhere. (c) The condition must be such that a child would not recognize it as dangerous. Here P, a child of seven, would not recognize the danger of being hit with a golf ball while playing on the course. (d) The usefulness to the occupier in maintaining the condition must be slight compared to the risk of injury to the child. Operating a golf course is a legitimate business activity, but D had the obligation to use reasonable care to prevent children from trespassing. The fact that D posted "No Trespassing" signs was not adequate. The fence around the course should have been kept in repair to prevent children from coming onto the course so easily. The danger of injury was substantial and the care required to prevent it was small. Children are too valuable to society to permit a landowner to escape liability when the conditions requisite to the application of the "attractive nuisance" doctrine are met. Therefore, the case was remanded to the trial court with directions to enter judgment in P's favor in accordance with the jury's verdict.

See Lyshak v. City of Detroit, 351 Mich. 230, 88 N.W.2d 596 (1958).

MODERN CONCEPT OF DUTY

1. It has been suggested by legal scholars and some courts that the mechanical or traditional approach to the liability of owners and occupiers of land be replaced by the test of ordinary negligence. One legal writer urges that "as in all other negligence cases, duty should be determined by balancing the foreseeable risk of harm generated by the landowner . . . against the expense and inconvenience of avoiding it." See Bloustein, "Torts," 1964 Annual Survey American Law 429, 430 and illustrative cases depicting absurdity of the traditional approach.

   e.g. A policeman injured by a fall into unguarded excavation on church property during robbery investigation was held to be licensee and recovery denied. Scheurer v. Trustees of Open Bible Church, 175 Ohio St. 163, 192 N.E.2d 38 (1963). Cases depicting the modern approach: Gould v. De Beve, 330 F.2d 826 (D.C.Cir.1964)—owners of housing development liable for injury to two year old trespassing boy who fell out of window due to faulty screen (plaintiff well within range of foreseeability); Crutchfield v. Adams, 152 So.2d 808 (Fla.1963)—three year old neighbor, injured by unguarded fan belt on pump machinery on defendant's land, granted recovery.

2. A recent California case, CASE 50, below, dispensed with the "magical" significance of the status of the injured party. It held that the land possessor's liability turns on several key factors, or negligence including:

   (a) the closeness of the connection between the injury and the conduct,

(b)   the moral blame attached to the conduct,

(c)   the policy of preventing future harm, and

(d)   the prevalence and availability of insurance.

3.   The factors in number 2, above, bear very little relationship to the traditional trilogy of trespasser, licensee and invitee. In effect, the court held that the proper test is whether, in the management of his property, the possessor of land acted as a reasonable person in view of the possibility of injury to others. See CASE 50, below.

See generally, Gregory, pp. 474–485; Keeton, pp. 408–417; P & W, pp. 517–522.

Modern concept of duty rejects common law classifications   **Case 50**

P was a social guest in D's apartment. While P was in the bathroom P tried to use the water faucet and it broke, severing tendons and nerves on his hand. D knew that the faucet was cracked and had previously complained to the manager of the building about it. However, D did not warn P of the condition of the faucet. P brought a civil action against D for his injuries. D moved for summary judgment. The judge concluded that P, as a social guest, was a licensee and under applicable state law should be obliged to take the premises as his hostess found them or permitted them to be. [Under the general rule an owner must warn a licensee of known concealed dangers which the licensee would not discover.] D's motion was granted and P appealed. Should D's duty to P depend on P's status as a trespasser, licensee or invitee?

Answer. No. Over the years much confusion has developed concerning the application of the common law principles governing the liability of the owner or possessor of land. This is the result of attempting to use old rules in our modern society. The common law classifications often do not reflect factors which should determine liability. Those factors include: "the closeness of the connection between the injury and the defendant's conduct, the moral blame attached to the defendant's conduct, the policy of preventing future harm, and the prevalence and availability of insurance." The United States Supreme Court has refused to apply the common law classifications in an admiralty case, and England has changed its common law by statute. Therefore, the proper test to determine liability is whether the owner or possessor of land has acted as a reasonable person in view of the probability of injury to others. Although the injured person's status as a trespasser, licensee or invitee may have some bearing on liability because of the facts which give rise to that status, such status is not determinative.

Applying that rule to the present case the court reasoned: D knew the faucet handle was defective and dangerous; the defect *was not obvious; D knew that P was about to come into contact with the defective faucet; and D did not warn P. Therefore, the trier of fact may reasonably conclude that the failure to warn constituted negligence and D's motion for summary judgment should be denied.*

See Rowland v. Christian, 69 Cal.2d 108, 70 Cal.Rptr. 97, 443 P.2d 561 (1968).

NOTE 1—California was the first state to discard the common law classifications of persons entering land and impose a general duty of reasonable care. A few states, including New York, have followed the California decision and adopted the modern approach. However, this is still the minority rule. See Basso v. Miller, 40 N.Y. 2d 233, 386 N.Y.S.2d 564, 352 N.E.2d 868 (1976).

NOTE 2—Courts which have adopted the modern approach are divided as to whether to include trespassers under the new rule or to continue to apply the common law standard of care to trespassers.

VI LIABILITY WITHOUT FAULT

Summary Outline

A. Introduction

B. Injury from Animals

C. Abnormal Activities

D. Defenses

INTRODUCTION

1. Liability without fault, the third basic category of tort liability, is a liability imposed by law on a person even though there has been no:

    (a) negligent act, or

    (b) wanton, willful or intentional wrong doing.

2. Liability without fault is sometimes called "strict liability", "absolute liability", or preventing damage "at one's peril".

3. Such liability has been imposed on two groups of persons:

    (a) owners or possessors of animals, for damage done by the animals, and

    (b) those who either maintain conditions or engage in activities which are abnormally dangerous to the general safety.

    CAVEAT—The student must not confuse strict liability with absolute liability. Absolute liability would impose liability for any harm caused by the dangerous animal or activity. Strict liability allows a defendant to assert some defenses even though the plaintiff is not required to show negligence. See CHART III and Defenses, below.

4. The concept of "fault", in "liability without fault", carries with it no meaning of moral wrong. The idea is that really neither party is "to blame", but in balancing the social equities, and determining who can best bear the loss, the loss has been shifted, by law, from plaintiff to the defendant. "The courts have tended to lay stress upon the fact that the defendant is acting for his own purposes, and is seeking a benefit or a profit of his own from such activities, and that he is in a better position to administer the unusual risk by passing it on to the public than is the innocent victim." Prosser, p. 495.

5. The reason for imposing liability without fault on the owners or possessors of animals is that such persons have control of such animals and can prevent their doing damage.

6. The reason for imposing liability without fault on one who maintains dangerous conditions or engages in extrahazardous activities (usually a business involving a threat of serious injury to persons in the immediate neighborhood) is that such person should bear the entire burden of his undertaking. He is the one who is in a position best able to bear it, usually by shifting the burden onto the public by an increase of the price of his product, or service or by carrying liability insurance.

INJURY FROM ANIMALS

1. Animals may be classified in three groups:

    (a) those which are considered safe and threaten no harm to human beings, such as: rabbits and canaries,

(b) domesticated animals which are considered safe, in the absence of knowledge or notice of some dangerous propensity for injuring human beings, such as: cattle, horses, sheep, goats, hogs, mules, burros, dogs and cats, and

(c) wild animals, which are considered by nature dangerous to human beings such as: lions, tigers, elephants, leopards, wolves, hyenas, bears, monkeys, and zebras.

2. Liability without fault is imposed in three types of animal cases.

(a) The owner or possessor of hard-hoofed domesticated animals is strictly liable for their *trespasses*, including both damage to the land and such other damage which might reasonably be expected to accompany such trespass.

e.g. D's bull trespasses on P's land and gores P's bull. D is liable both for injury to P's land and for the injury to P's bull. See Noyes v. Colby, 30 N.H. 143 (1855).

NOTE—Many Western States rejected this rule as contrary to local custom and the needs of the people. Thus where D's cattle wandered onto P's uninclosed land and caused damage, no liability was imposed on D in the absence of a showing of negligence. See Wagner v. Bissell, 3 Iowa 396 (1856).

(b) The owner or possessor of domesticated animals which are known to have propensities dangerous to mankind, whether those propensities be vicious or playful, is strictly liable for injury done by his animals by the exercise of such dangerous propensities on a human being. A trespass is not necessary to impose liability.

e.g. D's huge dog is playful and has a propensity for greeting his friends by standing on his hind feet and putting his front feet against the person's shoulders. D knows this. D and his dog are walking along the street and meet P, an old lady. D's dog gives P his usual friendly greeting and knocks P to the pavement, breaking her hip bone. D is liable to P even though he was neither negligent nor guilty of intentional wrong.

(c) The owner or possessor of a wild animal which is considered by nature dangerous to mankind, is strictly liable for any injury the animal does.

e.g. D's tiger gets loose through no fault of D, and claws P and kills P's cow and dog. D is absolutely liable to P for P's injury and for the destruction of P's cow and dog.

NOTE—One court considered the constitutional question presented by laws prescribing a different duty of care for different animals. A state law made the owners of dogs strictly liable for any injury caused by their dogs. Owners of livestock were required to keep livestock fenced off of public highways, but proof of negligence was necessary to find liability. The court held that the Equal Protection Clause of the Fourteenth Amendment was violated only when the classification of animals establishing the owner's duty was arbitrary and unreasonable. Here the statute which imposed different liability for domestic animals and livestock was a reasonable exercise of the police power of the state, and therefore, constitutional. Imposing strict liability in addition to fencing and other regulations on the owners of livestock would place a great burden on the livestock industry. Further, there are no comparable controls on dogs such as a statewide leash law. Thus a state may prescribe by statute different standards of care for different animals when it has a valid purpose, such as promoting an important industry in the state. See Selby v. Bullock, 287 So.2d 18 (Fla.1973).

3. Liability without fault is NOT imposed in three types of animal cases.

   (a) The owner or possessor of an animal considered always harmless is not liable for damage done by it, at least in the absence of negligence.

   e.g. D's canary flies into P's eye, or D's rabbit scratches P. D is not liable to P unless in some way he was negligent.

   (b) The owner or possessor of a domesticated animal is not liable for damage done by it, apart from trespass, unless the owner has knowledge or notice of the dangerous propensity (scienter) or there is negligence. See CASE 53, below.

   e.g. D gives P permission as a licensee to cross D's pasture and fish in the river flowing through D's land. While P is crossing D's pasture D's bull attacks and seriously injures P. The bull had never attacked a human being before and no facts could have given D notice that the bull might do such a thing. D is not liable to P.

   (c) An owner or possessor of domesticated animals which are being driven along a highway is not liable for damage caused by such animals trespassing upon property abutting the highway unless there is negligence. See Restatement, Second, Torts § 504(3).

   e.g. D is driving a herd of cattle along the highway when, without any notice to D or negligence on D's part, D's bull breaks away from the herd and plunges through the door of P's china shop abutting the highway and does considerable damage therein before he is driven out. In the absence of negligence, D is not liable to P for the damage done by the bull. This is an exception to the general rule that the owner or possessor of domesticated animals is strictly liable for the damage they do while trespassing. The reason seems to be the social interest in having such animals driven along the highway, or that the abutting landowners assume the risk of such damage when there is no negligence. See Tillett v. Ward, 10 Q.B.D. 17 (1882).

NOTE—Prosser states that today D might be held liable in a large city even if his conduct were not prohibited by a city ordinance, because the concept of what constitutes negligence can be different in a densely populated area as contrasted to sparsely populated rural areas. See Prosser, p. 498.

See generally, Gregory, pp. 488–495; Keeton, pp. 573–578; P & W, pp. 705–709; Prosser, pp. 496–503.

Strict liability for owners of wild animals Case 51

P was a child, age two years, seven months, when his father took him to D's monkey farm. After paying admission they purchased food to feed the animals which was encouraged by D. While P was feeding a chimpanzee, it grabbed his arm and injured him. Suit was brought on P's behalf for damages based on strict liability. D contended that liability should depend on negligence, that is, D should only be liable if he breached the duty of care reasonably required considering the nature and species of animal involved. May P recover?

Answer. *Yes. The court held that the general rule imposing strict liability for owners and keepers of wild animals should be adopted in the fast growing, populous and activity-oriented society of Florida. The risk of injury in such situations should not be placed on the community, but on the owner of the wild animal. Therefore, strict responsibility was placed upon those who, even with proper care, expose persons to the risk of a dangerous animal. P may recover because strict liability was imposed on D.*

See Isaacs v. Powell, 267 So.2d 864 (Fla.App.1972).

Strict liability—vicious propensities of dogs Case 52

P was a guest at a hotel. D, the owner of the hotel kept a dog there. P leaned over to pet the dog and it bit him. The dog had never bitten anyone before, but the dog had growled at people and D who kept the dog on a leash had told guests, "you would never know when a dog will turn on you." P sued for damages and received the jury's verdict. D appealed. Is P entitled to damages?

Answer. *Yes. The court stated the common law rule that "one who keeps a domestic animal which he has reason to know has vicious propensities abnormal to its class is liable for the harm the animal causes to others. . . . This liability is not based on negligence; it is applicable regardless of the care taken to guard*

CHART III

LIABILITY OF OWNER OR POSSESSOR OF ANIMAL FOR DAMAGE DONE BY THE ANIMAL

CATEGORY OF ANIMAL	COMMON LAW LIABILITY	STATUTORY LIABILITY
1. Animals Naturally Harmless (canaries, parrots, rabbits)	no liability unless negligence	no liability unless negligence
2. Domesticated Animals (cattle, horses, hogs, sheep, goats, mules, burros, cats and dogs) — A. trespassing	strict liability is general rule except no liability for trespassing of cats and dogs except no liability for damage done by animals being driven along highway for trespass on property abutting highway, unless negligence	strict liability often imposed as country became more settled except no liability in states wanting to encourage business in cattle, hogs, sheep and goats unless negligence
B. not trespassing	no liability is general rule, unless negligence strict liability if there is scienter, which is knowledge of vicious propensities	strict liability for dogs and cats often imposed by statute unless to a trespasser or tortfeasor
3. Wild Animals Naturally Dangerous to Mankind (lions, tigers, elephants, leopards, wolves, hyenas, bears, monkeys, zebras)	strict liability for damage done	strict liability for damage done

Note—Whether an animal is domesticated or wild is a question of time and place. Thus an elephant is a domesticated animal in India, but a wild animal in the United States. A dog was once wild, but is now domesticated.

against harm." P comes within the protection of the rule since he was a business visitor on D's premises. "The notion that a dog is entitled to one bite before it becomes a source of liability to its owner has been repudiated in Pennsylvania. . . . It is enough that facts are shown from which the vicious propensities may be found." Here there was sufficient evidence for the jury to conclude that D was aware of the dangerous propensities of his dog and therefore, the jury verdict in P's favor should stand.

See Zarek v. Fredericks, 138 F.2d 689 (3d Cir. 1943). See also Restatement, Torts § 518.

NOTE—The case above should emphasize that the old adage "every dog is entitled to at least his first bite" is not true. Many states have statutes imposing absolute liability on an owner or possessor of a dog for all damage done by it, and without scienter on the part of the owner or possessor.

e.g. Ohio Revised Code § 955.28, provides that "The owner or keeper shall be liable for any damage or injuries caused by a dog unless such damage or injury was to the body or property of a person who, at the time such damage or injuries were sustained, was committing a trespass on the property of the owner, or was teasing, tormenting, or abusing such dog on the owner's property". Under this statute, only nominal and/or compensatory damages may be recovered; however, the common law action still exists under which punitive damages may be awarded upon a showing of known vicious propensities. Plaintiff has the option of suing under the statute or pursuing the common law remedy.

Domesticated animals—liability of owners   **Case 53**

D was the owner of a cat which followed its natural bent for killing and eating birds. The cat climbed over a high fence into the pigeon roosts of P's valuable pigeons and killed 25 of P's choicest birds. P sues D for the trespass and for the destruction of his birds. D demurred to the complaint. How should the court rule on the demurrer?

Answer. *The demurrer should be sustained. At common law the owner of a cat was not liable for any damage done by its trespassing or by its following its natural bent for the reason that the damage it may do is usually trivial and no protection is needed against its depredations. Hence D is not liable for the actions of his cat in following its natural instincts.*

See Buckle v. Holmes, 2 K.B. 125, 54 A.L.R. 89 (1926).

NOTE—An owner or possessor of a dog, knowing of its propensities for attacking and biting human beings, is held strictly liable for an injury caused by the dog when following that particular trait. Thus domesticated animals are placed in the same category as wild animals where the owner knows or should know of their vicious trait. See Baker v. Snell, 2 K.B. 825 (1908).

Case 54 *Domesticated animals with vicious propensities—strict liability*

P and D owned neighboring farms. After P had fed hogs on his farm he saw a hog (a boar) which belonged to D. D's hog was standing nearby, but it did not move. It had escaped from D's farm previously and attacked P, forcing him to seek safety in his out-house. P went into his house. Later P went outside and looked for D's hog, but did not see it. As P was walking on his own property to his car, the boar attacked P and injured him. May P recover for his personal injuries from D?

Answer. Yes. The court held that where the owner of a domesticated animal knows or should have known of its vicious propensities, the owner is strictly liable. The jury found that D should have known of the boar's vicious propensities, although D did not have actual knowledge. Therefore, D is strictly liable for P's injuries. Even if P were negligent in failing to discover the boar, P's contributory negligence was no defense because his claim was based on strict liability. D contended that even if strict liability was imposed, P assumed the risk by leaving his house with the knowledge that the dangerous boar was somewhere on his farm, and therefore, P should not recover. However, assumption of the risk is not applicable in the present case. P did not voluntarily assume the risk because he did not have a free choice of alternatives. P only had a choice which D wrongfully imposed on him. P could remain inside of his house and surrender his right to walk over his property to his car, or P could leave his house at the risk of not reaching his car before D's hog attacked him. P's choice involved the exercise of a right of which D could not deprive him. Therefore, P did not voluntarily assume the risk.

See Marshall v. Ranne, 511 S.W.2d 255 (Tex.1974).

NOTE—There is strict liability for trespass by livestock for harm to land, its possessor, or a member of the possessor's family where such harm might be reasonably expected. The Restatement takes no position regarding liability to employees of the possessor. See Restatement, Second, Torts § 504(1) and (2).

ABNORMAL ACTIVITIES
1. Strict liability is the imposition of liability without requiring a showing of fault or negligence. It is applied where ultrahazardous or abnormally dangerous activity is conducted.

   e.g. P owned a garage where an automobile was kept for repair. D was blasting on property 125 feet away to construct a tunnel. D set off dynamite which damaged P's garage and the car inside by shock waves. P sought to recover damages based on strict liability. D contended that P could not recover unless negligence were shown. The court held that "one who engages in blasting must assume responsibility, and be liable without fault, for any injury he causes to neighboring property." That is the rule followed in almost all jurisdictions. Every person is entitled to the undisturbed possession and lawful enjoyment of her own property. Of course the mode of enjoyment may be limited by the rights of others. In the present case P had the right to undisturbed possession, and D had the right to build the tunnel, which was a lawful use of D's property. Where these rights conflict, P must prevail. Otherwise D could deprive P of all beneficial use of his property unless D were negligent. There is no need to show a physical trespass for P to recover where strict liability applies. The court noted that P was not seeking to prevent D from blasting, but merely sought damages caused by D's activities. P may recover damages without proof of D's negligence. See Spano v. Perini Corp., 25 N.Y.2d 11, 302 N.Y.S.2d 527, 250 N.E.2d 31 (1969).

2. Rylands v. Fletcher, CASE 55, below, is the leading case involving the doctrine of liability without fault for abnormally dangerous conditions and activities on land. In that case the doctrine was applied for non-natural use of land (maintaining a reservoir) which was likely to cause substantial harm to others (by flooding) even without negligence.

    e.g. The rule is commonly applied to blasting activities and to the manufacture or storage of explosives.

    CAVEAT—Where strict liability is imposed, the abnormally dangerous activity must be the proximate cause of the harm.

3. Nearly all states recognize and impose liability without fault for abnormally dangerous activities or conditions, either by express approval of the rule in Rylands v. Fletcher or under the term "nuisance."

    NOTE—There is a tendency to misuse the term "nuisance." In many jurisdictions the "Rule of Rylands v. Fletcher" is imposed under the name of "nuisance." See, Prosser, p. 512. In fact, nuisance is not a single tort, but rather a field of tort liability in which the interest in the use and enjoyment of land may be invaded by any one of several types of conduct: intentional and unreasonable conduct; or negligent, reckless, or ultrahazardous conduct. The Rule referred to here is based solely on ultrahazardous activity. See Chapter XIII, Nuisance, below.

4. The doctrine of such strict liability is applied if the following elements are present:

    (a) The occupier of land must either:

        (i) maintain a thing or condition on the land, or

        (ii) engage in an activity on the land.

(b) The use of the land for the thing, condition or activity must be "non-natural", "exceptional", "abnormal" or "extraordinary". These terms all mean the same thing.

(c) The maintenance of the thing or condition, or the activity engaged in, must threaten serious injury to others both because:

(i) it is in its nature inherently dangerous, and

(ii) it is located in a place where it threatens serious danger to others.

(d) The thing, condition or activity must cause damage. See Restatement, Second, Torts §§ 519–520.

5. The "thing" or "condition" maintained, should be distinguished from the "activity egaged in".

(a) The "thing" may be a lion, or a known vicious bull.

(b) The "condition" may be a huge tank of gasoline, a magazine of stored nitroglycerine, a powder factory, or a large reservoir of water.

(c) The "activity engaged in" may be blasting with dynamite, operating a powder plant or manufacturing highly explosive chemicals.

NOTE—These activities are highly dangerous and require exercise of great care.

6. The *location* of the thing, condition or activity is important.

(a) A lion in a circus tent is a far greater threat of harm than the same lion in a well constructed zoo.

(b) A 50,000 gallon tank of gasoline in a residential neighborhood is quite a different threat to safety than one 5 miles from the closest dwelling.

(c) Operating a powder factory or blasting with dynamite on the edge of a town or city is a threat to human safety, while, by contrast, doing the same things in the mountains or on the desert 25 miles from any human habitation or highway, would involve comparative safety.

7. It is common, usual, natural or normal to do some things on land, whereas it is unnatural, non-natural, exceptional, abnormal or extraordinary to do other things on the land.

(a) It is natural for one to maintain cows, pigs and chickens on his land, but quite unnatural to maintain an elephant or a known vicious dog thereon.

(b) It is natural to maintain a 1000 gallon tank of gasoline buried 6 feet deep in the ground at a filling station, but quite extraordinary to maintain a 20,000 gallon tank of gasoline above the surface on the same premises.

(c) It is natural to operate a powder plant on a section of land 20 miles from any human habitation, but quite non-natural to operate such a plant in the residential district of a city.

8. There are sound reasons for imposing such strict liability.

(a) There is always an extraordinary threat to the general safety from such conduct, and he who creates such threat should bear the entire burden for harm done.

(b) The mere requirement of the exercise of due care does not adequately protect the members of society from such unusual hazards; even utmost care does not remove threat of harm.

(c) The maintainer of such things and conditions on his land or the actor in such hazardous activities, is in a better position than anyone else to bear the burdens of injury, either by insurance, or by increasing the price of his product and shifting the loss to the public at large.

See generally, Gregory, pp. 495–514; Keeton, pp. 579–595; P & W, pp. 709–726; Prosser, pp. 505–516.

Absolute liability for ultrahazardous activity   **Case 55**

D built a large reservoir of earth and filled it with water in an area where there were many underground mining operations. He maintained the reservoir for some time before a leak therein was discovered. The water from the reservoir was percolating into P's underground shaft in which he was operating a mine. There was no negligence on the part of D in maintaining his reservoir for milling purposes. P sued D for damages without alleging negligence on D's part. D demurred to the complaint setting forth these facts. How should the court rule on the demurrer?

Answer. The demurrer should be overruled. The complaint states a cause of action or claim against D based on liability without fault. This is substantially the fact situation involved in Rylands v. Fletcher. All the elements to support strict liability exist in these facts: (1) D, the occupier of land, maintained a condition on the land in the form of stored water in a reservoir. (2) The use of the land for such purpose was extraordinary or unnatural. (3) The maintenance of the water in the reservoir threatened serious harm to others for two reasons. (a) Water is of such a nature that it is always on the move seeking to follow the force of gravity and reach a lower level. It is inherently dangerous and needs restraint. When it is stored in large quantities it may create a danger to others by flooding. (b) The water in this reservoir was on the surface, in an area where there were many mining operations below ground. Even with the utmost care the moving water was always a threat of serious harm to others who were working at a level below *that of the maintained stored water. (4) The maintenance of the water in the reservoir caused damage to the plaintiff in his mine. Therefore, D is liable to P for the injury suffered and the complaint states a cause of action. The demurrer should be overruled.*

See Rylands v. Fletcher, L.R. 3 H.L. 330 (1868).

NOTE 1—The landmark case of Rylands v. Fletcher has been followed in most states. It has been applied to gasoline stored in a rural community near a well, Yommer v. McKenzie, 255 Md. 220, 257 A.2d 138 (1969), and the use of hydrocyanic acid gas to fumigate a building, Luthringer v. Moore, 31 Cal.2d 489, 190 P.2d 1 (1948). The doctrine is not applied if the use of the land is natural or not dangerous, such as using a bulldozer to grade a hillside, Beck v. Bel Air Properties, 134 Cal.App.2d 834, 286 P.2d 503 (1955).

NOTE 2—A few states reject the doctrine because of the needs of people in those states.

e.g. D, while operating oil wells, stored salt water from the operations in large artificial pools and as a result polluted natural water holes six miles away from which P obtained water. The jury found that D was not negligent in maintaining the artificial pools. The Texas court held that D was not liable in the absence of evidence of negligence. The court reasoned that while the artificial storage of the water in England may be unnatural, in an arid state such as Texas it is not uncommon. Therefore, there is no liability without negligence in the storage of water in Texas. See Turner v. Big Lake Oil Co., 128 Tex. 155, 96 S.W.2d 221 (1936); Railroad Commission of Texas v. Manziel, 361 S.W.2d 560 (Tex.1962).

Case 56   *Absolute liability for blasting*

D was enlarging a river channel and this activity required much blasting with dynamite. P owned a hotel as close as 230 feet to some of the blasting. Vibrations from the blasting caused many water and heating pipes in the hotel to break, plaster was cracked and floor tile was split. Without alleging negligence P sued for the damage to his hotel described above. May he recover?

Answer. *Yes. This case involves not merely a thing or condition maintained on the land, but affirmative conduct or activity on the land which is highly dangerous and creates a serious threat to others around the area of activity. Within the sphere of such threatened danger the actor is absolutely liable for any harm which is caused by his affirmative conduct. This blasting case is a typical case for the application of the doctrine of liability without fault. (1) D has engaged in affirmative activity on his land. (2) Such activity on the land is abnormal and extraordinary. (3) Blasting is in itself inherently dangerous to others. (4) The blasting caused damage within the area of danger, that is, vibrations from the blasting* *damaged P's nearby hotel. For all these injuries D is strictly liable to P, the damage including that which was caused by concussion and the vibration of the earth. In such a case negligence or lack of it is immaterial. Indeed, in such cases all the care and caution it is possible for an actor to exercise, will usually not prevent injury.*

See Whitman Hotel Corp. v. Elliott & Watrous Engineering Co., 137 Conn. 562, 79 A.2d 591 (1951).

DEFENSES

1. In contrast to a negligence action *contributory negligence* is *not a defense* to an action based on strict liability.

   e.g. P turned his horses out to pasture on D's land. When P went to feed his horses, D's horse kicked and injured him. P sued D for damages claiming that D knew his horse had vicious propensities and he is, therefore, strictly liable. D defended by claiming that P was contributorily negligent. The court held that unless P voluntarily assumed the risk by placing himself in a position to be injured, knowing the probable consequences of his act, D is liable. Therefore, P recovered. See Sandy v. Bushey, 124 Me. 320, 128 A. 513 (1925). See also Fraser-Patterson Lumber Co. v. Southern Railway Co., 79 F.Supp. 424 (1948) where a statute imposed strict liability and the court held that contributory negligence was no defense.

2. As in a negligence action *assumption of risk generally* constitutes *a defense* to strict liability. See Prosser, p. 523.

   e.g. D blasts on his own land showering P's building with rocks. P, hearing on the rocks hit against his building negligently sticks his head out the window to see what is happening. D cannot set up contributory negligence as a defense. But suppose P knows what is going on, and that there is about to be another blast accompanied by another hail of rocks. P again puts his head out the window and his head is severely injured by the flying fragments. P's conduct may constitute an assumption of risk on P's part which will be a good defense to D.

3. An *Act of God* intervening in the maintaining of a dangerous condition on the land and the injury constitutes *a defense*.

   e.g. P sued D for damages alleging that D negligently maintained a dyke in connection with the operation of its hydroelectric plant and this resulted in damage to P's land when a hurricane caused the river to overflow. D defended by arguing that the hurricane was an act of God which D had no reason to anticipate. The defense was held valid and D was not liable. See Golden v. Amory, 329 Mass. 484, 109 N.E.2d 131 (1952).

   NOTE—An Act of God is an act of a force of nature which could not have been escaped from by any amount of foresight or reasonable degree of care, such as unprecedented flooding. Some states do not recognize an Act of God as a defense.

4. The *act of a third person* intervening in the maintaining of a dangerous condition on the land and the injury may constitute *a defense.*

    e.g. The noise and vibrations from D's blasting frightened a mother mink on P's mink farm and she killed a large number of her "kittens." P sued D for the value of the "kittens" claiming that D was strictly liable. D is not liable because the intervening act of the mink broke the chain of causation. The mother did not act to save herself. Her act was a peculiarity of disposition of the species and was not to be anticipated by D. See Madsen v. East Jordan Irrigation Co., 101 Utah 552, 125 P.2d 794 (1942); Foster v. Preston Mill Co., 44 Wash.2d 440, 268 P.2d 645 (1954).

    NOTE—As to defenses to strict liability in Products Liability cases see Chapter VII, Defenses, below.

    See generally, Gregory, pp. 514–517; P & W, pp. 729–736; Prosser, pp. 517–525.

VII PRODUCTS LIABILITY

Summary Outline

INTRODUCTION

INTRODUCTORY NOTE—Products liability is the general term used to describe the law governing the responsibility of manufacturers, wholesalers and retail sellers for harm caused by their goods or products to persons with whom they are not in privity of contract. The principles of products liability do not apply when the product sold fails to perform properly and there is only an economic loss to the buyer as opposed to personal injury. Damages for breach of the contract of sale is the usual remedy for economic loss because it is not a tort.

See Smith's Review, Contracts, Chapter XIV, Remedies for Breach of Contract.

1. The concept of products liability of a manufacturer or supplier applies to both defects in the product and defects in the design of the product. That is, a product may be manufactured according to specifications but it is the design itself which permitted or caused the injury alleged.

2. Products liability is usually based on:

   (a) negligence,

   (b) breach of an express or implied warranty, or

   (c) strict liability.

   See Prosser, p. 641.

   CAVEAT—In addition to the two basic tort theories of recovery in products liability cases, negligence and strict liability, there are also theories of recovery which have at least some historical antecedent in the law of contracts. Prosser refers to a seller's warranty as "a curious hybrid, born of the illicit intercourse of tort and contract, unique in the law." Prosser, p. 634. Prosser points out that although it had a historical basis in the law of tort, the seller's warranty "gradually came to be regarded as a term of the contract of sale, express or implied, for which the normal remedy is a contract action." Prosser, p. 635. Although there may still be some difficulties of precise definitional distinction, "whether it be tort or contract, a breach of warranty gives rise to strict liability, which does not depend upon any knowledge of defects on the part of the seller, or any negligence." Prosser, p. 636. Although recovery based on a warranty theory is contract oriented, court decisions have emphasized tort theories and consumer protection in permitting recovery.

3. Additional emerging theories of liability include:

   (a) violation of statute,

   (b) tortious misrepresentation, and

   (c) res ipsa loquitur.

   CAVEAT—The student should analyze each fact situation not only with regard to the theories above, but also on the basis of the relationship between the plaintiff and defendant. *e.g.* Is the plaintiff a purchaser, or a member of the purchaser's family or a foreseeable third party or an innocent bystander? Is the defendant a manufacturer or a wholesaler or a retailer? Is the unforeseeable plaintiff concept of the Palsgraf case relevant? It is also important that the student be aware of the curious overlapping of the warranty theory in negligence and strict liability.

1. The liability of the manufacturer and seller of goods to the purchaser and consumer has undergone considerable evolution.   **BACKGROUND**

    (a) First, the doctrine of *caveat emptor* applied, and the buyer assumed all risks for defects in the chattel bought.

    (b) Second, *caveat emptor* was superseded by casting the burden on the manufacturer and seller to use the care of a reasonable, prudent person to make certain that the goods sold did not harm the purchaser. Liability was imposed for negligence without regard to contractual privity.

    (c) Third, a contract theory of recovery based on breach of an express and/or an implied warranty under the Uniform Sales Act (now superseded by the adoption of the Uniform Commercial Code in all states except Louisiana) emerged.

        e.g. Liability for the condition of the goods sold was cast on the manufacturer and seller through the imposition of implied warranties as set forth in the UCC. See Sections 2–314 and 2–315. These implied warranties provide:

        (i) that the seller warrants that the described goods are of a merchantable quality if the seller is a merchant with respect to goods of that kind unless modified or excluded under UCC 2–316, and

        (ii) that the seller warrants that the goods shall be fit for the particular purpose where at the time of contracting the seller has reason to know any particular purpose for which the goods are required, and that the buyer is relying on the seller's skill or judgment to select or furnish suitable goods unless excluded or modified by a *conspicuous writing* under UCC 2–316.

    (d) Fourth, strict liability in tort, which is the most important theory under present law.

    NOTE 1—In addition to the common law and UCC warranties, the Federal Trade Commission has issued rules under the Magnuson-Moss Warranty Act, 15 U.S.C.A. §§ 2301–2312. These rules do not require firms to issue written warranties, but if they are issued, they must conform to the FTC rules. The rules establish requirements for: (1) the disclosure of written warranty terms, (2) the pre-sale availability of such warranties, and (3) the minimum requirements for informal dispute settlement mechanisms. Under the rules, the warrantor must disclose "in simple and readily understood language," the following items of information, among others:

(a) what is covered by and, where necessary for clarification, what is excluded from the warranty,

(b) what the warrantor will do in the event of a defect, malfunction or failure to conform with the written warranty, including a statement of what items or services will be paid for or provided by the warrantor, and, where necessary for clarification, those that will not be, and

(c) a step-by-step explanation of what the purchaser should do to have the warranty honored.

NOTE 2—Many statutes have been enacted to provide protection to the consumer. Remedies under such statutes are in addition to common law remedies. See *e.g.* Consumer Product Safety Act, below.

2. A supplier of goods for a consideration may be liable for his negligence in failing to make the goods safe for the purpose for which they are intended, and such liability may extend:

(a) to third persons who buy or use the goods, and

(b) to third persons who are injured in the area foreseen for their use.

3. Recovery by third persons in certain cases is specifically provided for under UCC 2–318 entitled Third Party Beneficiaries of Warranties Express or Implied. This section provides: "A seller's warranty whether express or implied, extends to any natural person who is in the family or household of his buyer or who is a guest in his home if it is reasonable to expect that such person may use, consume, or be affected by the goods and who is injured in person by breach of the warranty. A seller may *not* exclude or limit the operation of this section." This section refers to "vertical privity," that is it provides who, besides the immediate purchaser, may sue to enforce the seller's warranty.

NEGLIGENCE AND PRIVITY

1. Historically, privity of contract was a prerequisite to imposing liability for negligence on the manufacturer.

e.g. D contracted with the Postmaster General to supply mail coaches and maintain them. P, a coachman, was injured because the coach he was using had been manufactured negligently. P brought suit against D manufacturer, contending that D owed a duty of care to him to provide coaches in proper working order, and the negligent manufacture of the coach breached that duty. The court denied recovery because there was no privity of contract between P and D. D's obligation was held to be limited to the Postmaster General who had contracted with D. Third parties such as P may not sue either party to the contract. If the rule were otherwise the contracting parties would be exposed to potentially unlimited liability. Thus, under the common law rule P may not recover. See Winterbottom v. Wright, 10 M. & W. 109, 152 Eng.Rep. 402 (Ex. 1842).

2. Today most courts apply the doctrine stated in the leading case of MacPherson v. Buick Motor Co., which provides that lack of privity of contract between the purchaser and manufacturer is *not* a defense to liability founded on negligence. Thus, the risk of injury from defective products is shifted onto manufacturers and sellers who are in a better financial position to absorb the loss. See Prosser, "The Fall of The Citadel (Strict Liability to the Consumer)," 50 Minn.L.Rev. 791 (1966). See also CASE 57 below.

3. The duty of the manufacturer extends to providing notice to warn of latent defects in its product even if it is *not* negligently manufactured.

   (a) A manufacturer of cement-base paint was found liable for not having adequately warned that its paint could cause blindness upon coming into contact with one's eyes. The test in these cases is one of reasonable foreseeability which is a question of fact for the jury. Liability was imposed on defendant-manufacturer even though the product was *not* negligently produced. See Haberly v. Reardon Co., 319 S.W.2d 859 (Mo.1958).

   (b) Recovery was granted to a third party who was in no way connected with the owner of a defective vehicle. The owner of a Buick had experienced brake failure and took his automobile to a dealer for repairs. GM had notified its dealers of the particular defect, but had given no notice to its purchasers. The dealer's service manager forgot that the brakes were defective, and while moving the car struck plaintiff, the dealer's mechanic. The court found negligence in failing to warn the owner of the defect. Comstock v. General Motors Corp., 358 Mich. 163, 99 N.W.2d 627 (1959).

   (c) Intervening cause does not always insulate a manufacturer from liability as it does in the usual negligence situation.

      e.g. The service manager's negligence in forgetting the defect and subsequently striking the plaintiff with the defective vehicle, was *not* a valid defense to the action in the Comstock case.

   (d) It has been held that a manufacturer's implied warranty of fitness runs in favor of all intended users, and privity of contract need not be shown to recover. See Goldberg v.

Kollsman Instrument Corp., 12 N.Y.2d 432, 240 N.Y.S.2d 592, 191 N.E.2d 81 (1963).

4. In the law of negligence, liability may also be cast on the defendant-manufacturer for failure to warn adequately of improper design and/or for failure to test and inspect adequately.

5. A defect in the design of an automobile may not cause or contribute to an accident, but the defect may cause greater injuries than would have otherwise occurred. The trend of recent decisions and vast majority of jurisdictions hold the manufacturer responsible where a design defect unreasonably enhances injuries from an accident.

(a) Suit was brought against an automobile manufacturer after a car it manufactured was involved in an accident. It was not contended that the manufacturer was responsible for the initial accident, but that its back seat assembly was defectively designed so that the impact caused it to break away from the body of the car resulting in additional injuries which would not otherwise have been sustained in the accident. May a manufacturer be held responsible for enhanced injuries from an accident because of a design defect even though the defect did not cause the initial impact?

Answer. Yes. The court noted that although the design defect did not cause the initial impact, if the defect was a cause of the ultimate injury, liability should be imposed where the manufacturer could have reasonably foreseen that the defect would cause or enhance injuries on impact. This rule is in accord with the modern trend of decisions. See Volkswagen of America, Inc. v. Young, 272 Md. 201, 321 A.2d 737 (1974).

(b) P was injured in a head-on collision with another car. The impact allegedly caused the steering shaft to thrust forward into P's head. P sued D manufacturer alleging negligence in the design of the steering assembly because it would not absorb the force of such a head-on collision. The court held that a manufacturer's duty of design and construction extends to producing a product reasonably fit for its intended use and free from hidden defects. Although a manufacturer does not intend that its cars will be involved in collisions, it is easily foreseeable that an automobile may be involved in an injury-producing accident. Thus the manufacturer is under a duty to use reasonable care in the design of a vehicle to avoid subjecting the user to an unreasonable risk of injury in the event of a collision. The court emphasized that it was not making automobile manufacturers "insurers," but was merely applying common law principles of negligence. An automobile need not be crash-proof, but only designed to provide "a reasonably safe vehicle in which to travel." The case was remanded for trial based on those principles. See Larsen v. General Motors Corp., 391 F.2d 495 (8th Cir. 1968).

NOTE 1—The doctrine of "crashworthiness" which permits recovery for enhanced injuries was initially announced in the Larsen decision. The burden of proof to show "enhanced" injury is normally on the plaintiff.

NOTE 2—The court in Larsen also addressed the duty to warn consumers. "Where the danger is obvious and known to the user, no warning is necessary and no liability attaches for an injury occurring from the reasonable hazards attached to the use of chattels or commodities; but where the dangerous condition is latent it should be disclosed to the user, and non-disclosure should subject the maker or supplier to liability for creating an unreasonable risk." At the later trial the jury found for the defendant manufacturer. See Bowman, "Defense of an Auto Design Negligence Case," 10 For The Defense, No. 5, May, 1969.

Liability for negligence without privity   Case 57

D manufactured wheels which he supplied to the manufacturers of automobiles. D supplied a wheel to X, a car manufacturer. The wheel was made of defective wood, and D was negligent in failing to test or inspect it properly. X put the wheel on one of its automobiles and sold the car to wholesaler, Y, who sold it to retailer, Z, who sold it to H, the ultimate new car purchaser. While H's wife, W, was driving the car, the defective wheel collapsed, the car was overturned in a ditch, and W was injured. H and W sue D for their injuries, alleging the foregoing facts and that D's negligence in manufacturing the wheel caused the injuries. D demurred (moved to dismiss) on the grounds that there was no privity of contract between the plaintiffs and D, and that D owed no duty to them. The court overruled the demurrer. Was there error?

Answer. No. The complaint states a cause of action and there is no ground for the demurrer. There was a duty and the lack of privity of contract is immaterial in this tort action. A manufacturer or supplier of goods for a consideration undertakes obligations far beyond the terms of his contract to persons who are not named in his contract, provided injuries to such persons can be reasonably foreseen in case the supplier or manufacturer of the goods does not use the care of a reasonable, prudent person in the preparation, supplying or manufacturing of the goods. *This principle is applicable to this set of facts. (a) The contract which D made with X was the first step in a series of transactions which D not only could foresee, but actually expected would take place. Although the contract itself imposed obligations only on D and X, additional burdens are imposed by tort law. (b) D could reasonably foresee that the wheel would be placed by X on a car. (c) D could reasonably foresee that the automobile would be sold to a wholesaler such as Y, that Y, in turn, would sell it to a retailer such as Z, and that Z, in turn, would sell it to the ultimate consumer, H. (d) D could reasonably foresee that the ultimate purchaser would use the car, and that the wheel would be required to endure great strain and stress in ordinary use. (e) D could reasonably foresee that if the wheel was not capable of resisting such strain and stress, it would collapse and cause the car to run out of control. (f) D could reasonably foresee that such event would cause injury to the car, to the driver and other occupants of the car, and to others near the place where the wheel would collapse. (g) D could reasonably foresee that lack of due care in the manufacturing of the wheel, or in making proper tests and inspection, would cause the injuries indicated above. (h) Therefore, D owed a duty to all persons to whom injury might reasonably be foreseen, to use due care in making, testing, inspecting, and supplying the wheel. (i) D is liable for failure to use due care in such conduct when that negligence causes injury. (j) H and W are persons in the chain of events to whom such duty is owed. (k) The complaint, under the above principles, states a cause of action against D, and the demurrer must be overruled.*

See MacPherson v. Buick Motor Co., 217 N.Y. 382, 111 N.E. 1050 (1916).

NOTE 1—The principle of CASE 57, above, that the manufacturer owes a duty of care to all foreseeable users, and such duty does not depend on contract, has been extended to all foreseeable persons within the scope of use of the product.

NOTE 2—The principle of this case has also been applied to the design and construction of real property. A tenant was permitted to sue the architect and contractor who built an apartment with a back porch which was unsafe for lack of railings, and from which a baby fell and was injured. The lack of privity of contract between the parties did not prevent recovery. The foreseeability of danger was the test of liability, and not whether the property was personal or real. See Inman v. Binghamton Housing Authority, 3 N.Y.2d 137, 164 N.Y.S.2d 699, 143 N.E.2d 895 (1957).

WARRANTY THEORY

1. One theory of recovery in products liability cases is based on the concept of express and implied warranties in the UCC.

   (a) *Express* warranties are set forth at UCC 2–313. These include any *affirmation* of fact or promise made by the seller to the buyer; any *description* of the goods, and any *sample* or *model*.

   > *e.g.* P, a consumer, recovered the loss of value of his automobile that had been defectively manufactured by D automobile manufacturer. P's reliance on mass media advertising to the effect that D's product was trouble-free and

economical negated the necessity of privity of contract with D manufacturer. Recovery was based on breach of an express warranty in the sale to P. See Inglis v. American Motors Corp., 3 Ohio St.2d 132, 209 N.E.2d 583 (1965).

(b) The types of implied warranties under UCC 2–314 and 2–315 are set forth above. See Background, numbers 1(c) and 3. These warranties include the implied warranty of merchantability and the implied warranty of fitness for the particular purpose.

2. Persons using a particular product with the purchaser's consent have been permitted to recover on an implied warranty theory, even *without any showing of privity of contract* with the manufacturer.

(a) Plaintiff suffered personal injuries while driving her husband's vehicle which contained a defective steering mechanism. The manufacturer's warranty provided for replacement of defective parts, but disclaimed all other warranties, express or implied. The attempted disclaimer was found to be against public policy. The court also held that privity was unnecessary to fix liability, even though plaintiff was *not* the purchaser of the defendant's product. See Henningsen v. Bloomfield Motors, Inc., 32 N.J. 358, 161 A.2d 69 (1960).

(b) The implied warranty of fitness extends to a consumer of food and drink by virtue of UCC 2–314 which provides that *the serving for value of food or drink to be consumed on the premises or elsewhere is a sale.* Plaintiff, consumer, found a mouse in his soft drink. The court disposed of an intervening cause defense of tampering on the basis that defendant-bottler had impliedly warranted the fitness of its product, i.e. that it was fit for human consumption. See Paul v. Rodgers Bottling Co., 6 Cal.Rptr. 867 (1960).

3. Exclusion or modification of express and/or implied warranties is provided for at UCC 2–316. The *implied warranty of merchantability* may be disclaimed under this section, but UCC safeguards require mention of the word *merchantability* and the same must be conspicuous in the case of a writing. The *implied warranty* of fitness for a particular purpose may be excluded by general language in a conspicuous writing.

CAVEAT—The student should note that *all implied warranties* are excluded by expressions like *"as is", "with all faults",* or other similar language indicating plainly that there is no implied warranty.

4. Manufacturers or suppliers may attempt to limit liability in warranties through disclaimers. However, UCC 2–719(3) provides: "Consequential damages may be limited or excluded unless the limitation or exclusion is unconscionable. Limitation of conse-

quential damages for injury to the person in the case of consumer goods is prima facie unconscionable but limitation of damages where the loss is commercial is not."

5. Under UCC 2–719(3) retail customers and users of a product are ordinarily protected. Purchases by businesses are less often protected from disclaimers because such purchasers are deemed to have greater bargaining power when making the transaction.

NOTE—UCC 2–719(3), quoted in number 4, above, has been strengthened by statute or court decisions in many jurisdictions to prohibit the exclusion or modification of implied warranties.

6. Express and implied warranties also extend to third parties, such as friends of the buyer who use the product, in certain cases under UCC 2–318. For the full text, see Background number 3, above.

7. Under modern procedure, the plaintiff may plead his cause of action in the alternative, that is, in tort for negligence or strict liability, and in contract for breach of express or implied warranty.

Case 58   *Lost profits recovered based on warranty*

P bought a truck for use in his business of heavy duty hauling. The truck was manufactured by D and sold by a dealer under a conditional sales contract. In the purchase order D warranted the truck "to be free from defects in material and workmanship under normal use and service, its obligation under the warranty being limited to making good at its factory any part or parts thereof. . . ." The truck did not run smoothly from the start and D's dealer was not able to correct the problem. Thereafter the brakes failed resulting in a collision and damage to the truck. P paid for the truck repairs needed after the collision, but refused to make any further payments toward the purchase price. The truck was repossessed eleven months after the original sale. P sued the dealer and D for (a) the cost of repairing the truck after the brakes failed, (b) the money P had paid toward the purchase price, and (c) lost profits because of P's inability to make normal use of the truck. The lower court awarded P the money he paid toward the purchase price of the truck and lost profits because of the breach of warranty. However, it denied recovery for the cost of repairs after the brakes failed, because it was not shown that this resulted from a breach of warranty. P and D appealed. Was the decision proper?

Answer.   *Yes. D gave P an express warranty on the truck on which P relied. P gave notice of the defect and D was unable to repair it. D's failure to repair the truck in accordance with its warranty gives rise to damages for that failure. These damages proper-*

ly include the amount paid on the purchase price and lost profits. The express warranty and failure to repair the truck properly established liability. The following defenses were rejected by the court: (1) D contended that its obligation to P was limited by the warranty to repair or replace defective parts. However, D failed to correct the defect as warranted and, therefore, D is liable for damages resulting from that breach. (2) D contended that P must elect between the remedy of rescission and return of the purchase price, and damages for breach of warranty which would be P's lost profits. The court held that in a suit against the manufacturer for consequential damages, P was not required to make an election between remedies. P is not seeking to rescind his contract with the immediate seller, the dealer, but P is seeking all damages which arise from D's breach of warranty which properly include the money P paid and his lost profits. (3) D also contended that to impose strict liability for P's economic loss would make manufacturers liable for damages of unknown and unlimited scope. However, application of the rules of warranty prevent that result. D is liable for breach of its agreement with P. However, D would not be liable for P's commercial losses without the warranty because P could have shopped around until he found a truck that met his business needs. P would be charged with the risk that the truck would not match his expectations unless the manufacturer agreed that it would, which D did in the warranty. P was not permitted to recover for the damage caused by the failure of the truck brakes because there was no evidence that the defect caused the accident. The decision of the trial court was affirmed.

See Seely v. White Motor Co., 63 Cal.2d 9, 45 Cal.Rptr. 17, 403 P.2d 145 (1965).

1. The third and primary theory used in products liability cases is that of strict liability. In many jurisdictions, products liability means strict liability being imposed on the manufacturer and the seller without regard to privity or negligence.   **STRICT LIABILITY**

   (a) Strict liability was imposed on the manufacturer of a power tool that caused injury to plaintiff even though he was *not* the purchaser. The petition sounded in breach of warranty only. According to Justice Traynor "liability is not one of contract warranties nor of agreement, but rather is imposed by law. Imposition of strict liability is to ensure that the cost of plaintiff's injury or loss will be borne by the manufacturer rather than the injured party who is virtually powerless to protect himself". Greenman v. Yuba Power Products Inc., 59 Cal.2d 57, 27 Cal.Rptr. 697, 377 P.2d 897 (1963).

   (b) In a landmark case, strict liability was imposed on both the retailer and manufacturer for personal injuries sustained from an accident caused by a defective part in an automobile. In order to afford maximum protection to the injured party, the court held both defendants strictly liable. Justice Traynor stated that "it is for the defendants to adjust the cost of protection between themselves." Vandermark v. Ford Motor Co., 37 Cal.Rptr. 896, 391 P.2d 168 (1964).

(c) A waitress in a restaurant was putting bottles of coke into a refrigerator when a bottle exploded in her hand and injured her. The concurring opinion of Justice Traynor stated that the manufacturer should be held to strict liability when an article placed on the market, knowing that it is to be used without inspection, is defective and causes injury. This rule is based on public policy and does not depend on the care used by the manufacturer or his negligence. The majority of the court based liability on res ipsa loquitur. Thus recovery was permitted from the manufacturer. See Escola v. Coca Cola Bottling Co., 24 Cal.2d 453, 150 P.2d 436 (1944).

2. The Restatement, Second, Torts rule of strict liability, as set forth in § 402A, has been of significance in the jurisdictions which have adopted the concept of strict liability. Section 402A provides:

"(1) One who sells *any* product in a defective condition unreasonably dangerous to the user, or to his property, is subject to liability for physical harm thereby caused to the ultimate user or consumer, or to his property, if

(a) the seller is engaged in the business of selling such a product, and

(b) it is expected to and does reach the user or consumer without substantial change in the condition in which it is sold.

"(2) The rule stated in Subsection (1) applies although

"(a) the seller has exercised all possible care in the preparation and sale of his product, and

"(b) the user or consumer has not bought the product from or entered into any contractual relation with the seller."

NOTE 1—The student should note the sweeping language i.e. "any product," and its effect. The Restatement rule imposes liability with respect to ANY product, whereas traditionally the courts considered the issue on a product-by-product basis. The rule has been the subject of considerable criticism.

NOTE 2—Liability may be imposed where the product was designed, as contrasted to manufactured, so that it created an unreasonable risk of harm in foreseeable use. See Negligence and Privity, number 5, above.

3. Some courts have rejected the concept of "unreasonably dangerous" contained in Restatement, Second, Torts § 402A, but have retained the remainder of the definition. The unreasonably dangerous language in the definition has been rejected primarily because of its negligence overtones. See number 9, below.

4. Whether or not a product is "defective" is a fact question for the jury. "Products are defective which are dangerous because they fail to perform in the manner reasonably to be expected in light of their nature and intended function." Dunham v. Vaughan & Bushnell Manufacturing Co., 42 Ill.2d 339, 247 N.E.2d 401 (1969). That traditional definition has been expanded by courts to include any excessive, preventable danger, including a foreseeable misuse of the product. See numbers 8 and 9, below.

5. Most courts do not permit recovery by bystanders for injuries resulting from the *breach of warranty* by a manufacturer in the absence of negligence because they are neither the ultimate consumer, nor the user of the product.

e.g. One court denied recovery to a pedestrian hit by an automobile when a defective spring caused the hood to raise, blocking the vision of the driver. See Mull v. Ford Motor Co., 368 F.2d 713 (2d Cir. 1966).

6. The trend of recent decisions permits a bystander to recover on the basis of *strict liability* against the manufacturer, at least where the risk to which the bystander was exposed was reasonably foreseeable.

(a) A bolt from a mower flew 150 feet through the air and injured P. The court concluded that P was a foreseeable bystander and could recover. See Sills v. Massey-Ferguson, Inc., 296 F.Supp. 776 (N.D.Ind.1969).

(b) The driver and passenger of a vehicle were struck by a car which had been defectively manufactured. Both were permitted to recover from the manufacturer and the retail automobile dealer based on strict liability. The court rejected the defense that privity of contract should be used to restrict liability. See Elmore v. American Motors Corp., 70 Cal.2d 578, 75 Cal.Rptr. 652, 451 P.2d 84 (1969).

7. A manufacturer must take reasonable steps to warn consumers of known risks involved in its product and the failure to do so will subject the manufacturer to strict liability.

e.g. The Sabin polio vaccine was licensed by the government and first manufactured and sold by D. At that time there were no known risks and, therefore, there was no duty to warn. Later D learned that the vaccine was dangerous to about one person in a million, who usually had certain symptoms, but no effective warning was given to persons to be vaccinated. The court held D strictly liable to P who contracted polio as a result of taking the vaccine after D knew of the danger. D should have warned customers of the risk when D learned of it. Had the warning been given P could have made a reasoned choice and assumed the risk. See Davis v. Wyeth Laboratories, Inc., 399 F.2d 121 (9th Cir. 1968).

8. The liability of a manufacturer extends to products which are unreasonably dangerous, regardless of whether the defect is hidden or obvious.

e.g. P was employed as a printing press operator. P attempted to clean the printing plate while the press was in operation. P knew that this was dangerous, but this was the usual practice in the industry. While doing this P's hand was drawn into the machine and injured. There were no safety guards to prevent such an occurrence, and P could not reach the shut-off button when his hand was in the machine. P filed suit against the manufacturer of the machine based on negligence in failing to place guards on the machine. D contended that the danger created by the absence of safeguards on the machine was obvious, and therefore, D was not required to protect P. The trial court found that D was negligent, but denied recovery because P was contributorily negligent. On appeal the court held that a manufacturer is required to use due care in the design of a machine to avoid unreasonable risk to the operator. The mere fact that the danger is obvious will not bar recovery from the manufacturer. However, the obviousness of the danger may be considered insofar as it bears on the issue of whether P exercised the reasonable care required under the circumstances. P was awarded a new trial in which the fact that the dangerous condition of the machine was apparent will not, by itself, prevent recovery. See Micallef v. Miehle Co., 39 N.Y.2d 376, 384 N.Y.S.2d 115, 348 N.E.2d 571 (1976).

NOTE 1—In rejecting the latent (hidden) and patent (obvious) analysis the court overruled Campo v. Scofield, 301 N.Y. 468, 95 N.E.2d 802 (1950). That case had been relied upon by many courts to restrict the expansion of liability under the strict liability theory because many courts following the holding in Campo had refused to find liability where the danger was obvious to the user. Under present law most courts do not deny recovery merely because a defect is obvious.

NOTE 2—What constitutes reasonable care by the manufacturer will depend on the surrounding circumstances, and will involve a balancing of the likelihood of injury, the seriousness of the resulting harm, and the burden of the precaution which would avoid the harm. Unreasonable expense and decreased efficiency of the product may be considered under that standard.

9. A product is defective in design if either:

(a) it does not perform as safely as an ordinary customer would expect when used in a reasonably foreseeable manner, or

(b) the benefits of the design do not outweigh the risk inherent in the design. This is the so-called risk-benefit standard, under which the jury may consider:

(i) the danger posed by the design,

(ii) the likelihood that the danger would occur,

(iii) the feasibility of a safer design, and

(iv) the cost of the alternative design and any adverse consequences which would result therefrom.

e.g. P was injured while operating a high-lift loader at a construction site. P brought suit against D manufacturer contending that the loader was designed defectively thereby causing P's injury. The jury was instructed that strict liability for a design defect must be based on a finding that the product was unreasonably dangerous for its intended use. The jury found for D, and P appealed. The court held that the instruction was erroneous because the jury may have concluded that P had the burden of proving that the loader was "unreasonably dangerous." Once P shows that the injury was proximately caused by the product's design, if D seeks to avoid liability under the risk-benefit standard, the burden shifts to D to show that the product was not defective. That is so because D has special knowledge of the relevant factors. The judgment was reversed because the jury may have believed that P had the burden of proving that the loader was more dangerous than the average consumer contemplated, and because the instruction misinformed the jury that the defectiveness of the product must be evaluated in light of its "intended use." The product should be evaluated by its "reasonably foreseeable use." The court announced that the criteria in number 9, above, should be used to determine whether there was a design defect. See Barker v. Lull Engineering Co., 20 Cal.3d 413, 143 Cal.Rptr. 225, 573 P.2d 443 (1978). See also Knitz v. Minster Machine Co., 69 Ohio St.2d 460, 432 N.E.2d 814 (1982).

NOTE 1—The view of the court in the Barker case is contrary to that of the Restatement, Second, Torts § 402A. The Restatement, which has been adopted in a majority of jurisdictions, requires a product to be "unreasonably dangerous" for strict liability to apply. A product is unreasonably dangerous if it is "dangerous to an extent beyond that which would be contemplated by the ordinary consumer who purchases it, with the ordinary knowledge common to the community as to its characteristics." Comment i. See Wade, "On the Nature of Strict Tort Liability for Products," 44 Miss.L.J. 825 (1973).

e.g. "Good whiskey is not unreasonably dangerous merely because it will make some people drunk, and is especially dangerous to alcoholics; but bad whiskey, containing a dangerous amount of fuel oil, is unreasonably dangerous." Restatement, Second, Torts § 402A, comment i.

NOTE 2—The Barker case illustrates how the policy of strict liability has had an effect on the burden of proof. After the plaintiff shows injury and proximate cause, the burden of proof shifts to the defendant to show that the product was *not* defective.

10. The doctrine of strict liability in tort is not limited to sellers of personal property, but is also applicable to the bailor and lessor of such property. See Price v. Shell Oil Co., 2 Cal.3d 245, 85 Cal.Rptr. 178, 466 P.2d 722 (1970).

NOTE 1—Although the rule in the Price case has been applied in only a few states, Prosser states that there is no reason to distinguish between those who sell products and those who rent them. It can be expected that this rule will eventually be the prevailing view. See Prosser, p. 679.

NOTE 2—All cases in this area emphasize that the defendant is in the business of supplying such personal property. This follows the Restatement, see number 2, above.

11. Some products, such as drugs, by their nature cannot be made absolutely safe for their intended use. Where a product is *unavoidably unsafe* the seller is not held strictly liable if the product is prepared properly and a warning is given.

e.g. P received a blood transfusion from which she developed serum hepatitis. P sued the blood manufacturer and other parties connected with the transfusion contending that there was strict liability for using the infected blood. The court noted that at the time of the transfusion there was no way to detect or guard against the hepatitis virus in blood. The blood was prepared properly with a warning given to the physician. P may not recover because the blood could not have been made safe. Since it was "unavoidably unsafe," strict liability was not imposed. See Hines v. St. Joseph's Hospital, 86 N.M. 763, 527 P.2d 1075 (1974).

NOTE—Recovery based on strict liability is permitted because of policy considerations favoring the protection of consumers. That policy must yield when a more important policy is present, such as the protection of hospitals from suits based on the ill effects of drugs which are unavoidably unsafe. The court denied recovery in the Hines case, above, because of the greater public good which could be achieved by protecting health care institutions in these circumstances.

12. Courts have not imposed strict liability where services were rendered. However, one decision found liability where a defective product, a lotion, was applied to the plaintiff's hair in a beauty parlor. The court said that there was no legal distinction between the sale of a product for use and the use of that product on the person as a service at the store. See Newmark v. Gimbel's Inc., 54 N.J. 585, 258 A.2d 697 (1969).

PRODUCT MISREPRESENTATION

1. Misrepresentation is emerging as a basis for imposing liability against the manufacturer and seller of chattels. Such misrepresentation may be innocent, negligent or intentional.

    (a) P bought a new car and while driving it, a pebble from a passing car hit the windshield, shattering the glass and injuring P. P sued the car manufacturer for damages. The court held that P could recover without privity of contract with the manufacturer based on an express warranty in its advertising that the windshield was shatterproof. See Baxter v. Ford Motor Co., 168 Wash. 456, 12 P.2d 409 (1932). However, on a second appeal, 179 Wash. 123, 35 P.2d 1090 (1934), the court permitted P to recover based on strict liability for the misrepresentation, even though it was not intentional.

    (b) In a Tennessee case, plaintiff sued for a breach of warranty of a tractor that did not perform according to the manufacturer's advertisements. Recovery was granted on the basis of tortious misrepresentation. See Ford Motor Company v. Lonon, 217 Tenn. 400, 398 S.W.2d 240 (1966).

2. Section 402B of the Restatement, Second, Torts provides: "One engaged in the business of selling chattels, who, by advertising, labels or otherwise, makes to the public a misrepresentation of a material fact concerning the character or quality of a chattel sold by him is subject to liability for physical harm to a consumer of the chattel caused by justifiable reliance upon the misrepresentation even though

    "(a) it is not made fraudulently or negligently, and

    "(b) the consumer has not bought the chattel from or entered into any contractual relation with the seller".

    CAVEAT—Under this rule, strict liability is cast on the seller, even though the misrepresentation is innocent. See Ford Motor Co. v. Lonon, cited above, number 1(b).

3. In some jurisdictions, negligent misrepresentation imposes liability on the manufacturer, seller, and others.

e.g. D gave its Good Housekeeping seal of approval to a certain brand of shoes. P bought the shoes and slipped on her kitchen floor while wearing the slick-soled shoes. P brought suit for personal injuries against D. D moved to dismiss P's complaint on the ground that D's endorsement was merely a statement of opinion and not actionable. The court noted that D benefited from its endorsement by enhancing the value of its magazine for advertising purposes. D's seal and certification implied that D had taken reasonable steps to examine the product endorsed with some degree of expertise, and found it satisfactory. P alleged that D either did not test the product or tested it in a careless manner. Those allegations are sufficient to amount to a negligent misrepresentation and P may recover if she can prove her allegations. The fact that D limited its contract liability in the endorsement by guaranteeing a replacement or refund does not limit D's tort liability for negligent misrepresentation. However, P may not recover on a warranty or strict liability theory because D did not manufacture the product or supply it to consumers. See Hanberry v. Hearst Corp., 276 Cal. App.2d 680, 81 Cal.Rptr. 519 (1969). See also P & W, pp. 840–841, 962–963.

4. Intentional or reckless misrepresentation in products cases will result in a fraud action against the manufacturer. See Chapter VIII, Misrepresentation, below.

DEFENSES 1. Before specific defenses are analyzed it should be determined whether the plaintiff has established the necessary elements of his case. These requirements are the same whether the suit is based on negligence, warranty or strict liability:

(a) Plaintiff must show that he was injured by the product. If it is equally likely that the injury was caused by another product, he cannot recover.

(b) The plaintiff must have been injured because the product was defective.

(c) The product must have been defective when it left the defendant's possession. See Kerr v. Corning Glass Works, 284 Minn. 115, 169 N.W.2d 587 (1969).

2. The possible defenses available to the manufacturer and seller in a products liability case include:

(a) contributory negligence,

(b) assumption of the risk,

(c) intervening cause, and

(d) disclaimers, exclusions and limitations under the UCC.

CAVEAT—The student should analyze each defense on the basis of the theory of plaintiff's cause of action.

    (a) Contributory negligence is a defense to an ordinary negligence action, but it is generally not a valid defense to an action based on strict liability nor to a contract action. See numbers 3 and 4, below.

    (b) Assumption of the risk is a valid defense to strict liability. See number 7, below.

    (c) In comparative fault jurisdictions there is considerable conflict in court decisions as to whether the plaintiff's actions constituting contributory negligence are admissible where the theory of recovery is based on strict liability. See Werber, The Product Liability Revolution in Automotive and Related Industries—Proposals for Continued Legislative Response, 18 New England L.Rev. 1 (1982).

3. If the theory of recovery is negligence, then the contributory negligence of the injured plaintiff is a valid defense where the plaintiff fails to use a warranted product as a reasonable, prudent person just as in any negligence action.

4. If the theory of recovery is strict liability, then the contributory negligence of the plaintiff in failing to discover or take precautions against defects is *not* a defense.

CAVEAT—Traditionally, the seller or manufacturer was entitled to expect a normal use of its product. However, in strict liability cases it is the *foreseeable* use, or misuse, of the product that is considered. See McDevitt v. Standard Oil Co. of Texas, 391 F.2d 364 (5th Cir. 1968); Cintrone v. Hertz Truck Leasing & Rental Service, 45 N.J. 434, 212 A.2d 769 (1965). See also Strict Liability, number 8, above.

5. The defense of contributory negligence has been rejected in food cases. An action for breach of implied warranty for defective food is ex contractu (arising out of the contract) and the defense of contributory negligence is thus not applicable. See Brockett v. Harrell Brothers, Inc., 206 Va. 457, 143 S.E.2d 897 (1965).

6. It has been held that a cigarette manufacturer is not liable for disease caused by the use of its product when it was not reasonably foreseeable by the manufacturer. See Ross v. Philip Morris & Co., 328 F.2d 3 (8th Cir. 1964); Lartigue v. R. J. Reynolds Tobacco Co., 317 F.2d 19 (5th Cir. 1963). Because the dangers of cigarette smoking are now generally known, a manufacturer probably would not be held liable for the habits of the consumer because of public policy refusing to extend an implied warranty or because of assumption of the risk by the consumer. See P & W, pp. 785–786.

7. Assumption of the risk is generally a valid defense in a products liability case. The defense was said to have a dual meaning, however:

   (a) If it is equated to contributory negligence it is not a valid defense.

   (b) If it means voluntary exposure to a known risk, it is a valid defense. See Pritchard v. Liggett & Myers Tobacco Co., 350 F.2d 479 (3rd Cir. 1965). Federal legislation requires tobacco companies to print a warning of the hazardous nature of cigarette smoking on each package of cigarettes. See 15 U.S.C.A. § 1333. This warning creates an assumption of the risk.

8. Intervening cause may be a valid defense in a proper case. The basic issue is one of proximate causation. See Negligence and Privity, number 3, above.

9. Disclaimers, exclusions and limitations by the manufacturer in warranties may afford protection in certain cases under the UCC. See Warranty Theory, numbers 4 and 5, above.

10. A full warning placed on the label of the product may insulate the producer from liability as in the case of an unavoidably unsafe product. See Strict Liability, number 11, above. A warning may also make the defense of assumption of the risk available. See numbers 6 and 7, above.

11. A manufacturer need not produce a product which will not wear out. However, the mere lapse of time and continued use after the sale is no defense if the product was defective at the time of sale. See Mickle v. Blackmon, 252 S.C. 202, 166 S.E.2d 173 (1969) where a defective gearshift lever did not cause injury until the car was 13 years old.

12. Usually the statute of limitations begins to run at the time an injury is incurred. However, at least in products liability cases based on strict liability, some states limit by statute the time for recovery based on the date of purchase rather than the date of injury. The purpose of such statutes is to protect manufacturers and suppliers from strict liability claims after a period of many years.

CONSUMER PRODUCT SAFETY ACT

INTRODUCTORY NOTE—Products liability law evolved primarily through judicial decisions. In recent years a maze of statutes have been enacted to protect consumers in addition to their common law remedies. For example, the Occupational Safety and Health Act (OSHA) 29 U.S.C.A. §§ 651 et seq. (1970), the Poison Prevention Packaging Act, 15 U.S.C.A. §§ 1471 et seq. (1970), the Flammable Fabrics Act, 15 U.S.C.A. §§ 1191 et seq. (1972), and the Consumer Product Safety Act, 15 U.S.C.A. §§ 2051 et seq. (1972). The violation of these Acts, or a regulation issued under them setting a standard of care, would justify recovery on a negligence per se theory for violation of a statute. See Chapter III, Violation of Statute, above. See also P & W, p. 756. The Consumer Product Safety Act is treated here to illustrate the present statutory protection in one area.

1. The Consumer Product Safety Act, 15 U.S.C.A. §§ 2051 et seq., was passed in 1972. It has the following purposes:

    (a) to protect the public against unreasonable risks of injury associated with consumer products,

    (b) to assist consumers in evaluating the safety of products,

    (c) to develop uniform safety standards, and

    (d) to promote research into the causes and prevention of product-related injuries.

2. The Act covers all consumer products, except the following items which are regulated under other laws:

    (a) tobacco products,

    (b) motor vehicles and equipment,

    (c) pesticides,

    (d) firearms and ammunition,

    (e) aircraft,

    (f) boats,

    (g) foods, drugs and cosmetics.

3. An independent regulatory agency known as the Consumer Product Safety Commission was created to administer the Act. It is headed by five commissioners appointed by the President.

4. The Commission has jurisdiction over the manufacture of consumer products and their distribution in commerce. Businesses engaged solely in repair or service of consumer products are not covered.

5. The Consumer Product Safety Commission has authority to:

    (a) set safety standards for consumer products,

    (b) take action

        (i) against products determined to be hazardous, or

        (ii) against the manufacturers, distributors or retailers of the hazardous products,

    (c) collect and disseminate information on injuries and other related matters,

(d) conduct research, studies and investigations into product safety and means of improving such safety, and

(e) take appropriate court action to enforce the Act.

6. The Commission develops product safety standards by first publishing a notice in the Federal Register which:

   (a) identifies the product and the nature of the risk or injury associated with the product,

   (b) states the Commission's determination that a safety standard is necessary,

   (c) includes information with respect to any relevant existing standard,

   (d) invites any person to either submit an existing safety standard or offer to develop a proposed safety standard with respect to such product.

7. A period of 30 days after publication of the notice is prescribed during which such submissions and offers may be made. The Commission may proceed independently to develop its own standard if it desires, after the above notice has been given.

8. Within 60 days after the notice is published the Commission must conduct a rule making hearing pursuant to Section 553 of the Administrative Procedure Act. Within 210 days after publication of the original notice, the Commission must either withdraw the notice or proceed with the publication of the consumer product safety rule.

9. A product safety standard, once promulgated by the Commission, preempts any state or local standards dealing with the same hazard associated with the product.

10. If the Commission makes a finding that the consumer product represents an unreasonable risk of injury to the public which cannot be adequately corrected by any feasible safety standard, it may propose the promulgation of a rule declaring such product to be banned as a hazardous product. Such a banning rule must be adopted in accordance with the same administrative procedures for the promulgation of safety standards.

11. Any party adversely affected by a consumer product safety rule may seek review in a U. S. Court of Appeals. A consumer or consumer organization also has standing to seek review.

12. Upon review the Court will affirm the rule only if the findings upon which it is based are supported by substantial evidence on the record taken as a whole. Review of the decision rendered by the Court of Appeals may be brought in the U. S. Supreme Court.

13. The Commission may initiate proceedings on its own motion or any consumer may petition for a rule (safety standard).

14. Any consumer or consumer organization may petition the Commission to initiate a proceeding to issue, change or revoke a product safety rule. If a petition is denied, the Commission must publish notice of its reasons and the petitioner may obtain court review.

For a detailed discussion of rule making under the Administrative Procedure Act see, Smith's Review, Administrative Law, Chapter IV, Rules, Rule Making, and Hearings.

REMEDIES UNDER CONSUMER PRODUCT SAFETY ACT

1. The Commission may institute adjudicatory proceedings under the Administrative Procedure Act and make a determination if it believes either:

   (a) there is a product hazard arising from non-compliance with a standard, or

   (b) a product defect exists, regardless of whether or not it is covered by a standard.

2. If the Commission finds that a substantial hazard exists, it may order notification to every known person to whom the product was sold or delivered, and direct the manufacturer to:

   (a) recall the product and bring it into compliance or repair the defect, or

   (b) replace the product with an equivalent product which is in compliance or non-defective, or

   (c) refund the purchase price less a reasonable allowance for use.

3. If the Commission believes that a product causes an imminent risk of death or serious injury, it may institute proceedings directly in a U. S. District Court for condemnation or seizure of the product without the usual administrative proceedings.

4. A person may be subjected to civil penalties of up to $2,000 for each individual product involved in a violation of a standard. The civil penalties assessed for such related offenses may not exceed $500,000 in the aggregate.

5. Actual knowledge is not required to establish a violation, as the Act provides that a violator will be presumed to have the knowledge any reasonable man acting in the same circumstances would have.

6. Criminal penalties of fine and imprisonment are provided for willful violation after the Commission has given notice of non-compliance.

7. A private individual may bring suit to enforce a standard or banning rule if the Commission fails to act after the individual gives them 30 days' notice. Upon the filing of his complaint, the

private plaintiff may demand recovery of reasonable attorney's fees. If he does so, the Court will award such fees and other costs of the suit to *whichever* party prevails. Thus, if a "public interest" law firm loses a case after asking for attorney fees it may be required to pay the legal fees of the company sued.

8. If a violation of a product safety rule, or of any other Commission rule or order, results in injury to any person, such person is entitled to recover damages from any person who violated the rule or order which resulted in the injury. Reasonable attorney fees may be awarded at the discretion of the Court.

9. Compliance with the Commission's rules is not a defense to suit in state courts under appropriate state statutes or the common law, *e.g.,* a suit based on negligence or breach of implied warranty.

VIII

MISREPRESENTATION

Summary Outline

INTRODUCTION

1. "Misrepresentation" is a term which refers to a wide variety of tortious conduct. In describing such conduct courts frequently use the terms "fraud", "deceit", and "misrepresentation" interchangeably.

2. The separate and specific cause of action for INTENTIONAL misrepresentation is an "action in deceit." See Prosser, p. 684.

3. Fact situations involving an action in deceit generally involve business transactions. The injury involved is generally ECONOMIC, as contrasted to injury to person or property. In fact, recovery for physical harm is seldom permitted for actions in deceit.

4. Early cases considering actions for causing economic harm limited recovery to intentional misrepresentations which were intended to deceive. No recovery was permitted for loss caused by a misrepresentation negligently made with the honest belief that it was true. See Derry v. Peek, 14 App.Cas. 337 (1889).

5. Gradually the rule was broadened to include negligent statements directed to the plaintiff and, in a few cases, to deceitful statements which the defendant should know would cause harm to third persons. Some courts permitted an action based on negligence rather than deceit for a negligent misrepresentation. See Prosser 705–706; CASE 59 below.

6. As a general rule, strict liability in tort cannot be based on false representations honestly believed, because there is no intent to deceive. However, some cases permit recovery on the theory of warranty.

   e.g. D constructed a house with a septic tank system and sold it to P representing that the system was "adequate." P soon discovered that an outlet pipe had not been sealed and that was causing a contamination of all incoming water to the house which was from a well. P sued D for damages for D's misrepresentation. P was permitted to recover the cost of repairs and incidental expenses based on D's misrepresentation which was treated as a breach of warranty. The defenses that: (1) D originally had the work done by competent workmen, (2) D was not negligent in making the representation, and (3) D made the representation in good faith are not sufficient. P may recover for breach of warranty when it is later discovered that the statement is incorrect. See Sargent v. Janvrin, 109 N.H. 66, 242 A.2d 73 (1968).

ACTIONABLE MISREPRESENTATION

1. To support a cause of action or claim for *deceit* the following elements must be present:

   (a) a statement of a material fact,

   (b) the statement must be false,

(c) the defendant must know that the statement is false,

(d) the *defendant must intend to deceive* the plaintiff,

(e) the plaintiff relies on the statement justifiably, and

(f) the plaintiff is thereby damaged.

2. The *gravamen* of the cause of action is the defendant's *intent to deceive* the plaintiff. This kind of intent—intent to deceive—is known as "scienter."

3. An intent to deceive may exist when the defendant makes the statement:

(a) believing it to be untrue, or

(b) having no belief either as to its truth or untruth, or

(c) with reckless abandon as to whether it is or is not true, or

(d) knowing that he has no foundation for either believing the statement is true or untrue.

4. As a *general rule* an *action in tort cannot be based on false representations honestly believed but negligently made* because there is *no intent to deceive*. In some few situations recovery is permitted. See CASES 59 and 60, below.

5. The plaintiff's *reliance must be justifiable,* and not inherently ridiculous. This usually depends on the facts of the individual case and includes the intelligence, experience and capacity of the plaintiff, and the means available to him for observing, without necessarily making an investigation, of the truth or falsity of the defendant's representation. See Restatement, Second, Torts § 537.

(a) A plaintiff may not justifiably rely on the patently absurd statement of his oculist, or anyone else, that his glasses, being fitted to his face, would automatically adjust themselves to the condition of his defective eyes. Hence he cannot recover for such untrue statement. See Hirschberg Optical Co. v. Michaelson, 1 Neb. (Unof.) 137, 95 N.W. 461 (1901); Bishop v. Small, 63 Me. 12 (1874).

(b) P tells D that he will only buy a car from D if it has air conditioning and D states that it is so equipped. P took the car for a test drive and bought it. A few days later P discovered that the "air" knob was for ventilation and not for air conditioning as he thought. P sought to return the car because it did not have air conditioning. D refused to take back the car or install air conditioning in it and P sued for fraud. May P recover?

> *Answer.* No. When the falsity of a statement could have been discovered through ordinary care no recovery is permitted because of the misrepresentation. Ordinary care is a subjective standard, determined by the intelligence and experience of the misled individual. Here there is no rea-

son why P could not have easily determined whether the car had air conditioning. Thus P was not justified in relying on D's representation. Williams v. Rank & Son Buick, Inc., 44 Wis.2d 239, 170 N.W.2d 807 (1969). See also Babb v. Bolyard, 194 Md. 603, 72 A.2d 13 (1950).

NOTE—Reliance to be justified must normally have been intended or be reasonably foreseeable. Misrepresentation of opinion or quality may not usually be relied upon unless there is a special relationship between the parties.

6. Contributory negligence is not a defense in an action for *intentional* deceit where there is justifiable reliance on the misrepresentation. However, if the misrepresentation is only negligent (not intentional) contributory negligence of the plaintiff in relying on it will prevent recovery. See Restatement, Second, Torts §§ 545A, 552A.

7. The defendant's *statement must be* a statement *of* a *past or present fact. Neither* a *prediction* of things to come, *nor* a *promise* to do something in the future, *will support an action* for deceit.

    (a) D sells stock in X corporation to P, making two representations to P: (1) that these stocks will surely increase in value and (2) that thereafter D will procure for P a job. The stocks go down in value and D does not even attempt to procure P a job. P sues D for damages for deceit. The action will not lie. Neither representation is a statement of a fact, past or present; one is a *prediction* and the other is a *promise* to do something in the future.

    (b) D offered to buy one of several lots that P owned. D represented to P that he intended to build a house on the lot, but in fact had made plans to construct a parking garage. P relied on D's representations and sold the lot. When P learned of D's plans, P sued to rescind the agreement based on D's fraudulent misrepresentation because construction of a parking garage would substantially decrease the value of P's remaining lots. The court noted that D intentionally and falsely told P that he intended to purchase the land to build a dwelling thereon. D must have known that if he carried out his secret intention the value of P's remaining lots would be reduced by more than the purchase price which D paid. The general rule is that a statement of intention, even though it has been relied on, may be changed in good faith without affecting the obligations of the parties to the contract. A statement of intention does not relate to a fact that has a corporal and physical existence. In the present case D's statement of his intention induced P to sell the land. Although D's stated intention was subject to good faith change at any time, D did not change his stated intention in good faith. The evidence established that D intended to construct a parking garage throughout the negotiations for the lot, and notified his architect to prepare plans for the garage on the day following the purchase. Within two weeks D signed a contract for the erection of the garage. The state of a person's mind may be regarded as a fact. D misrepresented his state of mind and that misrepresentation is sufficient for P to rescind the contract of sale. See Adams v. Gillig, 199 N.Y. 314, 92 N.E. 670 (1930).

CAVEAT—The Adams case shows that the misrepresentation of a *present* state of mind or intention is treated the same as a misrepresentation of fact. However, in such circumstances the plaintiff must establish that the defendant had no intention of performing the promise when it was made. That renders it a misrepresentation of a present fact rather than an unenforceable promise. In the Adams case the plaintiff sustained her burden by showing the acts of the defendant before the purchase was completed and his acts immediately afterwards. An action to rescind a contract for misrepresentation could not be based solely on the mere nonperformance of a stated intention.

8. The *fact* stated *must be material* to the transaction. Misstatement of an *immaterial fact will not support* an *action*.

   (a) P bought a beautiful leather jacket from D because D stated "that D was a good and loyal alumnus of the college that P had attended". The jacket was exactly as it appeared and as represented by D, but D was not in fact an alumnus of that college, but of another, which had a long tradition of football rivalry with P's college, and the deceit was intentional. P sues D for damages for the deceit. The fact is totally immaterial to the transaction. Besides, there is no justification for P's relying on an immaterial fact. In this case it is immaterial to the transaction where D had gone to college. Such misstatement of an immaterial fact will not support an action, and P cannot recover.

   (b) Suppose in the case just given that D had represented that the jacket was made of "genuine cowhide exactly as it came from the cow", when in fact the original leather had been split and the jacket leather was only half as thick as represented, and D knew that fact, but it could not be discovered by P by inspecting the garment. Here is a misrepresentation of a material fact which will support an action for damages for deceit.

9. The statement of an opinion will not, as a general rule, support an action for deceit, both because it is not a statement of fact, and because it cannot justifiably be relied on. However, circumstances sometimes justify treating opinion as fact which will support an action for deceit.

   (a) D is a salesman of new automobiles. P is a prospective purchaser. D says to P: "P, this is the finest car on the market; it is the hottest thing on the road; it is really a clean job; it is the most economical car you can buy; you can't beat it for safety." P buys the car and finds it is not the "finest", not the "hottest", not "clean", not "economical" and not "safe". He sues D for deceit. The action should be dismissed. All these are statements of opinion, seller's talk, or "puffing". They are not intended as statements of facts, and P was not justified in relying on them. They are part of our common salesmanship practice of which the purchaser must take notice. As to them he must rely on his own judgment.

(b) Company A sold patents and equipment for the manufacture of vacuum cleaners to Company B. A made representations to B concerning the vacuum cleaner and B was allowed a full opportunity to test the product before the sale was finalized. After the sale B discovered that A had misrepresented the product. B sued A for deceit. May B recover?

Answer. No. B had the opportunity to examine and test the product. A's statements as to what the product would do, even though consciously false, should not have been taken literally by B. A and B stood on equal footing. B should have made an adequate investigation before completing the purchase. A's false statements as to performance, which B could have investigated but failed to do, do not give rise to an action for deceit. See Vulcan Metals Co. v. Simmons Mfg. Co., 248 F. 853 (2d Cir. 1918). See also Deming v. Darling, 148 Mass. 504, 20 N.E. 107 (1889).

(c) P had money to invest in X corporation stock, but did not want to buy such stock unless the corporation had a right to do business in P's home state. X corporation had been formed in state Y and P's home state was state Z. D owned stock in X corporation and wanted to sell such stock to P. D represented to P that X had a legal right to do business in state Z. Relying on such representation, P bought D's stock in X corporation. In fact, X had no right to do business in state Z. P sues D for damages for deceit. D's defense is that he merely represented the "law" and not a "fact" concerning X corporation. Is the defense good?

Answer. No. The general rule is that a misrepresentation of the law is no basis for an action for deceit. However, the general modern tendency is to treat a statement of law the same as a statement of fact when so intended, and not merely a statement of opinion. In this case the statement by D that X corporation had a legal right to do business in state Z, is the equivalent of saying that X had in fact complied with the statutes for foreign corporations and that X corporation had as a fact the right to do business in state Z. Therefore, the defense is not good. Of course, if the statement of law is made and understood to be merely opinion, then the defense is good. See Miller v. Osterlund, 154 Minn. 495, 191 N.W. 919 (1923). See also Restatement, Second, Torts § 545.

10. Many older decisions held that an action of deceit could not be based upon the mere silence concerning a material fact.

(a) D sold a house to P that was infested with termites. D did not disclose that fact and P could not discover it with a reasonable inspection. After taking occupancy P discovered the termites and sued D for knowingly concealing the fact. May P recover?

Answer. No. This was an arms length transaction and D had no duty to disclose the defect. P may not recover by the older rule. Swinton, Sele v. Whitinsville Savings Bank, 311 Mass. 677, 42 N.E.2d 808 (1942).

(b) Under recent decisions on the same set of facts, P has been permitted to recover. The court held that the vendor had a duty to disclose a latent dangerous condition of the property. A duty to disclose was found because the vendor had this special knowledge which was not available to vendee. See Obde v. Schlemeyer, 56 Wash.2d 449, 353 P.2d 672 (1960).

(c) D developed and advertised certain homesites. Purchasers of lots contracted with X, a building contractor, to construct a home on each purchaser's lot. The purchasers did not deal directly with D, but were influenced by D's advertising of the choice residential area. X completed the homes and delivered title which was received from D. After moving into their homes the purchasers discovered that trees and shrubs would not grow because of the saline condition of the soil. P and other purchasers sued D for (i) breach of an implied warranty of fitness, and (ii) fraud in the concealment of a material matter. They alleged that D knew or should have known that the lots would not sustain vegetation, and D graded the land so that it was impossible for P to discover the presence of salt areas. D asserted that no inquiry had been made and no assurance was given on the soil fertility. D also contended that there was no privity with P because P dealt only with X. In ruling on D's motion for summary judgment the court noted that the condition of the soil did not affect the structural qualities of the homes. (i) The court rejected P's contention that there was an implied warranty of fitness as in product liability cases because the injury in this case arose from the sterility of the soil rather than from the manufacture of a chattel, and there was no personal injury to P. (ii) "One who makes a fraudulent misrepresentation or concealment is subject to liability for pecuniary loss to the persons or class of persons whom he intends or has reason to expect to act or to refrain from action in reliance upon the misrepresentation or concealment." P was within the class of persons whom D intended to influence. Therefore, privity between P and D was not required. D's concealment of the soil condition was a material factor in inducing P to buy the homesite. P may maintain an action for fraudulent concealment. The case was remanded for trial of the factual issues presented. See Griffith v. Byers Construction Co. of Kansas, Inc., 212 Kan. 65, 510 P.2d 198 (1973).

11. Recent decisions have limited the older rule stated in number 10(a) by exceptions and held that an action for deceit may arise from fraudulent concealment and nondisclosure of material information as well as from affirmative misrepresentation in a business transaction.

   (a) If a question is asked by a prospective purchaser, it must be fully answered. An answer or statement which is a misleading half truth will give rise to an action for fraudulent misrepresentation. See Kraft v. Lowe, 77 A.2d 554 (D.C.Mun.App.1950). See also Junius Construction Co. v. Cohen, 257 N.Y. 393, 178 N.E. 672 (1931).

   (b) A party to a business transaction may have the duty to disclose because of a fiduciary or other similar relation of trust and confidence between them, such as an agent for an insurance company to a policyholder where the policy stated that the agent was authorized to settle claims and it was not necessary for the policyholder to obtain other assistance. See Stark v. Equitable Life Assurance Society of United States, 205 Minn. 138, 285 N.W. 466 (1939).

   (c) The relationship between the parties, trade custom or other circumstances may require the disclosure of a fact which goes to the essence of the transaction if it is known that the other party is about to act under a mistake as to such fact. This situation is illustrated in number 10(b), above.

   (d) A stockholder may sue for the benefit of the corporation where corporation officers and directors use "inside" information for personal profit. See Diamond v. Oreamuno, 24 N.Y.2d 494, 301 N.Y.S.2d 78, 248 N.E.2d 910 (1969). The federal securities laws also provide remedies for the misuse of information by insiders.

   (e) Any subsequently acquired information which makes untrue or misleading a previous representation upon which there is continuing reliance must be disclosed.

      e.g. D, an independent public accountant, audited financial statements of a publicly traded company and certified that information which was sent to stockholders in the company's annual report and filed with the SEC was correct. When D learned the financial statements were incorrect it failed to publicly disclose that fact. In a subsequent suit against D by stockholders and bondholders for losses sustained as a result of D's nondisclosure, the court held that D had a duty to correct its original representation when D learned that it was false and D knew that people were relying on it. That D did not profit from the nondisclosure and D only had a contract with the company to render accounting services are not valid defenses. D had a duty to disclose the subsequently acquired new information. See Fischer v. Kletz, 266 F.Supp. 180 (S.D.N.Y.1967).

(f) A duty to disclose may arise with respect to information which was not material when originally communicated to an individual. If the party making the representation subsequently ascertains that it has become material and that the other party is about to act upon it in a business transaction with him then he has an affirmative duty of disclosure.

See Restatement, Second, Torts, § 551.

See generally, Keeton, pp. 835–933; P & W, pp. 911–913, 936–942; Prosser, pp. 694–736.

Liability for negligent misrepresentation limited unless there is fraud Case 59

D, an accountant, examined the books of X, a merchant, for the purpose of procuring financing for X's import business. For this purpose D certified X's statement of financial condition. Through negligent error on the part of D in not verifying accounts receivable, the statement showed X's financial condition as being very good when, in fact, X was on the verge of insolvency. P bank relied on the statement with justification and made loans to X. Because of P's reliance on the statement and making the loans a substantial sum was lost when P was later discharged in bankruptcy. P bank sued D in tort for misrepresentation and fraud. (a) May P recover for misrepresentation? (b) May P recover for fraud?

Answer. *(a) No. (b) Yes. Under the general rule D is not liable to P because there was no intent by D to deceive. D was employed by X and owed a duty to X to use due care in preparing the financial statement. D knew that X would exhibit the statement to investors and use it to obtain credit. D owed the duty to those whom X showed the statement to prepare it without fraud. The court stated: "If liability for negligence exists, a thoughtless slip or blunder, the failure to detect a theft or forgery beneath the cover of deceptive entries, may expose accountants to a liability in an indeterminate amount for an indeterminate time to an indeterminate* *class." To prevent such unlimited liability D was held not liable for his negligence to persons whom the statement was shown by X.*

The court also considered a second allegation of P, that D was guilty of fraud because of D's certification that the statement "in our opinion, presents a true and correct view of the financial condition" of X. The pretense of knowledge is fraud. A jury could find that the failure to verify the invoices representing the faked accounts was such a fraud. The case was remanded for a new trial limited to the question of whether there was fraud.

See Ultramares Corp. v. Touche, Niven & Co., 255 N.Y. 170, 174 N.E. 441 (1931).

NOTE—The rule in CASE 59, above, is only applied where intangible economic interests are invaded that might result in almost unlimited liability. A substantial number of cases permit recovery without privity of contract, especially where the group affected by the negligent misrepresentation is small.

(a) D negligently told P that D would store P's goods on Dock F, knowing that P needed the information for insurance purposes. Half of P's goods were stored on Dock D and these were destroyed by fire. P could not recover from his insurer because of the misdescription of the goods. P was permitted to recover from D because it was D's negligent misrepresentation, knowing the purpose of the request, that resulted in P's inability to collect from his insurer. See International Products Co. v. Erie Railroad Co., 244 N.Y. 331, 155 N.E. 662 (1927).

(b) The successful bidder on a contract relied on a soil analysis made available to all bidders, on which the bid was based. The engineering firm was negligent in making the soil analysis and this caused the winning bidder to lose money on the contract. The bidder may recover from the negligent engineering firm. See Rozny v. Marnul, 43 Ill.2d 54, 250 N.E.2d 656 (1969); Texas Tunneling Co. v. City of Chattanooga, Tenn., 329 F.2d 402 (6th Cir. 1964).

(c) Where D, a public weigher, weighed A's beans and issued a certificate to B which B used to determine the amount he paid A for them, D was held liable to B for B's overpayment since this was caused by a negligent misrepresentation of the weight. D is liable because he knew the sole purpose of the weighing was to determine the amount B owed. See Glanzer v. Shepard, 233 N.Y. 236, 135 N.E. 275 (1922).

Case 60   *Innocent material misrepresentation justifies rescission of contract*

P told D's stockbroker that his corporation had some surplus funds from inventory and desired to purchase some listed securities. P emphasized that only listed securities would be considered because the money might be needed on short notice to put back into the business, and also as an additional safety. D's agent recommended 8% notes of X Company and represented that application had been made to list the securities, and that they would be listed. Based on this representation P invested in X Company's notes. A few months later, X Company went into receivership. P learned that no application had ever been made to list the securities he bought and the company never intended to list them. Immediately upon learning these facts, P rescinded the contract, offered to return the securities and demanded the return of his purchase price. When D refused to rescind the contract, P brought this action. The lower court dismissed the suit because P failed to show D's actions were willful. May P rescind the contract because of an innocent misrepresentation?

Answer. Yes. P relied on the misrepresentation to his detriment. The evidence presented by P showed that the misrepresentation was material. P said that he would not purchase any unlisted securities. Although P did not prove that the misrepresentation was willfully false or fraudulently made, that was not necessary. An innocent misrepresentation is sufficient in an action at law or equity for rescission. If P also sought damages for fraud or deceit, he would have to show that D's misrepresentations were knowingly made. In this case P only sought to rescind the contract and the facts established his prima facie case. The case was remanded for a new trial.

See Seneca Wire & Manufacturing Co. v. A. B. Leach & Co., Inc., 247 N.Y. 1, 159 N.E. 700 (1928).

SECURITIES—RULE 10b–5

1. Implied civil liability under Rule 10b–5 afforded recovery in situations of fraud and misrepresentation where none would otherwise be available under state statutes, or at common law.

2. It has been said that basically, Rule 10b–5 "requires"

   (a) disclosure of special knowledge by insiders, as well as

   (b) avoidance of active fraud and misrepresentation. See Superintendent of Insurance v. Bankers Life & Casualty Co., 404 U.S. 6, 92 S.Ct. 165, 30 L.Ed.2d 128 (1971), and 1972/73 Annual Survey of American Law, pp. 226–232.

3. Rule 10b–5 was adopted by the SEC under the provisions of Section 10 of the 1934 Act.

4. Section 10 of the 1934 Act provides that "it shall be unlawful for any person, directly or indirectly, by the use of any means or instrumentality of interstate commerce or of the mails, or of any facility of any national securities exchange (b) to use or employ, in connection with the purchase or sale of any security registered on a national securities exchange or any security not so

registered, any manipulative or deceptive device or contrivance in contravention of such rules and regulations as the Commission may prescribe as necessary or appropriate in public interest or for the protection of investors."

5. The language of Rule 10b–5 itself, was fashioned after the language of Section 17(a) of the 1933 Act, and provides as follows:

"Rule 10b–5. Employment of Manipulative and Deceptive Devices.

It shall be unlawful for any person, directly or indirectly, by the use of any means or instrumentality of interstate commerce, or of the mails, or of any facility of a national securities exchange

(1) to employ any device, scheme or artifice to defraud,

(2) to make any untrue statement of a material fact or to omit to state a material fact necessary in order to make the statements made, in the light of the circumstances under which they were made, not misleading, or

(3) to engage in any act, practice or course of business which operates or would operate as a fraud or deceit upon any person, in connection with the purchase or sale of any security."

6. Rule 10b–5 was originally adopted by the SEC in 1942 in an effort to protect defrauded sellers of securities from insiders buying on inside information and has been used administratively by the SEC.

7. The most significant impact of Rule 10b–5 is the fact that it has given rise to an *implied* civil cause of action in favor of an injured party, and with it has given rise to a vast volume of case law interpreting its scope. The first case recognizing the implied civil cause of action was Kardon v. National Gypsum Co., 69 F.Supp. 512 (E.D.Pa.1946).

e.g. A and B, father and son, and C and D, brothers, owned all of the stock in W Corporation, each of them owning one-fourth. All four were officers, and the four together constituted the entire Board of Directors. C and D entered into an agreement with G Corporation to sell the plant and equipment of W Corporation for $1,500,000. Subsequently, C and D purchased all of the stock of A and B in W Corporation for $500,000. At the time, A and B knew nothing whatsoever about the negotiations with G Corporation, and C and D did not make any disclosure. At the meeting at which the sale of A's and B's stock to C and D was consummated in answer to a question as to whether he had made any agreement for the sale of the stock, C answered "no". Subsequent to the purchase of A and B's stock, the transaction with G Corporation was concluded for $1,500,000. A and B now sue C and D claiming a violation of Section 10(b) of the Securities Exchange Act of 1934 through a violation of Rule

X–10(B)–5 (now Rule 10b–5). C and D move to dismiss the action on the basis that no civil remedy is available. Will the motion to dismiss be granted?

Answer. No. Although not expressly provided for in the statute, a remedy through a civil action based upon Section 10(b) and upon Rule 10b–5 is available to enforce the duties and liabilities created by the 1934 Act. The Court found that there was a duty imposed upon the defendants and that a breach of that duty had been shown. If the plaintiffs' cause of action were solely a common law action for deceit, they would of course have to prove a loss as part of their case. The action in this case is not in damages for deceit, but for a share of the profits of the transaction. The proper remedy in this case is an accounting to ascertain and restore to the plaintiffs their appropriate share of the profits, if any. Thus, the court awarded a decree against the defendants for an accounting as prayed for in the complaint.

See Kardon v. National Gypsum Co., number 7, above, 73 F.Supp. 798 (E.D.Pa.1947), supplemented 83 F.Supp. 613. See also Henn, p. 599.

8. Defendants in cases based on Rule 10b–5 have taken the position that the 1934 Act, and the rule adopted under it, should not be applied if the securities involved were neither registered on a national securities exchange nor traded in the over-the-counter market. The result in Kardon v. National Gypsum Co., number 7, above, has been consistently followed and this defense has been rejected, the only requirement being the use of the mails or any instrumentality of interstate commerce.

9. Actions under Rule 10b–5 afford a number of procedural advantages:

   (a) Such actions are enforceable in federal courts only.

   (b) There is no statute of limitations for fraud in the forum state.

   (c) Actions under the Rule provide a broad choice of venue and may be brought in the district where any act or transaction constituting the violation occurred, the district where the defendant is found or is an inhabitant, or the district where the defendant transacts business. See Cary, p. 795.

   (d) World-wide service of process is available, since once venue is determined, process may be served either in the district of which the defendant is an inhabitant, or wherever the defendant may be found. See Cary, pp. 795–796.

   (e) State statutes requiring the posting of security for expenses which are applicable in shareholder derivation actions are not applicable to actions brought under Rule 10b–5. See Cary, p. 796.

(f) Under the doctrine of "pendent jurisdiction", the original federal jurisdiction which vests on the basis of the plaintiff's Rule 10b–5 claim extends *also* to any *non-federal claim* which the plaintiff may have against the same defendant, so long as the non-federal claim bears the requisite relationship to the federal claim. In such cases the requirement of diversity of citizenship is immaterial. See Cary, pp. 796–797. See also Henn, pp. 22–24.

(g) Rule 10b–5 actions are free of many of the precise procedural requirements of statutory causes of action, such as those afforded by Section 11 of the 1933 Act and Section 17 of the 1933 Act.

10. Rule 10b–5 causes of action are applicable to a very broad range of transactions, including both sales and purchases of securities, and the Rule has been held applicable to a merger which although not a "sale" for Section 5 of 1933 Act purposes was held so for purposes of a Rule 10b–5 cause of action.

11. Because it gives rise to an "implied" cause of action, and because it has developed on a case by case basis, the full scope and ultimate impact of Rule 10b–5 are not yet fully determined and are still emerging. See SEC v. Texas Gulf Sulphur Co., 401 F.2d 833 (2d Cir. 1968), certiorari denied 394 U.S. 976, 89 S.Ct. 1454, 22 L.Ed.2d 756, on remand 312 F.Supp. 77 (1969). See also, Bromberg, Securities Law, Fraud, SEC Rule 10b–5 (1969); Henn, pp. 597–606, 749.

REMEDIES AND DAMAGES

1. The following remedies are available in a suit based upon misrepresentation:

   (a) damages for the tort of deceit, see numbers 3, 4 and 5 below,

   (b) damages based on negligence for making a statement without taking reasonable care to learn the truth,

   (c) contract damages for breach of warranty, and

   (d) rescission of the contract of sale and restitution of the consideration given by both parties.

2. A misrepresentation which induces D to make a purchase may be used as a defense:

   (a) In a suit for the balance due on the purchase price D may ask that the contract be rescinded and both parties must return any consideration given, or

   (b) D may make a counterclaim based on damages incurred because of the misrepresentation.

3. There are two rules for determining damages for deceit:

(a) "loss of bargain", and

(b) "out of pocket".

4. Under the "loss of bargain" rule, which is followed in most states, a plaintiff can recover the *benefit of his bargain*. That is, the plaintiff recovers the difference between the actual value of the property acquired and the value of the property if it had been as represented. See CASE 61, below.

5. Under the "out of pocket" rule, which is followed in a few states, a plaintiff is permitted to recover only the money he has actually lost, that is, the difference between the actual value of the property and the amount paid for the property. This rule makes the plaintiff whole, but denies him the benefit of his bargain.

NOTE—If the defendant seller has made fraudulent misrepresentations he may also have to pay punitive damages. See District Motor Co., Inc. v. Rodill, 88 A.2d 489 (D.C.Mun.App.1952).

See generally, Dobbs, pp. 594–608; Prosser, pp. 683–694.

Standards of damages for misrepresentation or deceit   **Case 61**

D represented that a tract of land contained four thousand cords of wood worth 50¢ a cord, that it was served with a good stream and was capable of producing crops. P visited the property only once before buying it, and due to a driving rainstorm and lack of knowledge regarding the exact location of the land, P did not get a satisfactory view of the property. These and other misrepresentations induced P to buy the land. Actually, there were only two hundred cords of wood on the land; there were only seven or eight acres of arable land instead of the thirty that were represented; and the stream was inadequate to irrigate the land. P sued for damages for the tort of deceit. May P recover the difference between the amount he paid for the land and the value of the land if it had been as represented?

Answer. *Yes. "The victims of fraud are entitled to compensation for every wrong which was the natural and proximate result of the fraud. . . . To facilitate its application the proximate result rule is often subdivided into four small auxiliary rules: (1) a defrauded party is entitled to all out-of-pocket losses; (2) he is entitled to the benefit of his bargain; (3) if the property was falsely represented as improved with or containing some items which are not there, he is entitled to the cost of installing them; and (4) he is entitled to all consequential damages." These are guides to be used in applying the general rule. The court wanted to avoid selecting one rule which would make future decisions inflexible. It* *said that it would apply the rule most likely to do justice in a particular case. In the present case D made representations to induce P to buy the land, P relied on them, and some material representations were false. P is made whole by awarding him the value of the land if it had been as represented. The jury concluded that in that event the land would have been worth $2,000.00, the purchase price from which was deducted the actual value of the land, $100.00. Therefore, the judgment of the lower court of $1,900.00 was affirmed.*

See Selman v. Shirley, 161 Or. 582, 91 P.2d 312 (1939).

IX

UNJUSTIFIABLE LITIGATION

Summary Outline

INTRODUCTION   1.   Suits for unjustifiable litigation may be divided into three categories:

   (a) malicious criminal prosecution (this is the traditional basis),

   (b) malicious civil action, and

   (c) abuse of process.

2.   Malicious civil actions include:

   (a) malicious institution of involuntary bankruptcy proceedings against another, see Balsiger v. American Steel & Supply Co., 254 Or. 204, 458 P.2d 932 (1968),

   (b) malicious liquidation proceedings,

   (c) malicious arrest,

   (d) malicious execution against property, and

   (e) more recently, malicious civil proceedings whether administrative or judicial.   See Melvin v. Pence, 76 U.S.App.D.C. 154, 130 F.2d 423 (1942) and CASE 62, below.

NOTE—The action of malicious prosecution began as a remedy for causing unjustifiable criminal proceedings to be initiated. Gradually the cause of action was expanded to include the wrongful initiation of civil suits, and is a developing area of tort law.   See Prosser, p. 870.

3.   The *interests protected* by this action are:

   (a) *physical integrity* and *freedom from restraint* (this interest is infringed by a wrongful arrest),

   (b) *reputation as an asset* (this interest is infringed by wrongfully charging one with a crime or insanity),

   (c) *feelings, dignity and honor* (this interest is infringed by the wrongful bringing of the proceedings), and

   (d) *financial integrity* (this interest is infringed by the expense imposed by having to defend in the proceedings wrongfully commenced).

MALICIOUS PROSECUTION   1.   The elements essential to a cause of action for malicious prosecution are:

   (a) commencement of legal proceedings,

   (b) the proceedings must terminate in favor of the defendant who is the plaintiff in the later malicious prosecution suit,

   (c) the proceedings must have been brought without probable cause, and

(d) there must be malice on the part of the person bringing the proceedings, meaning without legal justification.

CAVEAT—If the plaintiff in a suit for malicious prosecution has been arrested or confined, the student should distinguish the case from facts giving rise to the tort of false imprisonment. Malicious prosecution involves a valid, lawful arrest. By contrast, false imprisonment involves an arrest without legal authority, which is, a "false" arrest. In addition, malicious prosecution requires a showing of malice; malice is not required for false imprisonment, but if malice is shown the plaintiff may recover punitive damages. See Chapter II, False Imprisonment and False Arrest, and Legal Process and Arrest, above.

2. There is a "commencement of proceedings" if there is an issuance of some process, such as an indictment, information, or warrant for arrest although not served. If the court treats the proceedings as proper, it is immaterial that the court actually has no jurisdiction of the proceedings.

   (a) Criminal proceedings are usually initiated by making a charge to the police so as to cause them to issue an arrest warrant or procure an indictment.

   (b) Civil proceedings are usually initiated by filing a civil action.

3. The proceedings "terminate in favor of the defendant":

   (a) if the grand jury fails to indict and defendant is discharged,

   (b) if he is tried and acquitted,

   (c) if he is discharged by the committing magistrate on preliminary hearing,

   (d) if there is formal dismissal of the proceeding,

   (e) if there is abandonment of the proceeding by the county attorney, or

   (f) if any other act results in the termination of this particular proceeding, even though a new proceeding on the same cause may be later initiated.

NOTE 1—The reason for the requirement that the proceedings have ended in the defendant's favor is to prevent the prosecuting witness from being frightened out of continuing with bringing the defendant to justice by having to withstand the burdens and fear of a collateral civil suit while the prosecution continues. Otherwise, many proper criminal prosecutions would fail because the prosecuting witness would not want to testify.

NOTE 2—Where the defendant leaves the jurisdiction and the statute of limitations prevents the plaintiff from bringing the action to trial, the defendant may not later maintain an action for malicious prosecution because the proceedings are not considered to have ended in the defendant's favor. See Halberstadt v. New York Life Insurance Co., 194 N.Y. 1, 86 N.E. 801 (1909). If a criminal prosecution is voluntarily settled through plea bargaining, the accused may not later bring suit for malicious prosecution based upon the criminal charges which he settled. See Leonard v. George, 178 F.2d 312 (4th Cir. 1949), certiorari denied 339 U.S. 965, 70 S.Ct. 1000, 94 L.Ed. 1374.

4. The courts define *"probable cause"* as *"a reasonable ground of suspicion, supported* by *circumstances sufficient to warrant* an ordinarily *prudent man in believing the party is guilty of the offense."* Gallucci v. Milavic, 100 So.2d 375 (Fla.1958).

5. Probable cause *is a question of law for the court* and not a question of fact for the jury.

6. *"Malice" means* that the *proceedings* have been *brought for* some *purpose other than bringing the defendant to justice* which is the only proper purpose.

   e.g. A criminal prosecution is brought with malice if the primary purpose is not to prosecute the defendant, but for the purpose of compelling the defendant to pay a debt or surrender property. The factual determination of malice is a question for the jury.

7. The prevailing view, as to want of "probable cause," is as follows:

   (a) If a prosecuting witness submits the facts fully and honestly to a lawyer and he is advised that there is probable cause, such advice is conclusive that there is probable cause and he has a defense in malicious prosecution.

   (b) Either a discharge by a magistrate after a preliminary hearing, or a failure of a grand jury to indict, is conclusive that there is want of probable cause.

   (c) Conviction after a trial is conclusive that there was probable cause.

   (d) Acquittal after trial determines only that guilt was not proved beyond a reasonable doubt and is therefore, no evidence of want of probable cause. P, in his subsequent civil suit, must prove that D did not have probable cause in bringing the criminal prosecution.

   See Shoemaker v. Selnes, 220 Or. 573, 349 P.2d 473 (1960).

8. The law must usually take advantage of someone's ill will to set the criminal machinery in motion. Hence it will protect anyone who acts either:

   (a) upon probable cause, or

   (b) in good faith, to enforce the criminal law.

9. If a person acts wholly maliciously, he will be protected if there is probable cause. If there is no probable cause, but he acts in

good faith to enforce the criminal law, he is protected. Therefore, the plaintiff in the malicious prosecution case must prove both:

(a) lack of probable cause, and

(b) malice.

10. In malicious prosecution based on criminal proceedings, damage is presumed and need not be pleaded or proved. By contrast, if it is based on civil proceedings, damage must be pleaded and proved.

11. If a government officer acts with malice, so long as he is exercising his discretionary power, he is not liable in federal courts and in many state courts. This immunity from liability is based on public policy to permit government employees to perform their duties without fear of harassment by suits. See CASE 63, below.

e.g. A public prosecutor is absolutely privileged to initiate and continue criminal proceedings. See Restatement, Second, Torts § 656.

See generally, Keeton, pp. 1104–1130; P & W, pp. 1119–1143; Prosser, pp. 834–856.

Malicious prosecution—civil proceedings as basis for recovery   Case 62

P sued D for malicious prosecution. P showed that D had maliciously commenced a civil action against P without probable cause. P successfully defended against D's suit and now sues for damages. D contends that P may not sue for malicious prosecution unless P was arrested or P's property was seized, and neither element was present in the present case. Are the contentions valid?

Answer. *No. Most courts permit an action to recover damages for malicious prosecution of a civil suit. The reason for permitting such an action is that "costs" awarded the defendant when he successfully defends the civil suit against him are insufficient to cover the actual damages. Furthermore, there is no interest of the defendant to be protected when he brings a civil suit maliciously. The elements essential to support such an action are substantially the same as when a prior criminal proceeding is involved: (1) civil proceedings must be commenced; (2) such proceedings must have terminated in favor of the plaintiff in the malicious prosecution suit; (3) there must be want of probable cause, which is a question of law for the court; and (4) the question of "malice" is one of fact for the jury. It may be inferred from want of probable cause. In addition to compensatory damages the plaintiff may recover punitive damages if the jury decides to award them. Thus there is a remedy for* *damages when a civil suit is brought with malice and without probable cause.*

See Peerson v. Ashcraft Cotton Mills, 201 Ala. 348, 78 So. 204 (1917).

Case 63   *Public officers not personally liable for discretionary or willful actions in their employment*

P was arrested on the grounds that he was a German and, therefore, an enemy alien. After a hearing before the Enemy Alien Board, which found that P was a Frenchman, P was kept in custody from 1942 to 1946. After his release, P sued the successive attorneys general, directors of the Enemy Alien Control Unit of the Department of Justice and the District Director of Immigration at Ellis Island. He alleged that he was arrested and imprisoned "without any authority of law and without any reasonable or colorable cause" and the action was done "maliciously and willfully." The lower court dismissed the suit on the ground that the defendants had absolute immunity from liability. P appealed. On review the facts alleged by P were assumed to be true in determining whether P stated a cause of action. Was the lower court correct in dismissing the suit?

Answer. Yes. Public policy requires that persons who occupy government positions should be permitted to act freely and fearlessly in the discharge of their official functions. Of course, a public official should not be permitted to vent his spleen upon others because of personal motive not connected with the public good. However, it would be impossible to make such a determination without a trial, and to submit all officials to the burden of trial would inhibit them in the exercise of their duties. The court concluded: "In this instance it has been thought in the end better to leave unredressed the wrongs done by dishonest officers than to subject those who tried to do their duty to the constant dread of retaliation." Thus the suit was dismissed.

See Gregoire v. Biddle, 177 F.2d 579 (2d Cir. 1949), certiorari denied 339 U.S. 949, 70 S.Ct. 803, 94 L.Ed. 1363.

ABUSE OF PROCESS

1. The use of criminal or civil legal process primarily to accomplish a purpose for which it was not designed constitutes the tort of abuse of process. See Restatement, Second, Torts § 682.

2. An action for "abuse of process" differs from malicious prosecution in that the plaintiff does not need to show either:

   (a) want of probable cause, or

   (b) that the proceedings have terminated in his favor.

3. The gravamen of this cause of action is NOT the wrongful procurement of legal process or the wrongful initiation of criminal or civil proceedings. It is the MISUSE of process, *no matter how properly obtained,* for any purpose other than that which it was designed to accomplish. See Restatement, Second, Torts § 682, Comment a.

4. "Abuse of process" provides redress in "a group of cases in which legal procedure has been set in motion in proper form, with probable cause, and even with ultimate success, but nevertheless has been perverted to accomplish an ulterior purpose for which it was not designed." Prosser, p. 856.

5. The *elements essential* to a cause of action *for abuse of process* are:

   (a) an intentional, wrongful use of legal process, and

   (b) the primary purpose for which it is used is improper.

   e.g. D has a judgment against P for $200. He also has a $1000 promissory note signed by P which is due and unpaid. D knows that P has $1000 to his credit in B Bank, that P has a herd of cattle worth $2500, and a homestead worth $10,000, all within the county. He knows also that he has no right to levy upon the homestead. For the purpose of compelling P to pay the $1000 note, D, under the $200 judgment, levies execution upon the homestead and the cattle, and garnishes P's bank account. P immediately sues D for damages for abuse of process. May he recover?

   Answer. Yes. D had a right to make a levy on a sufficient number of P's cattle to satisfy his $200 judgment, or to garnish the bank account. This is so even though spite was an incidental motive. However, on the facts stated D abused his right of process under the judgment. The elements of the tort of abuse of process are present. First, D used the levy of execution and the garnishment wrongfully when he used them for the purpose of collecting an unpaid promissory note. Second, D used such processes for a purpose which was improper in the ordinary conduct of such process; the only proper purpose of such processes in this case was its use in forcing payment of the $200 judgment. D's levy upon P's homestead, knowing that it was exempt from execution, constituted an abuse. The levying execution upon $2500 of cattle and garnishing a $1000 bank account for the collection of a $200 judgment, is further abuse of process. The gravamen of this tort is exterior to the legal process itself; it is the attempt to collect this $1000 note by a type of illegal compulsion by outside negotiation or otherwise. See Hauser v. Bartow, 273 N.Y. 370, 7 N.E.2d 268 (1937). See also Ash v.

Cohn, 119 N.J.L. 54, 194 A. 174 (1937); Ellis v. Wellons, 224 N.C. 269, 29 S.E.2d 884 (1944).

See generally, Keeton, pp. 1130–1133; P & W, pp. 1144–1148; Prosser, pp. 856–858.

X | DEFAMATION

Summary Outline

INTRODUCTION

1. Defamation is a communication which injures a person's good name or reputation; it is usually calculated to bring one into the hatred, obloquy, contempt or ridicule of his fellows.

   e.g. D says or writes of P that he is a "petty thief". See Restatement, Second, Torts § 559.

2. The interest violated by defamation is the right of everyone to be secure in his acquiring, maintaining and enjoying a good reputation.

3. Defamation includes both:

   (a) libel, which is written or printed and seen, and

   (b) slander, which is spoken and heard.

   See Restatement, Second, Torts § 568.

4. Decisions by the United States Supreme Court have substantially modified the traditional rules pertaining to defamation. Those decisions are binding on the states as a matter of constitutional law.

5. In the landmark decision of New York Times v. Sullivan in 1964 the Supreme Court held that the law of defamation was controlled by the First Amendment guarantees of free speech and freedom of the press. This created certain constitutional privileges and defenses. See Constitutional Privileges, below.

6. In a series of decisions, beginning in 1964, the Supreme Court held that a public official or public figure must establish "actual malice" to recover damages for publication of defamatory matter. Actual malice was defined as knowing falsity or a reckless disregard for the truth.

7. Subsequently, in Gertz v. Welch the Court applied a number of constitutional privileges to defamation which were designed to accommodate freedom of the press with the states' interest in protecting the reputation of private persons.

   (a) The Court held that a state may not impose liability without fault in a suit by a private party against a media defendant, but states could adopt any other standard of media liability.

   (b) Where the New York Times test of knowing or reckless falsity is not met by a private party, damages are limited to actual injury suffered. Actual injury includes out-of-pocket loss, impairment of reputation and standing in the community, personal humiliation, and mental anguish and suffering. It does not include presumed or punitive damages.

   See Constitutional Privileges, number 4, below.

   NOTE—The Court reasoned in Gertz that a private person was entitled to greater protection than a public figure because a public figure has greater access to the media to rebut the defamation.

CHART IV BASIS OF LIABILITY FOR DEFAMATION		
TYPE OF CASE	CONSTITUTIONAL REQUIREMENTS	SUMMARY OF LIABILITY
Private person v. Nonmedia defendant	None expressly mandated	Publication tending to lower plaintiff's reputation Third party reasonably believes publication in defamatory sense Defendant liable regardless of intent (strict liability)
Private person v. Media defendant	Some showing of fault	State law controls. In most states the defendant must have known that the publication was defamatory, or defendant was negligent in determining whether it was defamatory.
Public official v. Media defendant	New York Times rule: Knowing or reckless falsity	Defendant actually knew the publication was false, or Defendant was subjectively aware of recklessness of publication Mere negligence is not sufficient to impose liability
Public official v. Nonmedia defendant	New York Times rule	Same standard as media defendant

NOTE 1—To use the CHART the student must first determine whether the plaintiff is a private person or a public figure, and then whether there is a media defendant or a nonmedia defendant.

NOTE 2—In the CHART the term public official includes public figures.

8. In the Gertz case there was a media defendant. The Supreme Court has not expressly stated whether the Gertz rule applies to suits by a private party against nonmedia defendants.

   (a) Some courts have applied the Gertz holding to both media and nonmedia defendants in libel and slander cases. One court reasoned that it would be "bizarre" to hold individual defendants liable without fault while the media were only liable for negligence. See Jacron Sales Co., Inc. v. Sindorf, 276 Md. 580, 350 A.2d 688 (1976).

   (b) Other courts have continued to apply the traditional common law defamation principles, reasoning that no first amendment protections apply where only private parties are involved. See Calero v. Del Chemical Corp., 68 Wis.2d 487, 228 N.W.2d 737 (1975).

CAVEAT—The law relating to defamation is now in the process of change as courts are rethinking and redefining the relationship of constitutional guarantees of free speech and freedom of the press to the protection given to a person's reputation.

COMMON LAW DEFAMATION

1. The essential elements of a cause of action for defamation, whether for libel or slander, include the following:

   (a) The language must be false and defamatory.

   (b) The words must be published to a third person.

   (c) The language must be "of or concerning" the plaintiff, that is, it must identify the plaintiff to a reasonable reader, listener, or viewer. See CASE 61, below.

   (d) The plaintiff's reputation must be injured among a substantial and respectable segment of the community, although it may be only a small group.

2. The language must be defamatory.

   (a) The court must first decide as a question of law whether the language can reasonably be construed as defamatory, before submitting it to the jury; then the jury decides whether the language used was in fact so construed and understood by the listener or reader.

   e.g. "D tells P, an employee, in the presence of others, "I am convinced that you are responsible for the missing drugs. I am also going to find out who else is implicated in it with you. Because of this, I have got to let you go." These words may be interpreted differently by reasonable men. The court should allow the jury to determine whether the words impute a crime to P and are thus defamatory and actionable per se. See Sokolay v. Edlin, 65 N.J.Super. 112, 167 A.2d 211 (1961).

   (b) It is defamatory per se to speak, write or print of a person that he is a "criminal", "liar", "bastard", "cheat", or "coward", because these injure his good reputation among other persons.

      (i) To call a lawyer a representative of the Communist Party is libelous because it lessens his reputation. See Grant v. Reader's Digest Association, 151 F.2d 733 (1945). See also Grein v. La Poma, 54 Wn.2d 844, 340 P.2d 766 (1959).

      (ii) To call a woman a "whore" or "ex-whore", even if this is not a criminal offense, is defamatory. See Hollman v. Brady, 16 Alaska 308, 233 F.2d 877 (1956).

(iii) To state that P "is a whore and hath had the pox, and hath holes one may turn his finger in them," is defamatory because it injures P's reputation by calling her a whore and also for attributing a loathsome disease to P.   See Miller's Case, Cro.Jac. 430, 79 Eng.Rep. 368 (K.B. c. 1618).

(c) It is not defamatory per se to speak, write or print of a person that he is "dead", "a labor agitator", or has refused to give "concessions to a union", unless extrinsic facts show the words have other or additional meaning from what appears on their face, because the words do not necessarily adversely affect one's reputation among his fellows.

e.g.   An article about P, an attorney, stated, "who would have believed an obscure lawyer could have been dug up out of the mud in Omaha to shake himself all over us. . . .   The only Daltons I ever knew about that were not killed in the Coffeyville, Kan., bank robbery about 45 years ago, died in the state penitentiary.   Of course, some may have escaped.   Might be. . . ."   These are words of general abuse which are not libelous per se.   Because of this special damages must be proved for P to recover.   See Dalton v. Woodward, 134 Neb. 915, 280 N.W. 215 (1938).

3. Publication means communication to a third person, one other than the person defamed.

(a) D storeowner said to P "You have stolen a handkerchief from us and have it in your pocket."   The charge was false, but no one else was present.   Later the charge was repeated in Greek in the presence of others, but no one except P understood Greek.   Since no one but P heard and understood the statement, there was no publication and hence no slander.   See Economopoulos v. A. G. Pollard Co., 218 Mass. 294, 105 N.E. 896 (1914).

(b) H tells P, or writes P a letter addressed only to P, that P is a thief.   It is no publication to tell or write a person himself that he is a thief.

(c) If a defamatory message is sent by telegram from A to B with defamatory content about B, the reading by telegraph company employees in the course of transmission does not constitute publication.   If the telegram is opened by the addressee himself there is still no tort because there has been no publication.   However, if the telegram is opened and read by the spouse of the addressee there is a publication if the sender should have reasonably anticipated the spouse's act.   See Western Union Telegraph Co. v. Lesesne, 198 F.2d 154 (4th Cir. 1952).

(d) Most courts hold that dictation of defamatory matter to a secretary is sufficient publication, unless it is privileged.

See Restatement, Second, Torts § 577h; Ostrowe v. Lee, 256 N.Y. 36, 175 N.E. 505 (1931); contra, Mims v. Metropolitan Life Insurance Co., 200 F.2d 800 (5th Cir. 1952).

4. At common law *once publication* of defamatory matter was *shown, strict liability attached* to the defendant, *whether* the *publication* was *intentional or negligent.* See CHART IV, above for present rules.

5. One who repeats or otherwise republishes defamatory matter is liable to the same extent as though he had originally published it. Restatement, Second, Torts § 578.

e.g. D left a defamatory writing, written by an unknown third party, on the wall in the men's room of his tavern after P informed him of it and asked D to remove it. P learned of the writing, which concerned his wife, after a patron called to arrange a tryst. D's failure to remove the libel after reasonable opportunity to do so constitutes a republication of the libel. D is libel for such republication. See Hellar v. Bianco, 111 Cal. App.2d 424, 244 P.2d 757 (1952).

NOTE—A vendor of newspapers and magazines is not liable if a publication he sells contains libelous matter if the vendor had no knowledge of the libel. The vendor is considered a secondary publisher without liability because he did not write the libel, and he cannot be expected to read all books and magazines for libelous material before selling the publications. See Bottomley v. F. W. Woolworth & Co., Limited, 48 T.L.R. 521 (1932). See also P & W, p. 1022.

6. The defamatory language must be "of or concerning" the plaintiff.

e.g. D wrote the book "U.S.A. Confidential." In referring to Neiman-Marcus department store's employees, D wrote "some Neiman models are call girls, . . . the salesgirls are good, too—pretty and often much cheaper—twenty bucks on the average . . . . most of the male sales staff are fairies." The store employed nine models, 382 saleswomen and 25 salesmen. The store and individual employees sued for libel. Do any employees have a cause of action even though no particular employee was named?

Answer. Yes. An imputation of gross immorality to *some* of a small group casts suspicion on all. Where no attempt is made to exclude the innocent, all in the group have a cause of action. However, where the group libeled is large, no one can sue. The nine models are a small class and they have a cause of action. The salesmen, of whom it was alleged that "most . . . are fairies" also have a cause of action. However, the class of saleswomen is large and the word "all" or similar terminology is not used to describe them. Therefore, no member of the large class, in the absence of circumstances pointing to a particular member of the class, has a cause of action. See Neiman-Marcus v. Lait, 13 F.R.D. 311 (1952). See also American Broadcasting-Paramount Theatres, Inc. v. Simpson, 106 Ga.App. 230, 126 S.E.2d 873 (1962).

7. The *language* used by a defendant may be either:

   (a) *defamatory on its face,* or

   (b) *defamatory* only *when extrinsic facts show* that *it is so.*

8. When language is not defamatory on its face, then the *plaintiff must* both *plead and prove* the *inducement or innuendo* which makes it defamatory.

   (a) When the defamatory meaning of the communication, or its application to the plaintiff, depends on extrinsic circumstances, these circumstances must be alleged in the "inducement."

   (b) In the "colloquium" it must be alleged that the publication was made of and concerning the plaintiff *and* of and concerning the extrinsic circumstances.

   (c) The function of the "innuendo" is the explanation of the communication itself, which must be set forth verbatim. See Restatement, Second, Torts § 564, Comment f.

See generally, P & W, pp. 997–1022.

CAVEAT—There are three terms which are frequently found in discussions of defamation. These are defamatory "per se"; defamatory "on its face"; and defamatory "per quod". Prosser, at page 748, footnote 47, indicates that uses of these terms are confusing, and thus, he avoids their use in his text.

   (a) A publication which is defamatory "per se" or "on its face" is one as to which the defamatory sense is clear, and which requires no extrinsic evidence to prove this. In such a case damages are available *without* the proof of special damages.

   (b) A publication which is defamatory "per quod" is one which requires additional evidence to show that it is defamatory. In such a case, damages are available *only* on the pleading and proof of "special" damages.

Common law libel—no fault required Case 64

D newspaper published a story in which it was said "There is Artemus Jones with a woman who is not his wife, who must be, you know—the other thing! . . ." thinking and intending that Artemus Jones represented only a character in fiction. But a real Artemus Jones turned up and sued D for libel, alleging that many of his friends and neighbors, as reasonable readers of D's newspaper, thought the story was about the plaintiff and identified him as having a mistress. D set up in defense that Artemus Jones was a fictional character, and that D published the story in good faith and with no intent to injure anyone. D contended that it had no knowledge of the plaintiff's existence and could not have intended to injure him, and therefore, there is no libel. Is the defense good?

Answer. No. The words used are defamatory on their face. They are "of and concerning" the plaintiff for they specifically name him. They were published to all who read that portion of D's newspaper. Being defamatory on their face and being published of and concerning this plaintiff, these words are such that the law conclusively presumes damage to the plaintiff. Hence, all the elements of a cause of action for libel are present. Once there is an intentional or negligent publication of defamatory matter the publisher is absolutely and strictly liable for the damage caused. It is no defense that the publisher was innocent of any wrongful intent or that he thought the name published represented only a fictional character, when it in fact identifies the plaintiff to a *reasonable reader* of the printed page.

See Hulton & Co. v. Jones, [1910] A.C. 20; Sweet v. Post Publishing Co., 215 Mass. 450, 102 N.E. 660 (1913). See also Prosser, p. 772.

NOTE—The Hulton case illustrates the common law rule. The holding would be different if the case were decided today. See Constitutional Privileges, number 2, below.

COMMON LAW SLANDER

1. Slander is oral defamation; it is spoken and heard. See Restatement, Second, Torts § 568.

2. In four instances words are slanderous per se, that is, they will support an action for slander without pleading or proving special damage. This means that damage is presumed without proof thereof:

   (a) Words imputing a crime to the plaintiff—limited to crimes which banish one from society, such as those punishable by death or imprisonment, or involve moral turpitude by most courts. This would not include a crime such as parking on the wrong side of the street.

   (b) Words imputing to the plaintiff a loathsome and communicable disease which banishes him from society—usually limited to venereal disease.

   (c) Words affecting the plaintiff in his trade, calling, business, profession, office—such as calling a doctor a "quack", a lawyer a "shyster", a merchant a "cheat", a carpenter an "incompetent wood butcher", an office holder "an acceptor of bribes" or "card carrying communist".

e.g. The statement "people cannot get money out of him . . . as he is threatening bankruptcy" was held actionable because the words adversely affected the business and good reputation of the person spoken of. See Reed v. Melnick, 81 N.M. 608, 471 P.2d 178 (1970).

(d) In some jurisdictions words imputing unchastity to a woman. See CASE 65, below.

NOTE—The examples above would also constitute slander under modern law, and subject the defendant to liability without proof of special harm in the absence of a constitutional privilege. See Restatement, Second, Torts §§ 570–574. However, number 2(d) might be restated by a modern court to avoid the sex based classification. The Restatement suggests that imputing serious sexual misconduct to another, regardless of sex, is actionable without proof of special damages. See Restatement, Second, Torts § 574.

3. When words are not slanderous per se, as above set forth, then the plaintiff must allege and prove that special damage has been caused by the alleged slander.

   e.g. The words "You are drunk," unless other facts show that the words have an additional meaning, are not actionable per se. Being drunk is a misdemeanor and the words are not actionable without proof of special damages. See Torres v. Huner, 150 App.Div. 798, 135 N.Y.S. 332 (1912); Restatement, Second, Torts § 575.

4. Whether defamation by radio or television constitutes slander or libel is not settled in the cases. Some courts hold that it is libel, while other courts hold it is slander. Still other courts hold that it is libel if with a script, but slander if without a script. The Restatement classifies such broadcasts as libel. See Restatement, Second, Torts § 568A.

5. It is often said that the basis for the difference between slander and libel lies in the fact that the spoken word is fleeting, temporary and ephemeral in duration, whereas libel takes the more permanent physical form of writing, printing, pictures and the like. See Prosser, pp. 753–754.

6. In determining whether a publication is libel, rather than slander, the following factors should be taken into account:

   (a) the area of dissemination,

   (b) the deliberate and premeditated character of its publication, and

   (c) the persistence or permanence of the defamatory conduct.

7. The use of a mere transitory gesture, as a substitute for spoken words, such as a nod of the head, a wave of the hand, or a sign of the fingers, is a slander, rather than a libel.

See Restatement, Second, Torts § 568, Comment d.

Case 65 *Proximate cause of damages for slander*

D told X and Y that P, who was having an affair with Mrs. F, would do all he could to keep Mr. F in the penitentiary so that P could continue his relationship with Mrs. F. Y told P of D's statement, adding that the rumor was spreading all over the country. This caused P to become both mentally and physically ill and he could not work. P sued D for slander. May P recover?

Answer. No. Unless the words spoken are actionable per se there must be proof of damages. Most courts permit a woman to maintain a suit for damages for the oral imputation of unchastity, but a man must prove damages. This rule is based on the assumption by courts that the damages to a man in such circumstances are not as great as they would be to a woman. Therefore, under the facts of the present case P must prove special damages which are the "natural, immediate and legal consequence of the words." The court concluded that D was not responsible for Y's repetition of the statement to P and would not be liable to P on that ground. However, even if D were responsible for the repetition to P, D would not be liable. P's special damages must flow from P's impaired reputation. There was no proof that anyone believed D's statements or that P's character suffered. P's illness must be attributed to apprehension of loss of character, and fear of harm to his character. For P to recover the loss of character must be a substantial loss, which has actually taken place. Since P's damages were not the result of his loss of character but only P's apprehension of such loss, P may not recover.

See Terwilliger v. Wands, 17 N.Y. 54 (1858).

NOTE—A modern court might not recognize the sexist common law rule applied in the Terwilliger case, above. The rule suggested by the Restatement would permit recovery by either a man or woman for the imputation of serious sexual misconduct. See Restatement, Second, Torts § 574.

COMMON LAW LIBEL

1. Libel is defamation which can be seen; it may take the form of writing, printing, effigy, moving picture film, picture, or statue, which, by its embodiment in physical form, has some quality of permanence. See Restatement, Second, Torts § 568.

    (a) In a motion picture the spoken words are considered part of the circumstances which explain the picture and are part of the libel. See Youssoupoff v. Metro-Goldwyn-Mayer Pictures, Limited, 50 T.L.R. 581 (1934).

    (b) A defamatory statement made on television or radio has been held to be libel rather than slander even though it is not reduced to writing. See Shor v. Billingsley, 4 Misc.2d 857, 158 N.Y.S.2d 476 (1956); Hartmann v. Winchell, 296

N.Y. 296, 73 N.E.2d 30 (1947). However, many courts hold such defamation to be slander. See Prosser, pp. 753–754. See also Common Law Slander, numbers 4–6, above.

2. Libel which is defamatory on its face, is known as libel per se. It does not need any extrinsic facts of explanation. Damage is conclusively presumed, and a jury may award nominal or substantial damages without either pleading or proof thereof. Such libel is deemed "actionable per se."

   e.g. D writes to X that "P is a burglar". The publication itself imposes strict liability on D. P can recover damages of any amount without either pleading damage and without proof of damage.

3. If the alleged libel is not defamatory on its face it is known as libel per quod. It requires extrinsic facts by inducement or innuendo to explain why it is defamatory or the sense in which it is defamatory. There are two distinct views in the cases:

   (a) One view is that the rule is identical with that set forth in number 2 above, that damage is conclusively presumed and it is not necessary to show special damages.

   (b) The other view requires allegation and proof of special damage unless, as in slander, there is: (i) an imputation of crime, (ii) an imputation of a loathsome disease, (iii) imputation of conduct or characteristics which would adversely affect the plaintiff in his trade, profession or office, or (iv) an imputation of unchastity to a woman. Prosser at page 763, says this rule is followed by a "great majority" of the courts which have considered the question.

1. Defenses to a defamation action include: **COMMON LAW DEFENSES**

   (a) truth,

   (b) consent, and

   (c) privilege, absolute or qualified. *Conditional*

2. Truth is an absolute and complete defense to a civil action for defamation—libel or slander.

   CAVEAT—Under present law, where a constitutional privilege is applicable truth is no longer an affirmative defense to be established by the defendant. The plaintiff must prove that the published matter was false and also establish the requisite fault with respect to its publication. See CHART IV, above. See also Restatement, Second, Torts § 581A.

3. It is a defense in defamation that the publication was made by accident and without either negligence or intent to publish.

e.g. D said to P: "P, you are a thief and a robber". When the words were spoken, D had no intention of saying them in the presence of any third person. No other person was in sight, and D had no reason to believe that the words would be heard by anyone other than P. But the words were heard by X who was concealed in a closet. D is not liable for defaming P, the publication being wholly by accident. By contrast, if D had reason to foresee that his communication would be overheard or read by a third person, then D would be liable because the publication was made negligently.

4. Consent by the person defamed that the defamatory material may be published is a defense.

e.g. D told P to his face when no one else heard it, "P, you are a perjurer". A friend of the two, X, then appeared and P said to D this, "D I wish you would tell X what you just told me." D then addressed X, "I told P he was a perjurer." P sues D for slander. P's consent is a complete defense to D. See Restatement, Second, Torts §§ 583–584.

PRIVILEGES
1. A privilege to publish defamatory words arises from the occasion in which they are published.

2. Privilege to publish defamatory material may be either:

(a) absolute, in which case it is a complete defense, or

(b) qualified or conditional, in which case it is a defense only if the publication is made without malice.

NOTE—Malice destroys the qualified privilege as a defense. See number 6, below.

3. Absolute privilege, a complete defense, exists when defamatory material is spoken or written on the following occasions:

(a) judicial proceedings,

e.g. Statements or arguments made during a judicial proceeding by attorneys or the judge are privileged on the ground of public policy unless the statement is made with malice. See Irwin v. Ashurst, 158 Or. 61, 74 P.2d 1127 (1938).

(b) legislative proceedings,

e.g. D is a member of the house of representatives in the state legislature (or a congressman). He addresses his colleagues in the house chamber: "P is our legal consultant. He is wholly ignorant of the law and is a shyster. We should fire him and hire another from whom we can get some intelligent legal advice." P sues D for slander. May he recover?

Answer. No. The office of a legislator gives its holder, D, complete immunity from civil liability for defaming P. The occasion of using these defamatory words is one of *absolute* privilege. D, being a member of the legislative department of the state, using the words in his role as legislator and on legislative business, cannot be held liable for slander even though he knew the words were untrue, used them to gratify his ill will against P and wholly for improper purposes. Of course, if D had used the same language about P on an occasion wholly divorced from any legislative functions, he would be liable like any other citizen. Such immunity from civil liability extends to all phases of the legislative process, including committee meetings, committee reports, arguments and voting. This absolute immunity does not extend to inferior legislative bodies such as town meetings and city councils. Using defamatory language in such meetings by councilmen is conditionally privileged by showing that the statement was made in good faith. See Mills v. Denny, 245 Iowa 584, 63 N.W.2d 222 (1954).

(c) executive proceedings in which government officers are charged with the responsibility of executing the laws.

e.g. D, Governor of State X, is required to make a report to the legislature on conditions in the state. In a report which he reads to the legislature, he charges A, B and C, large taxpayers, of evading the tax laws which make such evasion a criminal offense. He then releases to the newspapers of the state a copy of such report, explaining why such report was made in his executive capacity. A, B and C sue D for libel. May they recover?

Answer. No. Both of these publications were part of D's executive functions as governor and carry with them *absolute* immunity from civil liability for defamation. See also CASE 64, below.

4. A qualified or conditional privilege is prima facie a complete defense, but the privilege is lost in the following circumstances:

(a) "Malice" in the publishing destroys the privileges. "Malice" here means that the defamation is published with improper motive or for an improper purpose.

(b) Wanton or reckless conduct which causes the libel destroys the privilege. The privilege is not lost for a mistake due to inexperience. See Hutchinson v. New England Telephone & Telegraph Co., 350 Mass. 188, 214 N.E.2d 57 (1966).

5. There is no specific test for determining when the occasion will afford the protection of qualified privilege, because such occasions are of infinite variety in circumstances. In general three items are of importance:

(a) The publication must be for a proper purpose and made in a reasonable manner.

    (b) There must be either:

        (i)   a private interest which the law considers of such importance that it should be protected by the privilege, or

        (ii) a public interest in having the defamatory material published.

6.   The application of qualified privilege is shown in the following examples:

    (a) D, a director of a company received a letter stating that employee P was having an affair with X. D is privileged to show the letter to company officers to determine what action to take. D is not privileged to show the letter to P's wife because there is no legitimate purpose for so doing. See Watts v. Longdson, 1 K.B. 130 (1929).

    (b) D was engaged in the business of making investigations and reports for insurance companies. D reported that P was not qualified for a certain position. D was negligent in the investigation. P sued for damages. Does negligence in making a statement render an otherwise privileged statement libelous?

          Answer. No. Negligence in obtaining facts does not take the place of willful conduct from which malice can be inferred. D's statement does not lose its privilege merely because it was negligently made. See Johns v. Associated Aviation Underwriters, et al., 203 F.2d 208 (5th Cir. 1953).

    (c) The reports of a mercantile agency on the credit of individuals to subscribers are conditionally privileged. Such an agency supplies a legitimate business need and should have the protection of the privilege. However, where a report contains unreasonable or excessive publication of defamatory matter, the privilege may be lost. Similarly, the privilege is lost by reports made recklessly or without reasonable grounds. See Shore v. Retailers Commercial Agency, Inc., 342 Mass. 515, 174 N.E.2d 376 (1961).

    (d) Communications to law enforcement officials concerning persons suspected of committing some crime are privileged unless done with malice. See Brow v. Hathaway, 95 Mass. (13 Allen) 239 (1866); Faber v. Byrle, 171 Kan. 38, 229 P.2d 718 (1951). Malice may be shown if the informer acts with reckless disregard of the truth, such as reporting a rumor to police as though it were a fact for which the informer vouches. See Pecue v. West, 233 N.Y. 316, 135 N.E. 515 (1922).

    (e) P is D's employee who has applied to X for a job. X asks D about P's qualifications as an employee. D replies, "P is both a thief and an adulterer". D's reply is not for the purpose of giving information to X to protect X from incompetent or dishonest employees, but for the purpose of retaining P in his own employ. P sues D. The defense is *qualified* privilege. Of course, when D shows that he gave such defamatory material to X at X's request under these circumstances, he has made out a privileged occasion and a prima facie defense. But when it appears that D's motive for the remark was to retain P as his own employee and was for an improper purpose, that is, other than to give X honest information concerning P as a prospective employee of X, then such defamatory words were used "maliciously" and the privilege was thereby forfeited. There is an additional reason why the defense is not good. D's words went beyond the scope of the claimed privilege. For D to say that P was "an adulterer" has nothing to do with his capacity as an employee. Such defamatory words in this setting involve no privilege at all.

Federal officer acting within his authority has no personal liability Case 66

In 1950 the existence of the Office of Housing Expediter, the predecessor agency of the Office of Rent Stabilization, was about to expire. Congress had earmarked $2,600,000 for payment of terminal leave of employees of that agency. M and N, two agency officers decided that the money should be spent during the current fiscal year and devised a plan whereby they terminated themselves and other employees as permanent employees in order to become eligible to receive payment for accrued leave. They were re-hired the next day as temporary employees, with the intent to convert back to permanent employee status should the agency's life be extended. B opposed the plan at that time, but did not have authority to stop it. M and N carried out their plan and the life of the agency was extended. Three years later the plan was made the subject of much public criticism of the agency in Congress and in newspapers. When the plan was publicized, B was appointed acting director of the agency and B authorized issuance of a press release stating that M and N would be suspended as his first official act. The press release recounted the plan and how it came about. M and N sued alleging that the press release was libelous. B defended on the grounds that issuance of the press release was privileged. May the law of privilege be used as a defense by government officials in a civil suit for defamation?

Answer. *Yes. Privilege is an expression of policy designed to aid the effective functioning of government. In this case the integrity of the agency had been put in question. The press release stated B's position on the matter and named the officials responsible for instituting the plan which was contrary to the spirit of the terminal leave legislation and involved questionable ethics. The issuance of press releases was standard agency practice and the statement of* *the planned personnel change was appropriate in the circumstances. The claim of unworthy purpose does not destroy B's claim of privilege. The court held that one who is defamed by a federal officer acting within this authority, even if the action is malicious, has no recourse against the officer. M and N had no recourse against the government either, because the Federal Tort Claims Act expressly excludes suits for defamation. Thus, the suit for defamation was dismissed.*

See Barr v. Matteo, 360 U.S. 564, 79 S.Ct. 1335, 3 L.Ed.2d 1434 (1959), rehearing denied 361 U.S. 855, 80 S.Ct. 41, 4 L.Ed.2d 93. See also Heine v. Raus, 399 F.2d 785 (4th Cir. 1968).

NOTE—The rule in CASE 66 has been extended to all torts. See Norton v. McShane, 332 F.2d 855 (5th Cir. 1964).

Case 67   *Qualified privilege of fair comment recognized*

Three Cherry sisters were engaged in public entertainment. D's paper published a story on their performance in these words: "Effie is an old jade of 50 summers, Jessie a frisky filly of 40, and Addie, the flower of the family, a capering monstrosity of 35. Their long skinny arms, equipped with talons at the extremities, swung mechanically, and anon waived frantically at the suffering audience. The mouths of their rancid features opened like caverns, and sounds like the wailings of damned souls issued therefrom. They pranced around the stage with a motion that suggested a cross between the dance du ventre and fox trot,—strange creatures with painted faces and hideous mien. Effie is spavined, Addie is stringhalt, and Jessie, the only one who showed her stockings, has legs with calves as classic in their outlines as the curves of a broom handle." P, one of the sisters, sued D for libel, the complaint setting forth the above quotation verbatim. D set up in defense that the above article was written to expose the character of the public performance, that it was published as criticism in satire but without malice or ill will toward the plaintiff or her sisters. No malice was shown. May P recover?

Answer. No, as a matter of law. This is a defense of conditional privilege in the form of "fair comment". A publication may be justified on the ground of "fair comment" provided it: (a) deals with a matter of public concern or interest, (b) consists of opinion or comment rather than a statement of facts, and (c) is fair in the sense that it is not founded on misstatement of facts.

The reasoning is as follows: (a) When one publishes a book, a newspaper story, a magazine article, a composition in music or drama, or presents to the public a picture or statue, an opera, a recital, play or entertainment, there arises immediately a public interest in its quality, its characters, its author, its merits and the like. It invites public criticism, as well as public praise. There is no doubt that the entertainment which the plaintiff and her sisters presented was a matter in which the public had an interest. (b) The quoted article is wholly comment or opinion. It does not state facts beyond the fact of an entertainment, and the fact that the plaintiff and her sisters presented it, both of which facts were essential as the subject for opinion and comment. (c) The real question is whether the opinion is "fair" comment. The word "fair" here means that it must be the honest opinion of the writer or publisher, and that its purpose in being published is to give the public the benefit of such opinion so that it may be informed of the nature, character and quality of the performance. It means that it must not be published for the purpose of causing personal injury to the plaintiff, even though that may result. But "fair" comment is not limited to that which is agreeable, moderate, temperate, reasonable, wise or unprejudiced. It may be disagreeable, immoderate, intemperate, unreasonable, foolish and prejudiced. Nor is it limited in style to that which is staid and colorless. It may take the form of humor, denunciation, satire or ridicule. In this case the story takes the form of pungent satire and caustic ridicule. The fact that the writer or the publisher may or may not have been prejudiced is totally immaterial. The comment in this case is "fair". It made no misstatement of fact. It dealt only with the entertainment and the manner of its presentation in both of which the public had an interest and concern. It is limited to the realm of opinion expressed in colorful, humorous and biting satire. This makes out a case of conditional *privilege. When the occasion is one of* qualified *privilege there is a presumption that the publication was made in good faith and the burden is on the plaintiff to overcome such presumption by showing that the publication was "malicious" or for an ulterior purpose. The question of malice is one for the jury. Here the facts state there was no showing of such. Hence, P cannot recover.*

See Cherry v. Des Moines Leader, 114 Iowa 298, 86 N.W. 323 (1901).

CONSTITUTIONAL PRIVILEGES

1. The Constitution imposes some limitations on recovery for defamation because of the protection given to freedom of speech and freedom of the press by the First and Fourteenth Amendments.

2. A public official may not recover damages for a defamatory falsehood relating to his official conduct unless the statement was made with "actual malice."

   e.g. The New York Times published an advertisement by a committee seeking to raise funds for the civil rights movement. The ad described a "wave of terror" in Montgomery, Alabama including various acts of harassment by the police. The ad contained numerous inaccurate and untrue statements. P, an elected Commissioner whose duties included supervision of the police, brought a civil libel action against the newspaper and others. The newspaper contended that it acted in good faith in publishing the submitted ad, and that a public official should not be permitted to maintain a libel action for criticism of his official conduct. The jury awarded damages to P. On appeal the Court enunciated the following rule: "The constitutional guarantees require, we think, a federal rule that prohibits a public official from recovering damages for a defamatory falsehood relating to his official conduct unless he proves that the statement was made with 'actual malice'—that is, with knowledge that it was false or with reckless disregard of whether it was false or not." The Court reasoned that if a more relaxed standard were established, it would lead to self-censorship and inhibit discussion on matters of public concern, including criticism of official conduct of public officials. The civil judgment for damages against the newspaper was vacated because the defamatory statements concerned the official conduct of the plaintiff, a public official, and because there was no showing of "actual malice" by the defendant newspaper. The failure to check the accuracy of the published advertisement with news stories in its own files did not establish a reckless disregard for the truth. Therefore, P may not recover. See New York Times Co. v. Sullivan, 376 U.S. 254, 84 S.Ct. 710, 11 L.Ed.2d 686 (1964).

NOTE 1—The "actual malice" required by the New York Times rule should be contrasted to the "malice" or "express malice" sometimes required for punitive damages. Such malice involves personal ill will or a willful and wanton disregard of the personal rights and interests of the person defamed. See CASE 71, below.

NOTE 2—In a later case the Court equated reckless disregard of the truth with subjective awareness of probable falsity. "There must be sufficient evidence to permit the conclusion that the defendant in fact entertained serious doubts as to the truth of his publication." St. Amant v. Thompson, 390 U.S. 727, 88 S.Ct. 1323, 20 L.Ed.2d 262 (1968).

3. The constitutional privilege of the New York Times case covering public officials was subsequently extended to cover public figures.

(a) Two companion cases to New York Times were decided by the Court. The first case involved the Saturday Evening Post's charge that Coach Wally Butts of the University of Georgia had conspired with Coach Barr Bryant of the University of Alabama to fix a football game between their respective schools. The second case involved an erroneous Associated Press account of Brigadier General Edwin Walker's participation in a University campus riot. Because Butts was paid by a private alumni association and Walker had retired from the Army, neither could be classified as a "public official". However, the Court extended the constitutional privilege of the New York Times case to protect defamatory criticism of nonpublic officials who "are nevertheless intimately involved in the resolution of important public questions or, by reason of their fame, shape events in areas of concern to society at large." In both cases state court civil judgments for damages for libel were vacated because they were based on criticism of the conduct of the plaintiffs, and there was no showing of malice. The Court reasoned that the rule would obviate the fear of civil liability which might dissuade a timorous press from the effective exercise of First Amendment freedoms. See Curtis Publishing Co. v. Butts and Associated Press v. Walker, 388 U.S. 130, 87 S.Ct. 1975, 18 L.Ed.2d 1094 (1967).

(b) H and W were very wealthy and socially prominent. H sought a divorce from his wife on the grounds of extreme cruelty and adultery. H was granted the divorce, but the trial judge did not make a specific finding that W had committed adultery. Time magazine reported that H had been granted a divorce from W on the grounds of extreme cruelty and adultery. Subsequently, W brought suit for libel, and Time contended, inter alia, that W must show actual malice to recover because W was a public figure. The Court defined a public figure as one who has attained special prominence in society. The Court noted that W may have been prominent in Palm Beach, Florida society, but she lacked any prominent role in the affairs of society in general. She did not thrust herself into the forefront of any public controversy in order to influence the resolution of the issues. Since judicial proceedings are necessary to obtain a divorce, there was no public controversy. W did not freely choose to publicize her marital difficulties. Therefore, W was not a public figure for the purpose of determining the extent of the First Amendment protection afforded the publication. Furthermore, the fact that Time misinterpreted the court decision is not a valid defense. A publisher has the duty to determine whether his report of a decision is factually correct. W may recover if she can show negligence in the defamatory publication. She need not show actual malice. See Time, Inc. v. Firestone, 424 U.S. 448, 96 S.Ct. 958, 47 L.Ed.2d 154 (1976).

4. If the individual defamed is neither a public official nor a public figure the limitation of liability applicable in those situations does not apply, even though the event described is of public interest.

e.g. P, an attorney, was involved in a lawsuit of public interest by representing one of the parties. P was not a public official or a public figure. D made false statements about P in an article about the lawsuit, identifying P with various communist causes. P sued for libel. D contended that there was no liability under the New York Times rule because there was no malice. Is there liability?

Answer. Yes. Compensatory damages for the actual injury suffered may be recovered by P. P's actual injury includes impairment of reputation, personal humiliation and mental suffering as well as any out-of-pocket loss. The Court reasoned: "Public officials and public figures usually enjoy significantly greater access to the channels of effective communication and hence have a more realistic opportunity to counteract false statements than private individuals normally enjoy. Private individuals are therefore more vulnerable to injury, and the state interest in protecting them is correspondingly greater." However, First Amendment considerations require some limitation on liability. Punitive damages may not be recovered unless there was knowledge that the statement was false or there was a reckless disregard for the truth. This limitation of damages is necessary because otherwise the uncontrolled discretion of juries would inhibit the exercise of freedom of the speech and press. See Gertz v. Welch, 418 U.S. 323, 94 S.Ct. 2997, 41 L.Ed. 2d 789 (1974) which declined to follow the Court's plurality opinion in Rosenbloom v. Metromedia, Inc., 403 U.S. 29, 91 S.Ct. 1811, 29 L.Ed.2d 296 (1971).

5. The New York Times rule pertaining to public officials has also been applied to situations in which the publication is *by,* in contrast to being *about,* a public official. It is applicable "at the very least to those among the hierarchy of government employees who have, or appear to the public to have, substantial control over the conduct of government affairs." Rosenblatt v. Baer, 383 U.S. 75, 86 S.Ct. 669, 15 L.Ed.2d 597 (1966).

See generally, CHART IV, above; Gregory, pp. 1081–1129, Keeton, pp. 981–1041; P & W, pp. 1023–1057.

DEFENSES— PROCEDURAL ASPECTS

1. At common law truth was an affirmative defense which had to be established by the defendant. However, under present law the plaintiff may be required to show that the published matter was false, at least in situations where constitutional privileges are applicable. See CHART IV and Constitutional Privileges, above.

2. Privilege and consent are affirmative defenses. The burden of proving them rests on the defendant.

3. The burden of showing that a qualified or conditional privilege has been abused or that the publication was maliciously made is on the plaintiff.

4. If the facts concerning the occasion for publishing defamatory words are not in dispute, then the question of privilege is one of law for the court; otherwise it is for the jury under proper instructions from the court.

5. The defendant may show in mitigation of damages in a defamation action that he acted in good faith, that the reputation of the plaintiff is bad, or that he has published a retraction of the defamatory material. See Turner v. Hearst, 115 Cal. 394, 47 P. 129 (1896). None of these is a complete defense.

6. The so-called "single publication rule" may serve as a defense in libel matters, and more specifically as a defense to multiple litigation arising out of the publication of a book, magazine or newspaper.

   (a) At common law each sale or delivery of a single copy of a book or a magazine constituted a separate actionable publication.

   (b) The common law rule thus gave rise to as many causes of action as there were copies sold.

   (c) In an effort to limit the impact of this rule most American jurisdictions have adopted the "single publication rule". This rule provides that the entire edition of a magazine, book or newspaper is treated as only one publication, thus giving rise to only one cause of action. Similarly, all publications resulting from a single broadcast on radio or television would be included in the rule. See Ogden v. Association of the United States Army, 177 F.Supp. 498 (D.C.D.C. 1959); Restatement, Second, Torts § 577A.

   NOTE 1—The single publication rule only applies to multiple publications by the same publisher.

   e.g. An old movie shown on television could be the basis of an action for defamation even if an action against the original producer of the movie were barred by the statute of limitations. Assuming that the movie was defamatory, an action would lie against the television station. Under this rule the plaintiff could recover in a single action for all damages suffered, at least those within the jurisdiction of the court.

   NOTE 2—The "single publication rule" has not entirely eliminated the procedural problems with respect to interstate libel. In the situation where copies of one issue of a magazine or newspaper are circulated through several states the plaintiff may have a cause of action in each state. Although a court in a given state which has adopted the single publication rule may purport to dispose of all of the claims arising from the publication of that issue, it is not clear that a court in applying the rule could foreclose the courts of another jurisdiction from enforcing a separate cause of action in that state. See Prosser, p. 769.

See generally, Gregory, pp. 983, 1039–1040; Keeton, pp. 970–975; P & W, pp. 1019–1020.

XI RIGHT OF PRIVACY

Summary Outline

A.   Introduction

B.   Interests Protected

INTRODUCTION

1. The right of privacy, commonly referred to as the tort of invasion of privacy, involves the invasion of one of four distinct interests of the plaintiff.

2. Those wrongs which this tort protects against are:

    (a) unreasonable intrusion,

    (b) unreasonable disclosure of another's private life,

    (c) placing another in a false light, and

    (d) appropriation of another's name or likeness.

3. This separate tort action to redress an invasion of the right of privacy had its origin in an article in the Harvard Law Review in 1890 by Warren and Brandeis. See 4 Harv.L.Rev. 193 (1890).

4. The four interests protected by the tort, see number 2, above, are related in that all involve the right of a person to maintain his privacy and to live an individual life free from unreasonable or unwarranted prying or publicity. Prosser states that this is not one tort, but "four distinct kinds of invasion of four different interests of the plaintiff." Prosser, p. 804.

5. Damages for this tort include:

    (a) harm to the interest in privacy resulting from the invasion,

    (b) mental distress, including emotional distress and personal humiliation, and

    (c) special damages.

    NOTE—Punitive damages may be limited by the Supreme Court's decision in Gertz v. Welch. See Chapter X, Constitutional Privileges, above.

    CAVEAT—The "right of privacy" as a basis of tort liability should not be confused with the "right of privacy" which is constitutionally protected from state action. Although the Constitution does not specifically mention any right of privacy, the U.S. Supreme Court has recognized that right which has its roots in the First, Fourth, and Fifth Amendments and in the penumbras of the Bill of Rights, in the Ninth Amendment and in the concept of liberty guaranteed by the first section of the Fourteenth Amendment. The constitutional "right of privacy" served as the basis on which the Supreme Court struck down state laws imposing criminal sanctions for dissemination of birth control information and contraceptives. See Griswold v. Connecticut, 381 U.S. 479, 85 S.Ct. 1678, 14 L.Ed.2d 510 (1965). A later decision held that the constitutional right of privacy includes a woman's decision to terminate her pregnancy by abortion up to the time when the fetus becomes viable. See Roe v. Wade, 410 U.S. 113, 93 S.Ct. 705, 35 L.Ed.2d 147 (1973), rehearing denied 410 U.S. 959, 93 S.Ct. 1409, 35 L.Ed.2d 694.

1. Intrusion upon plaintiff's physical solitude or seclusion, either physically or otherwise, is the first of the four types of actionable conduct.

    (a) Recovery has been permitted for the humiliation and embarrassment which plaintiffs suffered when their landlord placed an eavesdropping device in their bedroom. See Hamberger v. Eastman, 106 N.H. 107, 206 A.2d 239 (1964).

    (b) Recovery for invasion of privacy based on intrusion was permitted for unauthorized wiretapping and electronic eavesdropping. However, the court held that keeping P under surveillance in public places by itself was not actionable, but it could be so "overzealous" as to render it actionable and that was a factual question for the jury to determine. In addition, recovery was denied for interviewing persons who knew P, thereby uncovering information of a personal nature, because such information was already known to others and thus could not invade P's privacy. Recovery was also denied for causing P to be accosted by girls with illicit proposals, and the making of harassing phone calls to P at odd hours, because neither of these activities involved intrusion for the purpose of gathering information of a private and confidential nature. See Nader v. General Motors Corp., 25 N.Y.2d 560, 307 N.Y.S.2d 647, 255 N.E.2d 765 (1970) and CASE 68, below.

    (c) Opening the personal mail of another may also be a tortious intrusion.

2. Intrusion does not depend on any publicity given to the information gathered to be actionable, but merely on an intrusion that would be highly offensive to a reasonable person. See Restatement, Second, Torts § 652B.

3. The second kind of actionable invasion is "disclosure". This is publicity, of a highly objectionable nature, given to private information about the plaintiff, even if it is true. The matter disclosed must be highly offensive to the reasonable person and not of legitimate concern to the public. See Restatement, Second, Torts § 652D.

    (a) Readers Digest published an article entitled "The Big Business of Hijacking" and described a number of incidents. The article stated: "P stole a 'valuable-looking' truck in Danville, Ky., and then fought a gun battle with the local police, only to learn that they had hijacked four bowling pin spotters." The article did not mention that the incident occurred eleven years previously. In the meantime P had reformed and assumed a place in respectable society. When the article was published naming P, his friends learned of P's past life and thereafter "abandoned and scorned" him. P sued for invasion of privacy, and the magazine moved to dismiss. The court noted that reports of current criminal activities, including the names of suspects and offenders, were the legitimate province of a free press. The facts of past crimes also serve a public purpose. However, the present article named a past offender who had reformed. P had not reattracted public attention to himself in some independent fashion, and the only public "interest" that would be served was that of curiosity. Therefore, the motion to dismiss was denied. At trial the following issues must be resolved: (i) whether P had become a rehabilitated member of society, (ii) whether identifying P by name would be highly offensive and injurious to a reasonable person, (iii) whether the information was published with a reckless disregard for its offensiveness, and (iv) whether any independent justification existed for disclosing P's identity. See Briscoe v. Reader's Digest Association, 4 Cal. 3d 529, 93 Cal.Rptr. 866, 483 P.2d 34 (1971).

(b) P was a prostitute in her younger days. She was also tried for murder and acquitted. Thereafter, P gave up her ways of sin and married, taking a respectable place in society. D made a motion picture of P's earlier life based on public records from P's murder trial and used P's true name. This caused P's friends who did not know of her past to scorn and abandon P. P sued for damages for a violation of her privacy. May P recover?

> ***Answer.*** Yes. The use of P's true name in connection with the incidents from her unsavory past was unnecessary. It held P up to the scorn and contempt of society and this is actionable. If D had based the film on the public record without identifying P, P would not have a cause of action. But D went further and used P's true name and permitted identification of P. Thus, P may recover for invasion of privacy. See Melvin v. Reid, 112 Cal.App. 285, 297 P. 91 (1931).

(c) Recovery was permitted by a plaintiff, against a newspaper which published a picture of her, taken at a "fun house", in which her dress was blown up by air jets, and except for her panties she was completely exposed from the waist down. Ordinarily the giving of publicity to what is already public, and what anyone present would be free to see, is not actionable. However, in this case, the plaintiff was singled out from the public scene and undue attention was focused on her in a situation where the court found "nothing of legitimate news value" in the photo. See Daily Times Democrat v. Graham, 276 Ala. 380, 162 So.2d 474 (1964).

CAVEAT—The First Amendment right of free speech and free press may be a valid defense to disclosure. The constitutional limits to recovery have not yet been defined. The Supreme Court has held that disclosure of facts which are obtained from public records is not actionable, thereby casting doubt on the viability of the decisions in number 3(a) and (b) above. The full extent to which disclosure of facts of a private nature is constitutionally permissible has not been decided. See CASE 70, below.

4. Placing the plaintiff in an objectionable "false light" before the public is the third type of actionable invasion.

   (a) Recovery was permitted by a female model when her photograph was altered from its original use in a book ad to use in a bawdy and suggestive bedsheet ad. See Russell v. Marboro Books, 18 Misc.2d 166, 183 N.Y.S.2d 8 (Sup.Ct. 1959). Note that recovery was allowed in this case, even though the plaintiff had signed a release consenting to the unrestricted use of her photograph.

   (b) Two professional female models were photographed on a Suzuki motorcycle for an ad and signed a release for use of the picture. The ad carried the legend, "You Get More Nookie on a Suzuki." The models sued and alleged that the ad "by reason of its smutty and pornographic implications and innuendoes . . . was done in a malicious violation of their right of privacy." They were permitted to recover as they were placed in a "false light." See Stern, Walter & Simmons, Inc., v. Seaboard Surety Company, 308 F.Supp. 252 (N.D.Ill., E.D.1970).

5. The Restatement has applied the standard of Gertz v. Welch, discussed in Chapter X, Constitutional Privileges, above, and concluded that false light must not only be highly offensive to the reasonable person, but also that the defendant must have known of the offensive nature or acted in reckless disregard to the false light in which the plaintiff would be placed in order to recover. See Restatement, Second, Torts 652E.

   NOTE—The gist of this invasion of privacy is placing the plaintiff before the public in an objectionable false light. In some situations this may also constitute the tort of defamation. In that event the plaintiff may base his suit on invasion of privacy and defamation, but there can only be one recovery for a single instance of publicity.

6. The fourth category of actionable invasion in the law of privacy is "appropriation" of plaintiff's name or likeness for the defendant's advantage.

   (a) Recovery was permitted by a woman whose picture was placed by mistake in a newspaper advertisement without her consent for a stage show describing her as an "exotic red haired Venus." See Flake v. Greensboro News Co., 212 N.C. 780, 195 S.E. 55 (1938).

(b) The result in (a) above should be contrasted to the case in which Pat Paulsen, the TV performer and comedian, sought redress for the unauthorized use of his picture in a poster. The poster bore the inscription "For President" and showed Paulsen wearing a ruffled cap and prim frock, holding an unlit candle in one hand and carrying a tire on his other. A banner was draped across his chest, "in the manner, if not the style of a beauty pageant contestant," saying "1968". Denying relief, the court said that "privacy in its usual sense is hardly the goal of an entertainer or performer." It held that "when a well-known entertainer enters the presidential ring, tongue in cheek or otherwise, it is clearly newsworthy and of public interest. A poster which portrays plaintiff in that role, and reflects the spirit in which he approaches said role, is a form of public interest presentation to which protection must be extended." Paulsen v. Personality Posters, Inc., 59 Misc.2d 444, 299 N.Y.S.2d 501 (1968).

7. Appropriation invades the interest of a person in the exclusive use of his own identity as represented by his name or likeness. The name or likeness must be appropriated by the defendant for his own use or to benefit his social or commercial standing. See Restatement, Second, Torts § 652C.

NOTE—In many fact situations where an action for invasion of privacy lies, there may also be a separate action for defamation, such as in the "false light" situation. Similarly, in "intrusion" or "publicity" situations there may also be a separate cause of action for intentional infliction of mental distress.

8. In contrast to a cause of action for defamation, truth is no defense to an action based on the right of privacy.

9. Right of privacy cannot be sustained:

(a) by one who has become a "public character" and a fit subject for "news",

(b) when there is a privilege of publication in libel or slander,

(c) when the person has consented to the publicity,

(d) unless the publicity is to the public or many people as distinguished from a very few,

(e) by a child too young to appreciate "privacy", or

(f) by a partnership or corporation which, as such, does not have a protectable interest in "privacy".

10. In addition to damages for emotional distress and personal humiliation, injunctive relief may be appropriate.

e.g. P was a free-lance photographer who kept Jacqueline Onassis and her children under constant surveillance in order to take and sell pictures of their daily activities. Mrs. Onassis sought to enjoin the various harassing activities of P. The court noted that legitimate social needs may warrant some intrusion into the privacy of a public figure. However, P's conduct was unreasonable, and at times even created a danger to Mrs. Onassis and her children. While the court recognized that some injunctive relief was warranted, it refused to grant an injunction which would unnecessarily infringe on P's reasonable efforts to "cover" Mrs. Onassis and her children. P was enjoined from: approaching within 25 feet of them, blocking their movements in public places, doing any act which would jeopardize their safety or harass or frighten them. P was also enjoined from entering the children's schools or play areas. See Galella v. Onassis, 487 F.2d 986 (2d Cir. 1973).

11. The "right to privacy" must be balanced against freedom of the press. See CASES 70 and 71, below.

    (a) A national magazine stated that a play portrayed the ordeal of the Hill family, which had been held prisoner in their home by three escaped convicts. In fact the play was fictionalized. Suit was brought under a state "right of privacy" statute, which provided for redress of false reports of matters of public interest. The Court held that if the magazine published the report with knowledge of its falsity, or in reckless disregard of the truth, the plaintiff may recover. On the other hand, if the jury found that the statements in the magazine were merely innocent or negligent misstatements, there may be no recovery. The case was remanded for further proceedings. See Time, Inc. v. Hill, 385 U.S. 374, 87 S.Ct. 534, 17 L.Ed.2d 456 (1967).

    (b) P, a child of ten, was involved in a street accident and a picture of P was taken. The picture was published in the newspaper the following day. Twenty months later D published the picture in connection with an article on traffic accidents and pedestrian carelessness entitled "They Ask To Be Killed." P sues D. May P recover?

    Answer. Yes. Although the original publication of the photograph was privileged as being newsworthy, D's later publication placed P in an unfavorable light, portraying P as an example of pedestrian carelessness. This exceeded the bounds of privilege and P may recover. The lapse of time before D's publication does not alter D's liability. See Leverton v. Curtis Publishing Co., 192 F.2d 974 (3d Cir. 1951).

See generally, Gregory, pp. 1131–1190; Keeton, pp. 1135–1170; P & W, pp. 1083–1118; Prosser, pp. 802–818.

Case 68   *Limitation on invasion of privacy actions*

U.S. Senator Thomas Dodd filed suit against newspaper columnists Drew Pearson and Jack Anderson for invasion of privacy and conversion. The defendants published newspaper articles dealing with Dodd's relationship with certain lobbyists for foreign interests. Factual data for the articles was obtained by two former employees of Dodd by entering his office without authority and removing papers which were copied and returned. The columnists knew how the information had been obtained when the articles were published. Was there an invasion of privacy or conversion?

Answer. No. The published information related to Dodd's qualifications as a U.S. Senator. Since he was a public figure, there was no invasion of privacy as to such truthful publication of his affairs. If the information was obtained by improperly intrusive means there is a cause of action against the columnists. Although the information was received knowing that it had been removed without authorization, since the columnists themselves did not remove the papers the court did not find them liable. The court said, "If we were to hold appellants liable for invasion of privacy on these facts, we would establish the proposition that one who receives information from an intruder, knowing it has been obtained by improper intrusion, is guilty of a tort. In an untried and developing area of tort law, we are not prepared to go so far." Since obtaining the information was not a tort, and the publication by itself was not an invasion of privacy because it involved a public figure, the combination of both acts cannot be tortious.

The court then considered whether there had been a conversion by copying Dodd's letters and office records. None of the information copied involved literary property, inventions or trade secrets which the law protects. Since there was no conversion of the physical contents of the files and the information copied is not subject to protection by suit for conversion, there can be no recovery on the theory of conversion. The suit was dismissed because there was no invasion of privacy by the columnists and no conversion of property.

See Pearson v. Dodd, 133 U.S.App.D.C. 279, 410 F.2d 701 (1969).

Case 69   *Right of privacy—publicity*

D operated a garage and put this notice in his garage window: "NOTICE Dr. M owes an account here of $49.67. And if promises would pay an account this account would have been settled long ago. This account will be advertised as long as it remains unpaid." Dr. M sued D for $5000 damages for interfering with his right of privacy, and because the notice was continued after suit was brought he asked for $1500 more. D asked that the complaint be *dismissed for want of facts to constitute a cause of action and set up truth as an affirmative defense.   Is either contention valid?*

Answer. No. *The fact that D had a claim against M for a debt is no justification for subjecting him to unwarranted publicity. The public as such is not interested in the personal and private relations which exist between D and M.   Neither is there any private interest or concern of D which should be protected by recognizing a privilege to make public the claim he has against M. These facts disclose a tort committed by D in subjecting M to unfavorable publicity which is unjustified.   It is an invasion of his right to be left alone.   The tortious conduct is an interference with his right of privacy.   The constituent elements of this tort have not yet been specifically determined, but certain characteristics of the wrong seem to be agreed upon.   The gravamen of the offense is the unjustifiable and unauthorized subjecting of a person to publicity among a large number of people.   It differs from libel and slander in that truth is not a defense.   Therefore, the plaintiff's facts show a cause of action.   This accords with the law in a majority of the states.*

See Brents v. Morgan, 221 Ky. 765, 299 S.W. 967 (1927).   See also Housh v. Peth, 165 Ohio St. 35, 133 N.E.2d 340 (1956), Tollefson v. Price, 247 Or. 398, 430 P.2d 990 (1967), and Prosser, p. 809.

Disclosure of public records protected   **Case 70**

Six persons were indicted for the rape and murder of V.   The case attracted publicity, but V's name was not disclosed publically because state law prohibited the publishing or broadcasting of the name of a rape victim.   At a court hearing five of the defendants pleaded guilty to rape or attempted rape, and the murder charge was dropped.   In the course of the proceedings a reporter examined the indictments, which were public records, and discovered the name of V.   The reporter disclosed V's name in a television broadcast when he described the court proceedings.   V's father brought a civil action for money damages against the broadcasting station and the reporter for broadcasting the name of his daughter, V.   He relied on the statute which prohibited such broadcasting and on his common law right to privacy.   The defendants contended that the statute was unconstitutional, and that V's name could be published because it was a matter of public interest.   The state supreme court held that the statute was constitutional as a legitimate limitation on the right of freedom of expression contained in the First Amendment in order to protect the right of privacy of the victim and her family.   An appeal was taken to the United States Supreme Court. May a state impose civil liability for the broadcast of information obtained from public records in the circumstances of this case?

Answer. No. *The prevailing law of invasion of privacy recognizes that the interests in privacy fade when the information in-*

volved already appears on the public record. When viewed in terms of the First Amendment, as made applicable to the states by the Fourteenth Amendment, and in light of the public interest in a vigorous press there are compelling reasons to support the general rule. The state statute limited the content of a publication contrary to the First and Fourteenth Amendments. This case does not involve the regulation of conduct, or a combination of speech and nonspeech which is sometimes permissible, such as "fighting words." Instead, the state imposed a sanction for the publication of truthful information contained in official court records which were open to public inspection. This was not constitutionally permissible. Therefore, V's father may not maintain an action for the disclosure of true information disclosed by public court documents.

See Cox Broadcasting Corp. v. Cohn, 420 U.S. 469, 95 S.Ct. 1029, 43 L.Ed.2d 328 (1975).

NOTE—The holding in the Cox case was limited to prohibiting states from using civil or criminal sanctions to prevent publication of information contained in public records. The Court declined to decide whether truthful publications may ever be subjected to civil or criminal sanctions. The Court stated: "At the very least, the First and Fourteenth Amendments will not allow exposing the press to liability for truthfully publishing information released to the public in official court records. If there are privacy interests to be protected in judicial proceedings, the States must respond by means which avoid public documentation or other exposure of private information."

Case 71   *Invasion of privacy—media defendant liable for "actual malice"*

P's husband died with 43 other persons when a bridge collapsed. A newspaper reporter, D, went to P's home to write a story on the impact of the tragedy on P and her children. P was not at home, but D spoke to the children. D's article stressed the family's abject poverty and contained many factual inaccuracies, including a fictitious conversation with P. After the article was published by D's employer, P brought suit against them contending that the story placed P and her family in a false light thereby invading their privacy and subjecting them to pity and ridicule. At the close of P's case the trial judge dismissed P's claim for punitive damages for failure to present evidence that the invasion of privacy was done maliciously. After D's defense was presented, the jury was instructed that liability could be imposed only if it concluded that the false statements had been made with knowledge of their falsity or in reckless disregard of the truth. The jury awarded compensatory damages to P and defendants appealed. They contended that the trial judge's finding of no malice negated the existence of "actual malice" which P must establish under the N.Y. Times v. Sullivan rule. Is the appeal meritorious?

Answer. *No. When the claim for punitive damages was dismissed, the common law standard of malice was used. That is, there was no evidence of personal ill will toward P or reckless or wanton disregard of P's rights. The "actual malice" standard in N.Y. Times v. Sullivan focuses on the truth or falsity of the material published. That standard was accurately reflected in the jury instructions that required a finding of knowing or reckless falsehood. There was ample evidence to support the jury verdict on that question. Therefore, D is liable for placing P in a false light, and D's publisher is liable under the doctrine of respondeat superior.*

See Cantrell v. Forest City Publishing Co., 419 U.S. 245, 95 S.Ct. 465, 42 L.Ed.2d 419 (1974).

NOTE—The private plaintiff in the case above did not thrust herself into a public controversy and had no access to the media. However, the Supreme Court limited its decision to the facts of the case and made no pronouncements concerning the rights of a private plaintiff who brings suit against a media defendant in a false light invasion of privacy case. The Court stated that "this case presents no occasion to consider whether a State may constitutionally apply a more relaxed standard of liability for a publisher or broadcaster of false statements injurious to a private individual under a false-light theory of invasion of privacy, or whether the constitutional standard announced in Time, Inc. v. Hill applies to all false-light cases." See Right of Privacy, number 11, above.

*

XII

INTERFERENCE WITH ADVANTAGEOUS RELATIONS

Summary Outline

A. Introduction

B. Interests Protected

INTRODUCTION

1. The tort of interference with advantageous relations is also known as interference with economic relations, interference with contractual relations, or interference with prospective advantage. The tort includes:

    (a) intentional interference with existing or prospective contracts, and

    (b) intentional interference with other forms of advantageous economic relations.

    NOTE—Intentional interference is necessary for the tort. The negligent interference with a contract is not a tort. See Restatement, Second, Torts § 766C.

2. The law also affords protection from interference with domestic relations. This includes:

    (a) intentional interference with husband-wife relations, and

    (b) in some circumstances, intentional interference with the relation of parent and child.

3. Interference with a contract to marry is not actionable as part of this tort. See Restatement, Second, Torts § 698.

4. The following factors are considered in determining whether the intentional interference with an existing or prospective contract is actionable:

    (a) the nature of the conduct,

    (b) motive,

    (c) the contractual interest involved,

    > *e.g.* A contract provision contrary to public policy will not normally be protected.

    (d) the interest promoted by the person who interferes,

    (e) the social utility of the interests involved,

    > *e.g.* Competition is desirable so lawful acts which promote competition may be permitted.

    (f) the proximity or remoteness of the conduct to the interference, and

    (g) the relations between the parties.

    > *e.g.* Statements made in good faith by a business advisor would normally be proper, especially if made in response to a specific question.

    See Restatement, Second, Torts § 767.

5. Damages for interference with contractual or prospective contractual relations include:

(a) lost profits,

(b) any consequential losses resulting from the interference such as additional expenses.

(c) punitive damages if the requirements for them are met, see Chapter XV, Punitive Damages, below, and

(d) emotional distress or actual harm to reputation, if that injury could be reasonably expected from the interference.

See Restatement, Second, Torts § 774A; CASE 72, below.

NOTE—The plaintiff has a cause of action for damages against the person who breached the contract as well as against the person who improperly induced the breach because both are wrongdoers. However, satisfaction of a judgment against one party reduces the damages which may be recovered against the other. For example, if P recovers lost profits from one party, P may not recover lost profits a second time from the other party.

1. The right to conduct a business or make contracts is a property right recognized by law. Wrongful interference with that right is a tort. **INTERESTS PROTECTED**

2. Intentionally inducing another person to breach a contract or intentionally interfering with the performance of a contract may constitute a tort. See Restatement, Second, Torts § 766; CASE 72, below.

(a) P operated a theatre and contracted with a famous opera singer to perform there. The contract also provided that the performer could not sing elsewhere during the term of the contract. D operated a competing theatre and persuaded the opera star not to perform for P. P sues D for damages for inducing the opera star to break her contract with P. May P recover?

Answer. Yes. It is a tort for a person to induce another to breach a contract. In such a situation contract damages against the person who breached the contract may not be a sufficient remedy. Therefore D, who induced the breach, should be responsible for damages in addition to the liability of the contractor. See Lumley v. Gye, 2 El. & Bl. 216, 118 Eng.Rep. 749 (1853).

NOTE—Lumley v. Gye is important because it was the first time that liability for the tort of interference with contractual relations was held to include methods of inducement which were not a tort. Prior to that decision it was necessary to show tortious inducement to breach a contract, such as fraud, defamation or violence in order to recover.

(b) B purchased an ice distributing business from D. Part of the contract of sale provided that D would not sell or distribute ice in a certain territory so long as B or one deriving title from B was operating the business. Subsequently, B sold the business to P, and D began to sell ice in the area contrary to the contract of sale with B. D purchased the ice from T, a competitor of P. P filed suit against D seeking to enjoin D from competing, and to restrain T from inducing D to violate the initial contract selling the business to B. T moved to dismiss. The court noted "that a person is not justified in inducing a breach of contract simply because he is in competition with one of the parties to the contract and seeks to further his own economic advantage at the expense of the other. . . . Whatever interest society has in encouraging free and open competition by means not in themselves unlawful, contractual stability is generally accepted as of greater importance than competitive freedom. Competitive freedom, however, is of sufficient importance to justify one competitor in inducing a third party to forsake another competitor if no contractual relationship exists between the latter two." Thus P must prove that T intentionally induced D to breach his contract to prevail against T. If T sold ice to D without knowledge of D's contract or without actively inducing D to violate his contract, T would not be liable for inducing D's breach of contract. P's complaint alleged that T intentionally and actively induced the breach, so T's motion to dismiss should be overruled. See Imperial Ice Co. v. Rossier, 18 Cal.2d 33, 112 P.2d 631 (1941).

(c) D induced theatres not to employ P's Wu Tut Tut Revue because wages paid to female performers were so low that they could not earn a living unless they engaged in prostitution. The court dismissed P's suit against D for damages because it found D's actions justifiable under the circumstances. See Brimelow v. Casson, 1 Ch. 302 (1924).

3. The giving of truthful information or honest advice when requested is not improper interference with contractual relations. The interference must be intentional. Therefore, the negligent interference with contractual relations is not a tort. See Restatement, Second, Torts §§ 766C, 772.

4. Privilege is the main defense to this tort. This defense may be applicable where the defendant was furthering a valid interest and only lawful means were used.

5. Competition may constitute a privilege. However, competition which violates the generally accepted standards of business ethics is designated "unfair" and may be a basis for tort liabili-

ty. Liability for such conduct is also imposed by statute in many states and covered in courses in unfair competition and trade regulation. See CASES 73, 74, and 75, below.

6. The privilege to engage in business and compete with others by lawful means is not absolute. It does not extend to one who tries to drive another out of business purely for spite or other malevolent reason where there is no legitimate business interest to protect. The gist of the tort is the defendant's malice.

   (a) D, a wealthy banker, established a barber shop, employed a barber to operate the business and used his influence to attract customers from P's barber shop. As a result P was forced out of business and P brought suit against D. P alleged that D's sole purpose in opening the barber shop was to injure P maliciously. D moved to dismiss the complaint on the ground that his motive was irrelevant in determining whether his actions constituted a civil wrong. The court noted that while competition was desirable, the purpose for which property was used may determine the rights of the parties. "To divert to one's self the customers of a business rival by the offer of goods at lower prices is in general a legitimate mode of serving one's own interest, and justifiable as fair competition. But when a man starts an opposition place of business, not for the sake of profit to himself, but regardless of loss to himself, and for the sole purpose of driving his competitor out of business, and with the intention of himself retiring upon the accomplishment of his malevolent purpose, he is guilty of a wanton wrong and an actionable tort. In such a case he would not be exercising his legal right, or doing an act which can be judged separately from the motive which actuated him." Therefore, P's complaint stated a cause of action and D's motion was denied. See Tuttle v. Buck, 107 Minn. 145, 119 N.W. 946 (1909).

   (b) P and D were rival wholesale fish dealers. D told P's wholesale customers that if they continued to purchase fish from P, D would open a retail store and sell fish at such low prices that they would be driven out of business. On the other hand, if P's customers bought fish from D they would be given substantial discounts. As a result many of P's customers ceased doing business with him and P went out of business. P sued D for damages contending that D acted maliciously for the purpose of forcing him out of business without any benefit to D. D moved to dismiss. The court reasoned that competition in business, although carried to the extent of ruining a competitor, is not ordinarily actionable so long as the methods used are not wrongful, such as fraud, misrepresentation or coercion. In the present case D acted to acquire the business of P's customers for himself. The ruining of P's business was incidental to that purpose.

D's methods were not unlawful. The "threats" to P's customers were lawful because D had a right to open retail markets to compete with them. D's statements related solely to the purpose of competing with P and gaining a business advantage. The fact that D's methods were ruthless or unfair in a moral sense did not make them illegal. In the absence of statutes regulating and prohibiting D's conduct, it is not actionable. D's motion to dismiss was granted. See Katz v. Kapper, 7 Cal.App.2d 1, 44 P.2d 1060 (1935).

NOTE—The Katz case may be distinguished from the Tuttle case based on the motive of the defendant in each case. The defendant in Katz sought to increase his own business, and acted to eliminate competition to accomplish that end. The defendant in Tuttle acted for the *sole* purpose of driving P out of business, which was a tort.

7. It is a tort to interfere with advantageous relations of a noncontractual nature intentionally. Thus, if D by fraud, duress or other tort induces another not to make a gift, D is liable for the loss of the gift. Restatement, Second, Torts § 774B.

   e.g. P alleged that X intended to will a large portion of his estate to P. However, false and fraudulent representations D made to X caused X to disinherit P. D contended that P did not state a cause of action on those facts. The court rejected D's contention. The court reasoned: "If the plaintiff can recover against the defendant for the malicious and wrongful interference with the making of a contract, we see no good reason why he cannot recover for the malicious and wrongful interference with the making of a will." Thus P's allegations, if proved, would entitle P to recover. See Bohannon v. Wachovia Bank & Trust Co., 210 N.C. 679, 188 S.E. 390 (1936).

8. The law also affords protection to domestic relationships against tortious interference. Direct and indirect interference with the marriage relationship and the relation of parent and child may be actionable. See Prosser, pp. 873–888.

   (a) H and W are married. T sees H taking narcotics. T seeks out W and tells her of the incident. T persuades W to leave H. T is liable to H for causing the separation. See Restatement, Second, Torts § 686.

   (b) W tells T, a close friend, that her husband, H, uses narcotics and asks T's advice. T advises W to separate from H which she does. The advice of T is privileged because of the relationship between W and T. Further, T only gave honest advice in response to W's question. Therefore, T is not liable to H. See Restatement, Second, Torts § 686.

   (c) A person who induces a child to leave home or not return home contrary to the wishes of a parent entitled to custody may be liable to the parent. The parent can recover for the loss of services and society of the child, and for emotional distress. See Restatement, Second, Torts § 700.

See generally, Keeton, pp. 1175–1176; P & W, pp. 1149–1210; Prosser, pp. 915–969.

Specific performance does not preclude tort damages   Case 72

P signed a contract with D to purchase D's house. D was induced by E to convey the house to him instead of P because E did not want P and his wife who were Negroes to move into the neighborhood. P sued D and E for specific performance, incidental damages caused by D's breach of contract, and for punitive damages. The trial court decreed specific performance and awarded compensatory and punitive damages. D and E appealed contending that if P were made whole by specific performance, the additional remedy of money damages could not be awarded. Is that contention valid?

Answer. No. *The appellate court affirmed. Where the tort is intentional, damages may include unforeseen expenses, mental suffering and injury to reputation. Since the acts of D and E were malicious, punitive damages were also proper. Limiting the award to specific performance would not make P whole. By inducing the breach of contract by D, E committed a tort against P. P may recover for the harm caused by that intentional tort whether or not such damages were expectable, in addition to obtaining specific performance of the contract.*

See Duff v. Engelberg, 237 Cal.App.2d 505, 47 Cal.Rptr. 114 (1965).

Unfair competition can be enjoined   Case 73

P News Service gathered news from all over the world at great expense. It made such news available in the early hours of the morning over a rotating bulletin board in Boston. D News Service copied this bulletin news and sent it by telegraph to its subscribers in Denver, Seattle, Los Angeles, and San Francisco, with little expense to itself, and before such news lost its value as news. P sued D for damages for unfair competition. May P recover?

Answer. Yes. *News as such has property value and when P gathered its news at great expense from points around the world, P was entitled to have its property interest protected from piracy by D. The difference in time between east and west coast cities made the news which was voluntarily published in Boston, still valuable as news in the West, three or four hours after publication in Boston. Although news events belong to the general public, D is not part of the general public in this case because it is a competitor of P. That* which may be legal by a noncompetitor can be illegal if done by a competitor. To appropriate something of another, even an event, and sell it as one's own is just as much unfair competition as misrepresenting one's product so that the general public will think that it is the product of someone else. The injunction was granted.

See International News Service v. The Associated Press, 248 U.S. 215, 39 S.Ct. 68, 63 L.Ed. 211 (1918). See also Pottstown Daily News Publishing Co. v. Pottstown Broadcasting Co., 411 Pa. 383, 192 A.2d 657 (1963).

Case 74   *State laws regulating business practices may not encroach on federal laws*

P secured design and mechanical patents on a "pole lamp" and began to market the lamps. They were a commercial success. D placed a substantially identical lamp on the market which sold at a lower price. P brought the present action alleging that D, by copying its design: (1) infringed on its patents and (2) caused confusion in the trade as to the source of the lamps and thereby engaged in unfair competition under state law. P's patents were found invalid for want of invention, but the court awarded damages to P under the state law because D's lamps were "a substantially exact copy" of P's. Can a state law prohibit the copying of an article as unfair competition when the article copied is not protected by a Federal patent or copyright?

Answer. No. The grant of a patent is the grant of a statutory monopoly. It is meant to encourage invention by rewarding the inventor with a right, limited to a term of years fixed by the patent, to exclude others from the use of his invention. A state cannot, consistent with the Supremacy Clause of the Constitution, extend the life of a patent beyond its expiration date or give a patent on an article which lacked the level of invention required by Federal patents. A state cannot encroach upon federal patent laws by granting protection which clashes with the objectives of federal laws. D copied and sold an unpatentable article. A state law forbidding unfair competition cannot prohibit this because that would be contrary to federal law which states that the item belongs to the public. Therefore, P was not given any relief and the suit was dismissed.

See Sears, Roebuck & Co. v. Stiffel Co., 376 U.S. 225, 84 S.Ct. 784, 11 L.Ed.2d 661 (1964).

NOTE—The Supreme Court has refused to extend the holding in CASE 74 above. Company P developed a secret process to grow a 17-inch crystal for use in the detection of ionizing radiation. Some of P's employees who worked on this process quit their employment and went to work for Company D. Shortly thereafter D began growing 17-inch crystals and competing with P. P sued D and the employees seeking injunctive relief and damages for misappropriation of trade secrets. The suit was based on the Ohio trade secret law. The U.S. Supreme Court held that the state's trade secret law was not preempted by the federal patent laws. "The only limitation on the States is that in regulating the area of patents and copyrights they do not conflict with the operation of the laws in this area passed by Congress. . . ." The Court concluded that there was no conflict between the trade secret law and federal laws. The purpose of both laws is similar—the maintenance of commercial ethics and the encouragement of invention. "Nothing in the patent law requires that States refrain from action to prevent industrial espionage. . . . A most fundamental human right, that of privacy, is threatened when industrial espionage is condoned or is made profitable; the state interest in denying profit to such illegal ventures is unchallengeable." The Court concluded that the state trade secret law involved in the present case was not an encroachment on the federal patent system, which was the criterion set by CASE 74 above. Therefore, the state law was held to be valid. P was able to recover for the misappropriation of the trade secret. See Kewanee Oil Co. v. Bicron Corp. et al, 416 U.S. 470, 94 S.Ct. 1879, 40 L.Ed.2d 315 (1974). See also 17 U.S.C.A. § 301.

False comparison of products held actionable   Case 75

P and D were competitors in manufacturing equipment for testing various commercial materials. D circulated a report to P's customers and potential customers that the United States government had tested the products of both P and D and concluded that P's products were 40 percent less effective than D's products. In addition, at a manufacturers' convention D's agent stated to prospective customers that "the government is throwing P out." P brought suit against D for trade libel or disparagement of property, contending that D's statements about P's products were false. D moved to dismiss on the grounds, inter alia, that even if P's allegations were true they were not actionable because D only stated that P's products compared unfavorably with its own. Should D's motion be granted?

Answer. No. The court recognized that statements which make an unfavorable comparison of products or exaggerate the quality of one's own products are not ordinarily actionable. In the present case D's statements were more than a mere unfavorable comparison, and therefore, D may not avail itself of the protection accorded to "unfavorable comparison." There is a difference between saying that one product is better than another and saying that the federal government has tested both products and found that one is 40 percent less effective. The former statement, arguably, expresses an opinion, the truth of which may be difficult to ascertain. The latter statement is more than an opinion because it implies that the party making it has the facts to prove it. Furthermore, because the evaluation of the products was allegedly made by the federal government, D's statement was given added authenticity. The additional statement that the government had "thrown out" P is also more than a mere comparison of products. Therefore, both of D's statements are actionable.

See Testing Systems, Inc. v. Magnaflux Corp., 251 F.Supp. 286 (E.D.Pa.1966). Accord, Restatement, Second, Torts §§ 623A, 626.

NOTE 1—If D's statements were true, truth would be a complete defense in CASE 75. See Restatement, Second, Torts § 634.

NOTE 2—In the factual situation presented in CASE 75 damages must be shown with reasonable certainty for plaintiff to recover. See Restatement, Second, Torts § 633.

XIII

NUISANCE

Summary Outline

INTRODUCTION   1.   The term "nuisance" describes a field of tort liability. It is not a single type of wrongful conduct or a separate tort. There are two types of nuisance:

(a) A *public* nuisance is the unreasonable interference with a right common to all members of the public.

(b) A *private* nuisance is the substantial and unreasonable interference with the use and enjoyment of land by the person in possession.

> *e.g.* The pollution of a stream which deprived eighty lower riparian owners of the use of water for purposes connected with their land would be a private nuisance. The large number of persons affected would not make the pollution a public nuisance because there was no interference with a right common to the public. However, if the pollution prevented swimming at a public beach, or deprived the public of their right to fish in the stream, then the pollution would also be a public nuisance because it interfered with a right common to all members of the public. See Restatement Torts, Second § 821B, Comment g.

2.   A nuisance may result from the failure to act or from the following types of conduct:

(a) intentional and unreasonable conduct,

(b) negligent conduct, or

(c) reckless or ultrahazardous conduct.

3.   The law affords a full spectrum of remedies for the various types of conduct which result in a nuisance:

(a) damages,

(b) injunction, and

(c) abatement, by self-help.

4.   Where a nuisance causes irreparable injury to one's use and enjoyment of land, a court may exercise its equitable powers and enjoin the nuisance.

5.   If money damages are sufficient, equitable injunctive relief is denied because the remedy at law is adequate. However, once jurisdiction is taken by a court, money damages may be awarded in addition to equitable relief.

6.   An action at law for damages will lie:

(a) for loss of the use of property during the existence of a temporary nuisance,

(b) for the permanent diminution in value of the plaintiff's property, or the cost of repairing or restoring the damaged property, or

(c) for demonstrable or calculable injury to plaintiff's interests.

7. Subject to the traditional limitations of the exercise of equity jurisdiction, an injunction may be an available remedy:

(a) in cases where recovery of damages is not adequate,

(b) where harm has not as yet occurred, but is threatened, or

(c) where the conduct is continuing.

8. The law of nuisance also permits the remedy of abatement by self-help, which is the privilege of removing or destroying the nuisance by the injured party by breaking or pulling it down. This privilege is subject to the limitations and risks of any other privilege, and it does not permit any act beyond that which removal of the nuisance requires.

CAVEAT—The student should be very careful in assessing any "definition" of nuisance.

(a) "There is general agreement that it is incapable of any exact or comprehensive definition." Prosser, p. 571.

(b) In any fact situation which appears to involve the law of nuisance, the student must be careful to distinguish the situation from that involving trespass to land, which protects the interest in *exclusive possession* of land, as contrasted to the use and enjoyment of land. There must be an entry upon the land for trespass but not for nuisance.

(c) Not infrequently courts or commentators make reference to an "absolute nuisance", or a "nuisance per se." Such a situation is generally one in which liability for conduct is imposed without regard to the defendant's wrongful intention, or negligent conduct. Prosser lists three situations in which these terms apply: (i) public nuisances designated by statute; (ii) intentional maintenance of something which interferes with the plaintiff's interests, and is clearly unreasonable in light of its surroundings; and (iii) abnormal and ultrahazardous activities. See Prosser, pp. 582–583; CASE 76 below.

NOTE—A nuisance per se should be contrasted with a nuisance per accidens. A nuisance per accidens means harmful conduct which may result in liability depending on the circumstances.

(d) In the field of the liability of owners and occupiers of land reference is often made to an "attractive nuisance." In these cases liability is imposed on some other theory (generally negligence), and the case is not one of "nuisance" at all. See Chapter V, Attractive Nuisance, above. See also Prosser, pp. 364–376 and 594–602.

PUBLIC AND PRIVATE NUISANCES

1. A public nuisance is an unreasonable infringement on the rights of the state or the community at large. It must affect an interest common to the general public rather than an interest peculiar to one person or only a few. See Restatement, Second, Torts § 821B.

   e.g. An obstruction to a public highway or an illegal liquor establishment.

2. "A private nuisance is a nontrespassory invasion of another's interest in the private use and enjoyment of land." Restatement, Second, Torts § 821D.

   NOTE 1—Nuisance should be contrasted to trespass. "A trespass is an invasion of the interest in the exclusive possession of land, as by entry upon it. . . . A nuisance is an interference with the interest in the private use and enjoyment of land, and does not require interference with possession." Restatement, Second, Torts § 821D, Comment d.

   NOTE 2—Actions for trespass and nuisance are not mutually exclusive. In some situations conduct may be actionable either as a trespass or as a nuisance. Both are areas of tort liability rather than a single type of tortious conduct. Both may result from intentional or unintentional conduct. However, where a trespass is intentional no harm is required for liability. Significant harm is necessary before liability is imposed for a private nuisance.

   e.g. In the operation of an aluminum reduction plant D caused certain fluoride compounds in the form of gases and particulates invisible to the naked eye to become airborne and settle upon P's land. The quantity of fluorides deposited on P's land prevented its use for grazing purposes and caused general deterioration of the land. P brought an action based on trespass because of its six year statute of limitations. D argued that at most a cause of action for nuisance, which had only a two year statute of limitations, was presented. P could recover substantially more damages if the action were based on trespass. The court held that the intrusion of fluoride particulates constituted a trespass and permitted P to recover on that theory. The court reasoned that the size of the object which invaded a person's property was irrelevant to the determination of whether the invasion constituted a trespass. The traditional concept of trespass which required a direct invasion by a visible, tangible object is now obsolete. Today it is known that there are atomic particles which can do great damage even though invisible to the naked eye. A force which cracks a foundation is just as real as a visible object, and therefore may constitute a trespassory invasion. D polluted the air and trespassed on P's land with invisible fluoride particles. P may recover for that trespass. See Martin v. Reynolds Metals Co., 221 Or. 86, 342 P.2d 790 (1959).

3. The following circumstances are considered in deciding whether there has been an unreasonable interference with a public right and there is a public nuisance.

"(a) Whether the conduct involves a significant interference with the public health, the public safety, the public peace, the public comfort or the public convenience, or

"(b) whether the conduct is proscribed by a statute, ordinance or administrative regulation, or

"(c) whether the conduct is of a continuing nature or has produced a permanent or long-lasting effect, and, as the actor knows or has reason to know, has a significant effect upon the public right." Restatement, Second, Torts § 821B(2).

e.g. A building contractor, D, was engaged in construction work on a building. A nylon string (chalk line) was placed across a sidewalk to mark the perimeter of D's excavation work. P tripped over the chalk line and injured himself. In a suit against D, D offered evidence to negate negligence and show contributory negligence by P. The trial judge refused to instruct the jury on the theory of nuisance as requested by P, and a verdict was returned for D. Should the jury have been instructed on the theory of nuisance?

Answer. No. P cannot proceed on the theory of a private nuisance because he was not injured in relation to a right which he enjoyed by reason of his ownership of an interest in land. Among the factors to be considered in determining whether there is a public nuisance is its frequency, continuity or duration. While the obstruction of a public sidewalk may constitute a public nuisance, that is not the situation in this case. The obstruction was temporary, and reasonably necessary for D's construction work. Furthermore, the duration or frequency of the alleged nuisance is a factor to be considered. That is, has it been in existence for some period of time rather than being an isolated instance of a temporary nature? The chalk line was only a temporary obstruction of the sidewalk. Therefore, P was not entitled to a jury instruction on nuisance, and could only recover if D were negligent. The verdict for D was affirmed. See Culwell v. Abbott Construction Co., 211 Kan. 359, 506 P.2d 1191 (1973).

4. A public nuisance is usually a criminal offense. Therefore, an action involving a public nuisance usually must be brought by the state.

5. A private individual has no civil cause of action for the invasion of a purely public right, unless the damage is different *in kind* from that sustained by the community in general. In all such situations it must be determined whether the damages were different *in kind,* or different only *in degree,* in which case no recovery is permitted for a public nuisance.

   (a) D's tanker ship struck an outcropping in the water causing 100,000 gallons of oil to be discharged into the coastal waters of the State of Maine. Commercial fishermen, clam diggers and businessmen sued for damages based on nuisance and other theories. The court noted that the plaintiffs had no individual property right with respect to the waters polluted by the oil spill. They may recover in tort for the invasion of a public right only if they suffered damage different in kind, rather than simply in degree, from that sustained by the public generally. The commercial fishermen and clam diggers have a special interest apart from the public generally because of their commercial use of the public right with which D interfered by polluting the water. To the extent that their pecuniary losses can be established, they may recover. However, the businessmen who lost customers because of the polluted waters and beaches, may not recover. They did not have a property interest in the water which belonged to the state, and there was no interference with their direct exercise of a public right. Their damage may be greater in *degree* than the public at large, but their injury was basically the same *in kind* as that to all businesses and residents of the area. See Burgess v. M/V Tamano, 370 F.Supp. 247 (D.C.Me.1973).

   (b) D obstructed a public highway with buildings and a fence. That caused P, whose property bordered that road, to detour two miles whenever he went from his farm into town. P sued to enjoin D from blocking the highway. The court denied relief. D's obstruction constituted a public nuisance. For P to obtain relief P's injury must be different in kind from that sustained by the general public. P's injury was different in degree from other travelers in that he used the highway more often, but his injury was not different in kind. Once P left his home, his right to travel on the public highway was no different from that of any other traveler. P was not denied access to his land by the obstruction, but he was merely required, like others, to travel a longer distance between his land and town. Thus P was not injured any differently than any other member of the community. Since P's injury was not different in kind from others, he may not obtain relief by injunction against the public nuisance. See Borton v. Mangus, 93 Kan. 719, 145 P. 835 (1915).

(c) P sought an injunction to prevent D from closing the outlets from a dam which would flood an area and close the only road leading to P's timber lands. The court granted the injunction because the obstruction of the highway would cause special damages to P, different in kind from those suffered by the general public. That is, P would be denied access to his business property. Further, the court noted that injunctive relief would prevent a multiplicity of suits, and P did not have an adequate remedy at law. See Pilgrim Plywood Corp. v. Melendy, 110 Vt. 12, 1 A.2d 700 (1938).

(d) If the highway in example (c) above were not made completely impassable, but passage was only rendered extremely difficult, inconvenient or dangerous, D's obstruction of the road should be enjoined. See Restatement, Second, Torts § 821C, Illustration 5.

NOTE—In situations where a person may bring an action based on a public nuisance he may obtain injunctive relief as well as special damages for the harm which is different in kind (rather than in degree) from the harm to the general public. However, the action does not then become an action for a private nuisance.

6. Liability for a private nuisance may arise from any of the three basic types of conduct considered in tort situations:

(a) intentional conduct,

(b) negligent conduct, or

(c) conduct as to which the law imposes liability, such as for abnormally dangerous conditions or activities.

See Restatement, Second, Torts § 822.

7. Only those persons who have property rights and privileges with respect to the use and enjoyment of the land affected have standing to bring an action based on a private nuisance. That includes:

(a) possessors of land,

(b) owners of easements and profits in land, and

(c) owners of nonpossessory estates in the land which are adversely affected by the alleged nuisance.

e.g. A landlord has standing to bring an action where the value of his estate is impaired by a permanent or continuing interference with the usability of the land.

8. The defendant's conduct may give rise to civil liability for both a public nuisance and a private nuisance. Separate and distinct analysis must be made for each cause of action.

    e.g. A house of prostitution has been held to be both a public and private nuisance. Therefore, a person living next to a bawdy house may seek damages and have its business enjoined. That action may be based on either: (a) the particular harm resulting from the public nuisance, or (b) the harm caused by the private nuisance. See Tedescki v. Berger, 150 Ala. 649, 43 So. 960 (1907).

    See generally, Gregory, pp. 521–524; Keeton, pp. 621–626; P & W, pp. 846–855.

ACTIONABLE CONDUCT

1. Liability for a private nuisance may arise from intentional conduct (or omission to act where there is a duty to act) which is unreasonable and causes substantial harm. Actionable conduct is deemed intentional when the defendant acts for the purpose of causing it, or knows that the resulting harm is substantially certain to result. Liability is imposed for such conduct, unless the utility of the defendant's conduct outweighs the gravity of the harm. See Restatement, Second, Torts §§ 822, 824–826. See also CASE 76, below.

    e.g. P owned an apartment building which had been renovated. D owned a building across the street which had been abandoned. It was unsightly and had been taken over by derelicts. P brought an action for damages contending that D maintained a nuisance by failure to supervise her abandoned building, and that depreciated the value of P's apartment. The court said that in determining whether D's building was a nuisance, its location and the surrounding area must be considered with other circumstances. An abandoned building in a deteriorating neighborhood might not be a nuisance. However, in P's neighborhood property owners were trying to upgrade housing standards. One bad building may eventually destroy an entire neighborhood. Therefore, P may recover damages which are the difference in market value of P's apartment before and after the nuisance. See Puritan Holding Co. v. Holloschitz, 82 Misc.2d 905, 372 N.Y.S.2d 500 (1975).

2. Actionable intentional conduct constituting a nuisance must be a *substantial* invasion of the plaintiff's rights. A slight inconvenience or petty annoyance is not actionable.

3. In the absence of the requisite intention, liability may be imposed for a nuisance, on a theory of negligence, i.e. failure to exercise reasonable care for the rights of the plaintiff.

4. Liability for a private nuisance may also be imposed "where the defendant carries on in an inappropriate place an abnormally dangerous activity such as blasting, . . . or where an enterprise such as a . . . slaughterhouse, . . . necessarily involves so great a risk to its surroundings that its location may be considered unreasonable." Prosser, pp. 575–576. In such cases liability is imposed on a theory of "absolute" or "strict" liability—liability without fault.

5. The pivotal element in the determination of a nuisance action is the reasonableness of the defendant's conduct. In each case the social utility of the defendant's conduct must be weighed against the gravity of the harm.

   (a) "The mere fact that an invasion of another's interest in the use and enjoyment of land is intentional does not mean that it is unreasonable." Restatement, Second, Torts § 826, comment b. See Stevens v. Rockport Granite Co., 216 Mass. 486, 104 N.E. 371 (1914).

   (b) The test of whether a particular use of property is a nuisance is determined by its effect on the average person, or by property in normal condition and used for a normal purpose. This is an objective standard. See Restatement, Second, Torts § 821F.

   e.g. P was very nervous and suffering from the effects of a sunstroke. P lived across the street from a church. Whenever the church bell was rung P went into convulsions. The bell did not disturb anyone else and the church refused to stop ringing the bell. P sued for damages claiming that the bell was a nuisance. May P recover?

   Answer. No. The test for a nuisance is its effect on the average person, not on someone who is supersensitive. If the ringing of the bell disturbed everyone in the vicinity it would have been a public nuisance. Since P was the only one affected he may not recover. See Rogers v. Elliott, 146 Mass. 349, 15 N.E. 768 (1888).

6. In determining whether the use of land is reasonable, the following factors are considered:

   (a) the extent of the harm,

   (b) the character of the harm, including its duration and frequency,

   (c) the social values of the conduct in question,

   (d) the suitability of the conduct in question and interest invaded to the character of the locality, and

   (e) the ease of preventing the harm, and the burden of avoiding it. See Restatement, Second, Torts §§ 827–828.

e.g. D purchased a house in a middle-class, residential neighborhood. D announced that the house would be used as a residence for persons paroled from the state prison, under a program to assist them in making a responsible adjustment to society. P sought to enjoin the proposed use of D's property on the ground of nuisance. P alleged that residents of the half-way house might commit criminal acts in the neighborhood, and the proposed use would depreciate land values in the area. In denying injunctive relief the court noted that the use of the land must be unreasonable to constitute a nuisance. The proposed use did not violate any zoning restrictions. The only grounds for an injunction were the fears and apprehensions of residents which were based on speculation. "Restraining the action of an individual or a corporation by injunction is an extraordinary power, always to be exercised with caution, never without the most satisfactory reasons." P's fear of what might occur, although genuine, rested completely on supposition and, therefore, injunctive relief was denied. See Nicholson v. Connecticut Half-Way House, Inc., 153 Conn. 507, 218 A.2d 383 (1966).

See generally, Gregory, pp. 517–532; P & W, pp. 861–872.

DEFENSES

1. The existence of a cause of action in nuisance must be based on one of the following theories:

   (a) nuisance resulting from intentional or reckless conduct,

   (b) nuisance resulting from abnormally dangerous conduct, or

   (c) nuisance resulting from negligence.

2. The availability of any particular defense depends on which of the theories listed in number 1 forms the basis for the claim of nuisance.

3. If the nuisance is intentional or results from reckless conduct, the "contributory negligence" of the plaintiff is NOT an adequate defense.

4. If the nuisance is the result of an abnormally dangerous activity, contributory negligence is not a defense unless the plaintiff has voluntarily and unreasonably subjected himself to the risk.

5. If the nuisance is based on negligence then the contributory negligence of the plaintiff may be a valid defense just as in other actions based on negligence.

   e.g. P fell and was injured when she caught her heel against a cement projection from a sidewalk. P sued the city for damages contending that the projection was a nuisance. The facts showed that P lived in the neighborhood and knew of the cement projection which had existed for two or three years. It was dark when she fell. The trial judge instructed the jury that contributory negligence was not a defense. The jury awarded damages to P. On appeal the court noted that where the danger is continuing, it may be characterized as a nuisance even though it grew out of a negligent act. The court held that "whenever a nuisance has its origin in negligence, one may not avert the consequences of his own contributory negligence by affixing to the negligence of the wrongdoer the label of a nuisance." The case was remanded for a new trial so the jury could determine whether P was contributorily negligent. See McFarlane v. City of Niagara Falls, 247 N.Y. 340, 160 N.E. 391 (1928).

6. Assumption of the risk may be a defense to nuisance to the same extent that it is permitted for other torts. See Restatement, Second, Torts § 840C.

e.g. P drives his car along a highway where D is conducting blasting operations. D has posted a sign on the road warning of the blasting and stationed a watchman to detour traffic. P sees the sign and the watchman but continues down the road and is injured by D's blasting activities. P may not recover because of assumption of the risk.

See generally, P & W, pp. 895–898.

1. When the plaintiff seeks to enjoin a nuisance there are two steps which the court takes in deciding the case.   **REMEDIES**

   (a) First, the court balances the interests of the parties to determine whether there is a nuisance.

   (b) Second, if a nuisance is found the court balances the conflicting interests again to make its decision as to whether or not to issue an injunction.

CAVEAT—The factors taken into account in determining whether or not the defendant's conduct constitutes a nuisance are similar to those which are taken into account in determining whether or not an injunction should issue as the appropriate remedy. However, the two issues, the existence of liability and the availability of injunctive relief, must be considered separately. This second balancing is essential. An award of damages may be reasonable, and issuance of an injunction "may lead to extortion if the injunction seriously curtails the defendant's enjoyment of his land." Restatement, Second, Torts § 941, comment c.

e.g. D constructed a building in good faith which encroached one foot on P's property. A court would not require removal of the building which would be very expensive, but rather would assess damages for the encroachment. If the injunction were granted P could demand an unreasonably large sum to sell the land to D. D's bargaining position would be so poor that D would pay the exorbitant demand by P for the land rather than tear down that part of the building which encroached on P's land.

2. After the plaintiff establishes the nuisance, the following general considerations are some of the factors evaluated by the court in determining the appropriate remedy:

   (a) the hardship of the injunction of the defendant compared with the injury to the plaintiff if the injunction is not granted,

   (b) the character of the conduct involved, including the motives of the parties, and

   e.g. If the plaintiff "moved to the nuisance" that factor would weigh against the plaintiff. In CASE 77, that fact influenced the court in its decision to require the developer to pay the defendant's relocation costs.

   (c) the interests of identifiable third parties and the general public.

   e.g. Defendant's business may provide essential services to the community such as telephone communications or electricity. The fact that a substantial number of persons would lose their jobs, or that the safety of third persons might be endangered in the absence of injunctive relief, could also be considered.

3. The unreasonable delay by a plaintiff in protesting the defendant's activities could also be a basis to deny an injunction.

4. The weight of each factor depends on its importance in any given case. See CASE 78, below.

5. Punitive damages may be recovered in most states where the defendant's conduct was malicious, or there was a reckless or wanton disregard for the property rights of another.

   e.g. Growers of gladiolus brought an action against the operator of an aluminum production plant for actual and punitive damages caused by the settling of fluorides from the plant on the plaintiffs' property. The trial court excluded certain evidence to support the claim for punitive damages, and that ruling was appealed. The appellate court held that a jury may award punitive damages if there was evidence of malice or wanton disregard of the property rights of the plaintiffs. Therefore, the trial court erred in excluding testimony that: (a) the plant manager allegedly stated, "It is easier to pay claims than it is to control fluorides," and (b) an electrostatic precipitator would remove 98 percent of the particulate matter from emissions. The case was remanded for submission of that evidence to the jury. See Reynolds Metals Co. v. Lampert, 324 F.2d 465 (9th Cir. 1963).

See generally, Gregory, pp. 536–546; Keeton, pp. 603–621; P & W, pp. 882–894.

Negligence not required for act to be a nuisance   **Case 76**

P owned nine acres of land near D's oil refinery. P had his residence, trailer accomodations and a restaurant on his land. P brought suit against D alleging that the oil refinery constituted a nuisance because it emitted nauseating gases and odors in great quantities two or three times each week. This impaired substantially P's use and enjoyment of his land. At trial D showed that the refinery was a modern plant of the type in general use and that there was no negligence in its operation. D moved to dismiss P's complaint. D reasoned that private nuisances are classified either as nuisances per se or at law, or as nuisances per accidens or in fact. Since D's business was lawful and not prohibited by any ordinance it could not be a nuisance per se. D contended that its business could only be a nuisance per accidens if it were constructed or operated negligently. D concluded that since there was no evidence that the refinery was constructed or operated negligently, P had failed to establish the existence of a nuisance. Should D's motion be granted?

Answer. *No. "A nuisance per se or at law is an act, occupation or structure which is a nuisance at all times and under any circumstances, regardless of location or surroundings. . . . Nuisances per accidens or in fact are those which become nuisances by reason of their location, or by reason of the manner in which they are constructed, maintained, or operated. However, contrary to D's contention, a lawful business may become a nuisance per accidens even though it is not constructed or operated negligently. Negligence and nuisance are distinct fields of tort liability. While negligence may create a private nuisance per accidens and both torts may coexist, negligence is not required for a nuisance. "An invasion of another's interest in the use and enjoyment of land is intentional in the law of private nuisance when the person whose conduct is a question as a basis for liability acts for the purpose of causing it, or knows that it is resulting from his conduct or knows that it is substantially certain to result from his conduct. . . . A person who intentionally creates or maintains a private nuisance is liable for the resulting injury to others regardless of the degree of care or skill exercised by him to avoid such injury." The evidence was sufficient to support a finding that D operated the refinery so as to intentionally and unreasonably impair P's use and enjoyment of his land in a substantial manner. Therefore, D's motion should be denied.*

See *Morgan v. High Penn Oil Co.*, 238 N.C. 185, 77 S.E.2d 682 (1953).

Case 77   *Nuisance enjoined, but plaintiff required to indemnify defendant*

For many years D maintained a cattle feedlot in an agricultural area remote from any city. The cattle produced one million pounds of wet manure per day. Despite good feedlot management and good housekeeping practices by D, the resulting odor and flies created an annoying and unhealthy situation on land nearby. P purchased land outside of a city and constructed a retirement community. Initially homes were built a substantial distance from D's business. As P's development became more successful, homes were constructed closer and closer to D's business. P and home owners filed suit against D, contending that D's business was both a private and a public nuisance as defined by state law. They sought an injunction against the continued operation of D's business. P showed that land near D's business could not be sold, and the home owners established that they could not enjoy outdoor living because of the odor and insects. (a) Should the operation of D's lawful business be enjoined because it has become a nuisance by reason of the newly established residential area? (b) If the nuisance is enjoined, may P, who developed the new town in a previously agricultural area, be required to indemnify D in moving its operations?

Answer. (a) Yes. (b) Yes. D's operations were both a public and private nuisance to the nearby residents. P showed special damages in the loss of sales because of the nuisance and, therefore, P may maintain an action based on the public as well as the private nuisance. D's feedlot operations should be permanently enjoined. However, a suit to enjoin a nuisance sounds in equity, and courts have a special responsibility in such cases. In addition to protecting the public interest, the operator of a lawful business must be protected from the knowing and willful encroachment by others "coming near the nuisance." If P, the developer, were the only party injured the doctrine of "coming to the nuisance" would bar injunctive relief. On the other hand if D located its business near the outskirts of a city, and the city grew toward the feedlot, D would have to abate the nuisance at its own expense. In the present case D established its business in a remote area, and there was no indication that a city would spring up nearby. D is required to move not because of any wrongdoing, but because of the legitimate regard of the court for the rights and interests of the public. P is entitled to injunctive relief, not because P is blameless, but because of the damage to the people who purchased homes in P's development. Therefore, P is liable to D because of the circumstances which P created. "It does not seem harsh to require a developer, who has taken advantage of the lesser land values in a rural area as well as the availability of large tracts of land on which to build and devel-

op a new town or city in the area, to indemnify those who are forced to leave as a result. Having brought people to the nuisance to the foreseeable detriment of [D], [P] must indemnify [D] for a reasonable amount of the cost of moving or shutting down." The case was remanded to determine the damages sustained by D as the reasonable and direct result of the granting of the permanent injunction against the nuisance.

See Spur Industries, Inc. v. Del E. Webb Development Co., 108 Ariz. 178, 494 P.2d 700 (1972).

NOTE—The rule of "coming to the nuisance" is not, by itself, an absolute doctrine preventing recovery. Rather, it is one of the factors considered by courts in balancing the equities in any given case to determine whether the nuisance is actionable. See Restatement, Second, Torts § 840D.

Injunction denied after balancing equities   Case 78

D operated a large cement plant. Neighboring land owners filed suit against D for an injunction and money damages. They alleged that dirt, smoke and vibrations from D's plant damaged their property. The trial court concluded that there was a nuisance and awarded temporary damages to each plaintiff for damages up to the time of trial. The court also determined the total amount of permanent damages for loss of value to their land amounted to $185,000. D had invested $45,000,000 in its plant and employed over 300 persons. The court denied plaintiffs' petition for an injunction because of the great disparity between the economic consequences of the nuisance and closing the business by an injunction. Plaintiffs appealed, contending that under established law where a nuisance has been found, and where substantial damage has been shown, an injunction should be granted. Should the court have enjoined the nuisance?

Answer. *No. Control of air pollution in any industry has greater ramifications than the rights of parties to a single private suit. Pollution control depends on technical research, economic impact of federal and state regulations, and the effect on public health. A court should not establish a policy for the control or elimination of air pollution as a by-product of private litigation. This is the direct responsibility of the government, not the courts. In this case money damages should be awarded to the plaintiffs for the permanent damage to their property. This will compensate them for their injuries and avoid the necessity of successive actions at law for damages as further damages are incurred. The case was remanded with instructions to award permanent damages to plaintiffs and grant a conditional injunction. That conditional injunction was to be vacated when D paid the permanent damages.*

See Boomer v. Atlantic Cement Co., Inc., 26 N.Y.2d 219, 309 N.Y.S.2d 312, 257 N.E.2d 870 (1970).

NOTE 1—CASE 78, illustrates the restraint exercised by most courts in such situations. The Boomer case involved a private nuisance, and the court concluded that its duty was only to resolve the controversy presented by the parties to the litigation. It stated that environmental control was "beyond the circumference of one private lawsuit," and was "a direct responsibility for government."

NOTE 2—The decisions of the lower courts in the Boomer case denied injunctive relief by balancing the equities and hardships of the parties. That is sometimes called the doctrine of comparative benefit. In doing that the trial court emphasized D's large capital investment and the contribution of D's business to the local economy including employment and taxes. In addition to those factors the Appellate Division noted that D's plant was located in an area zoned for quarrying and heavy industrial use, and that D used the most modern and efficient abatement devices. See Boomer v. Atlantic Cement Co., Inc., 55 Misc.2d 1023, 287 N.Y.S.2d 112 (1967), affirmed 30 A.D.2d 480, 294 N.Y.S.2d 452, reversed 26 N.Y.2d 219, 309 N.Y.S.2d 219, 257 N.E.2d 870 (1970).

NOTE 3—The highest court in the State of New York, the Court of Appeals, considered the granting of a postponed injunction to take effect at some time in the future, such as eighteen months from the decision. During that period D would be required to abate the nuisance by improved methods or continued plant operations would be enjoined. That remedy was rejected because it would require D to solve the industry wide pollution problem, the solution of which would depend on technical research in great depth and there would be no assurance that any significant technical improvement would occur. Moreover, techniques to eliminate pollution from cement making were unlikely to be developed by D's research alone. It was a nationwide problem of the entire cement industry. Thus it would be inequitable to enjoin D's business activities.

NOTE 4—Three farmers brought suit for damages against D power company, alleging that sulphur dioxide gas from D's plant settled on their land causing damage to vegetation. Damages were awarded to the plaintiffs, and D appealed. D contended that it was error to exclude testimony showing: (a) D used due care in the construction and operation of its plant, and (b) the social and economic utility of the plant outweighed any damage caused. The court rejected both of those propositions because the suit was based on nuisance, not on negligence. Whether there is a nuisance depends on the consequences of D's acts, not on the degree of care exercised by D. The fact that D was not negligent is not a defense to liability in this nuisance action. Further, the balancing of the utility of D's action activities, sometimes called the doctrine of comparative injury, is not applicable in a damage suit for nuisance. It is only used when injunctive relief is sought. Therefore, D's defenses were properly rejected, and the plaintiffs were entitled to damages for the nuisance. See Jost v. Dairyland Power Cooperative, 45 Wis.2d 164, 172 N.W.2d 647 (1969).

NOTE 5—The decisions in CASE 78, and Jost, NOTE 4, may be easier to understand if the student asks what relief the plaintiffs were seeking in each case. In Jost the plaintiffs asked only for money damages. The issue presented was whether private industry should pay for the damage to private property. In Boomer the plaintiffs sought damages *and* an injunction. The principal issue was whether a private business should be enjoined from operating. To obtain money damages the plaintiffs must only show unreasonable interference with the use and enjoyment of land. Other factors are weighed when an injunction is sought, such as the economic impact on the parties and the interests of the public.

*

XIV IMMUNITY

Summary Outline

INTRODUCTION

1. An "immunity" denotes the absence of civil liability for what would otherwise be tortious conduct if it were not for:

   (a) the relation between the parties, *e.g.* husband and wife, or

   (b) the status or position of the defendant, *e.g.* a public official. See Restatement, Second, Agency § 217, Comment b.

2. In a case in which an immunity applies there is an overriding public policy which protects the defendant from civil liability. See Restatement, Second, Torts, Chapter 45A, Introductory Note.

3. The immunity is conferred not because of the facts in a given situation, but rather because of the status or position of the defendant. The immunity does not deny or eliminate the tort; rather it negatives the liability for the otherwise tortious conduct. See Prosser, p. 970.

4. An immunity "avoids *liability* in tort under all circumstances, within the limits of the immunity itself." This should be contrasted to a privilege which eliminates the existence of the tort itself because the circumstances make it just and reasonable not to impose liability. See Prosser, p. 970.

5. This Chapter considers the following immunities:

   (a) intra-family immunities,

      (i) husband and wife, and

      (ii) parent and child,

   (b) charitable immunity, and

   (c) governmental immunity.

   CAVEAT—The traditional rules relating to intra-family, charitable, and governmental immunities have been under heavy attack and are in a state of change. Although "trends" toward or in favor of the gradual elimination of such immunities may be said to exist, each individual case must be carefully examined. "Trends" do not bind the courts of any given jurisdiction, nor do they replace the need for careful legal analysis of the principles underlying an immunity, or the principles of stare decisis. See Chapter II, Privilege, above.

INTRA-FAMILY IMMUNITIES

1. The basic rule, at common law, was that no action for personal torts could be maintained between husband and wife.

2. The rule has been sustained traditionally on two grounds:

   (a) the "legal identity" of husband and wife at common law; and,

(b) the idea that litigation between spouses would destroy the peace, harmony and unity of the family. See, *e.g.,* Lyons v. Lyons, 2 Ohio St.2d 243, 208 N.E.2d 533 (1965).

3. Gradually courts developed exceptions to the common law rule.

(a) Some courts have drawn a distinction between intentional torts and negligent torts. They have been more inclined to permit recovery for intentional torts than for negligent torts. The negligent torts in question generally involve automobile accidents in which insurance companies, and not the other spouse, are actually paying the damages. However, in some states, in suits involving members of the same family, the presence of liability insurance has served as the basis for *imposing* liability.

NOTE—One rationale for allowing recovery for intentional torts between spouses is that "the peace and harmony of the home has been so damaged that there is little danger that it will be further impaired." Prosser, p. 863. The court sustained a cause of action on behalf of a wife against her former husband for a rape committed upon her three weeks before they were divorced, because there was "no domestic harmony left to be disrupted." Goode v. Martinis, 58 Wn.2d 229, 361 P.2d 941 (1961).

(b) Some courts have drawn a distinction between "personal" torts and "property" torts. They have allowed recovery by one spouse for tortious property damage inflicted by the other spouse.

(c) Intra-family Offense Acts have been enacted in many jurisdictions. Such statutes provide civil and criminal remedies to victims of domestic violence. Offenses covered may include: threats of physical harm, assault and battery, burglary, sexual abuse, false imprisonment, kidnapping, child stealing, and damage to property. Civil remedies may include: money damages, moving expenses, medical expenses, and restitution.

4. Today, about one-half of the states have abolished the husband-wife immunity entirely and exceptions to it have been recognized in most other states. The Restatement no longer recognizes that immunity. See Restatement, Second, Torts § 895G.

5. The basic rule, at common law, was that a child could not recover from its parents for their personal torts. Justification for this rule was based on protection of parental discipline and control as well as protection of family unity and tranquility.

6. The trend of recent decisions, although it is still a minority view, is to end parent-child immunity entirely except as to:

(a) discipline of the children, and

(b) parental discretion as to food and care.

See Goller v. White, 20 Wis.2d 402, 122 N.W.2d 193 (1963), which was the first case to abolish the immunity.

7. The reasoning of New York courts in dealing with parent-child immunity is illustrated by the following decisions where immunity is abolished for breach of duty owed to the general public, but not for breach of duty arising by virtue of the parent-child relation.

(a) P was a passenger in a car driven by her son. P's son collided with another car driven by D, and P was injured. P sued her son and D for damages. The insurance company representing P's son pleaded that it was not liable to P because of parent-child immunity. P moved to strike the defense of immunity. The court analyzed parent-child immunity and concluded that it should not be applied to the present case. A rule which shields a wrongdoer from liability bears a heavy burden of justification. There has been judicial erosion of the intra-family immunity doctrine in New York and in other states. The doctrine does not apply if the child is of legal age. Since the statute of limitations is tolled until the child reaches majority, an action can be maintained at a later date. The doctrine is inapplicable where the suit is for property damage or an intentional tort. In some jurisdictions a child may sue a parent if the parent was operating the vehicle in connection with a business. Furthermore, since there is compulsory automobile insurance in New York, the present litigation is really between P and the insurance company. Therefore, the preservation of family harmony is not a valid reason to continue immunity. The court noted that by removing immunity as a defense it was not creating liability where none existed previously. Rather, the court was permitting recovery, previously denied, after liability was established. P's motion to strike her son's affirmative defense of immunity was granted. See Gelbman v. Gelbman, 23 N.Y.2d 434, 297 N.Y.S.2d 529, 245 N.E.2d 192 (1969).

(b) Three cases were consolidated on appeal. They all presented in varying contexts the issue whether a parent may be held liable to his child for failure to supervise an infant child adequately. The court held that parents were not liable. It is artificial to separate the parent and child as economic entities. The reality of the family is that it is a single economic unit. The fact that a parent is insured is not a sufficient basis to permit a cause of action in negligence. The court noted that few injuries to children could not have been avoided by closer parental supervision. In states where the immunity doctrine has been abrogated, the duty of parents to supervise their children has been recognized. The standard used is whether the defendant parent acted as a reasonable parent under the circumstances. That standard is not appropriate because the result may be "to circumscribe the wide range of discretion a parent ought to have in permitting his child to undertake responsibility and gain independence. . . . The mutual obligations of the parent-child relation derive their strength and vitality from such forces as natural instinct, love and morality, and not from the essentially negative compulsions of the law's directives and sanctions." Therefore, the court refused to abrogate parental immunity and permit children to maintain an action against parents for negligent supervision. The Gelbman case was distinguished because in that case the duty that the parent owed the child existed separately from the family relation. The duty to drive carefully is owed to the world at large. It is derived from the relationship of driver and passenger. The parent-child relationship is irrelevant to the duty owed and the determination of its breach. Where the duty is ordinarily owed to all other persons, the law should not withhold its remedy for breach merely because the parties are parent and child. Therefore, a child may recover damages from a parent for driving an automobile negligently, but not for failure to supervise the child adequately. See Holodook v. Spencer, 36 N.Y.2d 35, 364 N.Y.S.2d 859, 324 N.E.2d 338 (1974).

8. Other courts have allowed recovery for injuries to children arising out of their parents' business or employment, in contrast to injuries arising from the discharge of parental duties. See Dunlap v. Dunlap, 84 N.H. 352, 150 A. 905 (1930); Briere v. Briere, 107 N.H. 432, 224 A.2d 588 (1966).

9. Parental immunity has not barred suits between parents and children with respect to property torts. See Prosser, p. 861.

10. About one-third of the states have abolished parent-child immunity, and many other states have developed exceptions. The Restatement has rejected the concept of parent-child immunity. See Restatement, Second, Torts, § 895G.

11. Intra-family immunities apply only to suits between husband and wife or parent and child. The immunity does not extend to suits between siblings (brothers and sisters). See Herrell v. Haney, 207 Tenn. 532, 341 S.W.2d 574 (1960). See also Restatement, Second, Torts § 895H.

See generally, Gregory, pp. 735–747; Keeton, pp. 477–486; P & W, pp. 643–653.

1. Traditionally, charities, *e.g.* hospitals, schools and community organizations such as the Salvation Army and the Red Cross, **CHARITABLE IMMUNITY**

were held immune from tort liability. This immunity has been sustained on a number of theories:

(a) the "trust fund" theory, which holds that the donor to the charity gave the funds in trust for the purpose of the charity, and payment of such claims was not one of the purposes,

(b) the theory that "respondeat superior" does not extend to charities because they do not "profit" from the services of their employees,

(c) the "waiver" theory, which holds that the recipient of benefits from a charity thereby implicitly waives any claim against the charity, and

(d) the "public policy" theory, which reasons that using the charity's funds to pay tort claims would stifle charities by discouraging donors, and that there is a public interest in having charitable donors assured that their donations will be used solely for the charity's purposes. See Prosser, pp. 1020–1021.

2. In 1942, the landmark case of Georgetown College v. Hughes, 130 F.2d 810 (D.C.Cir. 1942) came to grips with these arguments, discounted them, and abandoned charitable immunity. See also Darling v. Charlestown Hospital, 33 Ill.2d 326, 211 N.E.2d 253 (1965); Pierce v. Yakima Valley Memorial Hospital, 43 Wn.2d 162, 260 P.2d 765 (1953); Abernathy v. Sisters of St. Mary's, 446 S.W.2d 599 (Mo.1969).

3. Today, about two-thirds of the states have abolished charitable immunity entirely. The remaining states have abolished it in part.

(a) In some states, recovery is allowed where liability insurance permits recovery without use of the charity's own funds. See Wendt v. Servite Fathers, 332 Ill.App. 618, 76 N.E.2d 342 (1947).

(b) In some states, recovery is allowed against charitable hospitals, but immunity remains for all other charities.

4. The modern rule is stated in Restatement, Second, Torts § 895E: "One engaged in a charitable, educational, religious or benevolent enterprise or activity is not for that reason immune from tort liability." The phrase "for that reason" means that a charitable institution may assert another immunity, if applicable, and thus avoid liability.

e.g. The federal government operates a hospital for veterans. In a suit against the hospital the government may not avoid liability because of charitable immunity, but it may claim governmental immunity if it has not consented to the suit.

CAVEAT—Because of the significant financial impact which abolition of immunity can make upon a charity, and because of the absence of liability insurance, some courts have made the abolition of immunity prospective only, with no retroactive effect. See Colby v. Carney Hospital, 356 Mass. 527, 254 N.E.2d 407 (1967). For the same reasons, some courts, while acknowledging the fact that the immunity should be abolished, reason that the legislature, and not the courts, should assume the task of abolishing it.

See generally, Gregory, pp. 747–750; Keeton, pp. 490–495; P & W, pp. 653–657; Prosser, pp. 992–996.

GOVERNMENTAL IMMUNITY

1. Governmental immunity, or sovereign immunity, means that the government may not be sued without its consent. It is based on the common law concept that the King can do no wrong, and that to allow suit would be inconsistent with the idea of sovereignty. See Prosser, pp. 970–971.

2. Governmental immunity applies to the federal government, state governments, and their agencies, unless such immunity has been waived.

3. The Federal Tort Claims Act was enacted in 1946 to waive sovereign immunity for certain torts committed by employees of the federal government. The Act, as amended, permits suit against the United States for negligent torts of government employees within the scope of their employment and most intentional torts likely to be committed by federal law enforcement officers. However, the Act contains a number of exceptions whereby governmental immunity is retained.

4. The immunity of the federal government is preserved with respect to acts or omissions which fall within the "discretionary function or duty" of any federal agency or employee. Discretionary functions are those which involve the personal judgment of the governmental official in decisions.

   (a) The government ordered fertilizer to be manufactured in its own plants to its own specifications. After the fertilizer was readied for shipment abroad, it exploded killing hundreds of people and causing great property damage. In a suit against the government, the trial court found negligence by government officials in the planning, manufacturing and storing of the fertilizer. On appeal, the Supreme Court construed the "discretionary function" exception to liability broadly. It held that the government was not liable for negligent decisions at the "planning or policy level." Since the negligence of the responsible government officials involved their discretion at the planning level, plaintiffs could not recover damages. See Dalehite v. United States, 346 U.S. 15, 73 S.Ct. 956, 97 L.Ed. 1427 (1953).

(b) A lighthouse maintained by the Coast Guard was not functioning and, as a result, a towing barge went aground. The owner of the barge sued the Coast Guard alleging negligence in the failure to check and repair the light or give warning that it was not operating. The government conceded that a "discretionary function" was not involved. It defended on the ground that the Act only imposed liability "in the same manner and to the same extent as a private individual under like circumstances." The government contended that since private persons do not maintain lighthouses, there should be no liability for the negligent performance of such "uniquely governmental functions." However, the Court observed that "it is hornbook tort law that one who undertakes to warn the public of danger and thereby induces reliance must perform his 'good samaritan' task in a careful manner." The Coast Guard did not have to undertake that service, but once it exercised its discretion to operate it, it was obligated to use due care in keeping the lighthouse in working order. If the light became extinguished it was obligated to use due care to discover that fact and repair it, or give warning that it was not functioning. If it failed in that duty at the operational level, it was liable under the Act. If the negligence occurred at the planning or discretional level in the agency, then the government would not have been liable. The Court concluded that the Coast Guard was negligent at the operational level and was, therefore, liable. This decision illustrates the expansion of the waiver of government immunity from the view of the Court in the Dalehite case number 4(a), above. See Indian Towing Co. v. United States, 350 U.S. 61, 76 S.Ct. 122, 100 L.Ed. 48 (1955).

5. Although a private person is subject to strict liability when engaging in "ultra hazardous activities," this does not apply to the federal government.

e.g. The Supreme Court held that the United States was not liable for damages from sonic booms caused by military planes where no government negligence was shown. See Laird v. Nelms, 406 U.S. 797, 92 S.Ct. 1899, 32 L.Ed.2d 499 (1972).

6. It is not always necessary for government liability to be predicated on the Federal Tort Claims Act. A "taking" may be within the purview of the "just compensation" requirements of the Fifth Amendment and provide a basis for suit.

e.g. The Court permitted recovery under the Fifth Amendment for the temporary takeover of a mine by the federal government. See United States v. Pewee Coal Co., 341 U.S. 114, 71 S.Ct. 670, 95 L.Ed. 809 (1951). See also CASE 12, above.

7. The immunity of state governments extends to their subordinate organizations, such as municipal corporations. However, the trend of modern law, both by statute and court decision, is to increase the area in which a state is liable to private citizens. See Nevada v. Hall, 440 U.S. 410, 99 S.Ct. 1182, 59 L.Ed.2d 416 (1979).

8. Courts have created liability in certain situations by dividing the functions of municipal corporations between:

    (a) "governmental" and "public" functions, as to which there is immunity,

    > *e.g.* police and fire department activities and education, and

    (b) "proprietary" and "private" functions, as to which there is no immunity. These are services provided by the city, but which could be provided by a private business.

    > *e.g.* A state would not be immune from suit for claims arising out of its operation of public transportation systems and airports, and the operation of plants providing water, gas or electricity. In most states the construction and maintenance of public streets and sewers is also considered a proprietary function so that governmental immunity is not a defense.

    NOTE 1—The trend of court decisions is to limit or abolish governmental immunity. Thus, courts tend to find that functions are proprietary rather than governmental. See P & W, pp. 661–663.

    NOTE 2—There is a further refinement to immunity for governmental functions. If due care is exercised by a city in a planning function, as distinguished from injuries arising from the day-to-day operations of government, a city is not liable for injuries arising therefrom. See CASE 79, below.

9. Criticism of the sovereign immunity of the states and their political subdivisions has led to an abolition of the immunity in many situations. Judge Traynor of the California Supreme Court has said that it "must be discarded as mistaken and unjust." See CASE 80, below.

10. Court decisions for many years have held that officers of the federal government and most state governments were immune from personal liability for torts which resulted from the use of their discretionary power.

    (a) It has been held that if a government officer acts with malice, so long as he is exercising his discretionary power, he is not liable for damages in federal court. This rule is based on the public policy to permit agency officials to perform their duties without fear of harassment by suits. See

Gregoire v. Biddle, 177 F.2d 579 (2d Cir. 1949), certiorari denied 339 U.S. 949, 70 S.Ct. 803, 94 L.Ed. 1363.

(b) The Supreme Court has held: "A judge will not be deprived of immunity because the action he took was in error, was done maliciously, or was in excess of his authority; rather, he will be subject to liability only when he acted in the clear absence of all jurisdiction." Stump v. Sparkman, 435 U.S. 349, 98 S.Ct. 1099, 55 L.Ed.2d 331 (1978).

NOTE—The constitutional aspect of sovereign immunity should also be considered. The Eleventh Amendment does not grant absolute immunity from suit to state officials. The immunity is qualified and must take into account the functions and responsibilities of the officials involved.

e.g. Suit was brought against the Governor of Ohio and other state officials alleging that they "intentionally, recklessly, willfully and wantonly" deployed the National Guard at Kent State University and ordered the Guard to commit unlawful acts which resulted in the death of certain students. This suit was brought by representatives of the estates of the students for damages. The suit was dismissed for lack of jurisdiction before an answer was filed to the complaint. This ruling was based on executive immunity under the Eleventh Amendment and, alternatively, the common law doctrine of sovereign immunity. Was the ruling correct?

Answer. No. A state government may not override private rights guaranteed by the Constitution. If that occurs, appropriate judicial action may be taken against the responsible officials. The case was remanded for further proceedings so that facts could be developed on: (1) whether the officers were acting within the scope of their duties, (2) whether they acted within the range of their discretion, and (3) whether they acted in good faith. The court did not attempt to define the limits of government immunity, but only held that the Eleventh Amendment did not bar all actions against state officials. See Scheuer v. Rhodes, 416 U.S. 232, 94 S.Ct. 1683, 40 L.Ed.2d 90 (1974).

11. Federal law provides that a civil action for money damages and equitable relief may be maintained against "any person" who, "under color of any statute" deprives any party of "rights, privileges or immunities secured by the Constitution and laws." 42 U.S.C.A. § 1983.

e.g. Suit based on section 1983 was brought against a city, which is included in the term "person." The Court found that federal law "creates a species of tort liability that on its face admits of no immunities." Thus, a municipality which was sued for violation of federally protected rights was not entitled to a qualified immunity from liability by asserting the good faith of officials as a defense. See Owen v. City of Independence, Missouri, 445 U.S. 622, 100 S.Ct. 1398, 63 L.Ed.2d 673 (1980), rehearing denied 446 U.S. 993, 100 S.Ct. 2979, 64 L.Ed.2d 850.

CAVEAT—The rule in number 11 has given rise to what is termed a "constitutional tort." That term "has been used to describe an area of the law encompassing that which is not quite a private (common law) tort, but which contains tort elements; it is not a 'constitutional law' matter per se, but it employs a constitutional test. . . . Involved in such a claim is an alleged deprivation of one of the rights secured by the Constitution (the tort) by one acting under color of state law." International Society for Krishna v. City of Evanston, Ill., 89 Ill.App.3d 701, 44 Ill.Dec. 664, 411 N.E.2d 1030 (1980).

See generally, Gregory, pp. 750–761; Keeton, pp. 455–470; P & W, pp. 657–677.

No liability if due care exercised in planning function   Case 79

Automobiles driven by A and B collided at an intersection and P, a pedestrian, was injured. P sued A, B, and the city for damages. A, who was also injured, sued B and the city. At the trial, P and A offered evidence to show that the yellow caution light was not on long enough to clear the intersection of traffic and that caused the accident. The city's evidence was that the traffic light was designed and installed by its Board of Safety after studying traffic at the intersection and that the timing of the light was adequate. It was also shown that there had been no other accidents at that intersection in three years. The jury returned verdicts against the city and it appealed. May a city government be held liable after its public planning body decided that the clearance interval provided by the yellow caution light at an intersection was adequate?

Answer. No. Although it is proper to hold municipalities and the state liable for injuries arising out of the day-to-day operation of government, such as the negligent maintenance of a highway, the court will not go behind the ordinary performance of planning functions by officials to whom those functions are entrusted. No civil action may be maintained for an erroneous estimate of a public need. In the present case safety studies were made concerning the timing of the light, and there was no evidence that the decision on the timing was arbitrary or unreasonable. In the absence of some evidence that due care was not exercised in the preparation for the timing of the light, or that no reasonable official could have adopted it, the city cannot be held liable. Therefore, P and A may not recover from the city.

See Weiss v. Fote, 7 N.Y.2d 579, 200 N.Y.S.2d 409, 167 N.E.2d 63 (1960).

Case 80   *Sovereign immunity abolished in some states*

P, who was a paying patient at Hospital C, fell while in the hospital and further injured the broken hip for which P was being treated. P sued the hospital and claimed that the fall was caused by its negligence. The hospital defended on the ground that it was a state agency exercising a governmental function, and therefore, it was immune from tort liability. P contended that the operation of the hospital was a proprietary function of government, and in any event, the rule of government immunity should be discarded. Should the state hospital be liable for its negligence?

Answer. Yes. The court re-evaluated the rule of governmental immunity from tort liability and concluded that it should be discarded. Historically the rule began as the personal prerogative of the king and seldom was used to deny compensation completely. Today, the rule of sovereign immunity creates injustice and should be discarded. The rule was originally court made. The fact that the state legislature has created exceptions to it by several statutes does not mean that the legislature has determined that sovereign immunity must be retained in all other areas. The argument that only the legislature has power to change a rule of such long standing is not valid. The rule has been narrowed regularly by state statutes and court decisions. The court has authority to make this final decision and discard the rule. The court added that its decision did not render the state liable for all harms that resulted from its activities. Basic policy decisions of government, within the constitutional limitations, are necessarily non-tortious. For example, harm done by the state's relocation of a highway would not be actionable if some stores lost business because of it. However, when state employees are negligent in caring for a paying patient in a state hospital, as they were in the present situation, then the state is liable.

See Muskopf v. Corning Hospital District, 55 Cal.2d 211, 11 Cal. Rptr. 89, 359 P.2d 457 (1961).

XV DAMAGES

Summary Outline

INTRODUCTION

1. "Damages" have been defined as a pecuniary compensation or indemnity, which may be recovered in the courts by one who has suffered loss, detriment or injury to his person, property or rights through the unlawful act or omission, or negligence of another.

2. In tort actions, the three major categories of damages are:

   (a) nominal,

   (b) compensatory, and

   (c) punitive.

   Each of these categories is discussed separately below.

3. The *availability* of one or more of these categories in any given case is a matter of law.

   e.g. As a matter of law, punitive damages are not awarded in an action based on ordinary negligence.

4. The *amount* of damages to be awarded in a tort action is a factual question and not one of law. It is the function of the jury to determine an award of damages upon instructions from the trial judge.

5. There may be a special problem when more than one person causes injury to the plaintiff.

   (a) If the defendants acted in concert they are joint tortfeasors and are jointly and severally liable.

   (b) If two or more defendants acted independently of each other, they are concurrent tortfeasors, and total damages must be apportioned among them, if possible.

6. Where there are multiple defendants the question of liability among them may arise, such as:

   (a) whether a defendant who has paid a judgment has the right of contribution from a codefendant for his share of the damages, and

   (b) whether a defendant may obtain indemnity from another tortfeasor for all damages paid to the plaintiff.

7. Other damage problems may arise, such as:

   (a) recovery of damages under wrongful death and survival statutes,

   (b) damages for loss of consortium, and

   (c) when remittitur or additur is permitted because the jury verdict is grossly excessive or grossly inadequate.

1. The term "nominal damages" means a trifling sum of money awarded to a party where there is no substantial loss or injury to be compensated, but rather only a technical invasion of his legally protected rights.

2. Nominal damages are symbolic of judicial recognition that a legally protected interest of the plaintiff has been violated by the defendant.

3. An award of nominal damages is usually made in the amount of one dollar, five dollars or ten dollars.

   (a) P can sue if he is wrongfully deprived of his right to vote, and obtain nominal damages. P does not have to show a loss, but only the interference with a legally protected right. See the dissenting opinion in Ashby v. White, Court of Queen's Bench, 1703, 2 Ld.Raym. 938, 92 Eng.Rep. 126, which was sustained on appeal.

   (b) Nominal damages should be distinguished from compensatory damages for small losses, such as the amount P paid for a telegram when it was not delivered. See Williams v. Western Union Telegraph Co., 136 N.C. 82, 48 S.E. 559 (1904).

4. No allegation or proof of loss need be shown by the plaintiff to receive an award of nominal damages.

   e.g. In actions for the torts of assault, battery, false imprisonment, conversion and trespass to land nominal damages are available. This means that nominal damages may be recovered without any pleading or proof of actual injury to the plaintiff. In addition, compensatory and punitive damages may be available.

5. An award of nominal damages may have the following results:

   (a) It may determine disputed property rights of the plaintiff, and thus avoid the possibility of an easement by prescription.

   (b) The plaintiff's reputation may be vindicated as, for example, in an action for libel or slander.

   (c) A judgment in favor of plaintiff usually shifts court costs to the defendant.

NOMINAL DAMAGES

1. The purpose of compensatory damages is to compensate the plaintiff for an actual injury or loss sustained through the act or default of the defendant.

2. Compensatory damages are distinguished from nominal damages in that proof of actual loss is a condition precedent to an award of compensatory damages.

COMPENSATORY DAMAGES

3. The object of compensatory damages is to place the plaintiff in as good a position as he occupied prior to his injury or loss. The law is concerned with "making the plaintiff whole" and not to provide him with means of profit for defendant's act.

4. The two categories of damages which fall within the scope of compensatory damages are:

   (a) general, and

   (b) special.

5. General damages are those which usually flow from, or are inherent in, the injury suffered. They need not be pleaded. For example:

   (a) In a personal injury action, physical and mental pain and suffering and future pain and suffering are all considered general damages which do not require special pleading. By contrast, future loss of earnings is considered special damages, and must be specially pleaded and proven. See Kenwood Tire Co. v. Speckman, 92 Ind.App. 419, 176 N.E. 29 (1931).

   (b) In an action for false imprisonment, the plaintiff may recover for loss of time caused by his unlawful detention, as well as for mental distress. These are items of general damages which need not be pleaded.

   (c) In a malicious prosecution action, injury to reputation and mental distress fall within the realm of general damages.

   (d) In actions for defamation, libel per se and slander per se permit the plaintiff to recover general damages upon his successfully maintaining a cause of action which include mental distress, injury to reputation, and loss of trade or business.

6. Special damages are the actual, but not the necessary result of the injury. However, they flow as a natural and proximate consequence from the defendant's wrong. These include: medical expenses, cost of prescriptions and corrective supports, and loss of earnings, present and future. In determining an award for impairment of earning capacity, the court may use mortality and annuity tables for computation purposes. See Mitchell v. Arrowhead Freight Lines, Limited, 117 Utah 224, 214 P.2d 620 (1950).

7. If the injured person does not incur medical expenses, either because they are rendered free or paid by insurance, he may still claim their value as special damages. This is because the wrongdoer should not benefit from money the plaintiff receives from a *collateral source*. This is the *collateral source rule,* which is followed in most jurisdictions. See Hudson v. Lazarus,

95 U.S.App.D.C. 16, 217 F.2d 344 (1954). See also CASE 81, below.

NOTE—The collateral source rule applies to payments from all forms of insurance and benefits from an employment contract, such as a pension, continued wages, or disability payments. Similarly the rule applies to payments received under social legislation such as Social Security.

8. Special damages must be specifically pleaded and proved. The following cases are illustrative of special damages:

   (a) In an action for conversion of personalty, special damages are recoverable for the value of the property at the time and place of the wrongful taking.

   (b) In a replevin action, plaintiff is entitled to special damages for wrongful detention. These damages are measured by the value of the chattel's use for the period during which it was wrongfully withheld.

   (c) In trespass to realty, special damages are recoverable for the decreased value of the land caused by harm to the land itself or improvements thereon.

   (d) In an action for false imprisonment or false arrest, plaintiff may recover special damages for injury to his health and reputation. He is also entitled to reimbursement for funds used to procure his release.

   (e) In a malicious prosecution action, special damages encompass loss of plaintiff's time, injury to health, and attorney's fees and court costs for defending the earlier proceedings.

   (f) In an action for defamation the rules pertaining to special damages vary.

      (i) Special damages must be proved in a *slander* action, except for the imputation of a crime, loathsome disease, unchastity to a woman, and that which affects the plaintiff's business.

      (ii) No special damages need to be proved where the *libel* appears "on its face" to recover more than nominal damages. See Prosser, p. 754. This is why it is more advantageous for a plaintiff to sue for libel rather than slander.

   (g) In misrepresentation actions, compensatory damages are awarded under two theories:

      (i) the loss of bargain rule, and

      (ii) the out-of-pocket rule. See Chapter VIII Misrepresentation, above for an analysis of these rules. See also

Rossen and Fairweather, "Damages in Fraud Actions", 13 Cleve.-Mar.L.Rev. 288 (May, 1964).

See generally, P & W, pp. 537–560.

Case 81 *Collateral source rule explained and upheld*

P was injured in a collision between his automobile and D's bus. P sued D for damages. At trial D requested permission to show that 80 percent of P's hospital bill and some other medical expenses had been paid by P's insurance carrier. The trial judge ruled that D could not show that P received payments for medical expenses from any collateral source, such as his own insurance carrier. The jury returned a verdict for P and D appealed. D contended that evidence concerning payments which P had received from his insurance carrier for medical expenses should have been admitted to prevent double recovery. Was the ruling of the trial court excluding the evidence correct?

Answer. Yes. Under the collateral source rule "if an injured party receives some compensation for his injuries from a source wholly independent of the tortfeasor, such payment should not be deducted from the damages which the plaintiff would otherwise collect from the tortfeasor." The reason for the rule is that a person who has invested years of insurance premiums to assure his medical care should receive the benefits of his thrift and foresight. The tortfeasor should not be given the benefit of his victim's providence. The rule reflects a policy judgment in favor of encouraging persons to carry insurance for personal injuries. If the collateral source rule were not applied, a person who did not purchase insurance would be in a better position than a person with insurance. This is so because the compensation for the injury would be reduced by the amount of the insurance coverage, and the victim's payment of premiums would have earned no benefit. The trial judge applied the collateral source rule correctly, and the judgment in favor of P was affirmed.

See Helfend v. Southern California Rapid Transit District, 2 Cal.3d 1, 84 Cal.Rptr. 173, 465 P.2d 61 (1970).

NOTE 1—In its decision the court noted that P did not receive a double recovery because he was obligated to refund benefits paid by his insurance carrier upon his tort recovery. However, the court concluded that the reasons for the rule justified its application even if P were not obligated to refund payments to his insurance company.

NOTE 2—New York does not follow the majority rule. In the leading case from that jurisdiction the plaintiff was a practicing physician. When injured through the defendant's negligence the plaintiff was not charged by his professional colleagues and a nurse for their medical treatments and physiotherapy. The court refused to allow special damages for the reasonable value of those services since they had been rendered to plaintiff gratuitously. The court reasoned that since damages are compensatory and not punitive, a defendant should not be required to pay a plaintiff for a friend's generosity. Although the plaintiff may have a moral obligation to reciprocate if the occasion should ever arise, that is too speculative to justify a recovery, and legal damages may not be awarded for a moral obligation. See Coyne v. Campbell, 11 N.Y.2d 372, 230 N.Y.S.2d 1, 183 N.E.2d 891 (1962).

PUNITIVE DAMAGES

1. Punitive damages, sometimes referred to as exemplary damages, are awarded as a punishment to the defendant for his acts which are aggravated, willful or wanton. They are awarded in addition to nominal and compensatory damages.

2. Punitive damages will not be awarded for negligence of the defendant, unless there is willful, wanton or reckless conduct that is tantamount to intentional wrongdoing.

   e.g. D, who was intoxicated, drove his automobile across the center of the highway forcing an oncoming vehicle off the road. D turned his car around following the other car onto the shoulder, and when it turned back onto the pavement, D collided with it injuring P. P brought suit against D for damages. The trial court instructed the jury that they were permitted, but were not required, to award punitive damages if they concluded that D's conduct was "wanton, reckless and grossly negligent." The jury awarded compensatory and punitive damages. D appealed, contending that it was improper to award punitive damages unless malice was shown. The court found no merit to D's contention. While malice is often an element in awarding punitive damages, it is not always an essential element. A jury may, in its discretion, award punitive damages to punish the wrongdoer, and also as an example and deterrent to others. The instructions of the trial judge were correct and the verdict was affirmed. See Sebastian v. Wood, 246 Iowa 94, 66 N.W.2d 841 (1954).

3. It is necessary that plaintiff be awarded either nominal or compensatory damages before punitive damages may be awarded.

4. An employer who participates in, ratifies, or authorizes the act of his servant or agent complained of will be subject to liability for punitive damages.

5. In determining an award of punitive damages, the following elements may be considered by the trier of fact:

   (a) the character of the defendant's conduct,

   (b) the seriousness of the loss or injury to the plaintiff,

(c) the defendant's financial status, i.e. wealth v. poverty,

(d) the expense of the litigation, including legal fees.

6. Punitive damages are discretionary. They may be awarded or withheld at the discretion of the jury.

   CAVEAT—A minority of courts do not permit the award of punitive damages. One court characterized them as "unsound in principle, and unfair and dangerous in practice." The court said that damages should be given as compensation for the injury sustained—nothing more and nothing less. By penalizing a defendant for his malice, elements of a criminal trial are brought into a purely civil action, without the usual safeguards. Further, the amount of punitive damages is left to the unguided judgment of the jury with no limit on the amount assessed and no check on the verdict of the jury. See Spokane Truck & Dray Co. v. Hoefer et ux., 2 Wash. 45, 25 P. 1072 (1891).

   See generally, P & W, pp. 560–569.

JOINT TORTFEASORS

1. Strictly defined, joint tortfeasors are those who have acted in concert in their tortious conduct, and are thus jointly and severally liable.

2. Liberal rules of joinder that have permitted joinder of multiple defendants in a wide variety of situations have broadened the meaning of joint tortfeasors to those who may be joined in a single action.

3. Technically, joint tortfeasors should be distinguished from concurrent tortfeasors. Concurrent tortfeasors are those who may be acting at the same time, but independently, and not in concert, whose conduct combines to injure the plaintiff.

4. Joint tortfeasors are each jointly and severally liable for the entire damages arising from the tortious conduct.

5. There is no apportionment of damages between joint tortfeasors. There may be apportionment among concurrent tortfeasors if the harms caused by each can be separated. See Prosser, pp. 313–323; CASE 82, below.

6. Where there are joint tortfeasors a plaintiff may wish to settle a claim against one of them, while reserving a cause of action against the other tortfeasors. This may be done by a release which extinguishes the cause of action against the tortfeasor who settles and obtains a release. The law relating to a release developed as follows:

   (a) At common law the release of one joint tortfeasor operated to release the other joint tortfeasors. The reason for the rule was that each tortfeasor was responsible for the entire amount of damages, and thus they were considered a single person.

(b) To avoid the common law rule a covenant not to sue, rather than a release, was used to preserve rights against other tortfeasors. In a covenant not to sue the plaintiff did not release the tortfeasor from liability, but merely agreed not to sue or attempt to enforce the claim against the party who settled. However, the amount paid for the covenant not to sue had to be credited against any judgment obtained against the other tortfeasors.

(c) Currently an increasing number of courts and legislatures are altering the common law rule so that a release does not automatically release other joint tortfeasors from liability.

7. An injured party is entitled to only one complete satisfaction of his claim. This equity rule, which prevents unjust enrichment, applies both to joint tortfeasors and concurrent tortfeasors. However, if a judgment against one tortfeasor is not satisfied, suit may be brought against the other tortfeasor since they are jointly and severally liable. See Prosser, pp. 299–301.

See generally, Green, pp. 724–739; Gregory, pp. 441–445; Keeton, pp. 323–324; P & W, pp. 406–410; Prosser, pp. 299–301, 313–323.

Joint and several liability of concurrent tortfeasors where damage cannot be apportioned   Case 82

Persons residing in Canada filed suit in federal district court against three companies, claiming that the defendants were discharging pollutants into the air in violation of various Michigan state laws. Jurisdiction was based on diversity of citizenship and the allegation that each plaintiff suffered damages of $11,000 or more. The plaintiffs sought to hold all three defendant companies jointly and severally liable, although there was no contention that there was a conspiracy by the companies. The defendants moved to dismiss on the ground that the complaint failed to allege that any one of the defendants caused $10,000 damage to any plaintiff. Thus, the defendants contended that the damages involved were less than the federal diversity minimum jurisdictional amount. The plaintiffs argued that since the pollutants from each defendant mix in the air so that it is impossible to separate the act of each defendant, all defendants should be considered together. May the independent actions of multiple defendants be considered together to create joint and several liability?

Answer. *Yes. Where the injuries are factually and medically separable, and damages may be allocated with reasonable certainty, liability for such injuries must be apportioned. However, if lia-*

bility cannot be divided among the tortfeasors, they are jointly and severally liable even though there was no common duty, common design or concerted action. Applying this rule to the present case the aggregate claim of each plaintiff against all three defendants is sufficient to meet the jurisdictional requirement for diversity in federal court. This is so because the injury caused by each individual defendant cannot be apportioned. If the rule were otherwise, it would impose an impossible burden on the plaintiffs in order to recover, which would be manifestly unfair. Therefore, the motion to dismiss for lack of jurisdiction was denied.

See Michie v. Great Lakes Steel Division, National Steel Corp., 495 F.2d 213 (6th Cir. 1974).

NOTE—The decision above illustrates the trend of current decisions, and is the rule followed by most courts. The Michie decision was based on an earlier Michigan case which involved an automobile collision. The court held that the same rule should apply in order to prevent injustice even though the present case involved a nuisance. See Maddux v. Donaldson, 362 Mich. 425, 108 N.W.2d 33 (1961).

CONTRIBUTION

1. Contribution is the right of one of several joint defendants who has discharged a liability common to all defendants to recover from the other defendant or defendants the aliquot (fractional) share for which the other defendant or defendants are liable.

2. At common law the basic rule was that as between joint tortfeasors who have acted in concert, there was no right of contribution.

3. The reason underlying this rule was that the joint tortfeasor was guilty of a wrongdoing and the court would not be a party to a dispute between wrongdoers. See Merryweather v. Nixan, 8 Term.Rep. 186, 101 Eng.Rep. 1337 (1799).

4. The common law rule has been severely criticized and many states have statutes permitting contribution between joint defendants in certain situations, especially where the injury was caused by negligence or mistake as distinguished from willful misconduct. See Prosser, pp. 305–310; Knell v. Feltman, 85 U.S. App.D.C. 22, 174 F.2d 662 (1949).

5. The rule against contribution does *not apply* in the case of indemnity, as contrasted to contribution. See Indemnity, below.

See generally, Keeton, pp. 552–555; P & W, pp. 392–396; Prosser, pp. 305–310.

1. Indemnity shifts the *entire* loss from the defendant tortfeasor to **INDEMNITY** another.

2. Indemnity, wherein the entire loss is transferred, should be contrasted to contribution, wherein the damages may be apportioned. "Contribution is appropriate where there is a common liability among the parties, whereas indemnity is appropriate where one party has a primary or greater liability or duty which justly requires him to bear the whole of the burden as between the parties." Hendrickson v. Minnesota Power & Light Co., 258 Minn. 368, 104 N.W.2d 843 (1960). See CASE 83, below.

3. A right of indemnity may arise by virtue of an agreement between the parties.

4. The right of indemnity also may arise by virtue of the relationship between the parties, such as those in which one individual is held liable for the actions of another by operation of law.

   (a) Situations involving vicarious liability, such as the liability of the master for the torts of a servant, would fall within this category. See CASE 31, above.

   (b) Similarly, there may be indemnity in favor of one who was guilty of mere passive neglect against one who was an active wrongdoer.

   (c) In a case involving an automobile accident it was held that a defendant guilty of ordinary negligence has no right to indemnity from one who was grossly negligent. See Panasuk v. Seaton, 277 F.Supp. 979 (D.Mont.1968).

See generally, Keeton, pp. 555–559; P & W, pp. 399–403; Prosser, pp. 310–313.

Passive negligence—indemnity permitted   **Case 83**

P was injured while riding on a school bus as the result of the horseplay of two other students, A and B. The bus driver, D, saw the activity of A and B, knew it was his responsibility to maintain discipline on the bus, but made no effort to do so because of the traffic on the road. P brought suit against A, B and D. D cross-claimed against A and B seeking contribution or indemnity. The trial court permitted the jury to apportion the negligence of the defendants under the state comparative negligence statute. D was found 76 percent negligent and A and B each twelve percent negligent. D appealed, contending that he was entitled to contribution or indemnity from A and B. Is D's contention valid?

   Answer. Yes. The court held that D had no right to contribution from A and B because there was no common liability for P's injury. D is liable because he failed to use reasonable care to prevent the injury caused by A and B. Thus, D is liable only because he failed to prevent the misconduct of A and B. D's negligence may be classified as passive or secondary, while the wrongdoing of A and B is active or primary. Examining the relative culpability of the wrongdoers the court concluded that D was entitled to indemnity from A and B. The nature of the legal responsibility of D was different from A and B. It was improper for the trial court to permit the jury to compare D's negligence with that of the students. Once the jury found D negligent, he was 100 percent responsible for damages, but only in the posture of secondary liability. Since the jury found A and B equally negligent, each of them was fifty percent responsible for P's injuries. D is entitled to complete indemnity from A and B who are jointly liable on D's indemnification claim. If either A or B pays his fifty percent share to P and also indemnifies D for paying the balance due to P, then such defendant (A or B) is entitled to contribution from the other.

See Hillman v. Wallin, 298 Minn. 346, 215 N.W.2d 810 (1974).

WRONGFUL DEATH

1. At common law no tort action could be brought for causing the death of another person. The reason for this rule was that the cause of action was personal to the injured party and did not survive his death. That rule was changed by statute in 1846 to permit suit for wrongful death. All states have statutes which allow such suits.

2. The basis of damages for wrongful death is the pecuniary loss to the survivors by reason of the death and not the total amount of decedent's future earnings. See Coliseum Motor Co. v. Hester, 43 Wyo. 298, 3 P.2d 105 (1931). Probable future earnings may be shown as evidence of the pecuniary loss in a proper case.

   NOTE—Under this rule if the decedent spent all of his earnings on himself, pecuniary loss to the survivors would be nothing, or only nominal damages. This is so because the survivors could not show any pecuniary loss.

3. Mental suffering of the survivors is not an element of damages.

4. Damages for a wrongful death can be determined by computing the annual earnings available to survivors after subtracting amounts of money the decedent spent on himself and paid for taxes. Using annuity tables the present worth of the earnings available to survivors over the decedent's life expectancy can be calculated. Even where state law permits damages for non-pecuniary benefits, such as the loss of service and counsel, the jury award must bear some reasonable relation to the loss suffered. See DeVito v. United Air Lines, 98 F.Supp. 88 (D.C.N.Y. 1951).

5. In the wrongful death of an infant, the value of his human companionship to the family is recoverable in many jurisdictions. See CASE 84, below.

6. Wrongful death statutes must be distinguished from survival statutes.

    (a) A *survival statute* gives survivors of the decedent the right to recover damages for injuries to the deceased preceding his death, such as conscious pain and suffering and pecuniary loss, including property damage and hospital bills, suffered prior to death. A statute is necessary to create this right because at common law any right of action for tort damages did not survive the death of the injured part.

    (b) A *wrongful death* statute provides recovery for loss to the survivors themselves.

7. Wrongful death and survival statutes are completely independent of each other as each is based on a different theory. A suit under one statute cannot be regarded as an election precluding a later suit under the other statute. See CASE 85, below.

    (a) P, as executrix, sued for the benefit of herself and was compensated under the wrongful death statute for the death of her husband. P then sued for the benefit of the estate for: (1) property damage to the testator's vehicle involved in the accident, (2) medical expenses, and (3) curtailment of testator's life expectancy. P can recover for (1) and (2), but not for (3) because that was not a cause of action arising before death. See Farrington v. Stoddard, 115 F.2d 96 (1st Cir. 1940).

    (b) D negligently injured V in an accident. V sued and recovered for permanent injuries, but later died from those injuries. V's widow can subsequently maintain an action for wrongful death. V's damages for personal injuries in the first suit do not affect the recovery in the second suit which is based on the pecuniary value of V's society, comfort and protection. See Blackwell v. American Film Co., 189 Cal. 689, 209 P. 999 (1922).

8. Most wrongful death statutes specifically designate the persons who may recover under the statute. In other states courts must interpret the statute.

    e.g. A state statute limited the right to recover for wrongful death to "heirs" and "personal representatives" of a deceased. P was the minor stepchild of deceased, and sought to recover under the statute. The court noted that a cause of action for wrongful death was wholly statutory in origin. Based on the statute P cannot recover for the wrongful death of her stepfather. "Heirs" refers to persons eligible to inherit from decedent's estate if he had died intestate. P was never formally adopted so she had no right to inherit. The determination of the legislature is conclusive in these circumstances. See Steed v. Imperial Airlines, 12 Cal.3d 115, 115 Cal.Rptr. 329, 524 P.2d 801 (1974).

9. Most states have a statute which fixes the factors which can be taken into account in calculating recovery under the wrongful death statute. Some states have set a maximum amount of damages for the pecuniary injuries caused by the wrongful death. Therefore, the amount of recovery allowed may vary from state to state.

See generally, Green, pp. 1042–1068; P & W, pp. 570–590; Prosser, pp. 898–914.

Case 84 *Child's value and his companionship to family recoverable in wrongful death action*

The parents of a 14 year old boy sued D for damages in negligently causing his death. Evidence was introduced at the trial concerning the boy's dependability, trustworthiness and ambition. The jury returned a verdict of $14,000.00 plus funeral expenses. The judge said that since no boy his age "could have had the earning capacity indicated by this verdict," he ordered a new trial unless a remittitur were filed. That ruling was appealed. In a wrongful death action, is the award of damage limited to the probable pecuniary loss to the beneficiary?

Answer. *No. Past decisions of many courts interpreted wrongful death statutes in accordance with the philosophy and social conditions which the legislature no doubt had in mind when the statute was enacted. The rule limiting damages to pecuniary loss was established more than one hundred years ago when children as young as five years old worked to earn their keep. Today, although the statute defines pecuniary loss as the pecuniary value of life, it must be interpreted broadly. "[A]n individual member of a family has a value to others as part of a functioning social and economic unit. This value is the value of mutual society and protection, in a word, companionship. The human companionship thus afforded has a definite, substantial, and ascertainable pecuniary value and its loss forms a part of the 'value' of the life we seek to ascertain." If there is a wage-profit capability in the infant, that is the expectation of an excess of his wages over his keep, that loss may also be considered. However, damages for grief and sorrow are not recoverable since it is forbidden by the statute. The court reversed the order granting a new trial subject to remittitur and remanded the case for entry of judgment on the verdict of the jury.*

See Wycko v. Gnodtke, 361 Mich. 331, 105 N.W.2d 118 (1960). See also Lockhart v. Besel, 71 Wash.2d 112, 426 P.2d 605 (1967); Selders v. Armentrout, 190 Neb. 275, 207 N.W.2d 686 (1973).

NOTE—CASE 84, above shows the trend of modern decisions. Under this rule verdicts have been sustained by the Michigan Supreme Court based on past expenditures of the parents and the loss of future companionship.

e.g. The court found that compensation to the parents in a wrongful death suit for loss of the society and companionship of their 21-year old daughter was reasonably set at $1000 per year for the average life expectancy of the parents. However, the court stated that such award must be reduced to its present worth. See Currie v. Fiting, 375 Mich. 440, 134 N.W.2d 611 (1965).

Wrongful death and survival statutes independent of each other   Case 85

P brought an action against D oil company on the ground that it negligently caused the death of her husband in a fire at D's gasoline station. The first count of P's complaint was based on the state's wrongful death statute, which permitted suit for pecuniary losses as a result of death from tortious conduct. Recovery under that statute was generally limited to loss of support to certain dependents. The second count of P's complaint sought damages for decedent's physical and mental suffering and lost wages between the date of the accident and death nine days later. P also sought recovery for the destruction of decedent's personal property (clothing) at the time of the injury. This claim was based on the state survival statute. May P recover under both statutes?

Answer. Yes. *Unless P is permitted to recover under both statutes her recovery would be incomplete. "There may be a substantial loss of earnings, medical expenses, prolonged pain and suffering, as well as property damage sustained, before an injured person may succumb to his injuries. To say that there can be recovery only for his wrongful death is to provide an obviously inadequate justice. Too, the result in such a case is that the wrongdoer will have to answer for only a portion of the damages he caused. Incongruously, if the injury caused is so severe that death results, the wrongdoer's liability for the damages before death will be extinguished. It is obvious that in order to have a full liability and a full recovery there must be an action allowed for damages up to the time of death, as well as thereafter." Therefore, P may recover under both the wrongful death statute, for pecuniary loss to herself and under the survival statute, for the injuries to deceased and his property resulting from D's tort.*

See Murphy v. Martin Oil Co., 56 Ill.2d 423, 308 N.E.2d 583 (1974).

LOSS OF CONSORTIUM

1. Consortium is the right of one spouse to the services, companionship, society, conjugal affection and sexual intercourse of the other spouse. See Guevin v. Manchester Street Railway Co., 78 N.H. 289, 99 A. 298 (1916); Schuttler et ux. v. Reinhardt et ux., 17 N.J.Super. 480, 86 A.2d 438 (1952). In the parent-child relationship consortium is their mutual companionship.

2. At common law only the husband could recover for loss of consortium. Married women did not have a separate cause of action for loss of consortium.

3. The trend of the law today, however, and the law in almost all jurisdictions, is to recognize the wife's separate action for the loss of her husband's consortium. The gist of the action is loss of conjugal rights and is an interest of personality which the court should protect. See Rodriguez v. Bethlehem Steel Corp., 12 Cal.3d 382, 115 Cal.Rptr. 765, 525 P.2d 669 (1974). See also Hitaffer v. Argonne Co., 87 U.S.App.D.C. 57, 183 F.2d 811 (1950); Montgomery v. Stephan, 359 Mich. 33, 101 N.W.2d 227 (1960); Diaz v. Eli Lilly and Co., 364 Mass. 153, 302 N.E.2d 555 (1973).

4. In a few jurisdictions each spouse has been held to have a cause of action for loss of the other's consortium on the theory that it is a constitutionally protected right under the Equal Protection Clause of the 14th Amendment. These courts reason that if the husband's right is protected, and the wife's is not, the wife's "equal protection" has been denied. The Supreme Court has not as yet passed upon the issue. See Krohn v. Richardson-Merrell, Inc., 219 Tenn. 37, 406 S.W.2d 166 (1966), certiorari denied 386 U.S. 970, 87 S.Ct. 1160, 18 L.Ed.2d 129 (1967).

5. When a child is injured a parent may recover for expenses and any loss of services actually provided by the child. However, courts have not permitted recovery solely for loss of companionship or consortium in parent-child situations.

    (a) X was injured when a lighting fixture fell on her in D's airline terminal. X's nine children filed suit against D alleging that D's negligence deprived them of the services, society, companionship, guidance and instruction of their mother. D demurred (moved to dismiss) for failure to state a cause of action. Should the demurrer be sustained?

    Answer. Yes. Strong policy reasons argue against extension of liability to loss of consortium of the parent-child relationship. These reasons include the inadequacy of money damages to compensate the children, the difficulty in measuring damages, and the danger of imposing disproportionate liability on the defendant. X may have relatives and friends who are also deprived of her companionship. At some point liability must cease. The court concluded that recovery for loss of consortium should be limited to the spouse of the injured person. See Borer v. American Airlines, Inc., 19 Cal.3d 441, 138 Cal.Rptr. 302, 563 P.2d 858 (1977).

(b) In a companion case the California court held that a parent has no cause of action for the loss of consortium of a child. See Baxter v. Superior Court, 19 Cal.3d 461, 138 Cal.Rptr. 315, 563 P.2d 871 (1977). However, a few courts permit a parent to recover for the loss of a child's consortium. See Shockley v. Prier, 66 Wis.2d 394, 225 N.W.2d 495 (1975).

NOTE—The decisions which deny recovery for loss of consortium within the parent-child relationship only apply to *negligent* torts. An action may be maintained for *intentional* interference with parental consortium. See Rosefield v. Rosefield, 221 Cal. App.2d 431, 34 Cal.Rptr. 479 (1963).

See generally, Dobbs, § 8.11; Franklin, pp. 259–266; Green, pp. 1099–1110; Keeton, pp. 1182–1190; P & W, p. 1208; Prosser, pp. 888–896; Shulman, pp. 546–557.

1. If money damages found by the jury are "grossly excessive" or "grossly inadequate" the trial court may, in its discretion:

REMITTITUR AND ADDITUR

(a) grant a motion for a new trial,

(b) order the plaintiff to either release the defendant from that part of the jury's award of damages which the court finds excessive, or submit to a new trial. This is known as a *remittitur.*

(c) order the defendant to pay a greater sum than awarded by the jury, or in lieu thereof, submit to a new trial. This is known as an *additur.*

2. The purpose of remittitur and additur is to cure an erroneous award of damages by the jury. Both are time-saving methods which avoid the necessity of a new trial or an appeal. Both are discretionary with the trial judge or appellate court.

3. The most common situation in which a remittitur is utilized occurs where the defendant asks for a new trial because of what he considers an excessive verdict for the plaintiff.

e.g. P alleged a violation of his civil rights and brought an action for alleged police brutality after being wrongfully arrested. P's actual damages consisted of medical expenses and one month's lost wages, which amounted to $95.00. There was no permanent injury and no punitive damages had been pleaded. The jury awarded P $17,500.00. The defendant moved for a remittitur, or in the alternative a new trial. Should the court grant a remittitur?

Answer. Yes. The jury's verdict, considering the circumstances of the case and the actual damages proved, "shocked the conscience of the court" and the court ordered a remittitur of $11,500.00 or, in the alternative, a new trial. In determining the amount of the remittitur the court considered jury awards in two similar cases. One case awarded damages of $5,000.00 and the other case awarded damages of $5,100.00. The court required P to remit $11,500.00 of his $17,500.00 award, permitting a $6,000.00 recovery, or a new trial would be granted. See Collum v. Butler, 288 F.Supp. 918 (E.D.Ill.1968), affirmed 421 F.2d 1257 (7th Cir.).

4. Courts may use one of the following theories in determining the amount of remittitur:

   (a) The verdict is reduced to the highest amount which the jury could have reached without being subject to a new trial or further remittitur. The reasoning for this rule is that the jury has decided to award the plaintiff the highest possible award, and, therefore, the court should cut off only that which is excessive.

   (b) The verdict should be reduced to that amount which the court believes a "properly functioning jury should have reached". Under this theory the court places itself in the position of the jury.

5. When additur is considered in Federal courts, the following Constitutional problem must be considered: the Seventh Amendment to the Constitution provides that "the right of trial by jury shall be preserved, and no fact tried by a jury, shall be otherwise reexamined in any Court of the United States, than according to the rules of the common law". Although remittitur was recognized at common law, additur was not recognized, and it, therefore, can be unconstitutional.

   e.g. The Supreme Court reasoned that since remittitur was recognized at common law and since it merely cut off the excessive amount of a jury verdict, it did not deprive any party of his rights. However, an additur is not something included in a jury verdict. There is no authority in common law to increase the amount of damages. Permitting the defendant to agree to pay additional damages or submit to a new trial without the consent of the plaintiff deprives the plaintiff of his rights under the Seventh Amendment. Therefore, the additur was not permitted in that case. See Dimick v. Schiedt, 293 U.S. 474, 55 S.Ct. 296, 79 L.Ed. 603 (1934).

6. Additur is permitted in Federal courts under the following circumstances:

   (a) where the trial is before the court without a jury, see Traylor v. United States, 396 F.2d 837 (6th Cir. 1968), appeal after remand 418 F.2d 262, and

(b) where the amount of damages is not in dispute, as in an action to recover excessive insurance premiums paid, and the jury has properly determined liability. This is permitted because it is, in effect, simply granting summary judgment on the question of damages. See Decato v. Travelers Insurance Co., 379 F.2d 796 (1st Cir. 1967).

7. Decisions of state courts are split as to the constitutionality of additur under state constitutions.

*

APPENDIX:
EXAMINATION QUESTIONS AND ANSWERS

SUGGESTED APPROACH TO ANSWERING ESSAY EXAMINATIONS IN LAW

1. Remember that you are taking an essay examination. The complete essay examination answer must contain not only the "answer" to the question, but of greater importance, must also contain your analysis, the applicable black letter law, and an explanation of how you have applied the black letter law to the facts and reasoned to the "answer."

2. Begin by reading the question, thoroughly.

3. Next, reread the question; read it as it is written, not as you think it is written.

4. As you read, spot key concepts, ideas, issues and applicable legal terms, principles and concepts.

5. Organize your thoughts into an orderly logical sequence.

6. Analyze the fact pattern and the key issues, terms, principles and concepts which you have spotted.

7. Work out a game plan for your answer, including the sequence of those things which you are going to write about, the priority for writing, the space to be allocated to each and an allocation of your time for writing.

8. Make a brief word-phrase outline of your proposed answer.

9. Use at least 25% of the time allotted for answering the question to all of the things outlined above before you begin to write the answer.

10. Begin writing with a short clear decisive answer to the question precisely as it is asked. For example, if the question reads: "Rule on plaintiff's motion," your answer should be: "Motion

granted," or "motion overruled." The balance of your answer explains how you reasoned to that conclusion.

11. Write your answer in clear, professional, lawyer-like English prose using full and complete legal terminology. Remember: This is an essay examination, in the English language, at the graduate level, in a learned profession.

12. Be certain to include full sentences of black letter law on each of the key issues.

13. Do not merely rehash the facts. A complete answer requires analysis, black letter law and application of that black letter law to the facts. Rehashing of the facts is not enough.

14. Use short, complete, simple sentences. Avoid long, wandering, convoluted sentences which deal with several issues and subjects.

15. Reason to a lawyer-like conclusion. If you have time and space, add a wrap-up concluding sentence to your answer.

16. Reread your answer to make certain that you have made no unintended errors or omissions, and to ensure clarity and completeness of your answer.

17. Use the full time allotted for the question—no more and no less.

TEST SPECIFICATIONS AND SELECTED QUESTIONS FROM THE MULTISTATE BAR EXAMINATION

Set forth below are the Test Specifications for Torts from the Multistate Bar Examination.

The questions which follow the Test Specifications have been selected from the Multistate Bar Examination and are reprinted here with the permission of the National Conference of Bar Examiners and Educational Testing Service. Their inclusion in this Review is designed to acquaint the student with the kind of question which he or she is apt to encounter in the Multistate Bar Examination, or in any so-called multiple choice examination on the subject of Torts.

The Directions on the Examination itself provide as follows: "Each of the questions or incomplete statements below is followed by four suggested answers or completions. You are to choose the *best* of the stated alternatives. Answer all questions according to the generally accepted view, except where otherwise noted."

On the Multistate Bar Examination itself three hours are provided for 100 questions. A total of 200 questions are given in six hours.

The lettered answers are the "official" answers provided by the National Conference of Bar Examiners and the Educational Testing Service. The explanation of those answers was prepared by the authors and in no way have they been approved by the National Conference of Bar Examiners or the Educational Testing Service.

The actual questions have been renumbered for purposes of this Review.

Multistate Test Specifications For Torts

Torts

Note—The Torts questions are to be answered according to current principles of general applicability, except that you are to assume that there is no comparative negligence rule, no No-Fault Insurance Act, and no automobile guest statute unless the specific question informs you to the contrary.

I.   The intentional torts

    A.   Basis of liability
        1.   Assault and battery
        2.   False imprisonment
        3.   Trespass to land
        4.   Trespass to chattels and conversion
        5.   Intentional infliction of mental distress
    B.   Privileges and defenses

II.   Strict liability

    A.   Basis of liability
        1.   Defective products
        2.   Abnormally dangerous things and activities
        3.   Animals
    B.   Defenses

III.   The negligence action

    A.   Risk and duty
    B.   Standard of conduct
        1.   General
        2.   Statutory
        3.   Special classes of persons
    C.   Proof of fault, including *res ipsa loquitur*
    D.   Causation
        1.   Cause in fact
        2.   Legal or proximate cause
        3.   Multiple actors
    E.   Apportionment of liability, including contribution and indemnity
    F.   Special problem areas
        1.   Owners and occupiers of land
        2.   Mental distress
    G.   Liability for acts of others
        1.   Vicarious liability and agency

      2. Joint enterprise
      3. Independent contractors and nondelegable duties
  H. Defenses
      1. Assumption of risk
      2. Contributory fault and last clear chance
      3. Comparative negligence

IV. Nuisance: public and private

V. Defamation

  A. Basis of liability
  B. Common-law privileges and defenses
  C. Constitutional limitations

VI. Privacy

  A. Basis of liability
  B. Common-law privileges and defenses
  C. Constitutional limitations

VII. Misrepresentation

  A. Deceit
  B. Negligent misrepresentation

(Approximately half of the Torts questions will be devoted to topics included under III and approximately half to topics included under the remainder of the subject matter outline. This Torts outline is an elaboration of the Torts outline previously published, but no topics that were not previously covered are included and no topics that were previously covered are excluded.)

QUESTIONS Questions 1–5 are based on the following fact situation.

Walker, a pedestrian, started north across the street in a clearly marked north-south crosswalk with the green traffic light in his favor. Walker was in a hurry, and so before reaching the north curb of the street, he cut to his left diagonally across the street to the east-west crosswalk and started across it. Just after reaching the east-west crosswalk, the traffic light turned green in his favor. He proceeded about five steps farther across the street to the west in the crosswalk when he was struck by a car approaching from his right which he thought would stop, but did not. The car was driven by Driver, 81 years of age, who failed to stop his car after seeing that the traffic light was red against him. Walker has a bone disease, resulting in very brittle bones, which is prevalent in only 0.02 per cent of the population. As a result of the impact Walker suffered a broken leg, and the destruction of his family heirloom, a Picasso original painting that he was taking to his bank for safe-keeping. The painting had been purchased by Walker's grandfather for $750 but was valued at $500,000 at the time of the accident.

Walker has filed suit against Driver. Driver's attorney has alleged that Walker violated a state statute requiring that pedestrians stay in the cross walks, and that if Walker had not violated the statute he would have had to walk 25 feet more to reach the impact point and therefore would not have been at a place where he could have been hit by Driver. Walker's attorney ascertains that there is a statute as alleged by Driver, that his measurements are correct, that there is a state statute requiring observance of traffic lights, and that Driver's license expired two years prior to the collision.

1. In determining whether Driver was negligent, his conduct will be judged on the basis of

   (a) that of a reasonable 81-year-old man under the circumstances of this case

   (b) an absolute liability standard

   (c) that of a reasonable man under the circumstances of this case

   (d) the standard set by the state traffic light statute, unless Driver has a valid excuse

2. Walker's conduct in violation of the crosswalk statute was

   (a) a concurring factual cause of his injury

   (b) the sole factual cause of his injury

   (c) a supervening factual cause of his injury

   (d) a legal condition and not a factual cause of his injury

3. The violation of the crosswalk statute by Walker should not defeat his cause of action against Driver because

   (a) Driver violated the traffic light statute at a later point in time than Walker's violation

   (b) pedestrians are entitled to assume that automobile drivers will obey the law

   (c) Walker was hit while in the crosswalk

   (d) the risks that the statute was designed to protect against probably did not include an early arrival at another point

4. The failure of Driver to have a valid driver's license

   (a) makes Driver liable to Walker because Driver is a trespasser on the highway

   (b) would not furnish a basis for liability

   (c) proves that Driver is an unfit driver in this instance

   (d) makes Driver absolutely liable for Walker's injury

5. If Walker establishes liability on the part of Driver for his physical injuries, should Walker's recovery include damages for a broken leg?

   (a) No, since only 0.02% of the population have bones as brittle as Walker's

   (b) No, unless a person of ordinary health would probably have suffered a broken leg from the impact

   (c) Yes, because Driver could foresee that there would be unforeseeable consequences of the impact

   (d) Yes, even though the extent of the injury was not a foreseeable consequence of the impact.

Questions 6–8 are based on the following fact situation.

Soldier had been drinking heavily in a bar, and had become involved in an argument with Bartender, an employee of Owner, who had refused to serve Soldier any more drinks. Soldier said to Bartender, "If you weren't the bartender here, I would break your skull," and while saying this Soldier leaned over from his side of the bar and tapped Bartender on the hand. At Bartender's instruction, two bouncers took Soldier into the men's room, doused his face with cold water, and locked him in the room for an hour to sober him up. Although Soldier was not yet sober, the bouncers then escorted him out in the cold weather, where he fell, was later picked up by the police, and sent to the hospital for frost bite.

6. If Bartender can successfully sue Soldier, Bartender's claim would most likely be for

   (a) assault for placing Bartender in fear of bodily harm

   (b) slander for humiliating Bartender in the performance of his duties.

   (c) battery for tapping the hand of Bartender

   (d) intentional infliction of emotional distress

7. If Soldier sues Owner, a claim for relief that would likely succeed would be for

   (a) false imprisonment in that Owner, through his agents, locked Soldier in the men's room for an hour

   (b) negligence for refusing to serve him as a guest

   (c) strict liability for his failure to serve persons in public accommodations

   (d) trespass *ab initio* for denying Soldier continued access to the premises after having been invited as a public guest

8. If Soldier sues Owner for damages resulting from frost bite, Soldier's claim for relief would most likely be based on the theory that

  (a) Soldier was a licensee and entitled to stay until closing hours.

  (b) Owner had a duty to his customer to ensure his safety

  (c) the bouncers acted unreasonably in ejecting Soldier

  (d) Owner may eject only those customers who are disturbing the peace and quiet of the premises

---

Questions 9–10 are based on the following fact situation.

Peter was rowing a boat on a mountain lake when a storm suddenly arose. Fearful that the boat might sink, Peter rowed to a boat dock on shore and tied the boat to the dock. The shore property and dock were the private property of Owner.

While the boat was tied at the dock, Owner came down and ordered Peter to remove the boat, because the action of the waves was causing the boat to rub against a bumper on the dock. When Peter refused, Owner untied the boat and cast it adrift. The boat sank.

Peter was wearing a pair of swimming trunks, nothing else. He had a pair of shoes and a parka in the boat, but they were lost when Owner set it adrift. Peter was staying at a cabin one mile from Owner's property. The only land routes back were a short rocky trail that was dangerous during the storm, and a 15-mile road around the lake. The storm continued with heavy rain and hail, and Peter having informed Owner of the location of his cabin, asked Owner to take him back there in Owner's car. Owner said, "You got here by yourself and you'll have to get back home yourself." After one hour the storm stopped, and Peter walked home over the trail.

9. A necessary element in determining if Peter is liable for a trespass is whether

  (a) Owner had clearly posted his property with a sign indicating that it was private property

  (b) Peter knew that the property belonged to a private person

  (c) Peter had reasonable grounds to believe the property belonged to a private person

  (d) Peter had reasonable grounds to believe his boat might be swamped and sink

10. If Peter asserts a claim against Owner for loss of the boat, the most likely result is that Owner will

    (a) have no defense under the circumstances

    (b) prevail because Peter was a trespasser *ab initio*

    (c) prevail because the boat might have damaged the dock

    (d) prevail because Peter became a trespasser when he refused to remove the boat

---

Questions 11–13 are based on the following fact situation.

Lowe Ricard, a flamboyant character, posed as a trick-shot artist with the Great Wild West Show which was scheduled to appear in Big City the following week. He asked Jane Witt, a nineteen-year-old university student, to try out as his partner in one of his trick-shot demonstrations. Although Miss Witt told Ricard she was afraid of getting hurt, she agreed to try out because this was her one chance to break into show business. Miss Witt, clad only in a yellow bikini furnished by Ricard, who said it was the costume required in the act, went with him in his sports car to an uninhabited area near Big City for the tryout. Ricard requested Miss Witt to stand 75 feet away and hold a lighted cigarette between her lips. Using a high-powered rifle, Ricard three times in as many tries shot a cigarette out of her mouth. He was enthusiastic about her performance and immediately offered her the job. Miss Witt accepted and was told to report to the Wild West Show's headquarters the following Monday.

Miss Witt reported on Monday, as instructed, to the headquarters, where a large number of people were working. In their presence, Miss Witt was informed that Ricard was not connected with the show in any way. She was told that he had been a trick-shot artist with the show for many years, but had been discharged a year ago because of failing eyesight and mental instability. At this point Miss Witt became hysterical, requiring sedation and hospitalization for a severe nervous reaction.

Miss Witt went to a Big City attorney for advice on whether to sue Ricard. Investigation shows that Ricard is a man of some wealth, and has done this sort of thing before.

11. Ricard's mental instability is no defense to an action for either assault or battery

    (a) because he is over 21 and has not had a guardian appointed to take care of him

    (b) if he has the money to pay for the harms he caused

    (c) if he had the state of mind required for the particular tort

(d) because the reasonable man test is used as a standard for these torts

12. The best argument for rejecting the defense of consent in an action by Miss Witt for either assault or battery is that

(a) she is under 21

(b) she was misled about the job opportunity

(c) she was misled as to Ricard's ability as a sharpshooter

(d) a person cannot legally consent to humiliating acts

13. In establishing the intent required of Ricard in an assault action, the most relevant evidence is proof of his

(a) intent to fire the gun in Miss Witt's direction

(b) intent to create risks of injury to Miss Witt

(c) knowledge that guns are dangerous instruments

(d) knowledge that Miss Witt feared harm when he fired at her

---

Questions 14–16 are based on the following fact situation.

A water pipe burst in the basement of Supermart, a grocery store, flooding the basement and damaging cases of canned goods on the floor. The plumbing contractor's workmen, in repairing the leak, knocked over several stacks of canned goods in cases, denting the cans. After settling its claims against the landlord for the water leak and against the plumbing contractor for the damage done by his workmen, Supermart put the goods on special sale.

Four weeks later Dotty was shopping in Supermart. Several tables in the market were covered with assorted canned foods, all of which were dirty and dented. A sign on each of the tables read: "Damaged Cans—Half Price."

Dotty was having Guest for dinner that evening and purchased two dented cans of tuna, packed by Canco, from one of the tables displaying the damaged cans. Before Guest arrived, Dotty prepared a tuna casserole which she and Guest ate. Both became ill and the medical testimony established that the illness was caused by the tuna's being unfit for consumption. The tuna consumed by Dotty and Guest came from the case that was at the top of one of the stacks knocked over by the workmen. The tuna in undamaged cans from the same Canco shipment was fit for consumption.

14. If Dotty asserts a claim against Canco based on negligence, the doctrine of res ipsa loquitur is

(a) applicable, because the tuna was packed in a sealed can

(b) applicable, because Canco as the packer is strictly liable

(c) not applicable, because the case of tuna had been knocked over by the workmen

(d) not applicable, because of the sign on the table from which Dotty purchased the tuna

15. If Guest asserts a claim against Dotty, Dotty most likely will

(a) be held strictly liable in tort for serving spoiled tuna

(b) be held liable only if she were negligent

(c) not be held liable unless her conduct was in reckless disregard of the safety of Guest

(d) not be held liable because Guest was a social visitor

16. If Guest asserts a claim against Supermart, the most likely result is that Guest will

(a) recover on the theory of res ipsa loquitur

(b) recover on the theory of strict liability in tort

(c) not recover, because Supermart gave proper warning

(d) not recover, because Guest was not the purchaser of the cans

---

Questions 17–20 are based on the following fact situation.

Tenant is an unmarried female, aged twenty-five. She occupies an apartment, under a written lease which has two years to run, in a building owned by Landlord. Landlord occupies the manager's apartment in the same building. One evening, while Tenant was out, Landlord entered her apartment using his pass key, and changed the lock on the door. When Tenant returned and found her key would not work, she rang Landlord's bell. Landlord answered it and told Tenant he had changed the lock on her apartment because she was using the apartment for prostitution. This statement about Tenant was not true and Landlord had no reason to believe it to be true. In fact a nephew of Landlord had recently married and Landlord wanted to induce Tenant to vacate so he could rent her apartment to his nephew.

Landlord also told Tenant that if she did not vacate in three days he would file suit to evict her and in that suit would allege, as grounds for eviction, that she had been using the premises for prostitution.

Tenant consults a lawyer as to her rights against Landlord. She informs her lawyer that although she had never engaged in any immoral conduct in the apartment, she has been having an affair with a young man named Bill who works in the office with her. They have frequently taken week-end trips together and have registered at hotels as husband and wife, but to the best of her knowledge, no one knows about this matter. She also informs the lawyer that Art and Bart, two tenants in the apartment building, have separately told her that they heard Landlord's statement to her but do not believe it to be true.

17. If Tenant sues Landlord for defamation, she will

   (a) have to prove some special damages because the defamation was oral

   (b) have to prove some special damages because of her conduct with Bill

   (c) have to prove she was discharged from her employment as a result of Landlord's statement

   (d) not have to prove any special damages

18. In the light of recent and significant trends in tort law, which of the following situations would obtain if Landlord's statements to Tenant had not been heard by any person other than Tenant?

   (a) Tenant would have a claim for relief for defamation because of Landlord's motives.

   (b) Tenant would have a claim for relief for defamation if she could establish that Landlord's statements caused her to suffer extreme emotional distress.

   (c) Tenant would have a claim for relief for intentional infliction of emotional distress.

   (d) Tenant would have no claim for relief against Landlord.

19. The fact that Art and Bart did not believe Landlord's statements to be true

   (a) establishes a complete defense to a claim for relief for defamation

   (b) establishes that Landlord had no reasonable basis for his statement

   (c) establishes that Tenant did not sustain damage

   (d) may tend to diminish the amount of damages that Tenant might recover

20. If Landlord filed suit to evict Tenant and alleged in his complaint that Tenant had used the premises for prostitution, such an allegation would be privileged in a subsequent defamation action

   (a) absolutely

   (b) only if Landlord believed the allegation to be true

   (c) only if Landlord believed the allegation to be true and had reasonable grounds for such a belief

   (d) only if the allegation were proved to be true

ANSWERS

1. **D** is correct. The standard of care established by statute, which requires observance of traffic lights, is the standard which should be used. Walker was within the class of persons that the statute was designed to protect; he was injured in a way that the statute was intended to prevent; and the accident would not have occurred if the statute had not been violated. **C** states the standard which is generally applicable; Driver's age is included in the phrase "under the circumstances." However, that is not the best answer because the statute conclusively establishes the standard of care to be used in this factual setting. **A** does not state the standard correctly. **B** is not correct. Although a violation of a statute is said to be negligence per se, that does not mean that the complete cause of action has been established by merely showing that the statute has been violated. It means that the breach of a legal duty has been established. The plaintiff must still prove the remaining elements of the cause of action. See Chapter III, Violation of Statute, pp. 65–69.

2. **A** is correct. Causation in fact refers to a series of events which may be traced to each other and lead to the event in question. Walker's conduct was not the "sole factual cause" of his injury so **B** is not correct. **C** is incorrect because negligence cannot be a supervening cause. **D** is not correct for the reasons stated in Answer 2 **A**. See Chapter III, Proximate Cause, pp. 77–85.

3. **D** is correct. Walker's early arrival at the place of the accident was not a risk that the statute was designed to prevent. In other words, Walker's violation of the statute was not the proximate cause of his injury. **A** refers to the doctrine of last clear chance which is not applicable because Walker was not contributorily negligent. **B** and **C** are not correct because they do not deal with the issue raised by the question, which is, why is Walker not contributorily negligent when he violated the statute.

4. **B** is the correct answer. The general rule is that statutes which require a license do not create liability where the actor is competent but unlicensed. This is because the failure to obtain a license, by itself, is not the proximate cause of the injury. Negligence must be shown. For these reasons **A**, **C** and **D** are incorrect. See Chapter III, Violation of Statute, number 9, pp. 68–69.

5. **D** is correct. Driver's negligence created a risk of danger and was the proximate cause of Walker's injuries. A tortfeasor must take the plaintiff as he finds him. While the *extent* of Walker's injury was more than it would have been for a normal person, that does not limit damages once liability is established. For that reason **A** and **B** are incorrect. **C** is self-contradictory. See Chapter III, Proximate Cause, number 11, pp. 81–82.

NOTE—Walker may also recover $500,000 which was the present value of his Picasso painting if Driver's liability is established. This is so because it is foreseeable that goods in Walker's possession would be damaged. The tortfeasor is responsible for their full value.

6. **C** is correct because there was an impermissible touching of Bartender without his consent. Although the touching was slight, it was not privileged. Intent to harm is not required for battery. See Chapter II, Battery, pp. 12–14.

    A is not correct because Soldier's words did not show a present intent to do anything. Further, there was no act which threatened bodily harm or that would cause immediate apprehension of bodily harm. See Tuberville v. Savage, CASE 1, p. 11. **B** is not correct because the tort of slander requires defamatory words which injure a person's good name or reputation. Recovery for intentional infliction of emotional distress requires "outrageous" conduct. The circumstances must be aggravated and the injury real and substantial. Those circumstances are not shown in the fact pattern so **D** is not correct.

7. **A** is correct. All the elements of false imprisonment were present when Soldier was locked in the men's room. The owner is responsible for the acts of his employees within the scope of their employment and which are related to the owner's business. This is based on the doctrine of respondeat superior. See Chapter II, False Imprisonment and False Arrest pp. 20–25; Chapter III, Master-Servant, pp. 86–88.

    There is no liability for refusing to sell drinks to persons who are intoxicated. In fact, liability has been found in some situations where drinks were served to persons who were known to be intoxicated. Thus **B** and **C** are incorrect. The doctrine of trespass ab initio has been rejected by most courts, and therefore, **D** would not be the "best" answer. See Chapter II, Trespass to Land, number 6, p. 26.

8. **C** is correct. The bouncers knew that Soldier was not sober and the weather was cold. They could reasonably foresee that Soldier might not be able to take care of himself and would suffer some injury. Thus Soldier's injury was foreseeable and the owner should be held liable because of respondeat superior. **A** is not correct because Soldier was an invitee, and Owner was not required to permit intoxicated customers to remain. **B** is not correct because Owner's duty to a customer is not all inclusive as the answer suggests. **D** is not correct because Owner's right to have customers ejected is not so limited.

9. **D** is correct. Peter was privileged to dock his boat because of necessity. See Chapter II, Defenses—Necessity, number 1, pp. 39–40 **A**, **B** and **C** are not correct because none of those factors prevent Peter from asserting the defense of necessity.

10. **A** is correct. Peter was privileged to tie his boat to Owner's dock because of necessity. Owner is responsible for preventing Peter from exercising that privilege. See Chapter II, Defenses—Necessity, number 1, pp. 39–40. For that reason **D** is incorrect. **B** is not correct: first, an entry on land to save goods which are in danger of being lost is not a trespass, and second, the doctrine of trespass ab initio has been rejected by most courts. See Chapter II, Trespass to Land, number 6, p. 26. **C** is not correct. However, if the boat damaged the dock, Peter would be liable for such damage.

11. **C** is the correct answer. The Restatement, Second, Torts § 895J states the rule which is applied in most states: "One who has deficient mental capacity is not immune from tort liability solely for that reason." This rule applies both to intentional and negligent torts. **A** is not correct because insane persons are responsible for their own torts just as normal persons. That rule is based on public policy and recognition of the difficulty in distinguishing between mental illness and lack of emotional balance which is not a defense to tort liability. **B** is incorrect because liability is not based on ability to pay damages. **D** is not correct because the reasonable, prudent person standard is the test for negligence, not for intentional torts.

12. **C** is correct. If consent is given because of fraud, deceit or substantial mistake induced by the defendant, it will not prevent recovery. In this fact pattern Ricard fraudulently misrepresented his ability as a trick-shot artist, which was a material fact. See Chapter II, Defenses—Consent, pp. 34–35; Chapter VIII, Actionable Misrepresentation, pp. 176–185; Restatement, Second, Torts § 892B.

    A is not correct. Miss Witt, age 19, was old enough to appreciate the danger, and therefore, could consent to it. Certain statutes establish an age of consent to protect a class of persons. E.g., the age of consent to sexual intercourse for the crime of statutory rape. Such statutes are not relevant to the present facts. **B** is not correct because that misrepresentation related to a collateral matter. The misrepresentation must be material to negate consent. **D** is incorrect. Whether or not an act is "humiliating" does not affect the validity of a consent.

13. **A** is correct. In the tort of assault the defendant must wrongfully and intentionally set a force in motion against plaintiff. That is what Ricard did, and it may be inferred that he intended the natural consequences of his act, which is, causing Miss Witt to apprehend imminent harm. These elements show an assault. See Chapter II, Assault, pp. 9–12.

    B is incorrect because the tort of assault does not require a showing of intent to create risks or injury, but only of creating the apprehension of harm. **C** is not correct because it only shows knowledge; it does not show the required intention. **D**

is incorrect. Assault requires that the plaintiff, as a reasonable person, be apprehensive of immediate bodily injury, but not that the defendant know that the plaintiff had been placed in fear.

14. **C is correct.** The doctrine of res ipsa loquitur requires that the injury be caused by an instrumentality within the exclusive control of the defendant. That requirement has been eased by courts in some cases where the plaintiff can show that when the goods were purchased from a retail store, they were in the same condition that they left the defendant manufacturer's possession. Due to the fact that the tuna in the undamaged cans was fit for consumption, an inference is warranted that the problem arose due to the exterior damage, so Canco would not be liable based on res ipsa loquitur. In a real sense the fact that Dotty used the contents is not adequate to eliminate res ipsa loquitur since this was the contemplated use. See Chapter III, Res Ipsa Loquitur and CASE 33, pp. 90–96.

A is not correct because the can was damaged. Therefore, it was not purchased in the same condition that it left Canco's possession. An argument can be made that the contents were not touched in any way and that merely denting the exterior of the can was not sufficient to avoid the application of res ipsa loquitur. That argument can be answered by the fact that tuna in undamaged cans from the same shipment was fit for consumption. The choice between **A** and **C** was close, but credit was given only for **C.** **B** is incorrect for two reasons: (1) The question concerns the doctrine of res ipsa loquitur and the answer refers to recovery on a different theory, strict liability. (2) Intervening cause such as damage to the cans after they left the possession of Canco, is a valid defense to recovery under res ipsa loquitur and strict liability. See CASE 33, p. 93; Chapter VII, Defenses, pp. 168–170. **D** is incorrect because there is an implied warranty of fitness that covers the goods sold, i.e., the tuna was fit for human consumption. In addition, the warning was inadequate. See Chapter VII, Warranty Theory, number 2(b), p. 159.

15. **B is correct.** Guest is a licensee to whom Dotty owed the duty of using due care not to injure by active negligent conduct. **A** is not correct because this is not a "transaction" in goods within the meaning of the UCC. Dotty did not sell the food to Guest so there is no strict liability. **C** states an improper standard. **D** is not the best answer because the mere fact that Guest was a social visitor (a licensee), does not insulate Dotty from liability. Dotty may be held liable to a social visitor under some circumstances, e.g., if she failed to warn Guest of a known concealed danger, she would be responsible for injuries caused by that dangerous condition. She would also be liable if Guest were injured by her negligence. See Chapter V, Analysis of Duty, pp. 125–132.

16. **B** is correct. Restatement, Second, Torts § 402A imposes strict liability for "any" defective product sold. This includes food which is not fit for human consumption. **A** is not the best choice because the tuna was not within the exclusive control of Supermart. Dotty opened the can to prepare the tuna casserole. Thus an element usually required for res ipsa loquitur, exclusive control by defendant, is missing. Moreover, recovery is more likely under a strict liability theory because a showing of negligence is not required. Under res ipsa loquitur, recovery is based on negligence and the doctrine is merely used to create an inference of negligence which may be disregarded by the jury. See CASE 34, pp. 93–94. **C** is incorrect. The warning, "damaged cans," does not prevent recovery because the tuna in the cans was sold for the purpose of being consumed and the warning was inadequate. **D** is incorrect because privity of contract is not required to recover from the seller of goods. See Chapter VII, Strict Liability, pp. 161–167.

17. **D** is the correct answer. Imputing unchastity to a woman is slanderous per se. That means that damages are presumed without proof. For that reason **A** and **B** are incorrect. **C** is an example of special damages, but such special circumstances do not have to be proven when the statement is slanderous per se. See Chapter X, Common Law Slander, pp. 206–208.

18. **C** is correct. The modern view is stated in Restatement, Second, Torts § 46(1): "One who by extreme and outrageous conduct intentionally or recklessly causes severe emotional distress to another is subject to liability for such emotional distress and for bodily harm resulting from it." Restatement Comment C notes that this area of the law is in a stage of development and the limits of this tort have yet to be determined.

NOTE 1—There is a trend toward recognizing a right to recover for a severe disturbance of mental or emotional tranquility resulting from an unprivileged act committed intentionally or recklessly. This is so even though there is no physical injury or independent tort. See Chapter II, Emotional Distress, pp. 17–20. See also cases collected at 64 A.L.R.2d 100, 119.

NOTE 2—The relationship between the parties in a suit for the intentional infliction of emotional distress is important. Where a landlord-tenant relationship exists, and the landlord engages in conduct which is malicious or in reckless disregard of the sensibilities of the tenant, courts have generally allowed recovery even though there was no physical injury to the tenant. See cases collected in 17 ALR2d 936, 938.

A and **B** are not correct because publication is necessary for defamation. If no one heard Landlord's statement, an element for that tort would not be present. **D** is incorrect for the reasons given for the correctness of **C**.

19. **D** is correct. Landlord's false statement was slander per se (see answer 17), and it was published to Art and Bart, so Miss Witt has a cause of action. Damages are presumed. However, since the statement was not believed, the damage to Miss Witt's reputation was not as great as it would have been if the statement were believed. **A** is incorrect because the elements of slander are present. **B** is incorrect. The fact that someone does not believe a statement does not show there was no basis for it. **C** is not true because the slander is actionable per se. Thus damages are presumed. Further, Tenant may have suffered emotional distress as a result of the slanderous statement. See Chapter X, Common Law Defamation, pp. 202–206.

20. **A** is correct. Statements made in judicial proceedings are absolutely privileged. Malice will destroy a qualified privilege, but not an absolute privilege. Therefore, **B**, **C** and **D** are not correct. See Chapter X, Privileges, pp. 210–215.

*

TABLE OF CASES

References are to Pages

*

INDEX

†